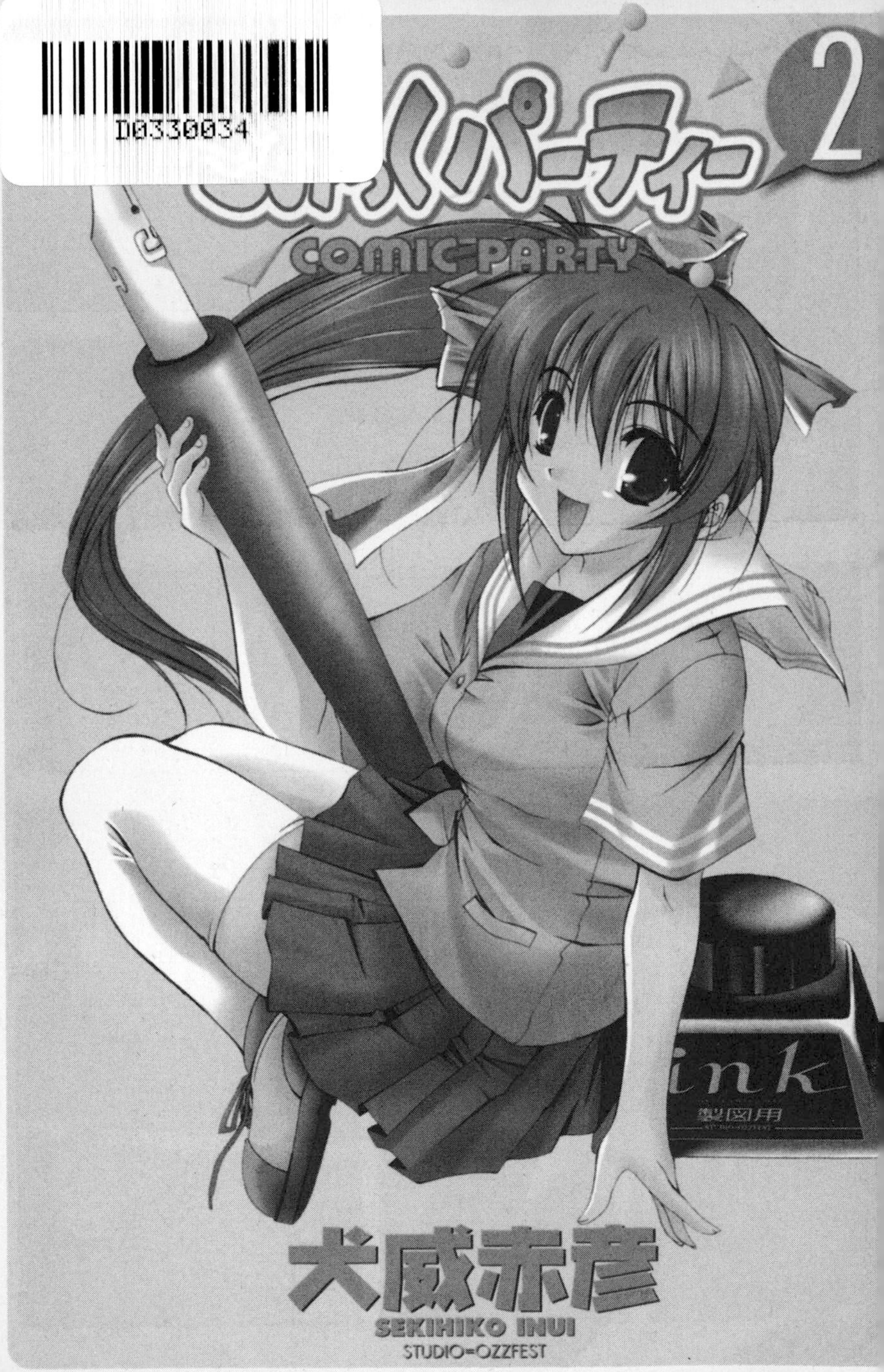

パーティー
2
COMIC-PARTY
ink
製図用
犬威赤彦
SEKIHIKO INUI
STUDIO=OZZFEST

Comic Party Vol. 2
Created by Sekihiko Inui

Translation - Mike Kiefl
English Adaptation - Ross Richie
Associate Editor - Nicole Monastirsky and Troy Lewter
Retouch and Lettering - Keiko Okabe and Louis Csontos
Cover Artist - Anna Kernbaum

Editor - Nora Wong
Digital Imaging Manager - Chris Buford
Pre-Press Manager - Antonio DePietro
Production Managers - Jennifer Miller and Mutsumi Miyazaki
Art Director - Matt Alford
Managing Editor - Jill Freshney
VP of Production - Ron Klamert
President and C.O.O. - John Parker
Publisher and C.E.O. - Stuart Levy

A  Manga

TOKYOPOP Inc.
5900 Wilshire Blvd. Suite 2000
Los Angeles, CA 90036

E-mail: info@TOKYOPOP.com
Come visit us online at www.TOKYOPOP.com

ISBN: 1-59182-855-4

First TOKYOPOP printing: August 2004
10 9 8 7 6 5 4 3 2 1
Printed in the USA

VOLUME 2
BY
SEKIHIKO INUI

HAMBURG // LONDON // LOS ANGELES // TOKYO

STORY SO FAR

KAZUKI SENDO HAD ALWAYS LOVED DRAWING AND PAINTING WITH HIS GIRLFRIEND, MIZUKI TAKASE. BUT WHEN CLASSMATE TAISHI KUHONBUTSU PULLS THEM INTO A DOUJINSHI CONVENTION, KAZUKI ENTERS A WHOLE NEW WORLD. SOON HE FINDS HIMSELF PASSIONATELY DRAWING MANGA AND CRAMMING TO GET INTO ALL THE CONVENTIONS. AS KAZUKI GETS ACQUAINTED WITH THE DOUJINSHI LIFESTYLE AND MEETS NEW FRIENDS, HE STARTS TO DRIFT AWAY FROM MIZUKI AND HIS "NORMAL" WAY OF LIVING. SURE, HIS NEW CAREER AS A STRUGGLING ARTIST HAS BEGUN, BUT AT WHAT COST TO HIS FRIENDS AND FAMILY? THUS BEGINS THE STRUGGLE OF A TALENTED ARTIST...

COMIC PARTY

COMIC PARTY™

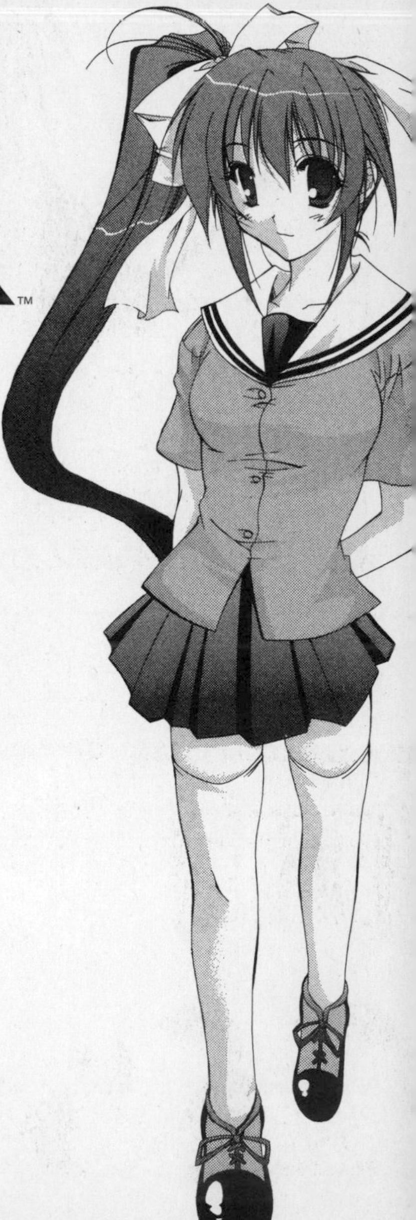

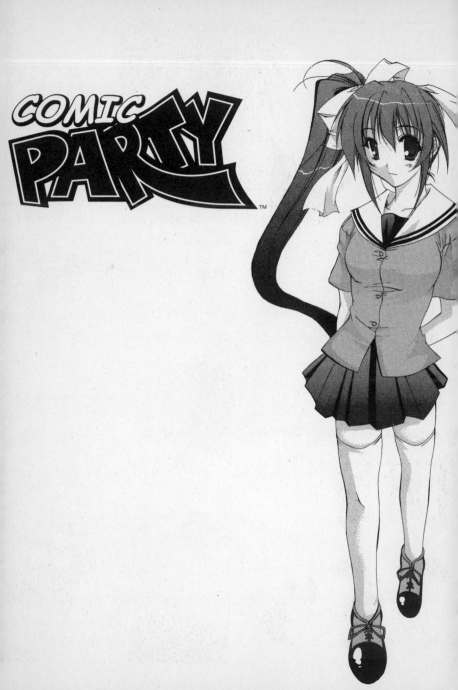

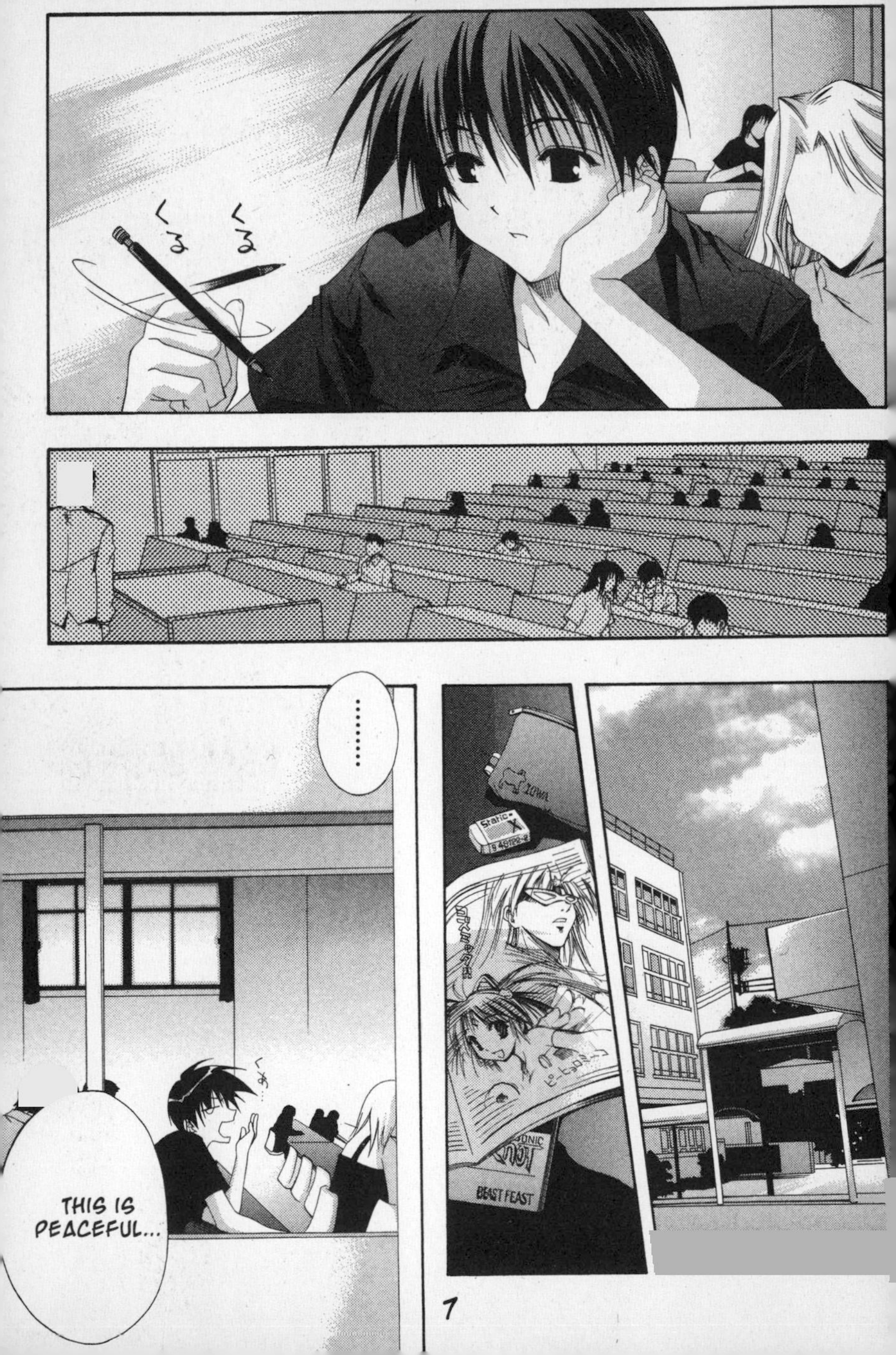
くる くる
Static-X
BEAST FEAST
......
THIS IS PEACEFUL...

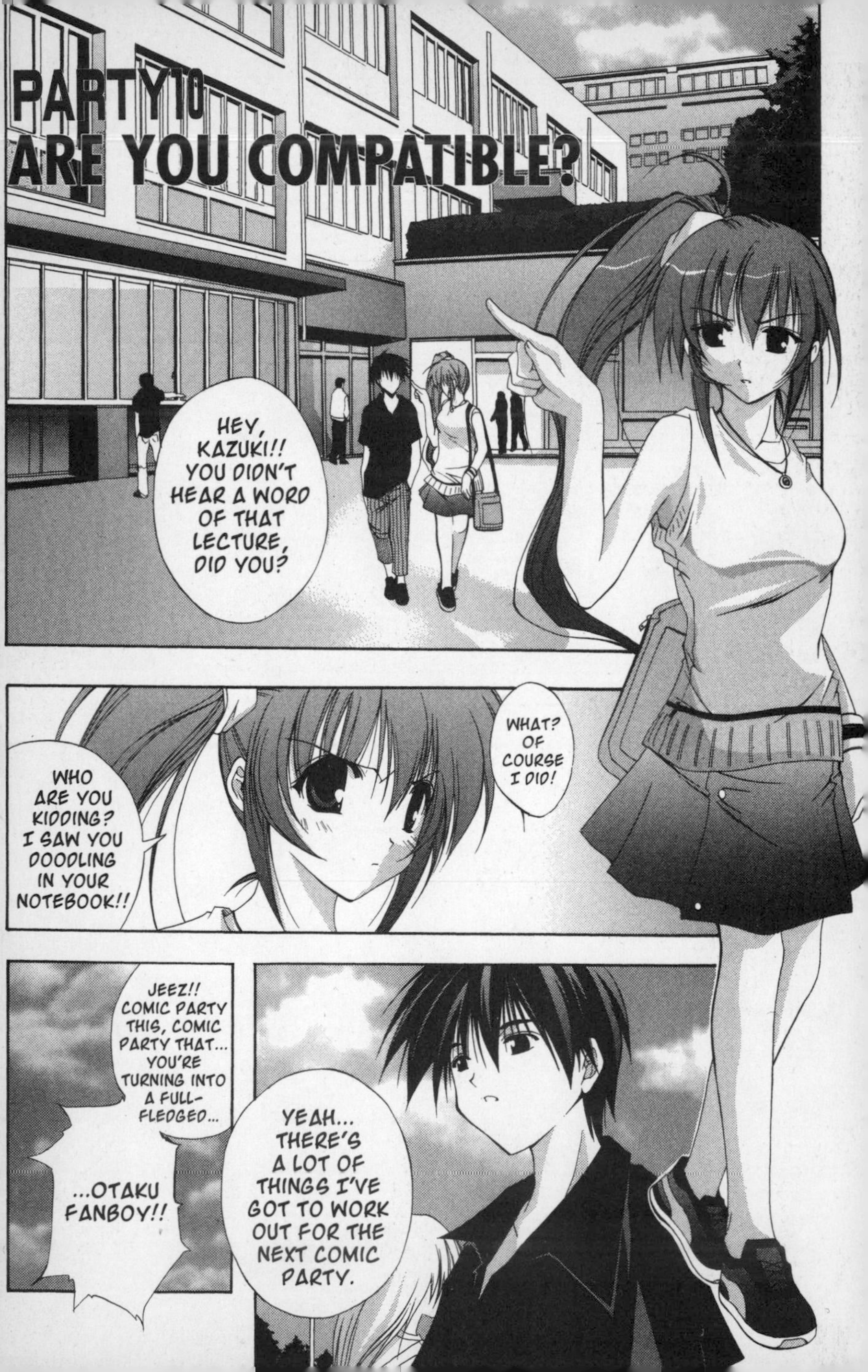
PARTY10
ARE YOU COMPATIBLE?
HEY, KAZUKI!! YOU DIDN'T HEAR A WORD OF THAT LECTURE, DID YOU?
WHAT? OF COURSE I DID!
WHO ARE YOU KIDDING? I SAW YOU DOODLING IN YOUR NOTEBOOK!!
YEAH... THERE'S A LOT OF THINGS I'VE GOT TO WORK OUT FOR THE NEXT COMIC PARTY.
JEEZ!! COMIC PARTY THIS, COMIC PARTY THAT... YOU'RE TURNING INTO A FULL-FLEDGED...
...OTAKU FANBOY!!

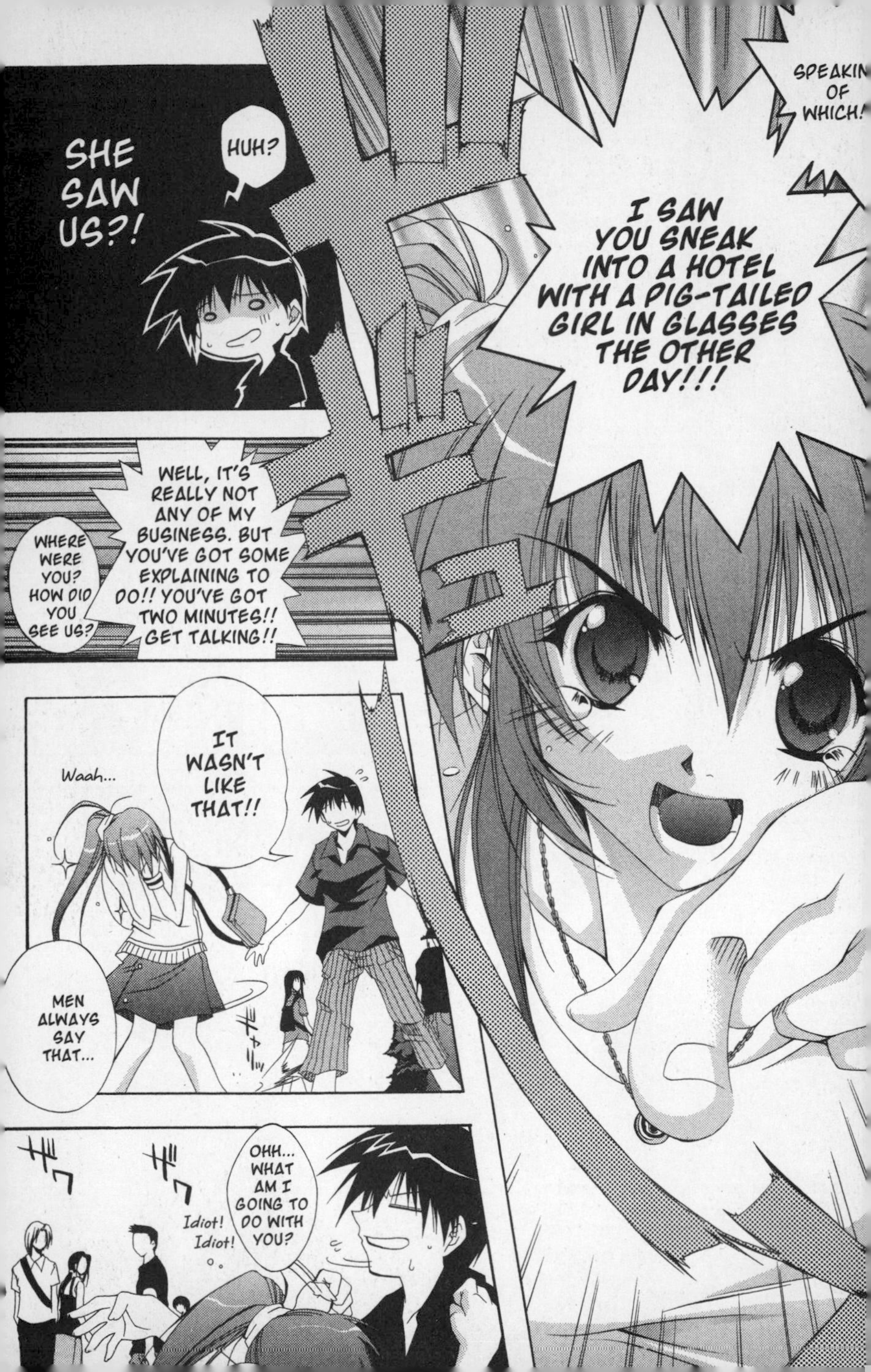
SPEAKIN OF WHICH!
I SAW YOU SNEAK INTO A HOTEL WITH A PIG-TAILED GIRL IN GLASSES THE OTHER DAY!!!
HUH?
SHE SAW US?!
WELL, IT'S REALLY NOT ANY OF MY BUSINESS. BUT YOU'VE GOT SOME EXPLAINING TO DO!! YOU'VE GOT TWO MINUTES!! GET TALKING!!
WHERE WERE YOU? HOW DID YOU SEE US?
IT WASN'T LIKE THAT!!
Waah...
MEN ALWAYS SAY THAT...
OHH... WHAT AM I GOING TO DO WITH YOU?
Idiot! Idiot!

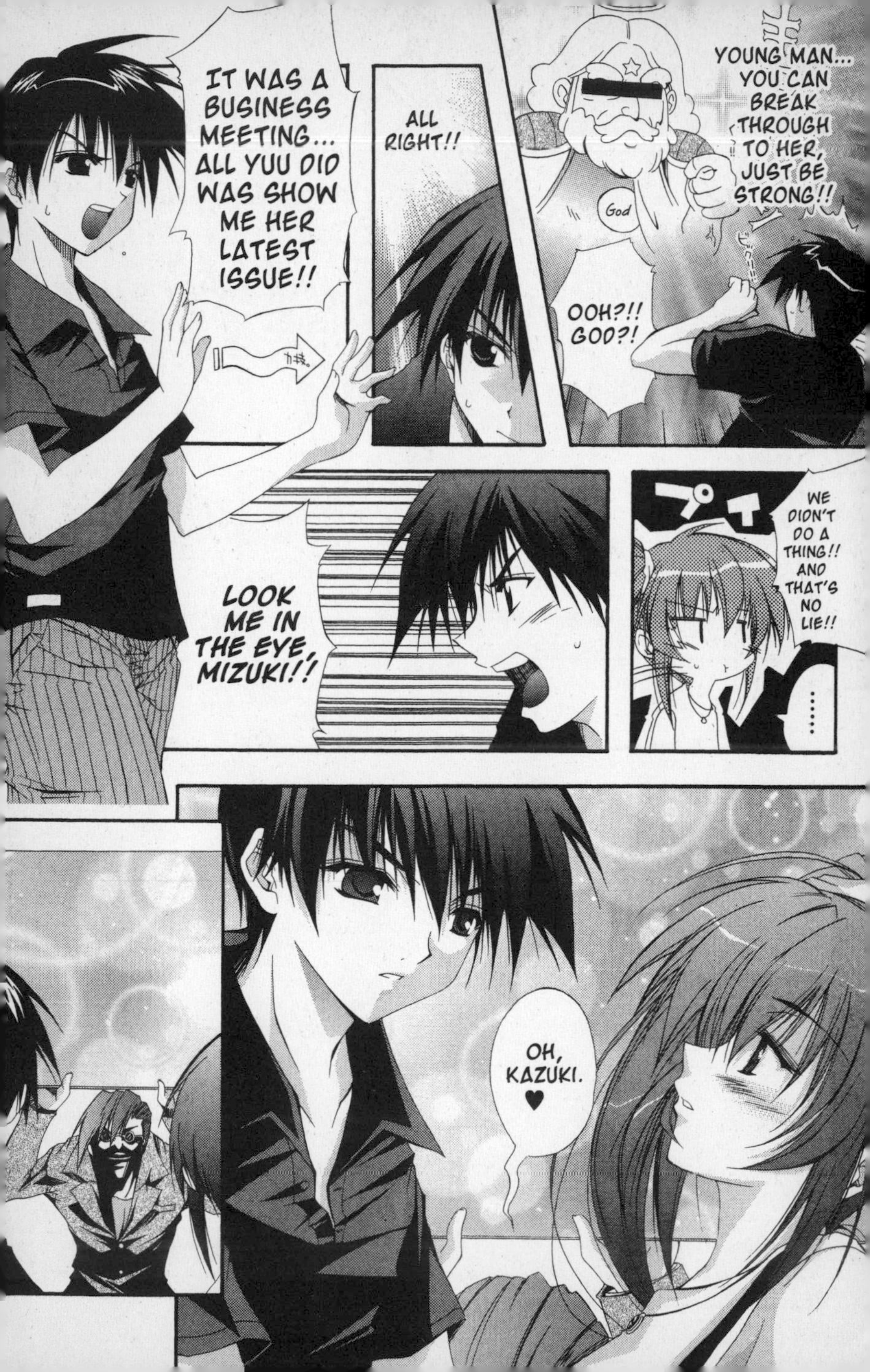

YOUNG MAN... YOU CAN BREAK THROUGH TO HER, JUST BE STRONG!!
God
OOH?!! GOD?!
ALL RIGHT!!
WE DIDN'T DO A THING!! AND THAT'S NO LIE!!
......
LOOK ME IN THE EYE MIZUKI!!
IT WAS A BUSINESS MEETING... ALL YUU DID WAS SHOW ME HER LATEST ISSUE!!
OH, KAZUKI. ♥

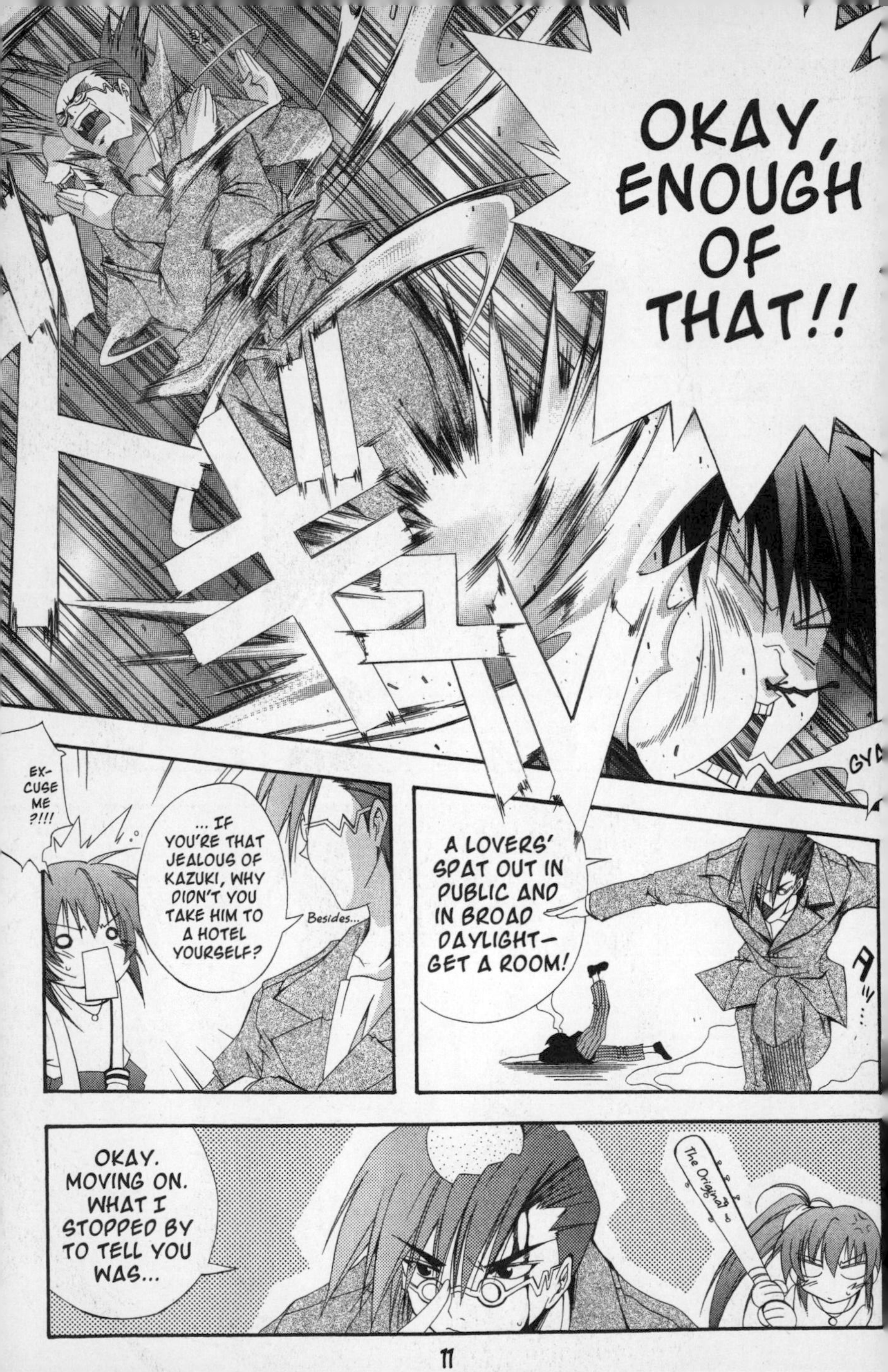
OKAY, ENOUGH OF THAT!!
GYA
A LOVERS' SPAT OUT IN PUBLIC AND IN BROAD DAYLIGHT— GET A ROOM!
Besides...
... IF YOU'RE THAT JEALOUS OF KAZUKI, WHY DIDN'T YOU TAKE HIM TO A HOTEL YOURSELF?
EX-CUSE ME ?!!!
The Original
OKAY. MOVING ON. WHAT I STOPPED BY TO TELL YOU WAS...

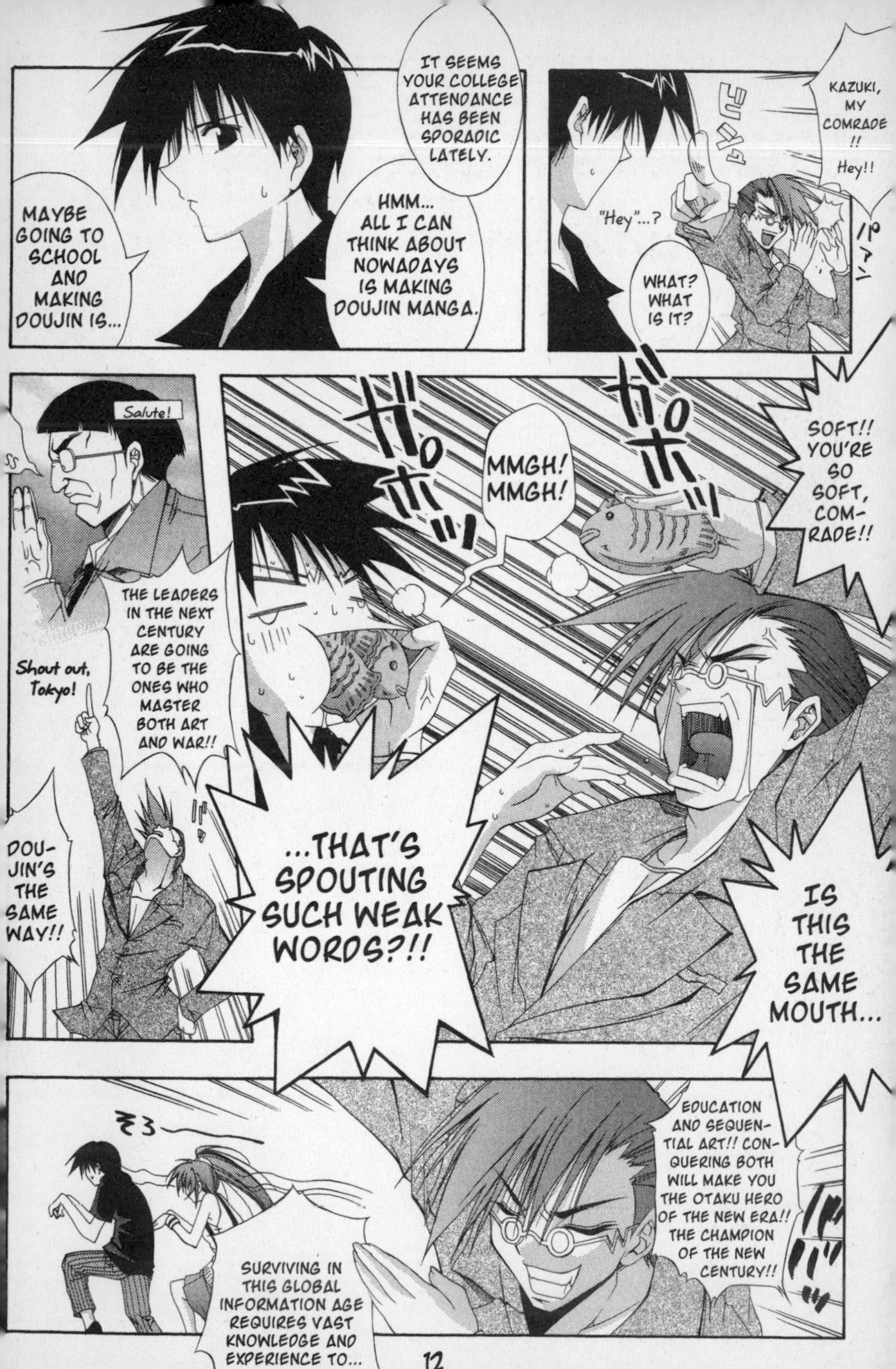
KAZUKI, MY COMRADE !!
Hey!!
"Hey"...?
WHAT? WHAT IS IT?
IT SEEMS YOUR COLLEGE ATTENDANCE HAS BEEN SPORADIC LATELY.
HMM... ALL I CAN THINK ABOUT NOWADAYS IS MAKING DOUJIN MANGA.
MAYBE GOING TO SCHOOL AND MAKING DOUJIN IS...
SOFT!! YOU'RE SO SOFT, COM-RADE!!
MMGH! MMGH!
IS THIS THE SAME MOUTH...
...THAT'S SPOUTING SUCH WEAK WORDS?!!
Salute!
THE LEADERS IN THE NEXT CENTURY ARE GOING TO BE THE ONES WHO MASTER BOTH ART AND WAR!!
Shout out, Tokyo!
DOU-JIN'S THE SAME WAY!!
EDUCATION AND SEQUEN-TIAL ART!! CON-QUERING BOTH WILL MAKE YOU THE OTAKU HERO OF THE NEW ERA!! THE CHAMPION OF THE NEW CENTURY!!
SURVIVING IN THIS GLOBAL INFORMATION AGE REQUIRES VAST KNOWLEDGE AND EXPERIENCE TO...

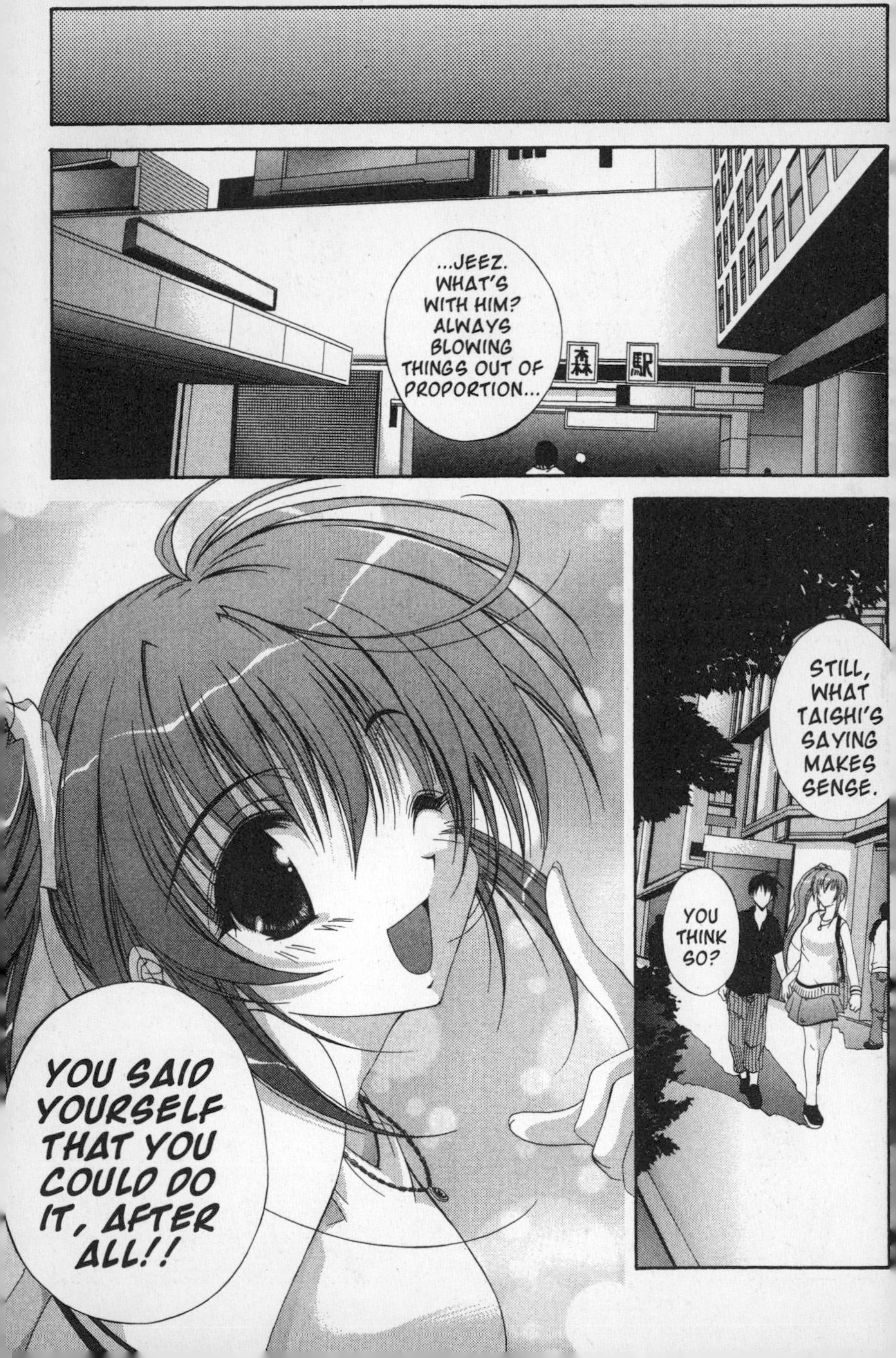
...JEEZ. WHAT'S WITH HIM? ALWAYS BLOWING THINGS OUT OF PROPORTION...
森 駅
STILL, WHAT TAISHI'S SAYING MAKES SENSE.
YOU THINK SO?
YOU SAID YOURSELF THAT YOU COULD DO IT, AFTER ALL!!

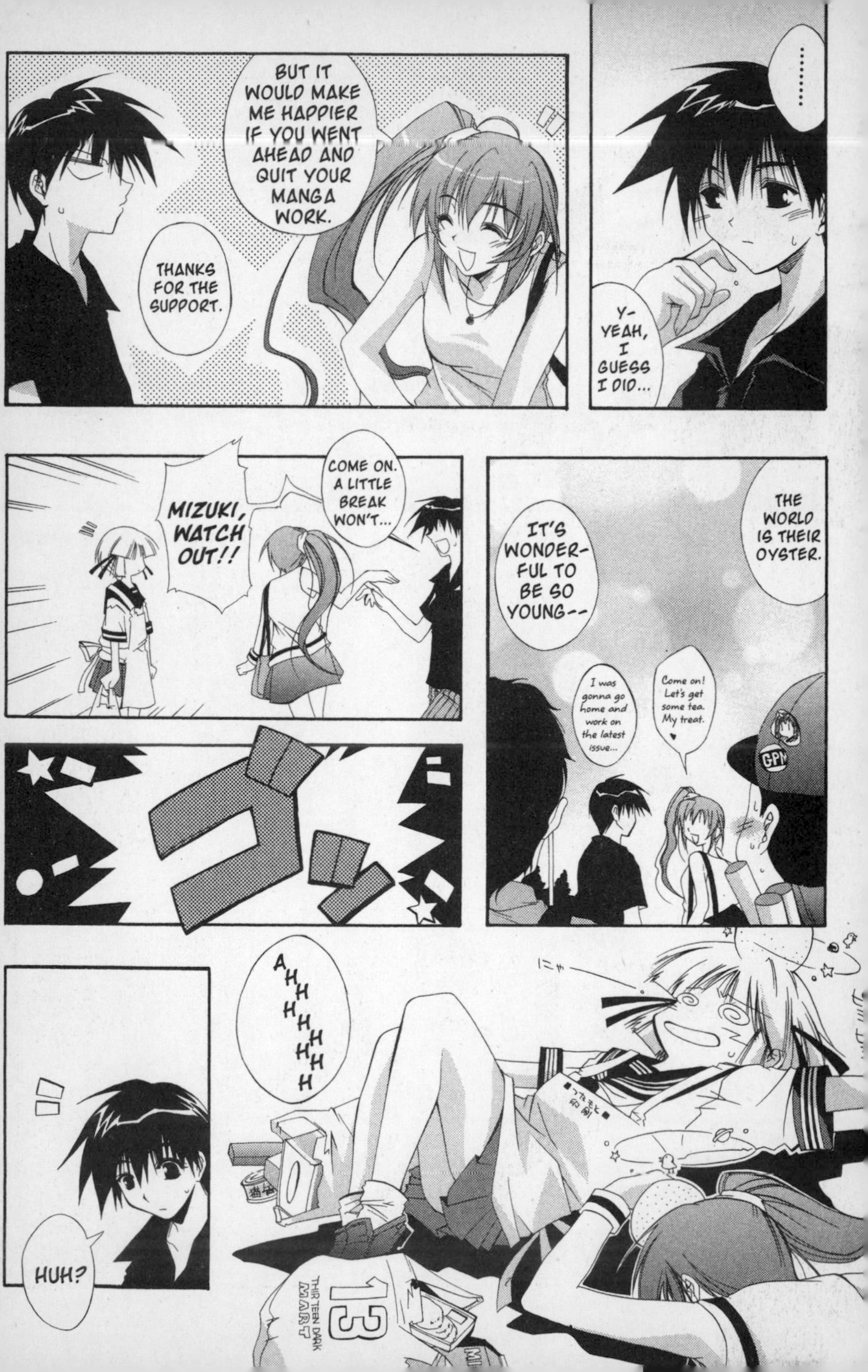
……
Y-YEAH, I GUESS I DID...
BUT IT WOULD MAKE ME HAPPIER IF YOU WENT AHEAD AND QUIT YOUR MANGA WORK.
THANKS FOR THE SUPPORT.
THE WORLD IS THEIR OYSTER.
IT'S WONDERFUL TO BE SO YOUNG--
Come on! Let's get some tea. My treat.
I was gonna go home and work on the latest issue...
GPM
COME ON. A LITTLE BREAK WON'T...
MIZUKI, WATCH OUT!!
AHHHHHHHHH
にゃー
13
THIR TEEN DARK MART
HUH?

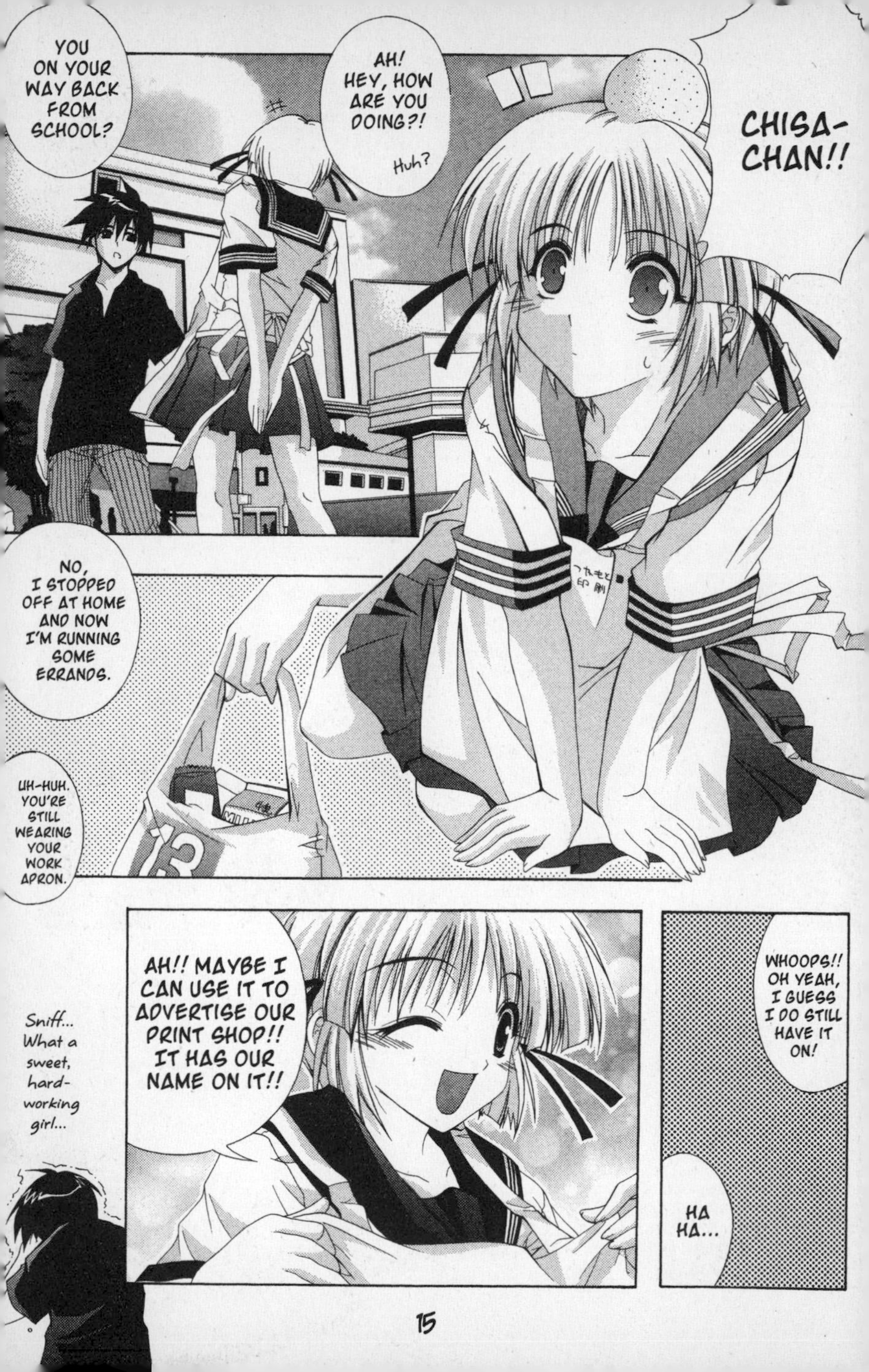
CHISA-CHAN!!
AH! HEY, HOW ARE YOU DOING?!
Huh?
YOU ON YOUR WAY BACK FROM SCHOOL?
NO, I STOPPED OFF AT HOME AND NOW I'M RUNNING SOME ERRANDS.
UH-HUH. YOU'RE STILL WEARING YOUR WORK APRON.
WHOOPS!! OH YEAH, I GUESS I DO STILL HAVE IT ON!
HA HA...
AH!! MAYBE I CAN USE IT TO ADVERTISE OUR PRINT SHOP!! IT HAS OUR NAME ON IT!!
Sniff... What a sweet, hard-working girl...

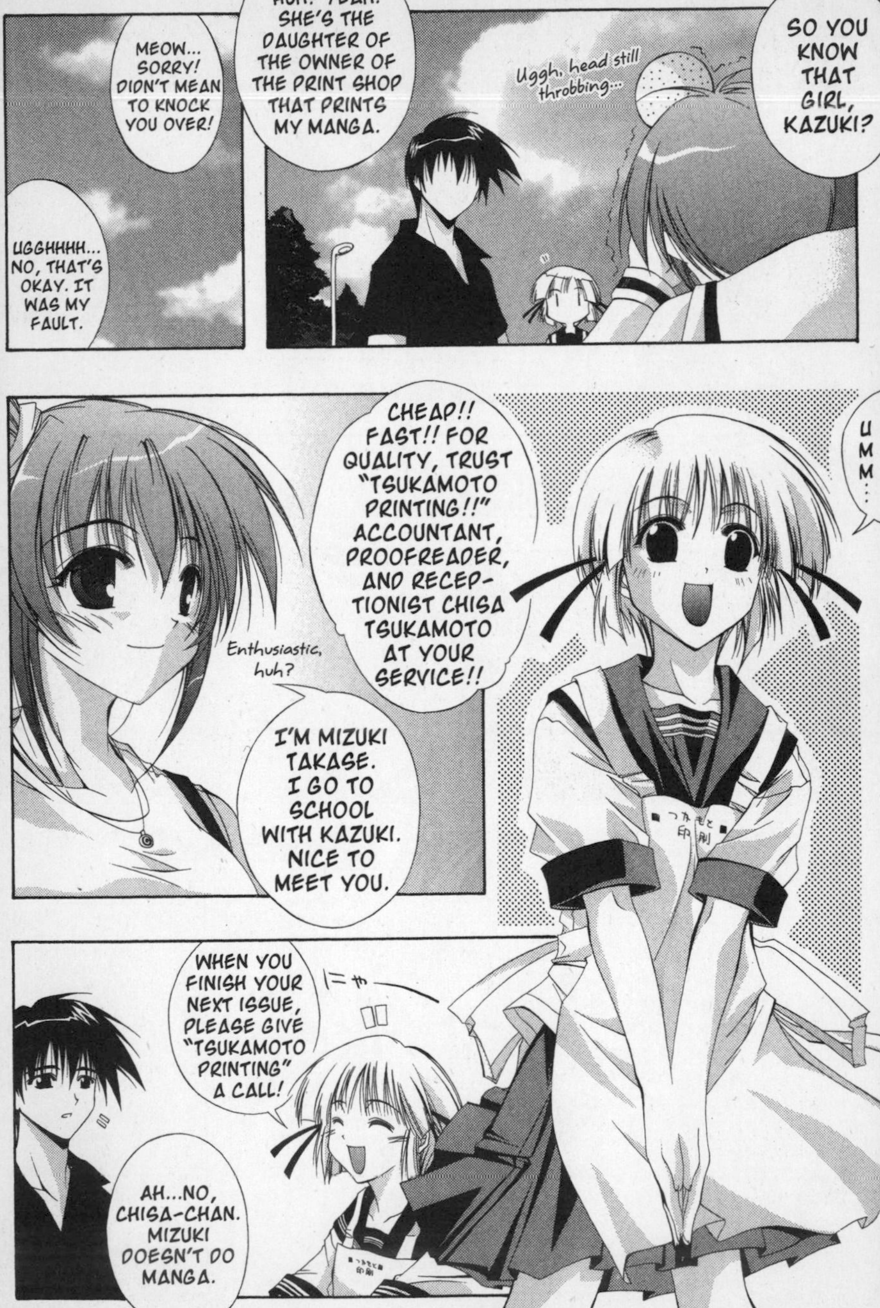
SO YOU KNOW THAT GIRL, KAZUKI?
Uggh, head still throbbing...
HUH? YEAH. SHE'S THE DAUGHTER OF THE OWNER OF THE PRINT SHOP THAT PRINTS MY MANGA.
MEOW... SORRY! DIDN'T MEAN TO KNOCK YOU OVER!
UGGHHHH... NO, THAT'S OKAY. IT WAS MY FAULT.
UMM...
CHEAP!! FAST!! FOR QUALITY, TRUST "TSUKAMOTO PRINTING!!" ACCOUNTANT, PROOFREADER, AND RECEP- TIONIST CHISA TSUKAMOTO AT YOUR SERVICE!!
Enthusiastic, huh?
I'M MIZUKI TAKASE. I GO TO SCHOOL WITH KAZUKI. NICE TO MEET YOU.
WHEN YOU FINISH YOUR NEXT ISSUE, PLEASE GIVE "TSUKAMOTO PRINTING" A CALL!
AH...NO, CHISA-CHAN. MIZUKI DOESN'T DO MANGA.

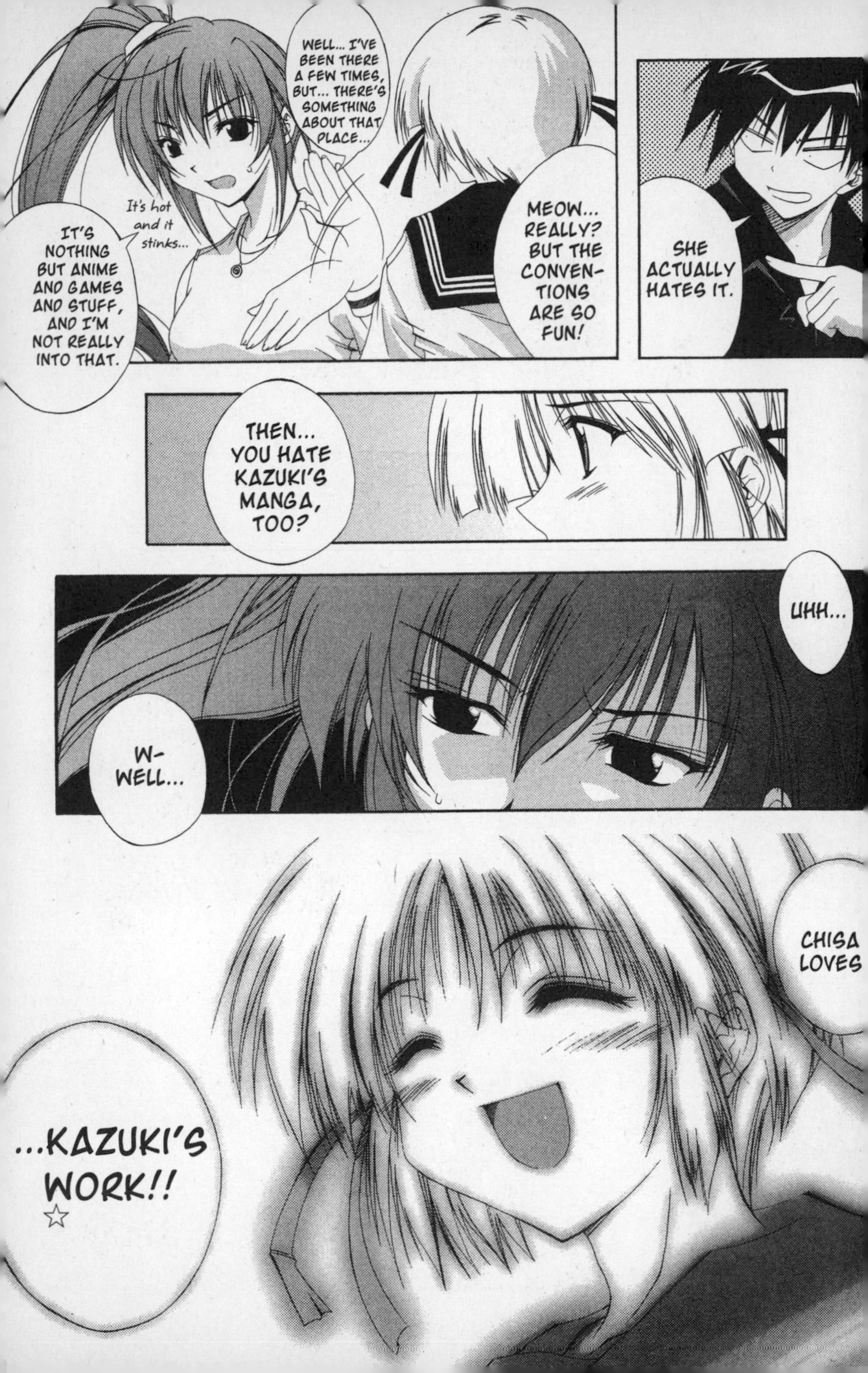
SHE ACTUALLY HATES IT.
MEOW... REALLY? BUT THE CONVEN-TIONS ARE SO FUN!
WELL... I'VE BEEN THERE A FEW TIMES, BUT... THERE'S SOMETHING ABOUT THAT PLACE...
It's hot and it stinks...
IT'S NOTHING BUT ANIME AND GAMES AND STUFF, AND I'M NOT REALLY INTO THAT.
THEN... YOU HATE KAZUKI'S MANGA, TOO?
UHH...
W-WELL...
CHISA LOVES
...KAZUKI'S WORK!! ☆

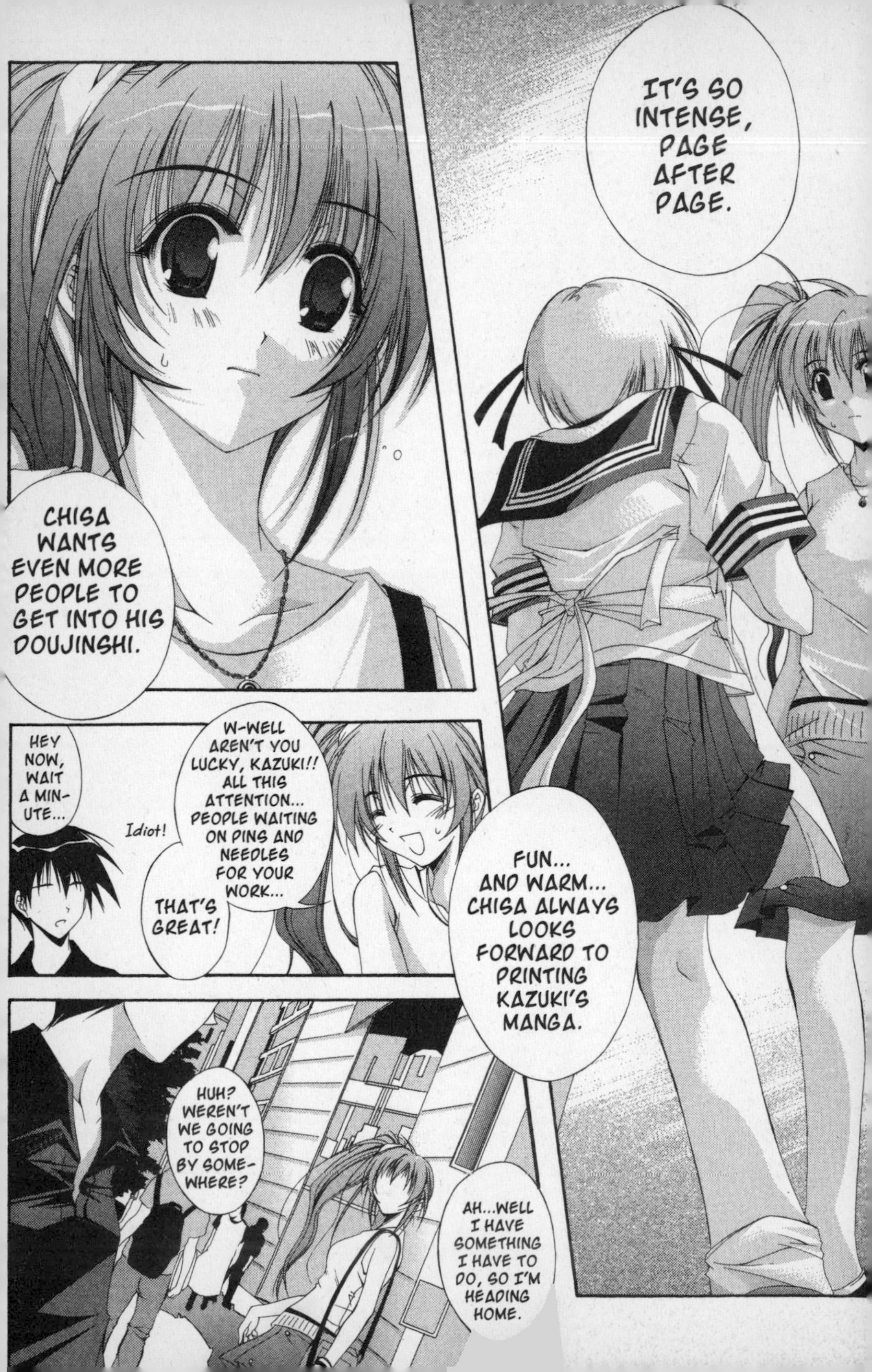
IT'S SO INTENSE, PAGE AFTER PAGE.
FUN... AND WARM... CHISA ALWAYS LOOKS FORWARD TO PRINTING KAZUKI'S MANGA.
CHISA WANTS EVEN MORE PEOPLE TO GET INTO HIS DOUJINSHI.
W-WELL AREN'T YOU LUCKY, KAZUKI!! ALL THIS ATTENTION... PEOPLE WAITING ON PINS AND NEEDLES FOR YOUR WORK...
THAT'S GREAT!
Idiot!
HEY NOW, WAIT A MIN-UTE...
HUH? WEREN'T WE GOING TO STOP BY SOME-WHERE?
AH...WELL I HAVE SOMETHING I HAVE TO DO, SO I'M HEADING HOME.

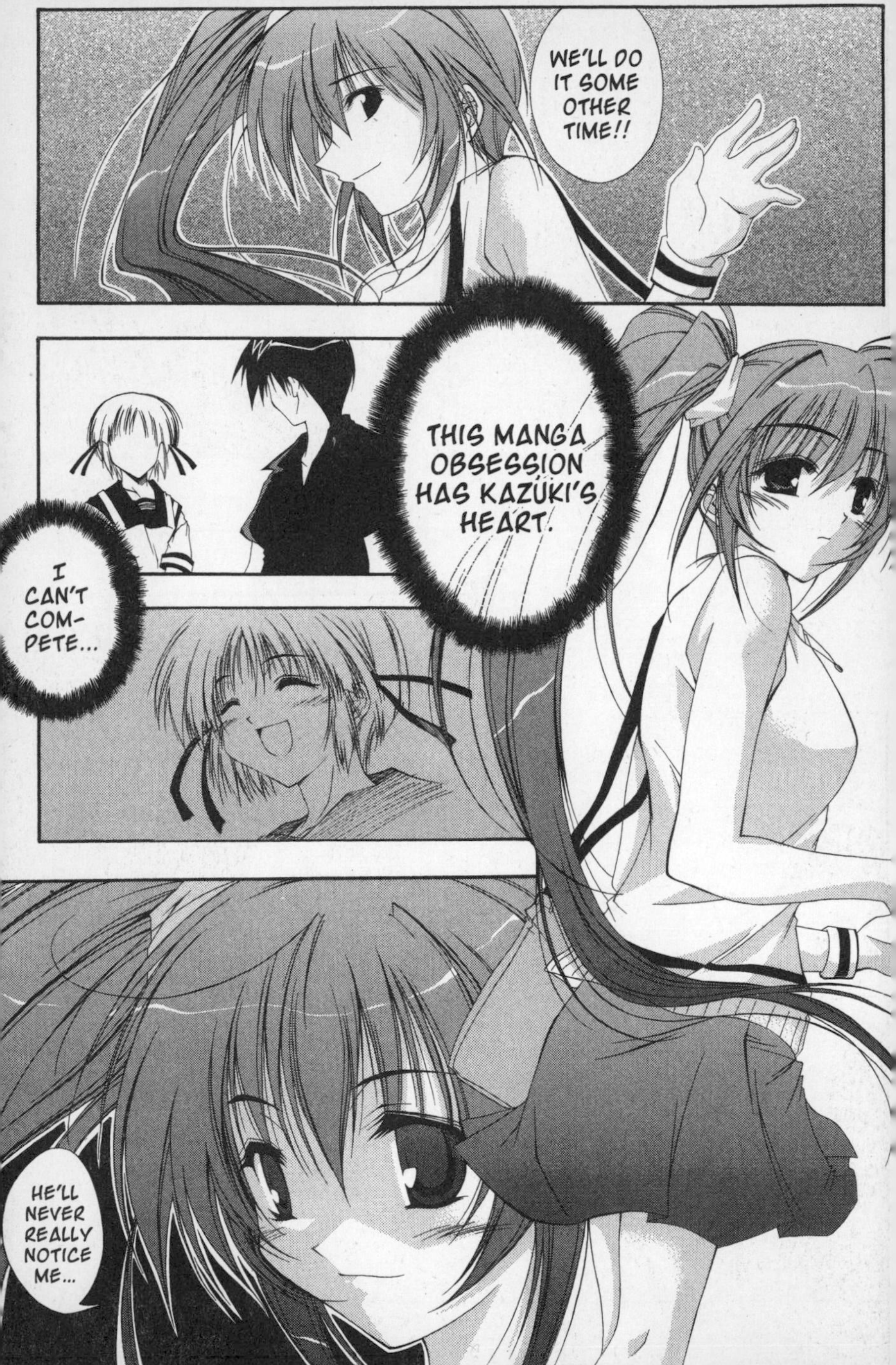
WE'LL DO IT SOME OTHER TIME!!
THIS MANGA OBSESSION HAS KAZUKI'S HEART.
I CAN'T COM-PETE...
HE'LL NEVER REALLY NOTICE ME...

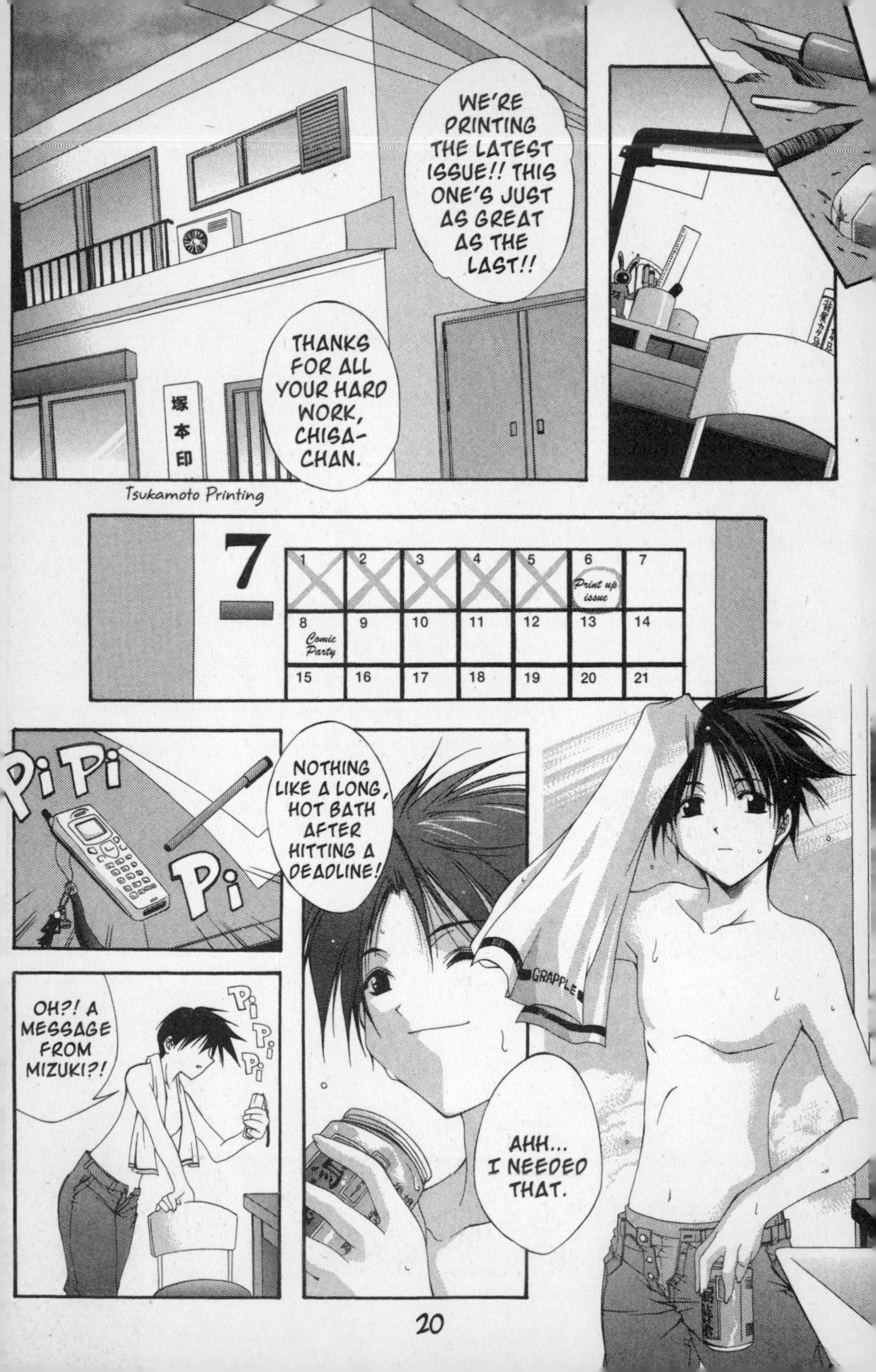
WE'RE PRINTING THE LATEST ISSUE!! THIS ONE'S JUST AS GREAT AS THE LAST!!
THANKS FOR ALL YOUR HARD WORK, CHISA-CHAN.
塚本印
Tsukamoto Printing
7
1 2 3 4 5 6 7
Print up issue
8 9 10 11 12 13 14
Comic Party
15 16 17 18 19 20 21
GRAPPLE
AHH... I NEEDED THAT.
NOTHING LIKE A LONG, HOT BATH AFTER HITTING A DEADLINE!
Pi Pi
Pi
OH?! A MESSAGE FROM MIZUKI?!
Pi Pi Pi Pi

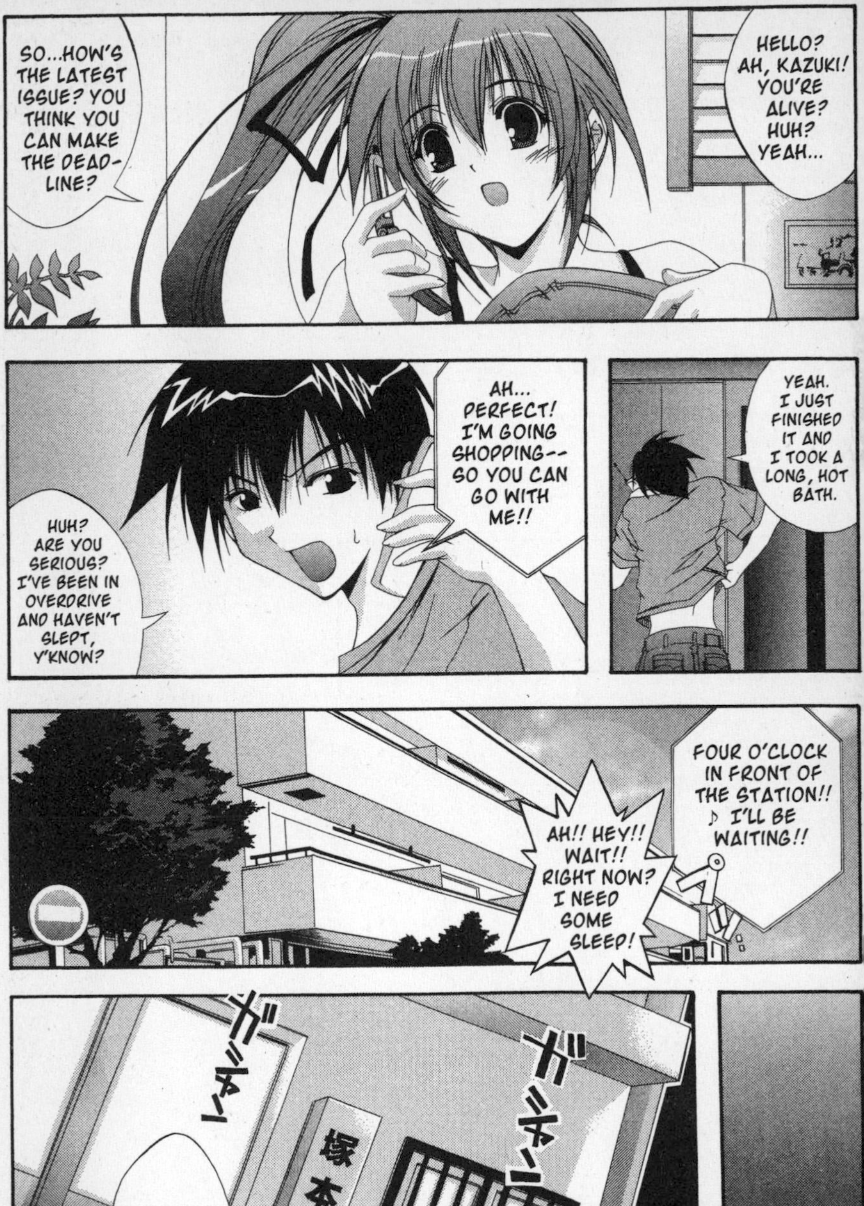
HELLO? AH, KAZUKI! YOU'RE ALIVE? HUH? YEAH...
SO...HOW'S THE LATEST ISSUE? YOU THINK YOU CAN MAKE THE DEAD-LINE?
YEAH. I JUST FINISHED IT AND I TOOK A LONG, HOT BATH.
AH... PERFECT! I'M GOING SHOPPING-- SO YOU CAN GO WITH ME!!
HUH? ARE YOU SERIOUS? I'VE BEEN IN OVERDRIVE AND HAVEN'T SLEPT, Y'KNOW?
FOUR O'CLOCK IN FRONT OF THE STATION!! ♪ I'LL BE WAITING!!
AH!! HEY!! WAIT!! RIGHT NOW? I NEED SOME SLEEP!
ガシャーン
ガシャーン
塚本印刷
OH NO...

Tsukamoto Printing

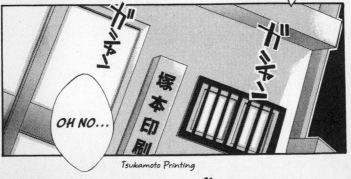

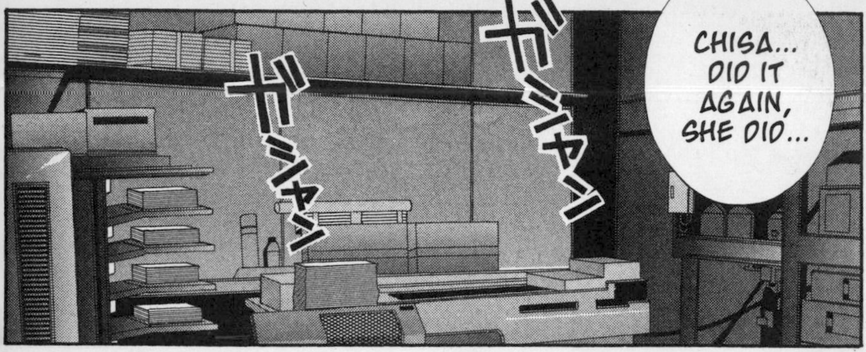
CHISA... DID IT AGAIN, SHE DID...
ガシャン
ガシャン

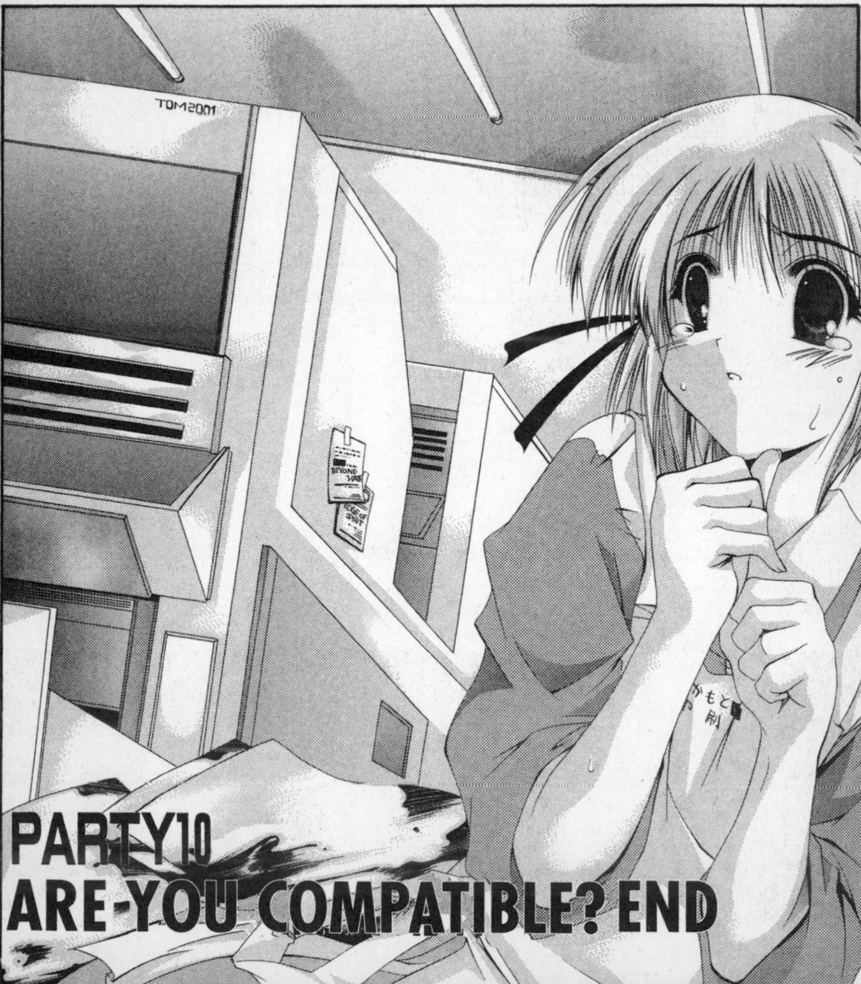
PARTY10
ARE-YOU COMPATIBLE? END

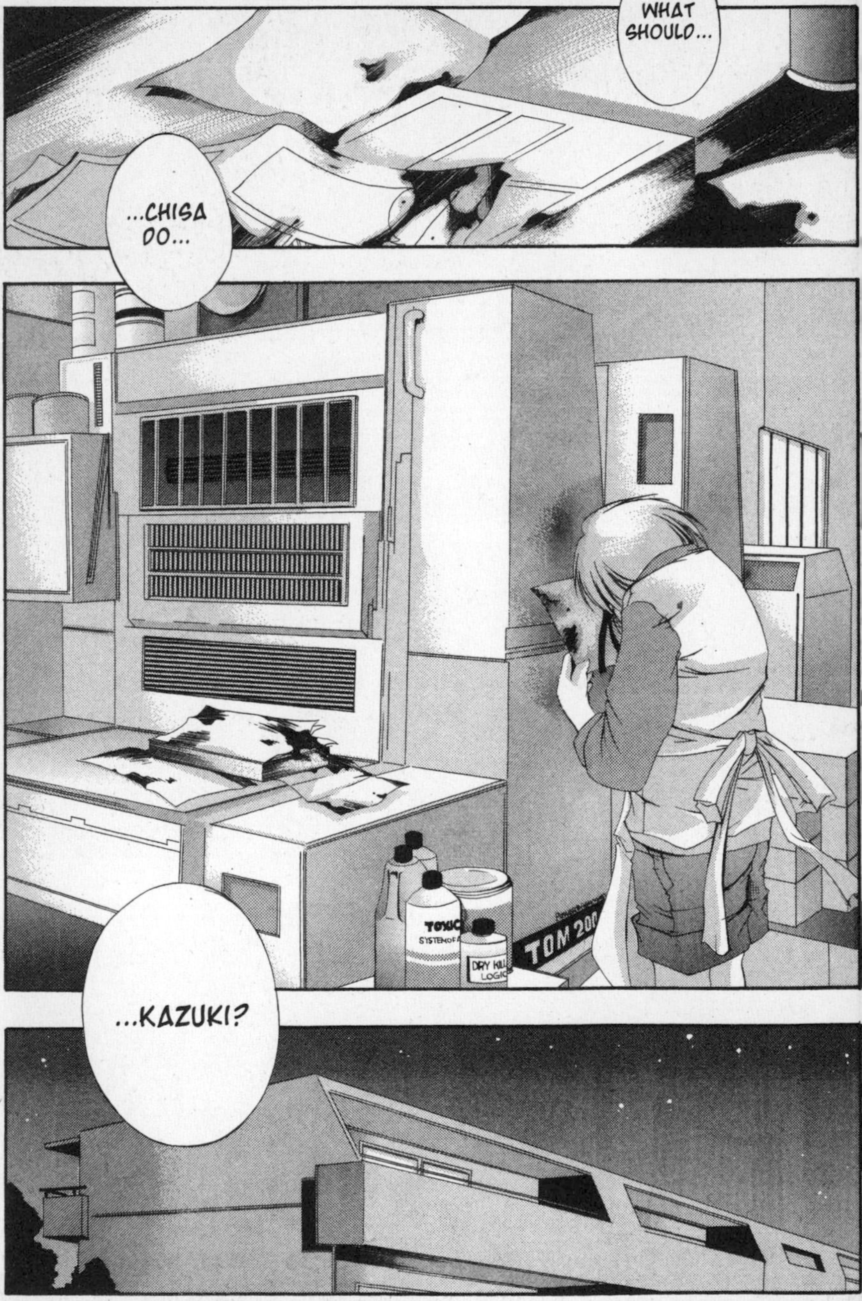
WHAT SHOULD...
...CHISA DO...
...KAZUKI?

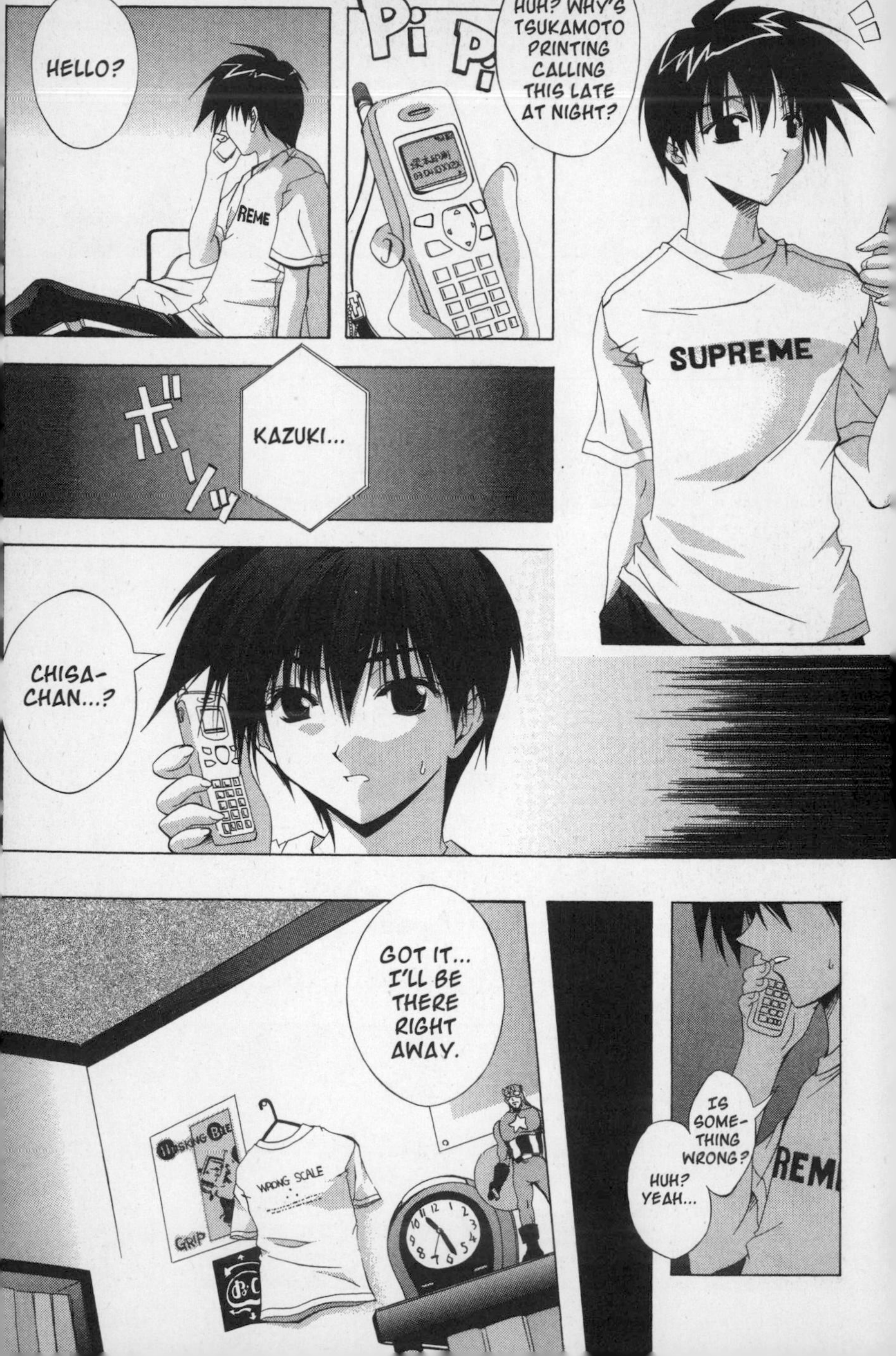
HUH? WHY'S TSUKAMOTO PRINTING CALLING THIS LATE AT NIGHT?
SUPREME
Pi Pi
HELLO?
REME
ボーッ
KAZUKI...
CHISA-CHAN...?
IS SOMETHING WRONG?
HUH? YEAH...
REME
GOT IT... I'LL BE THERE RIGHT AWAY.
WRONG SCALE
GRIP

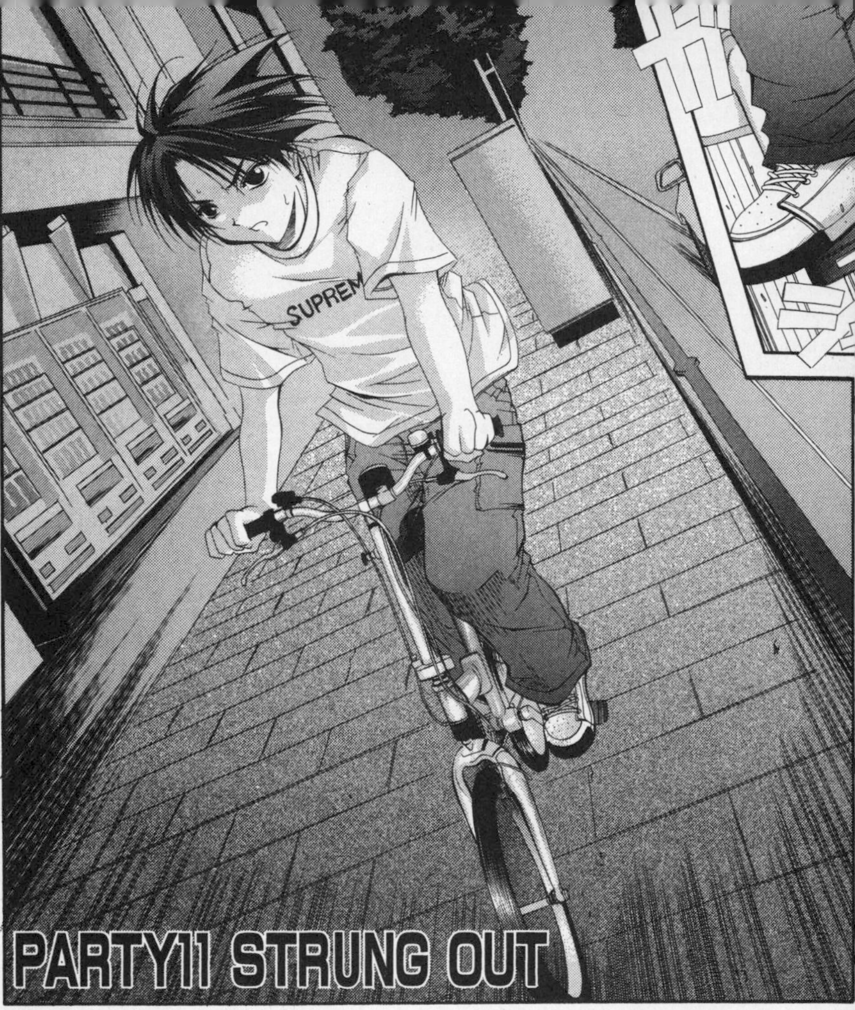
SUPREM
PARTY11 STRUNG OUT

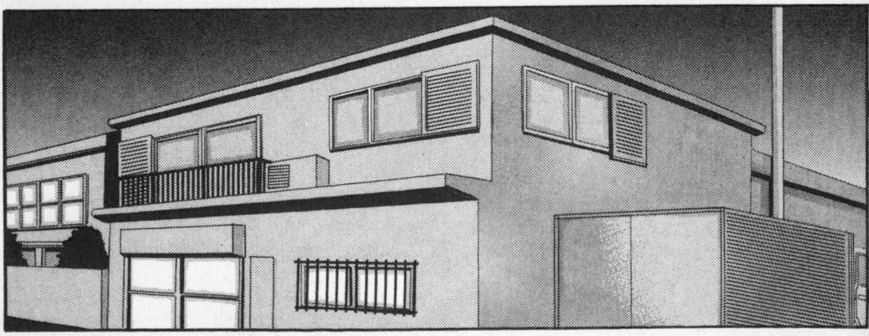

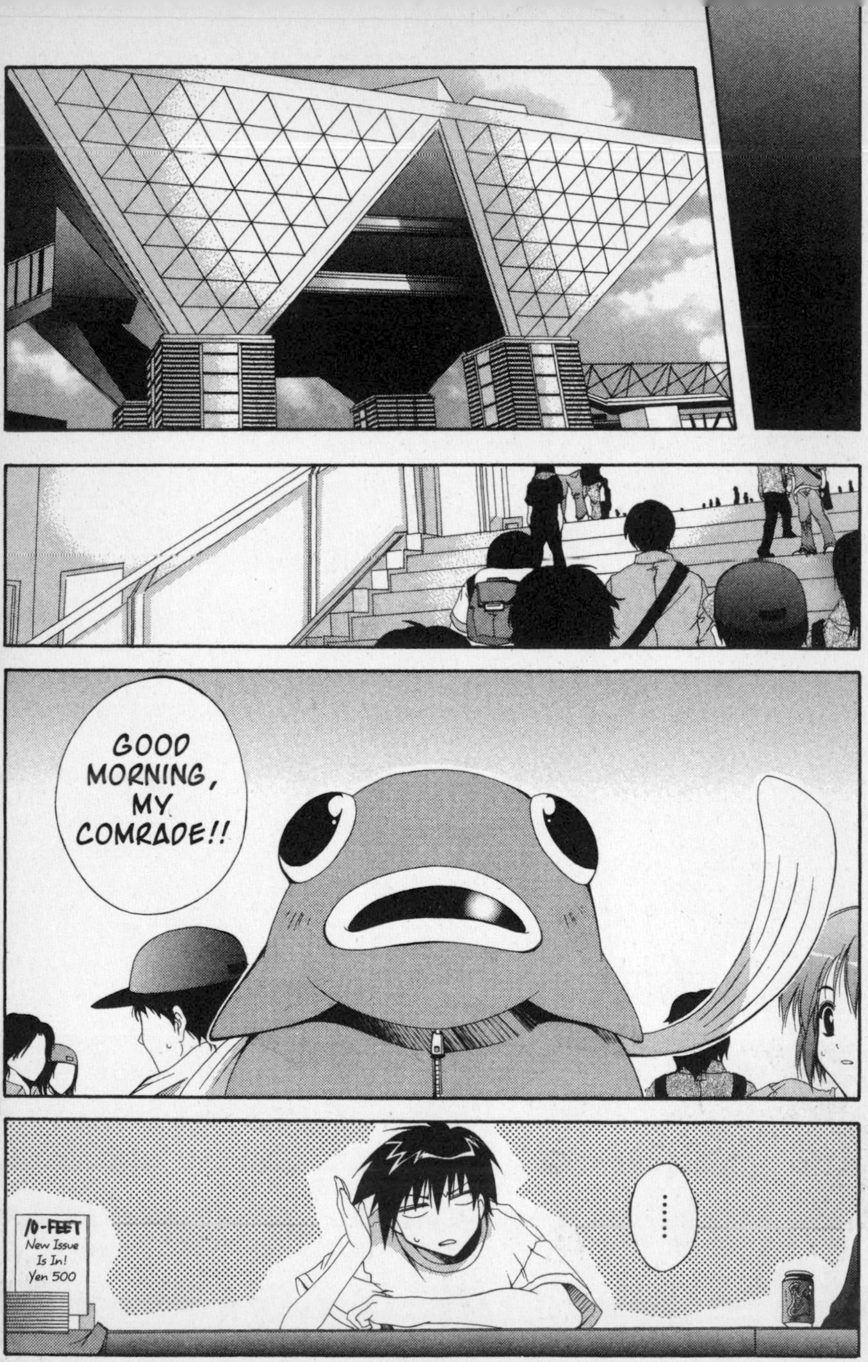
GOOD MORNING, MY COMRADE!!
......
10-FEET
New Issue Is In!
Yen 500

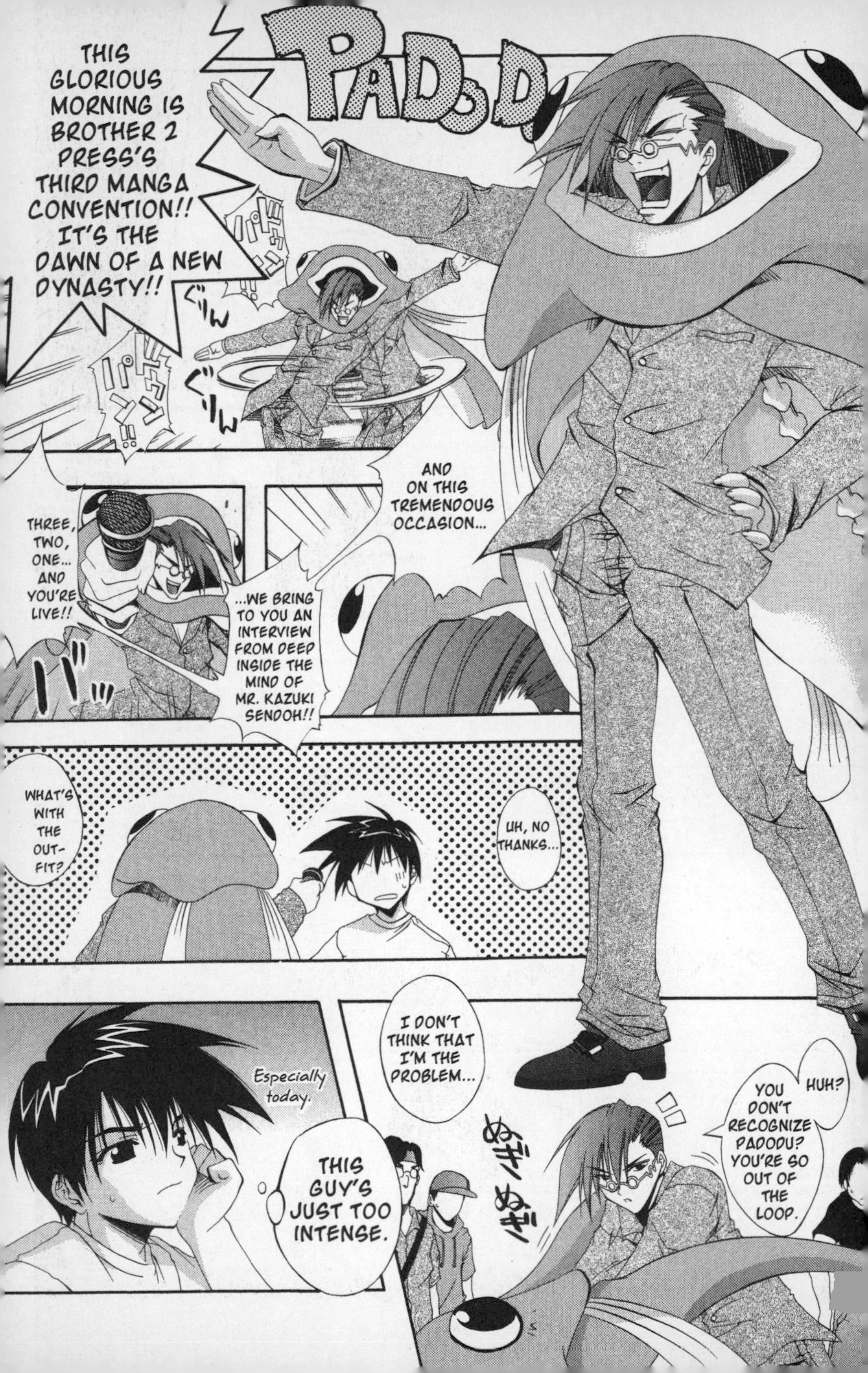
PADoDU
THIS GLORIOUS MORNING IS BROTHER 2 PRESS'S THIRD MANGA CONVENTION!! IT'S THE DAWN OF A NEW DYNASTY!!
AND ON THIS TREMENDOUS OCCASION...
...WE BRING TO YOU AN INTERVIEW FROM DEEP INSIDE THE MIND OF MR. KAZUKI SENDOH!!
THREE, TWO, ONE... AND YOU'RE LIVE!!
UH, NO THANKS...
WHAT'S WITH THE OUT-FIT?
HUH?
YOU DON'T RECOGNIZE PADODU? YOU'RE SO OUT OF THE LOOP.
ぬぎ ぬぎ
I DON'T THINK THAT I'M THE PROBLEM...
Especially today.
THIS GUY'S JUST TOO INTENSE.

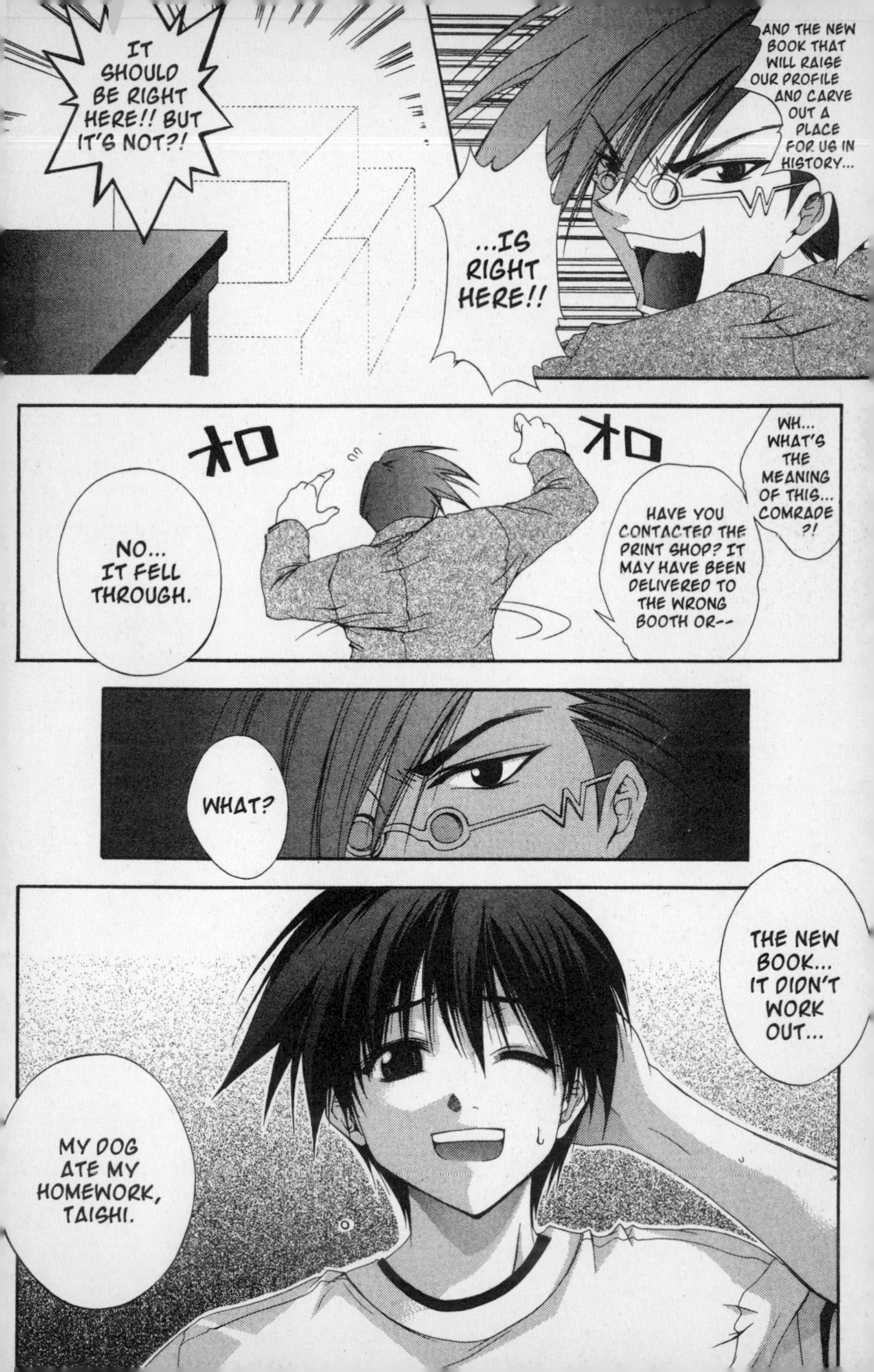
AND THE NEW BOOK THAT WILL RAISE OUR PROFILE AND CARVE OUT A PLACE FOR US IN HISTORY...
...IS RIGHT HERE!!
IT SHOULD BE RIGHT HERE!! BUT IT'S NOT?!
WH... WHAT'S THE MEANING OF THIS... COMRADE?!
オロ
HAVE YOU CONTACTED THE PRINT SHOP? IT MAY HAVE BEEN DELIVERED TO THE WRONG BOOTH OR--
オロ
NO... IT FELL THROUGH.
WHAT?
THE NEW BOOK... IT DIDN'T WORK OUT...
MY DOG ATE MY HOMEWORK, TAISHI.

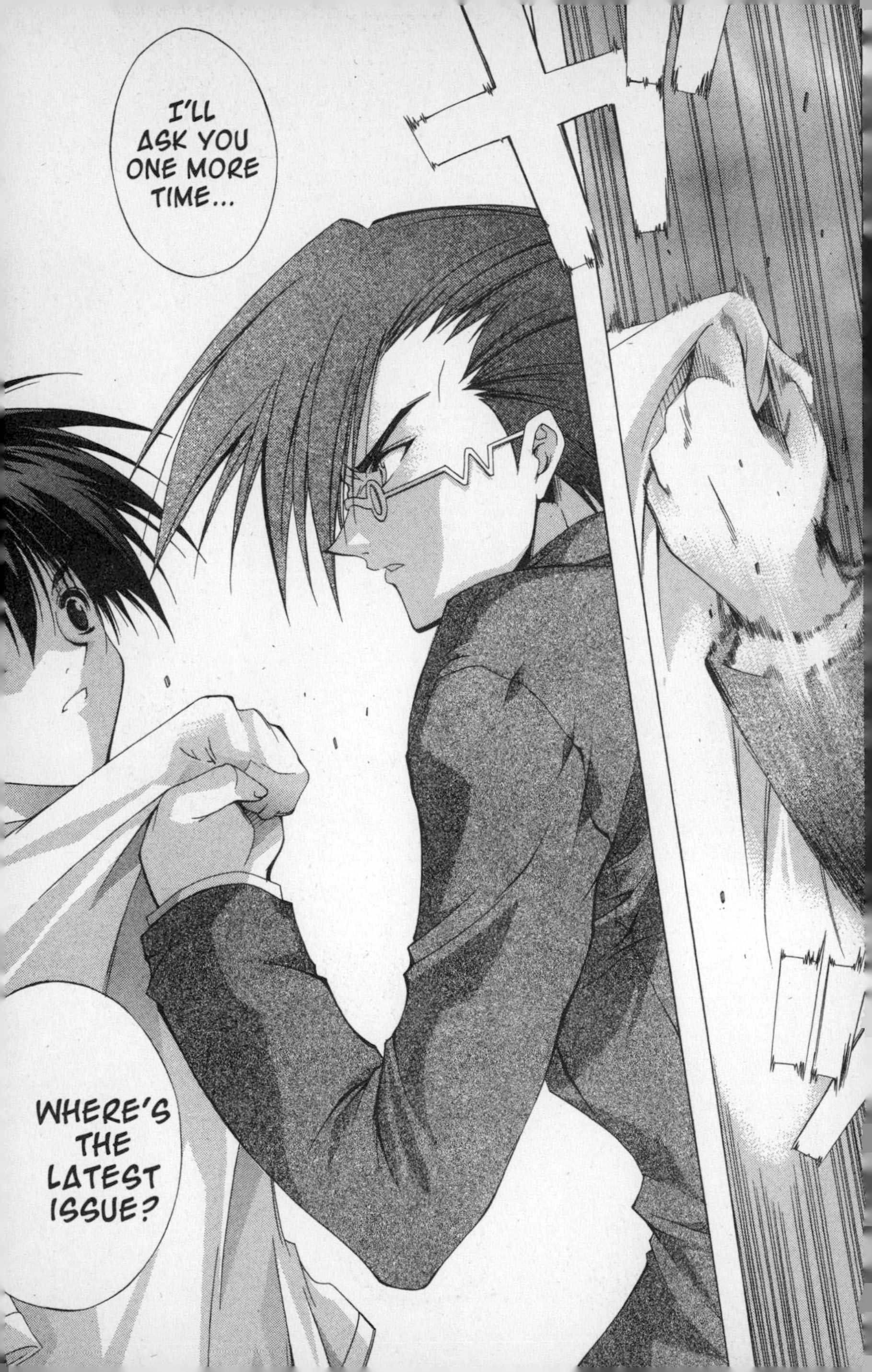
I'LL ASK YOU ONE MORE TIME...
WHERE'S THE LATEST ISSUE?

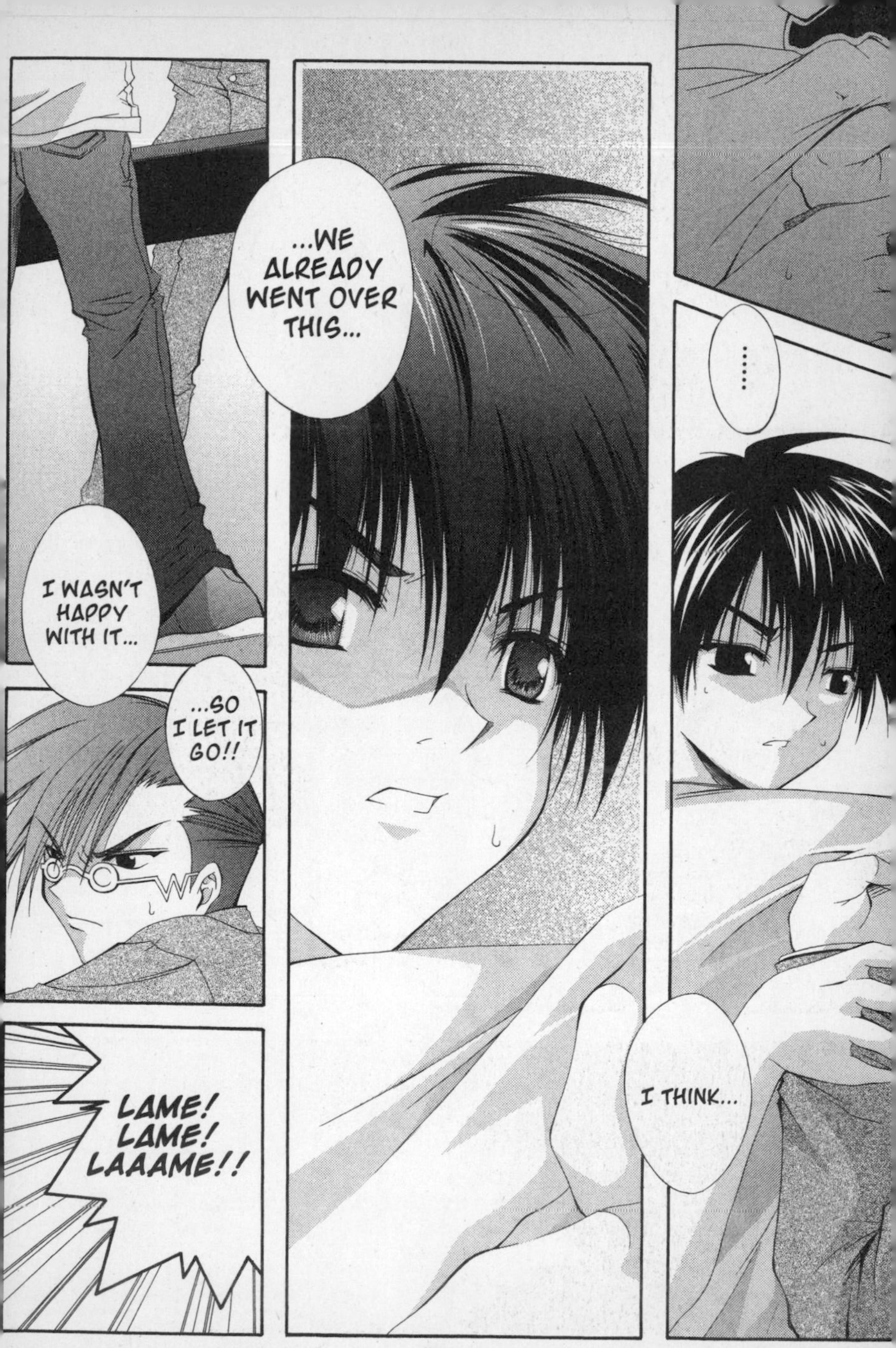
......
I THINK...
...WE ALREADY WENT OVER THIS...
I WASN'T HAPPY WITH IT...
...SO I LET IT GO!!
LAME! LAME! LAAAME!!

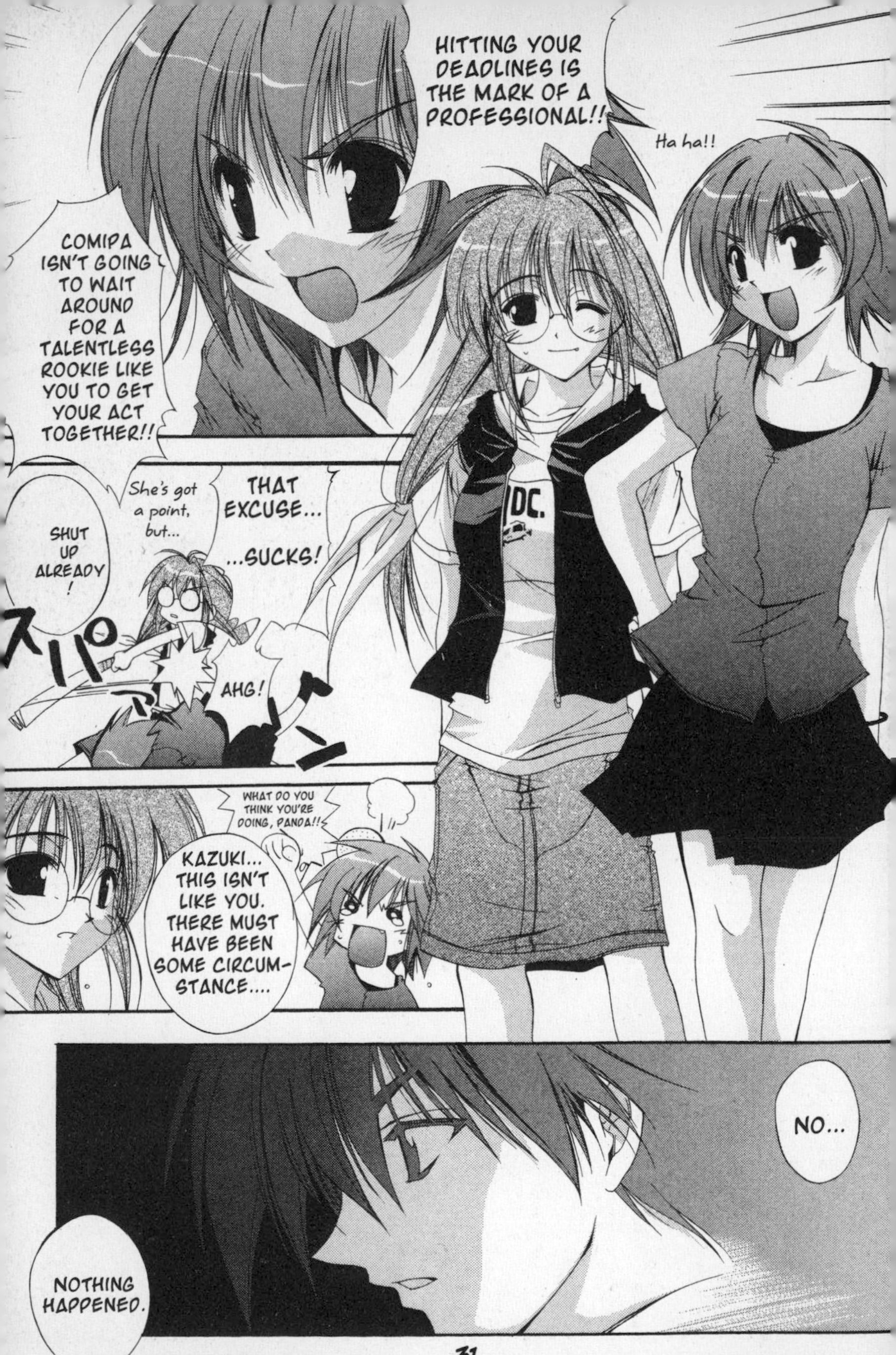
HITTING YOUR DEADLINES IS THE MARK OF A PROFESSIONAL!!
Ha ha!!
COMIPA ISN'T GOING TO WAIT AROUND FOR A TALENTLESS ROOKIE LIKE YOU TO GET YOUR ACT TOGETHER!!
THAT EXCUSE...
...SUCKS!
She's got a point, but...
SHUT UP ALREADY!
AHG!
スパーン
WHAT DO YOU THINK YOU'RE DOING, PANDA!!
KAZUKI... THIS ISN'T LIKE YOU. THERE MUST HAVE BEEN SOME CIRCUM-STANCE....
NO...
NOTHING HAPPENED.

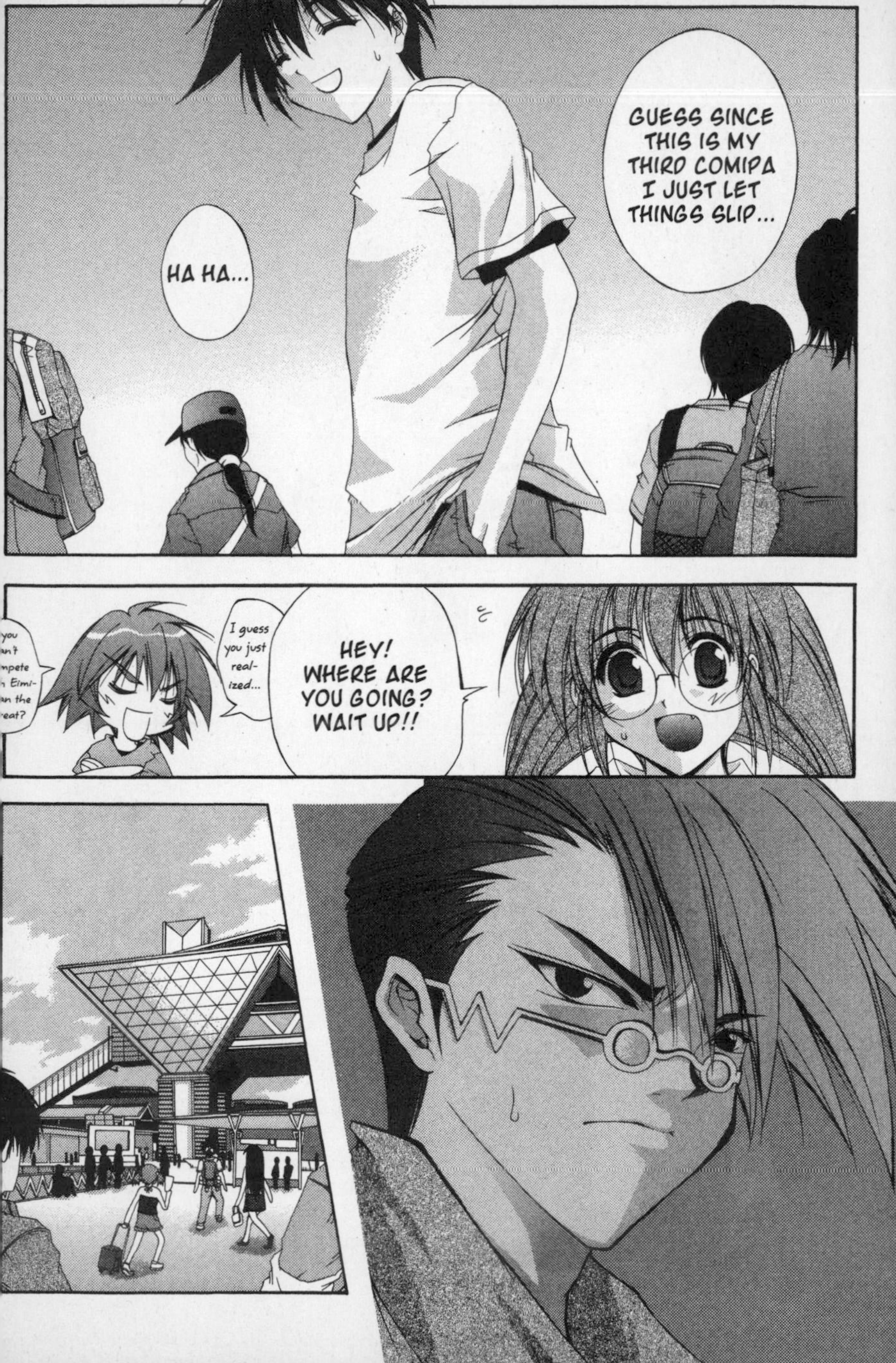
GUESS SINCE THIS IS MY THIRD COMIPA I JUST LET THINGS SLIP...
HA HA...
HEY! WHERE ARE YOU GOING? WAIT UP!!
I guess you just realized...
you an't mpete n Eimi- an the reat?

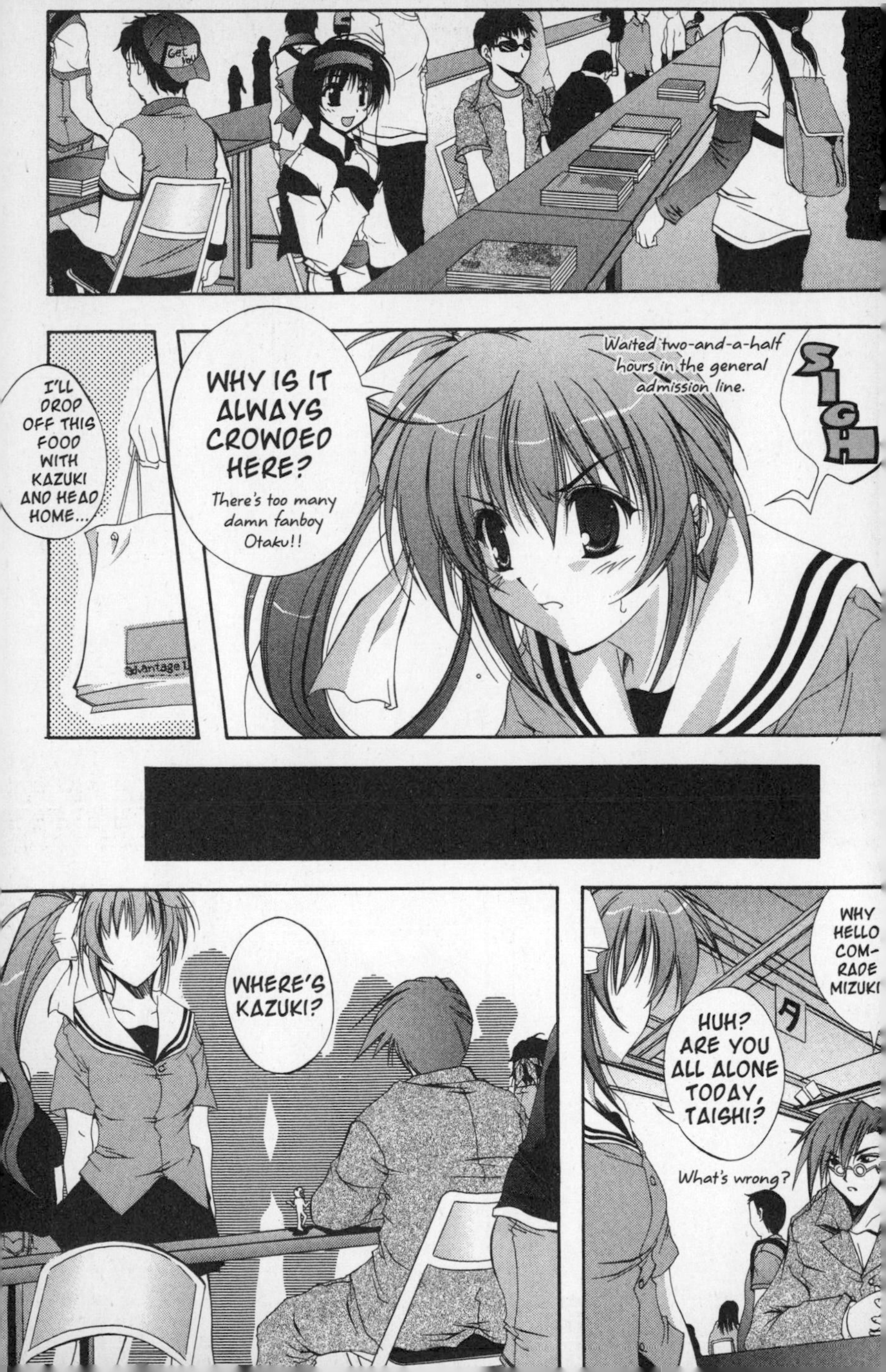
Waited two-and-a-half hours in the general admission line.
SIGH
WHY IS IT ALWAYS CROWDED HERE?
There's too many damn fanboy Otaku!!
I'LL DROP OFF THIS FOOD WITH KAZUKI AND HEAD HOME...
WHY HELLO COMRADE MIZUKI
HUH? ARE YOU ALL ALONE TODAY, TAISHI?
What's wrong?
WHERE'S KAZUKI?

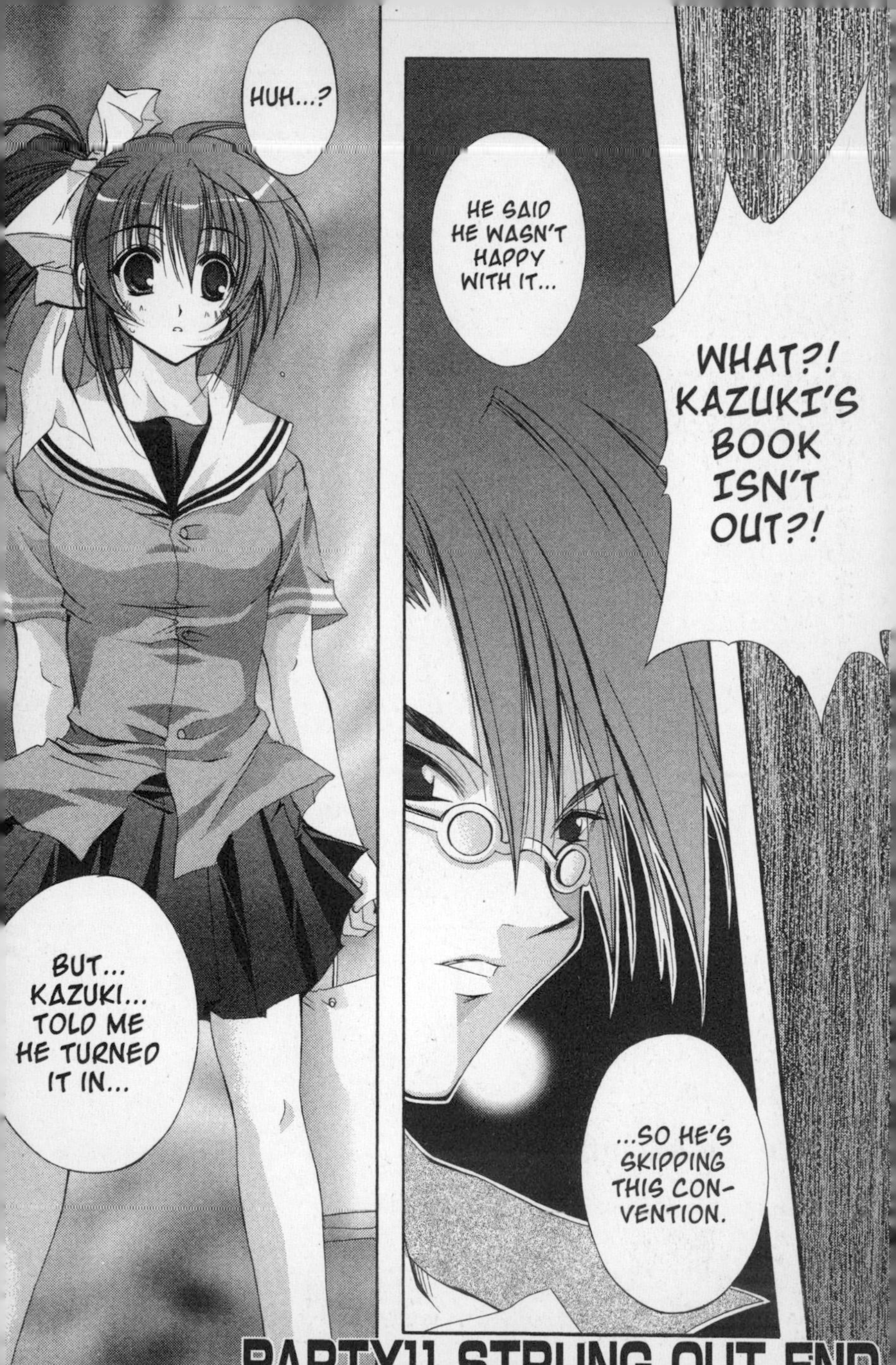
WHAT?! KAZUKI'S BOOK ISN'T OUT?!
HE SAID HE WASN'T HAPPY WITH IT...
...SO HE'S SKIPPING THIS CON-VENTION.
HUH...?
BUT... KAZUKI... TOLD ME HE TURNED IT IN...

PARTY11 STRUNG OUT END

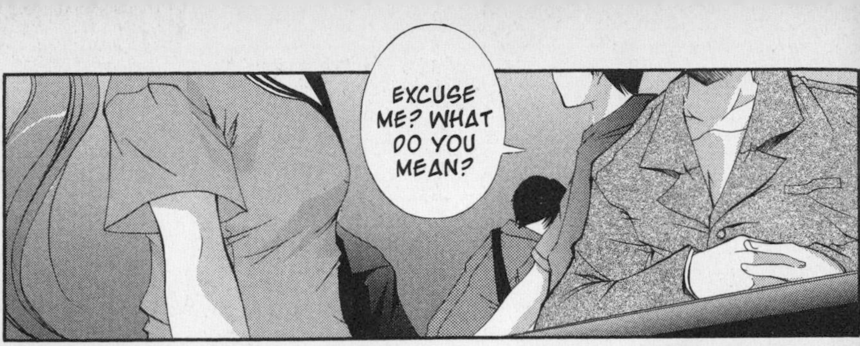
EXCUSE ME? WHAT DO YOU MEAN?

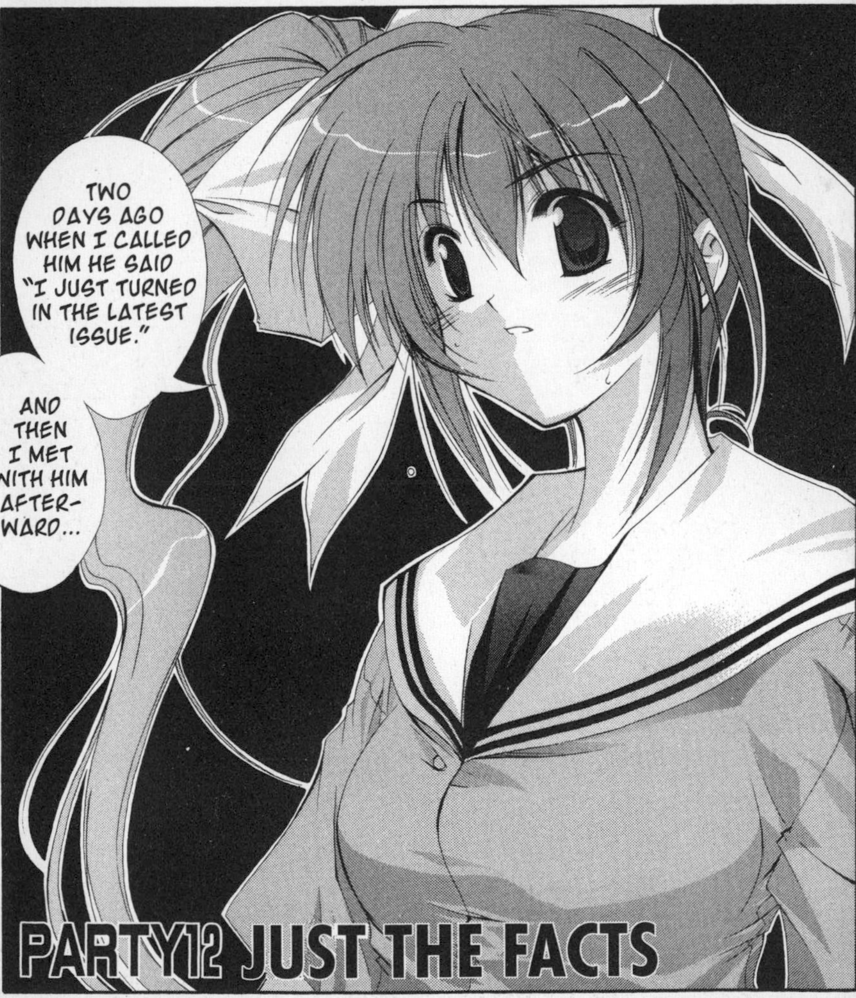
TWO DAYS AGO WHEN I CALLED HIM HE SAID "I JUST TURNED IN THE LATEST ISSUE."
AND THEN I MET WITH HIM AFTER-WARD...
PARTY12 JUST THE FACTS

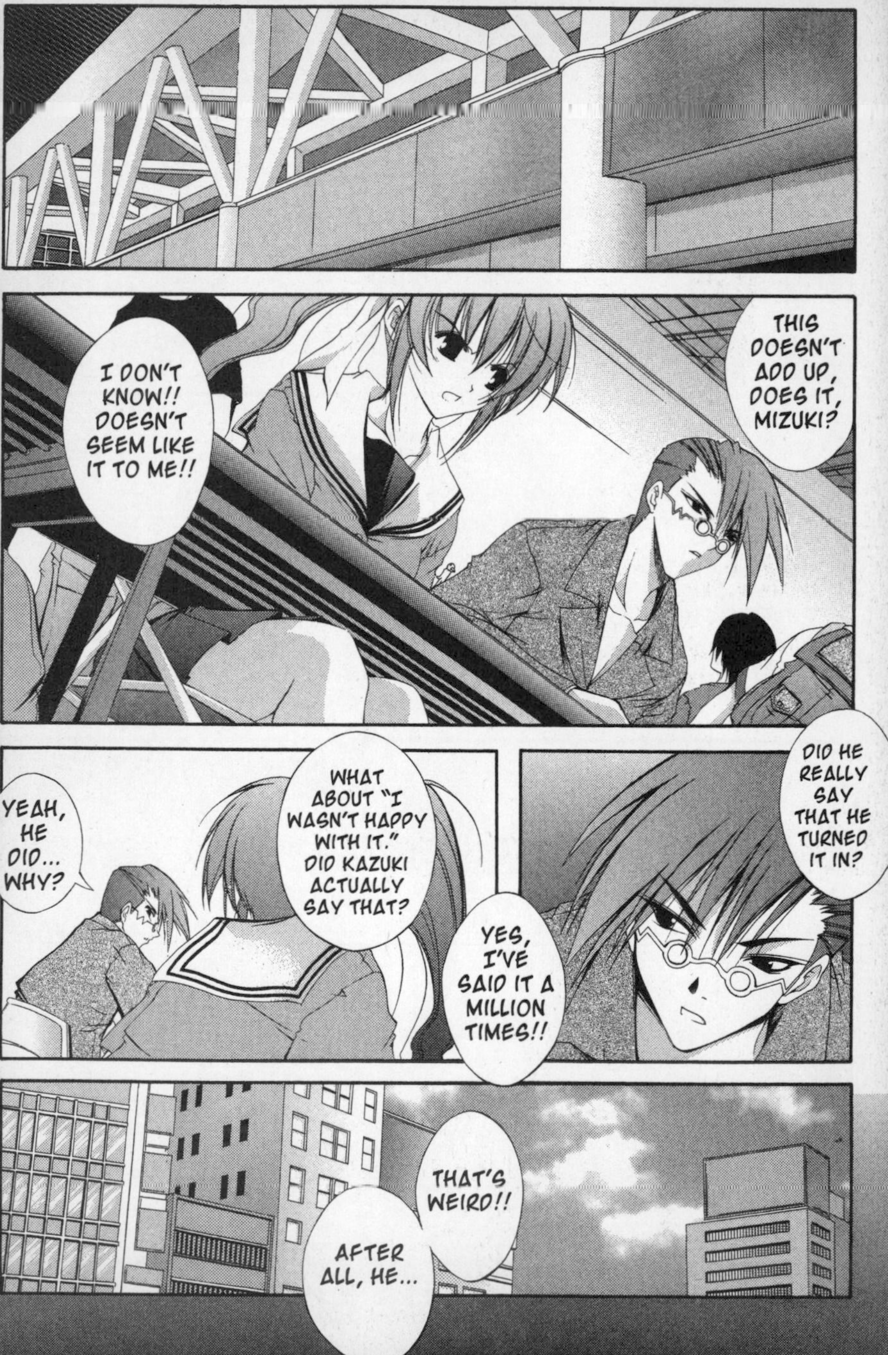
THIS DOESN'T ADD UP, DOES IT, MIZUKI?
I DON'T KNOW!! DOESN'T SEEM LIKE IT TO ME!!
DID HE REALLY SAY THAT HE TURNED IT IN?
YES, I'VE SAID IT A MILLION TIMES!!
WHAT ABOUT "I WASN'T HAPPY WITH IT." DID KAZUKI ACTUALLY SAY THAT?
YEAH, HE DID... WHY?
THAT'S WEIRD!!
AFTER ALL, HE...

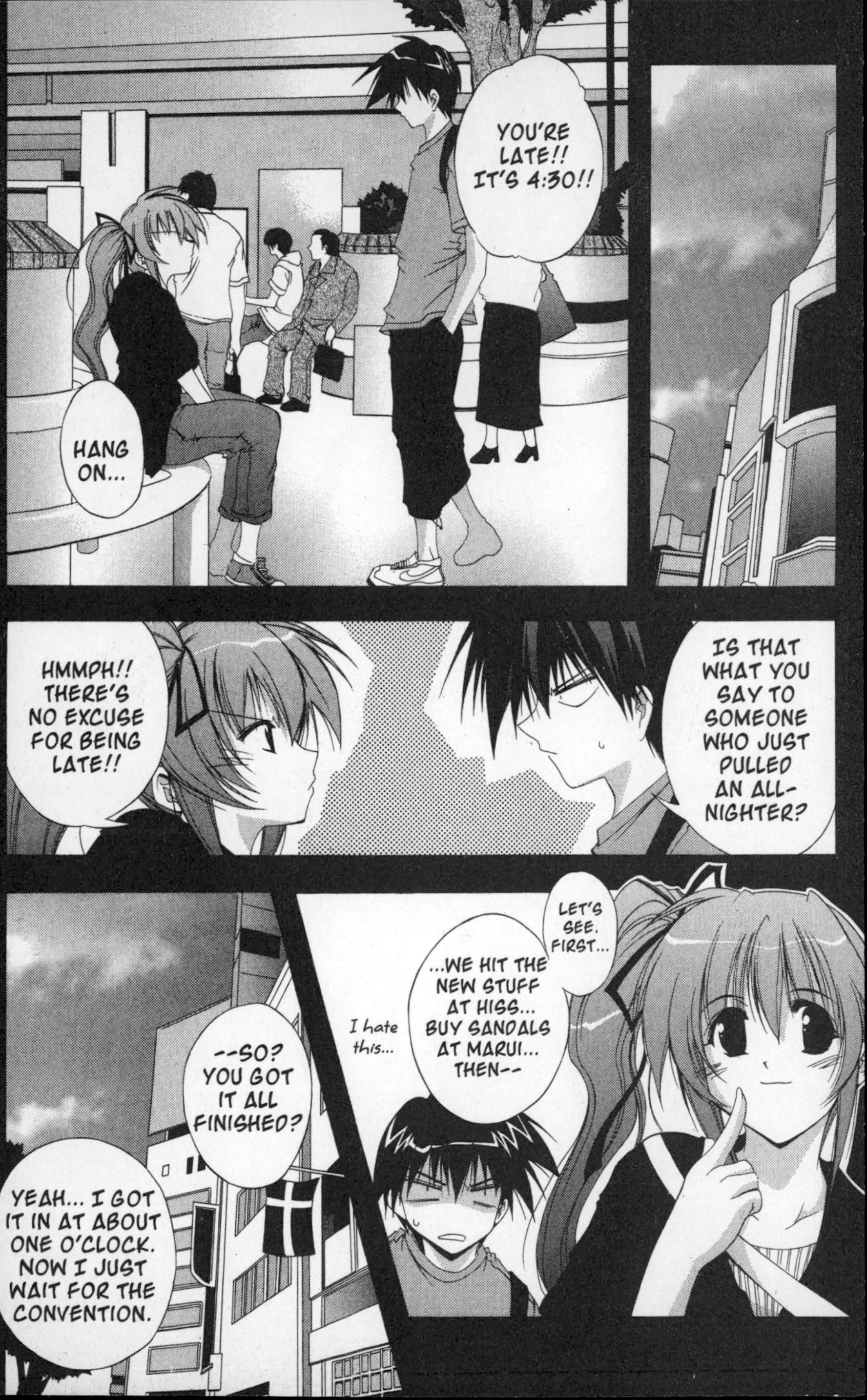
YOU'RE LATE!! IT'S 4:30!!
HANG ON...
IS THAT WHAT YOU SAY TO SOMEONE WHO JUST PULLED AN ALL-NIGHTER?
HMMPH!! THERE'S NO EXCUSE FOR BEING LATE!!
LET'S SEE. FIRST...
...WE HIT THE NEW STUFF AT HISS... BUY SANDALS AT MARUI... THEN--
I hate this...
--SO? YOU GOT IT ALL FINISHED?
YEAH... I GOT IT IN AT ABOUT ONE O'CLOCK. NOW I JUST WAIT FOR THE CONVENTION.

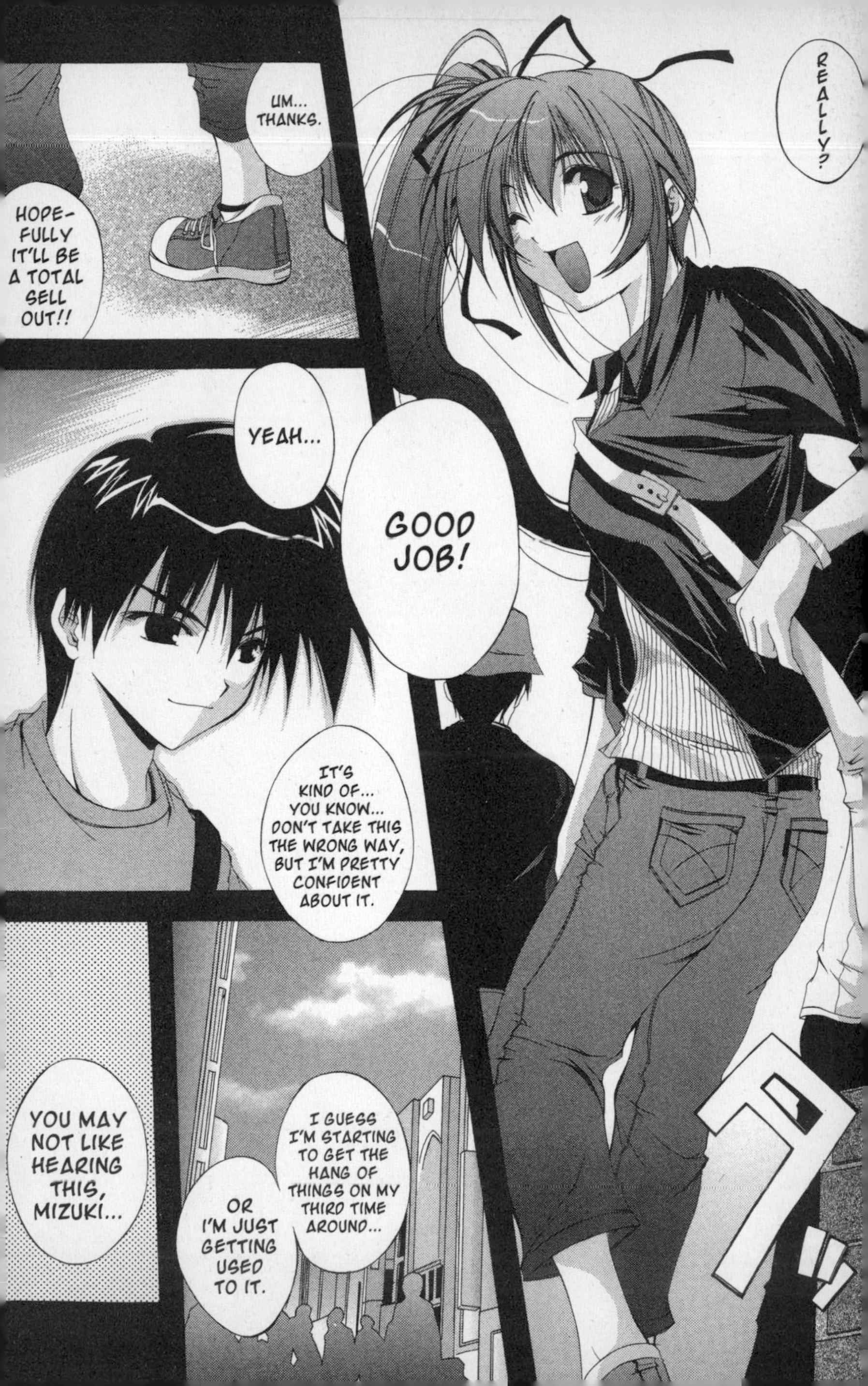
REALLY?
GOOD JOB!
UM... THANKS.
HOPE-FULLY IT'LL BE A TOTAL SELL OUT!!
YEAH...
IT'S KIND OF... YOU KNOW... DON'T TAKE THIS THE WRONG WAY, BUT I'M PRETTY CONFIDENT ABOUT IT.
I GUESS I'M STARTING TO GET THE HANG OF THINGS ON MY THIRD TIME AROUND...
OR I'M JUST GETTING USED TO IT.
YOU MAY NOT LIKE HEARING THIS, MIZUKI...

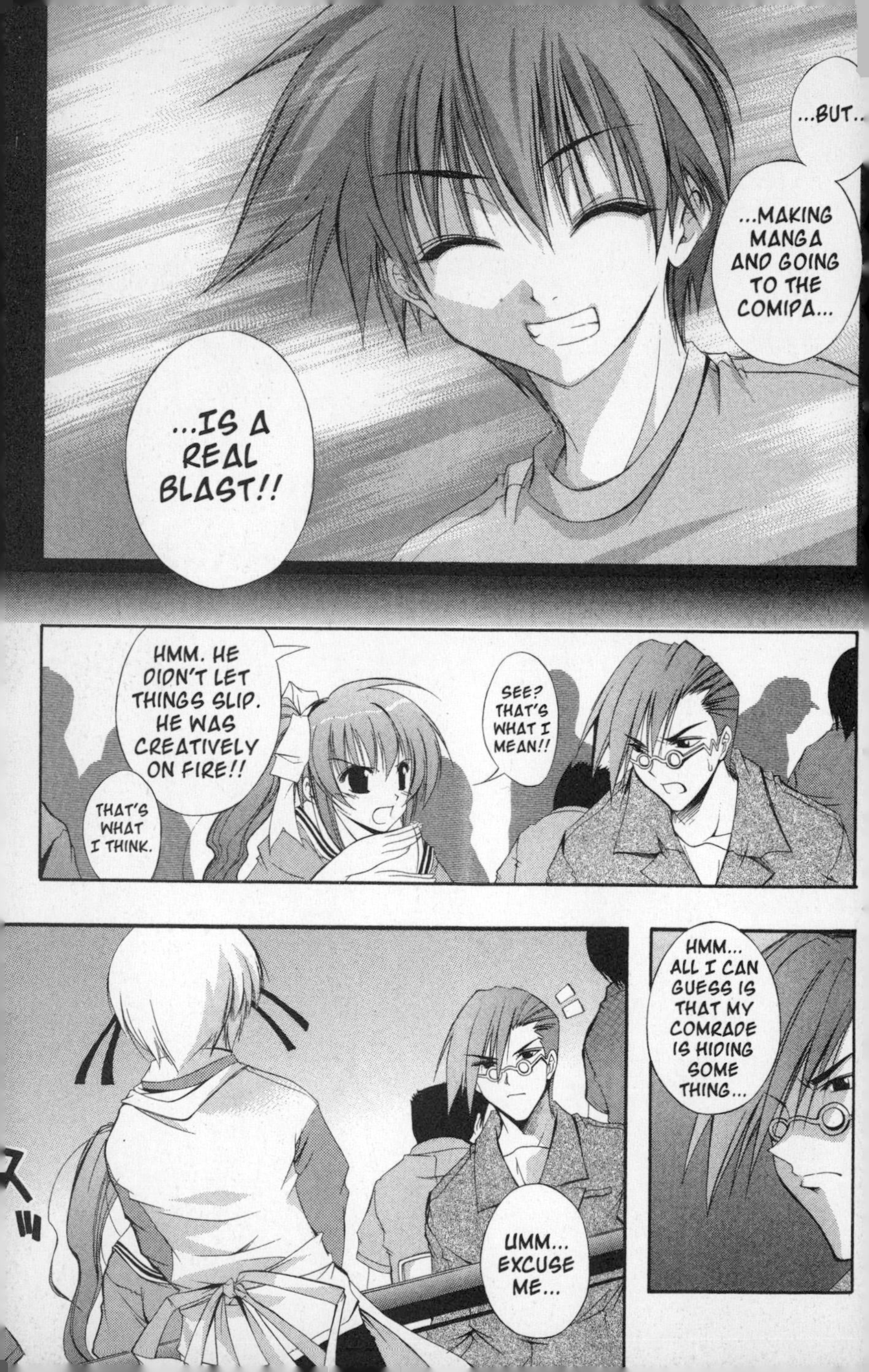
...BUT...
...MAKING MANGA AND GOING TO THE COMIPA...
...IS A REAL BLAST!!
SEE? THAT'S WHAT I MEAN!!
HMM. HE DIDN'T LET THINGS SLIP. HE WAS CREATIVELY ON FIRE!!
THAT'S WHAT I THINK.
HMM... ALL I CAN GUESS IS THAT MY COMRADE IS HIDING SOME THING...
UMM... EXCUSE ME...

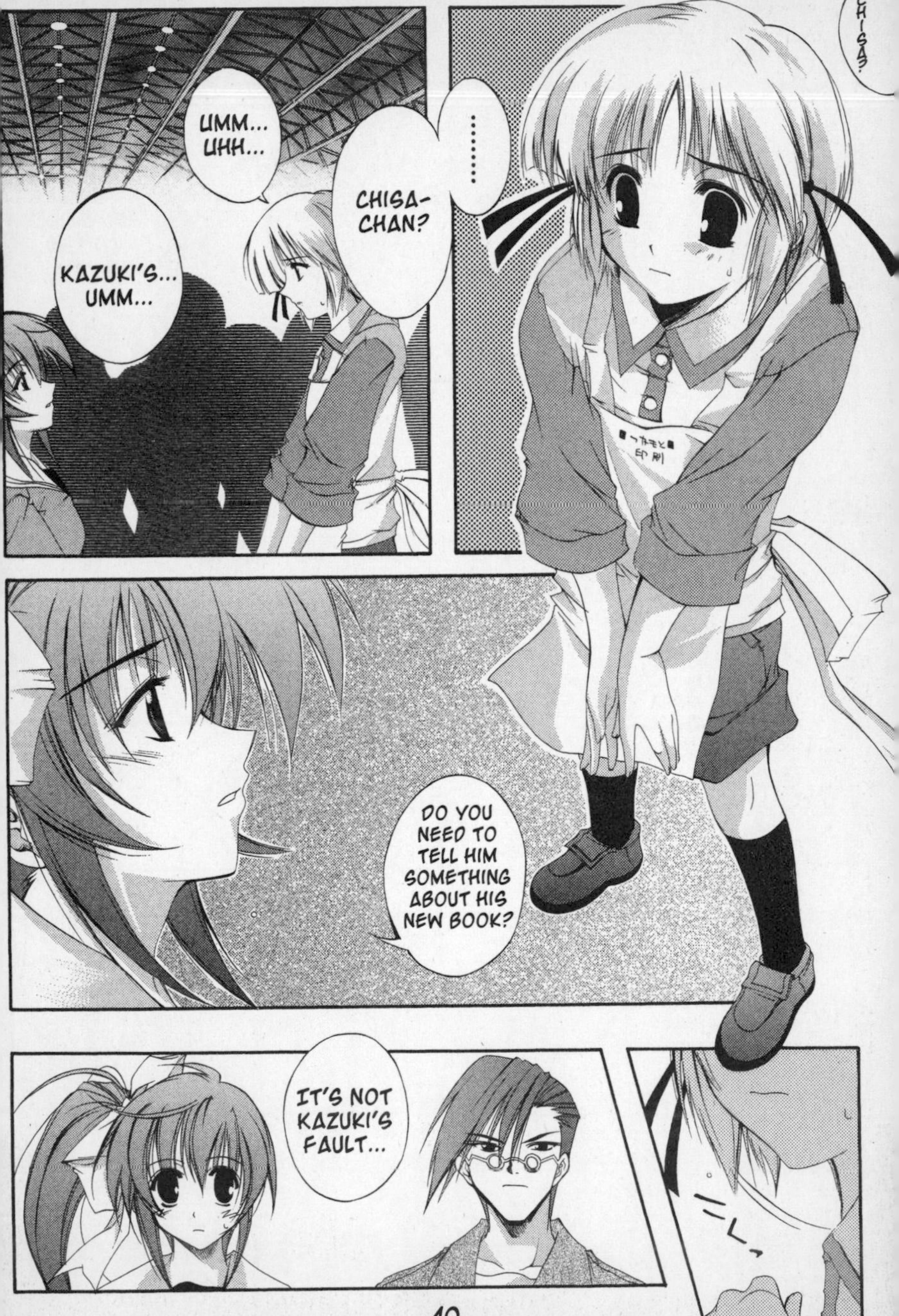
CHISA?
......
CHISA-CHAN?
UMM... UHH...
KAZUKI'S... UMM...
DO YOU NEED TO TELL HIM SOMETHING ABOUT HIS NEW BOOK?
IT'S NOT KAZUKI'S FAULT...

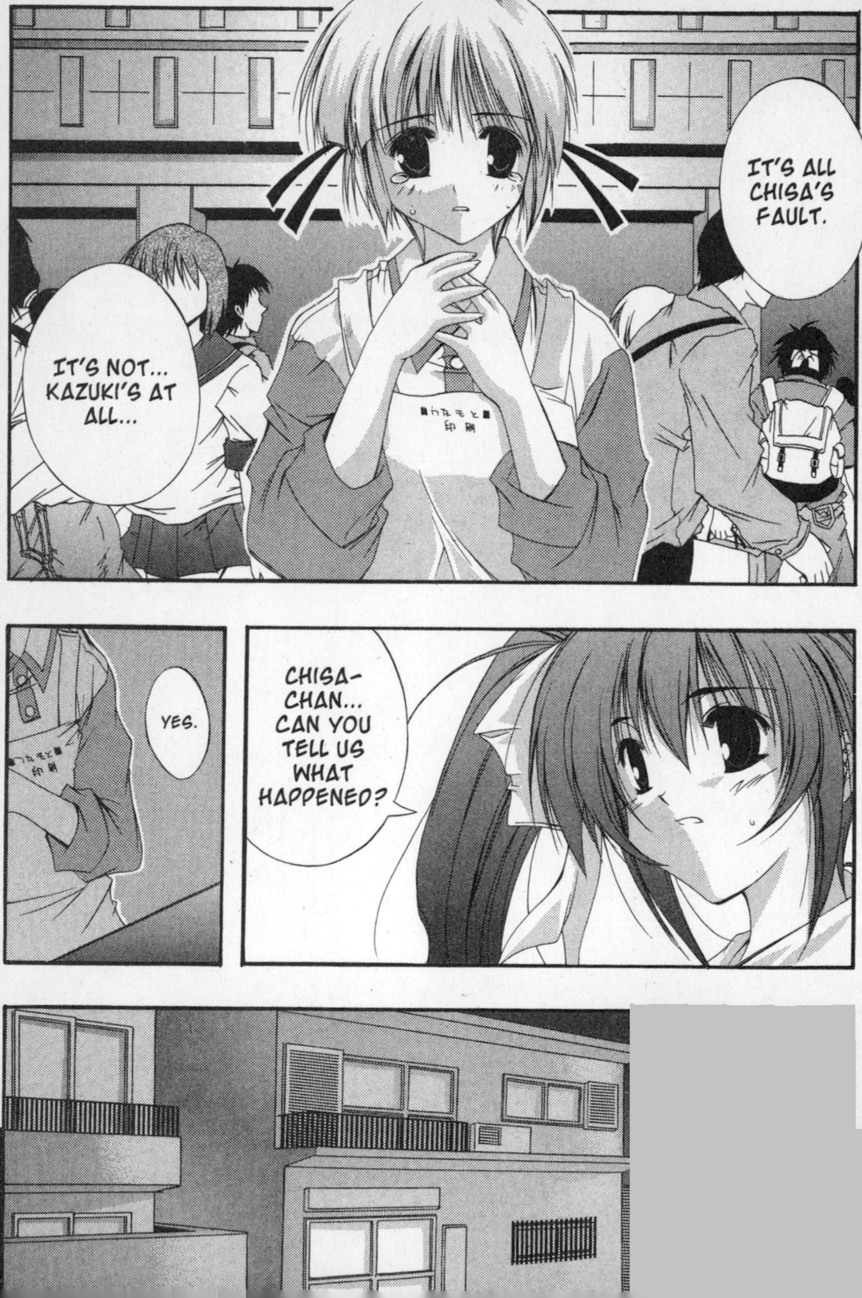
IT'S ALL CHISA'S FAULT.
IT'S NOT... KAZUKI'S AT ALL...
CHISA-CHAN... CAN YOU TELL US WHAT HAPPENED?
YES.

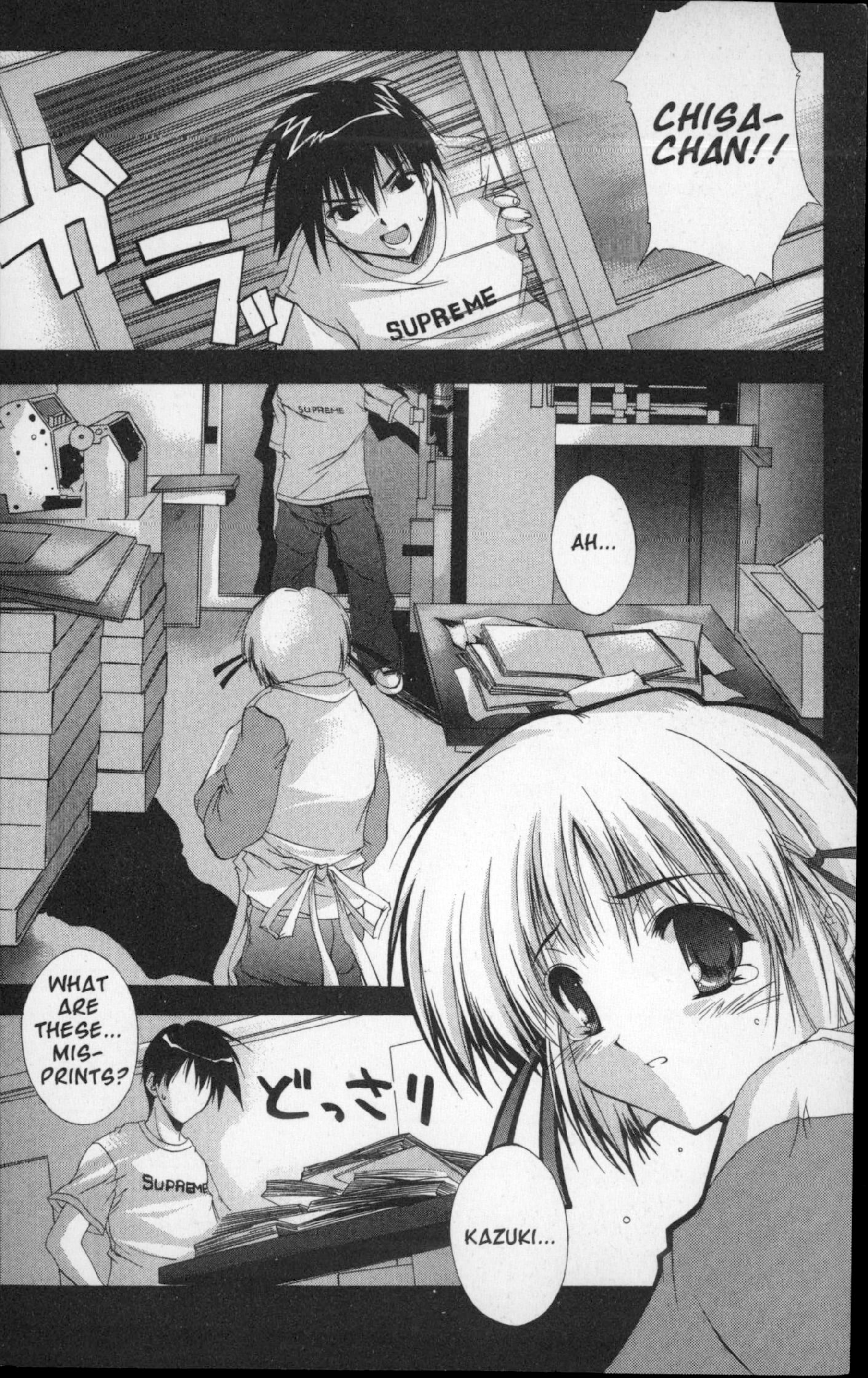
CHISA-CHAN!!
ガラッ
SUPREME
AH...
KAZUKI...
WHAT ARE THESE... MIS-PRINTS?
どっさり

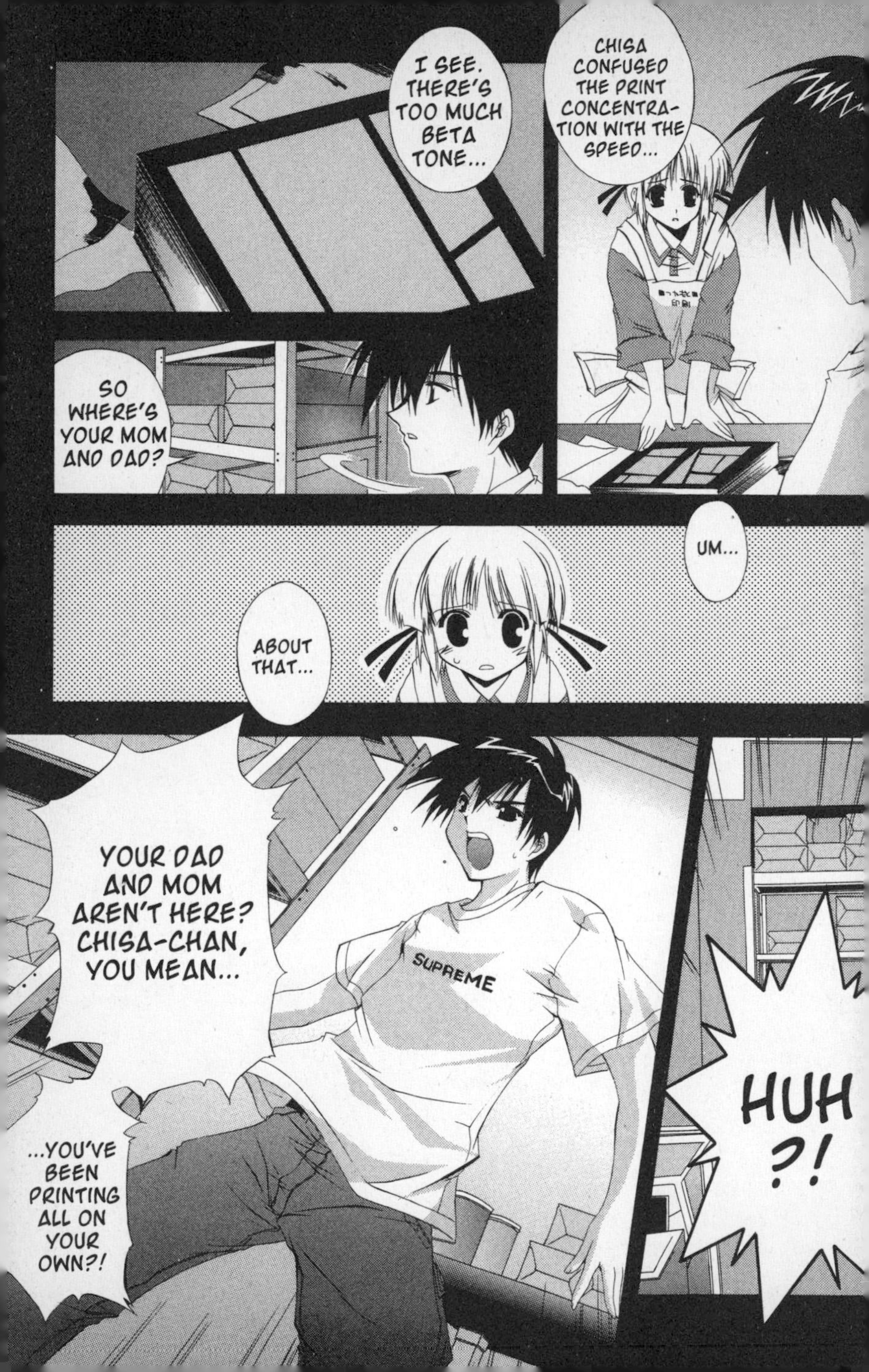
CHISA CONFUSED THE PRINT CONCENTRATION WITH THE SPEED...
I SEE. THERE'S TOO MUCH BETA TONE...
SO WHERE'S YOUR MOM AND DAD?
UM...
ABOUT THAT...
HUH?!
YOUR DAD AND MOM AREN'T HERE? CHISA-CHAN, YOU MEAN...
SUPREME
...YOU'VE BEEN PRINTING ALL ON YOUR OWN?!

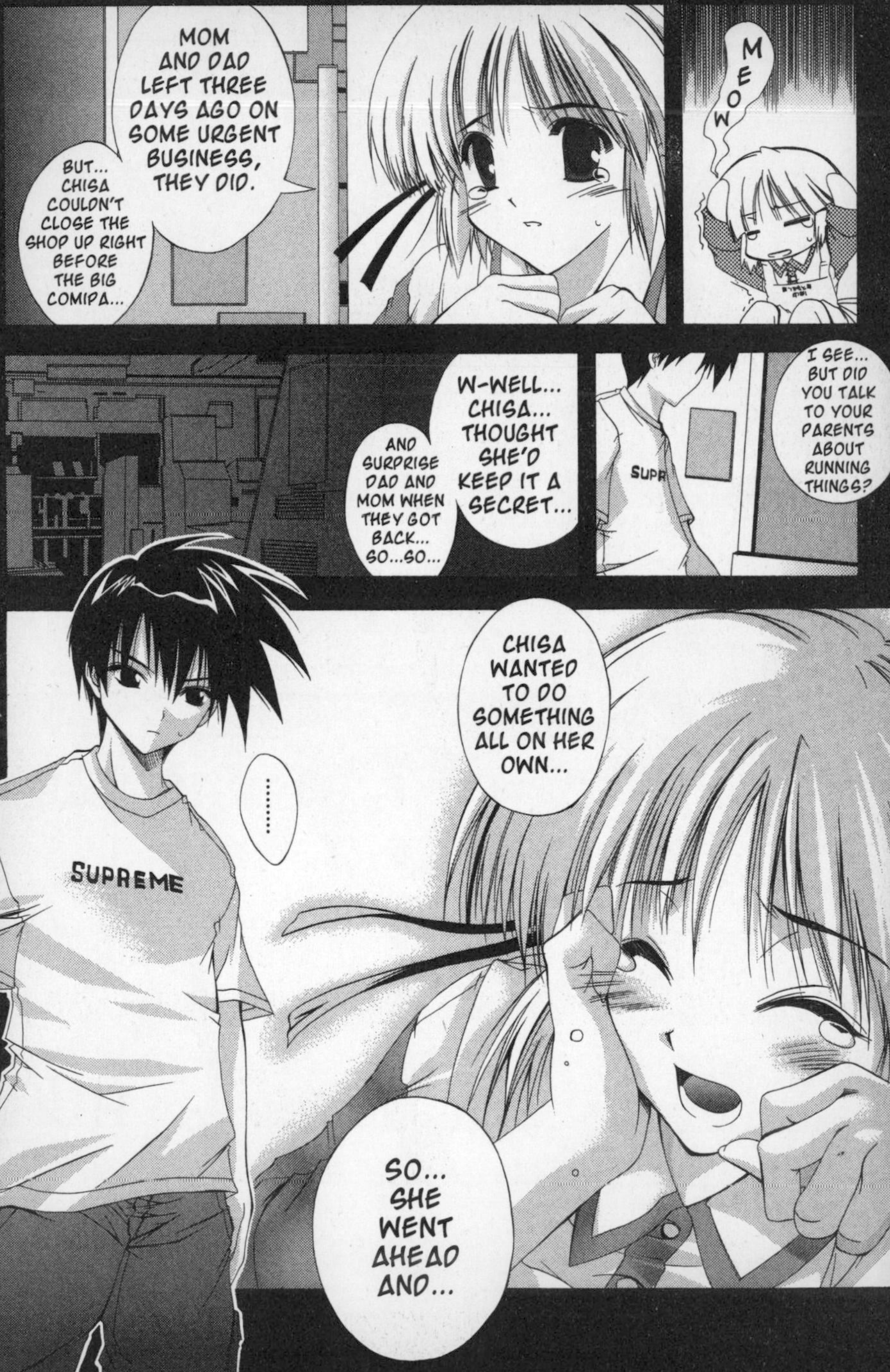
MEOW
MOM AND DAD LEFT THREE DAYS AGO ON SOME URGENT BUSINESS, THEY DID.
BUT... CHISA COULDN'T CLOSE THE SHOP UP RIGHT BEFORE THE BIG COMIPA...
I SEE... BUT DID YOU TALK TO YOUR PARENTS ABOUT RUNNING THINGS?
SUPR
W-WELL... CHISA... THOUGHT SHE'D KEEP IT A SECRET...
AND SURPRISE DAD AND MOM WHEN THEY GOT BACK... SO...SO...
CHISA WANTED TO DO SOMETHING ALL ON HER OWN...
......
SUPREME
SO... SHE WENT AHEAD AND...

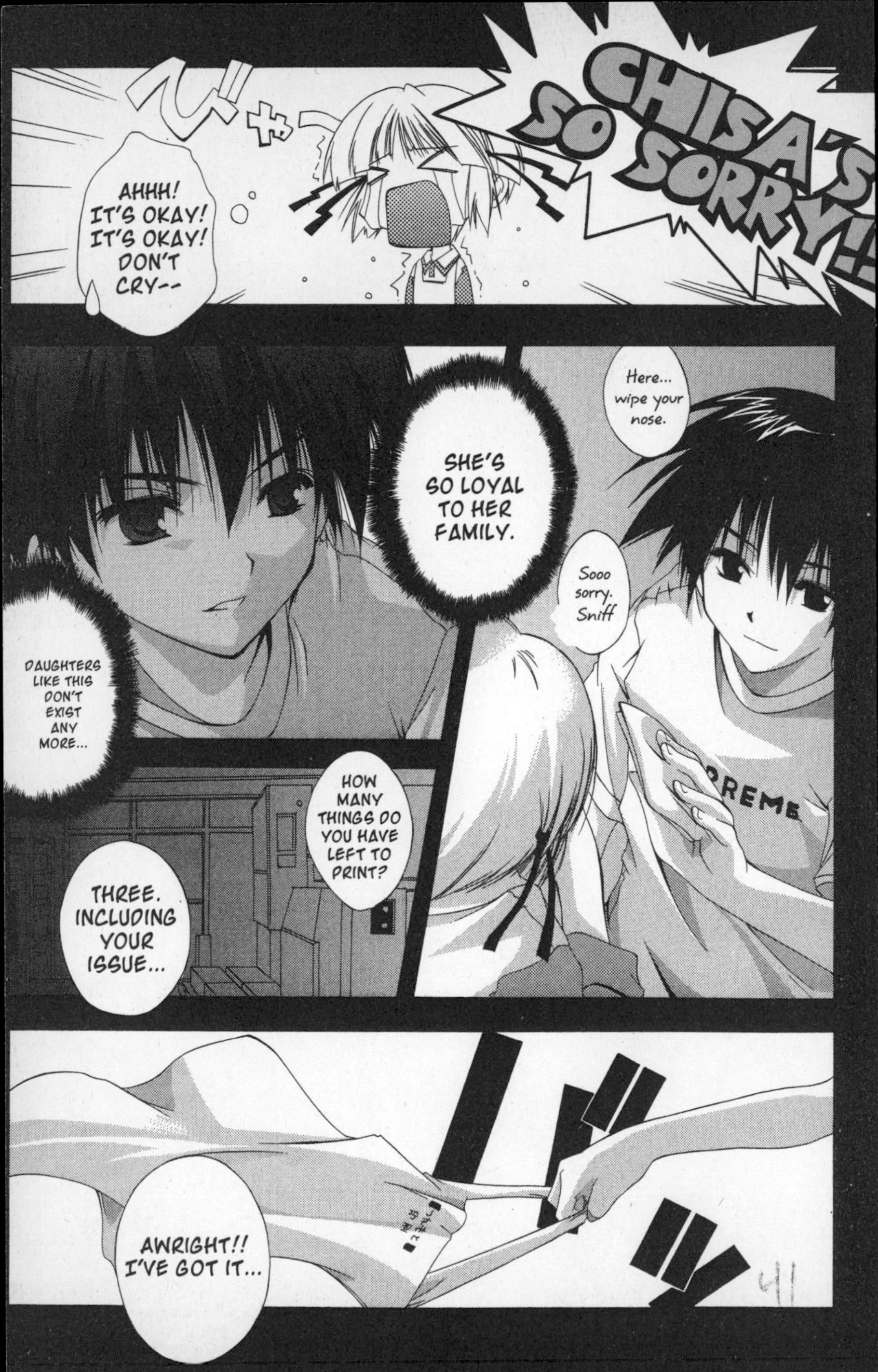
CHISA'S SO SORRY!!
AHHH! IT'S OKAY! IT'S OKAY! DON'T CRY--
Here... wipe your nose.
Sooo sorry. Sniff
SHE'S SO LOYAL TO HER FAMILY.
DAUGHTERS LIKE THIS DON'T EXIST ANY MORE...
HOW MANY THINGS DO YOU HAVE LEFT TO PRINT?
THREE. INCLUDING YOUR ISSUE...
AWRIGHT!! I'VE GOT IT...

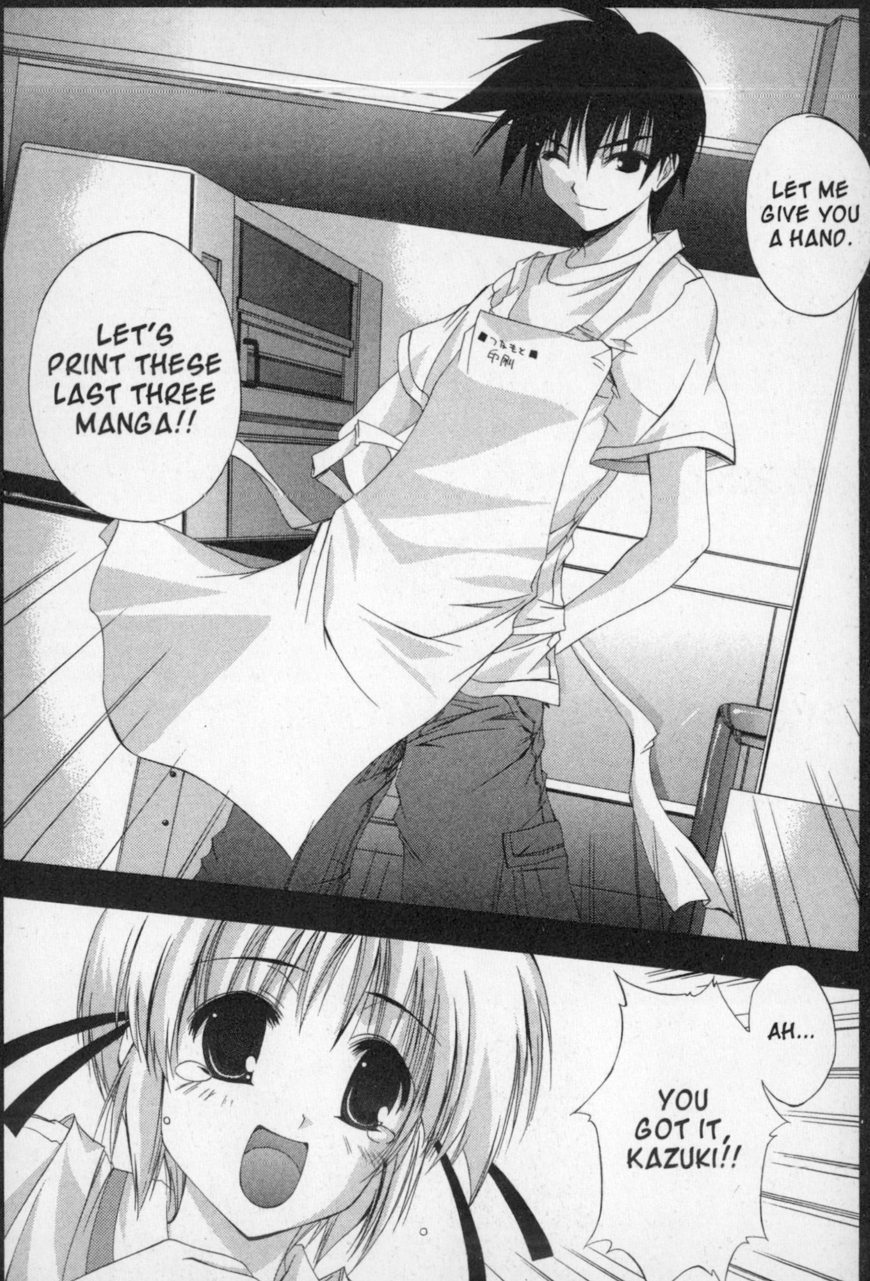
LET ME GIVE YOU A HAND.
LET'S PRINT THESE LAST THREE MANGA!!
AH...
YOU GOT IT, KAZUKI!!

PARTY12 JUST THE FACTS END

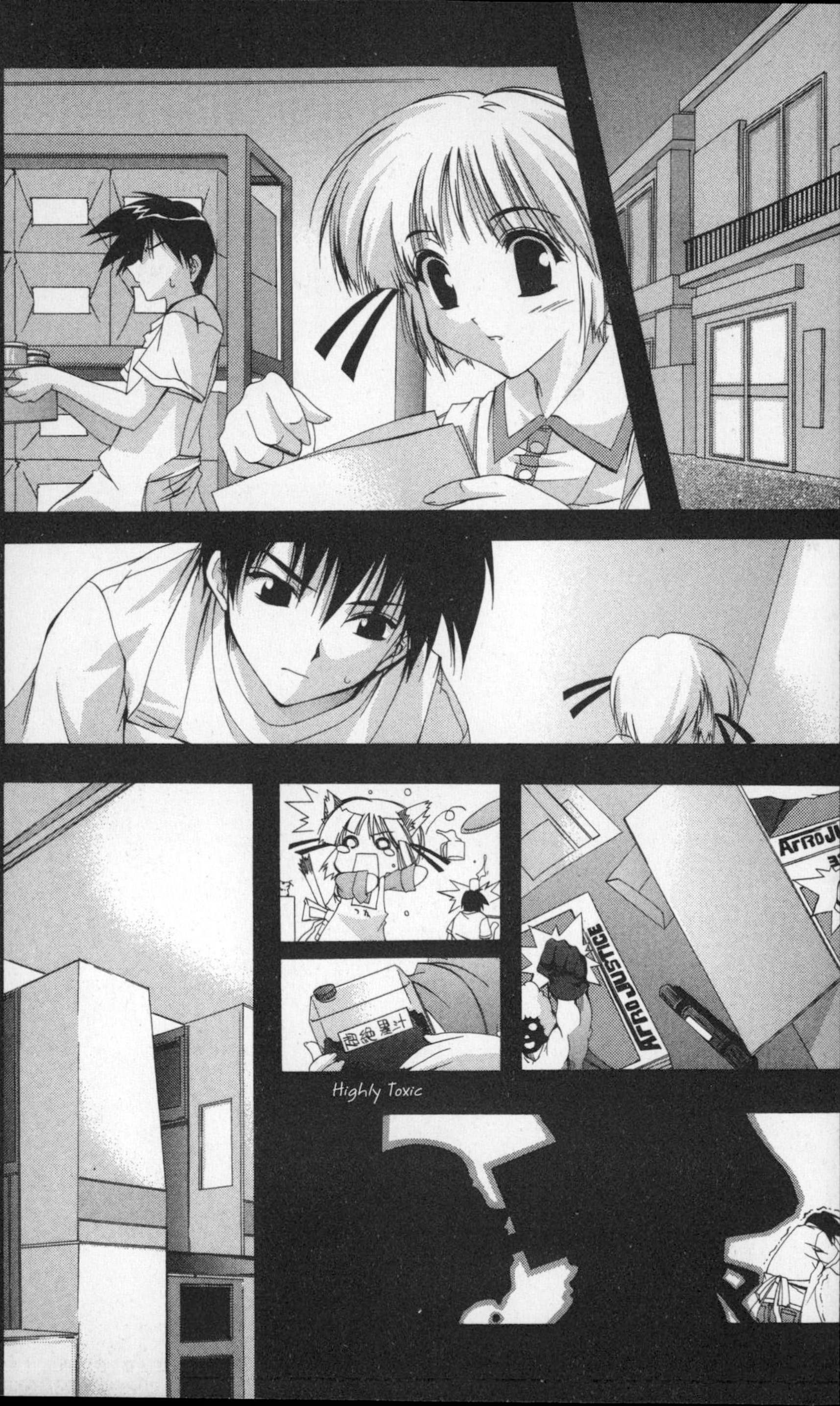
ARRO JUSTICE
超絶墨汁
Highly Toxic

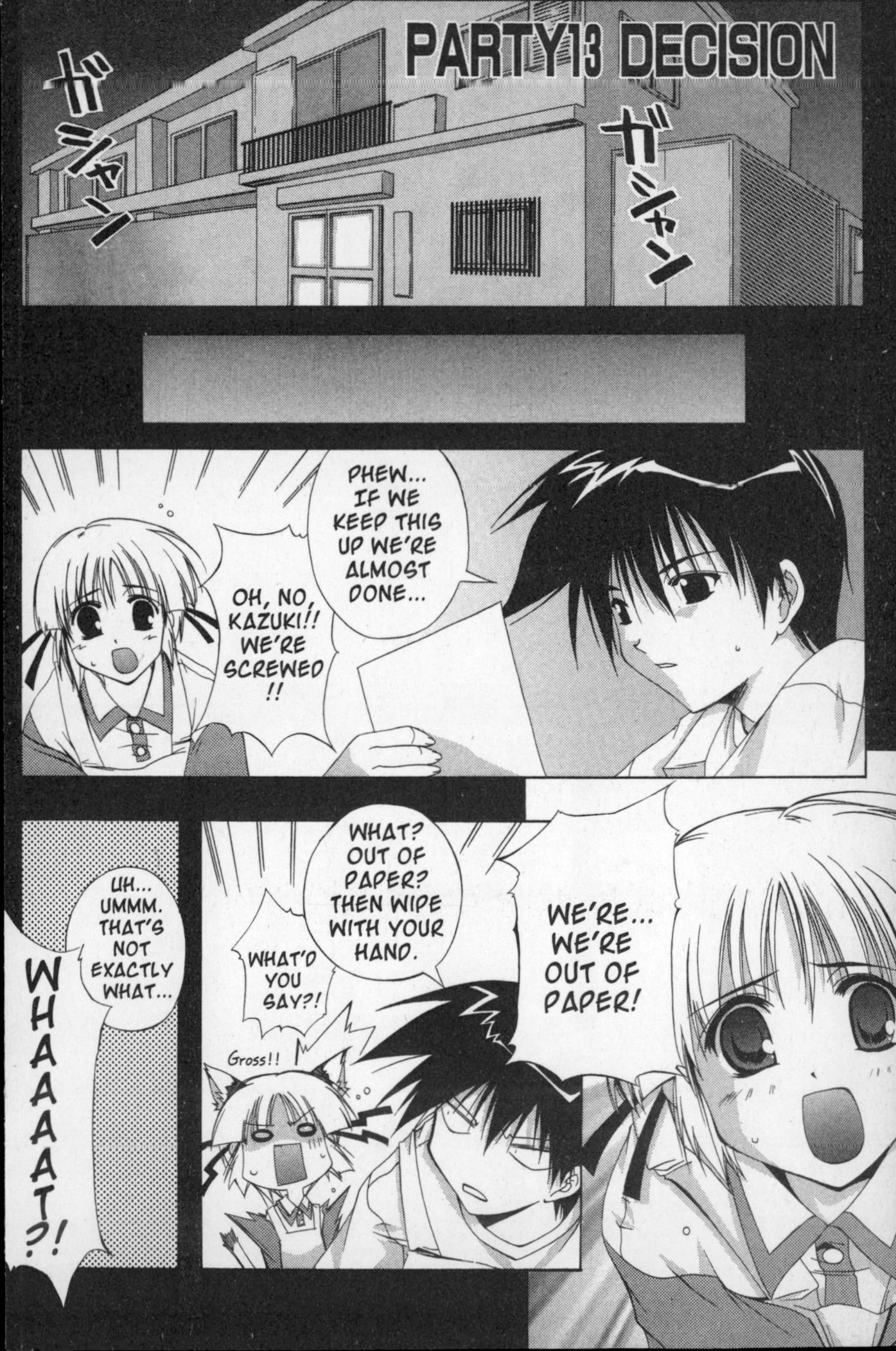
PARTY13 DECISION
ガシャン
ガシャン
PHEW... IF WE KEEP THIS UP WE'RE ALMOST DONE...
OH, NO, KAZUKI!! WE'RE SCREWED!!
WE'RE... WE'RE OUT OF PAPER!
WHAT? OUT OF PAPER? THEN WIPE WITH YOUR HAND.
WHAT'D YOU SAY?!
Gross!!
UH... UMMM. THAT'S NOT EXACTLY WHAT...
WHAAAAAT?!

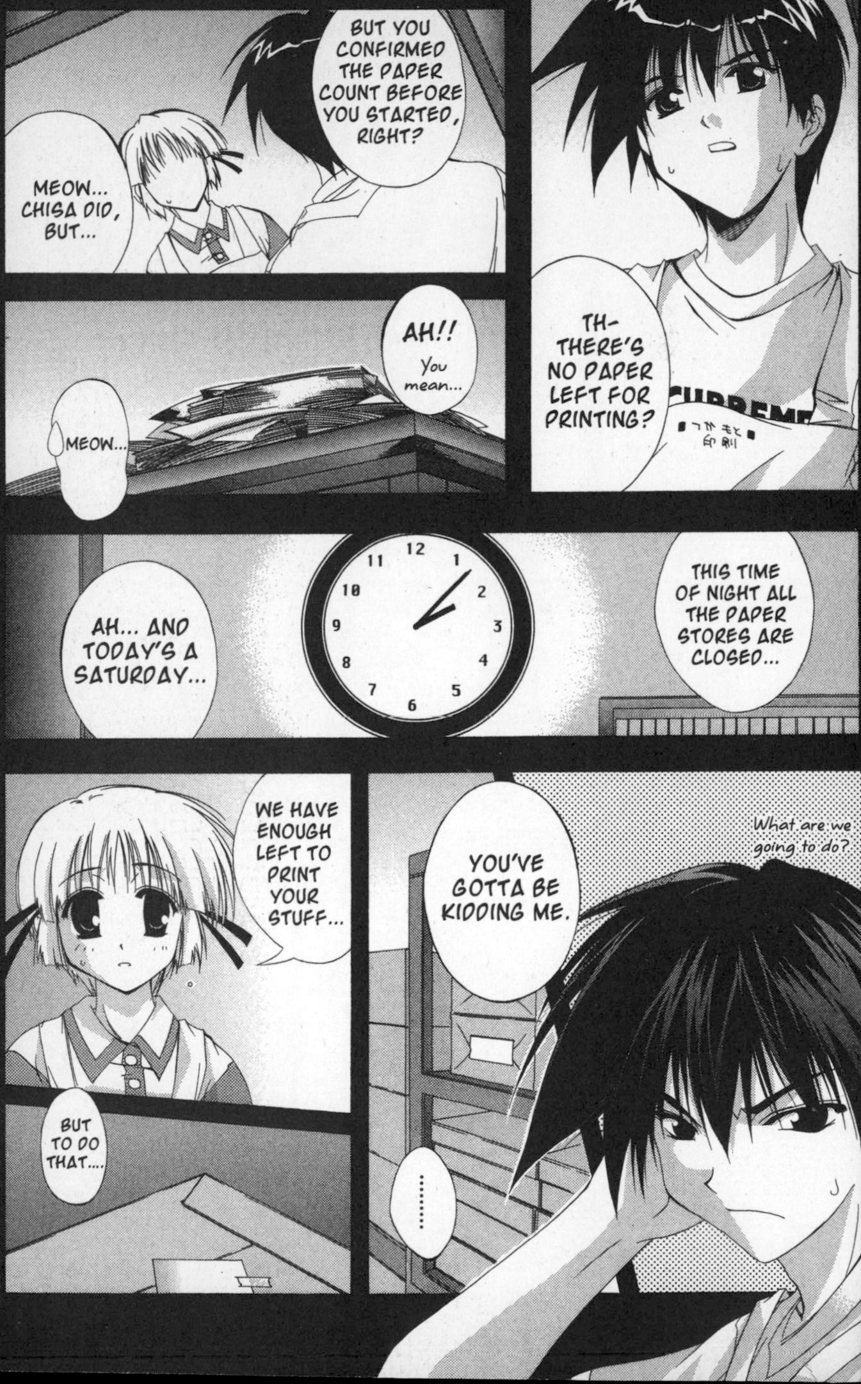
TH- THERE'S NO PAPER LEFT FOR PRINTING?
BUT YOU CONFIRMED THE PAPER COUNT BEFORE YOU STARTED, RIGHT?
MEOW... CHISA DID, BUT...
AH!! You mean...
MEOW...
THIS TIME OF NIGHT ALL THE PAPER STORES ARE CLOSED...
AH... AND TODAY'S A SATURDAY...
What are we going to do?
YOU'VE GOTTA BE KIDDING ME.
......
WE HAVE ENOUGH LEFT TO PRINT YOUR STUFF...
BUT TO DO THAT....

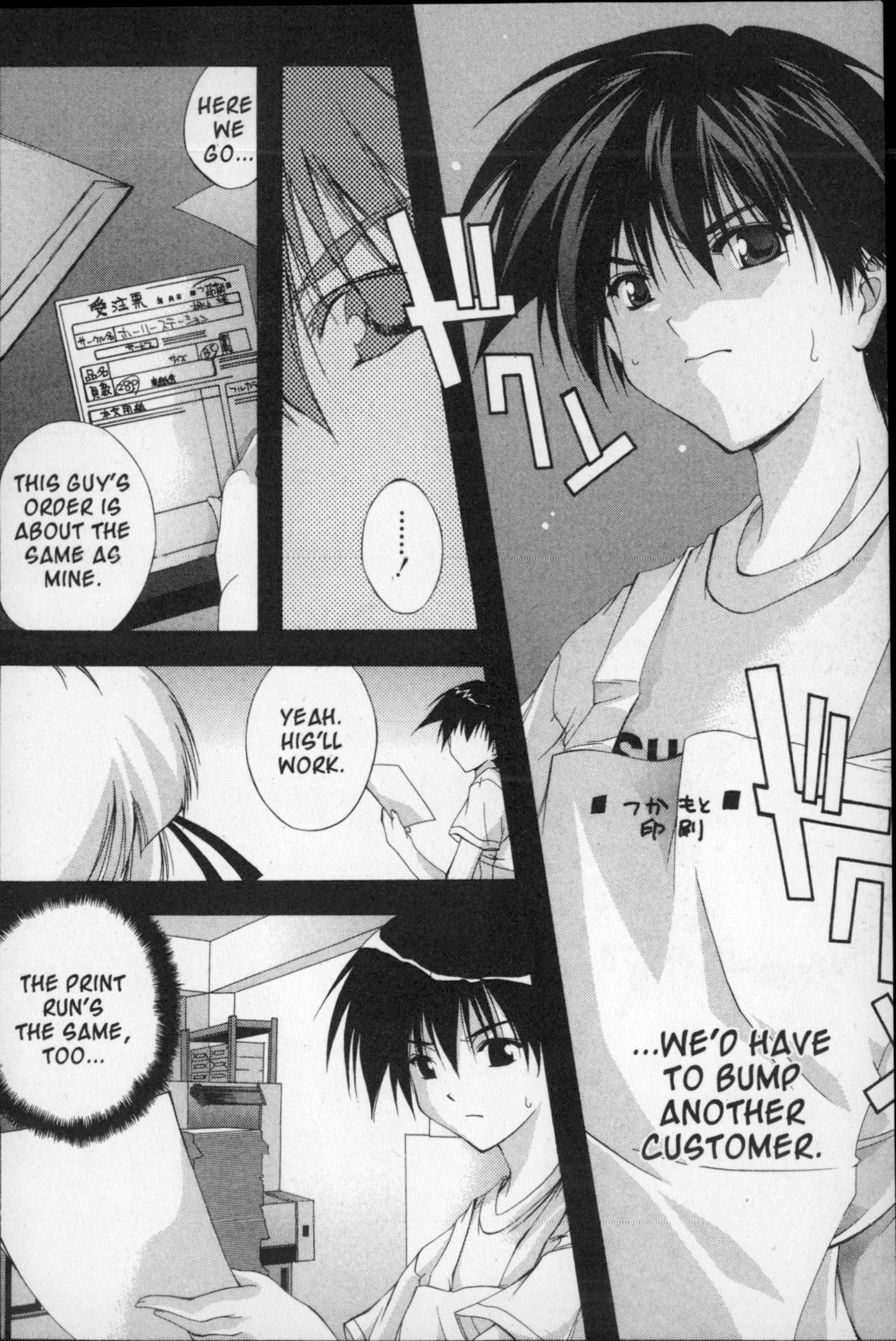
ギクッ
ギクッ
つかもと印刷
...WE'D HAVE TO BUMP ANOTHER CUSTOMER.
......!
HERE WE GO...
受注票
サークル名 ホーリーステーション
品名
頁数
本文用紙
THIS GUY'S ORDER IS ABOUT THE SAME AS MINE.
YEAH. HIS'LL WORK.
THE PRINT RUN'S THE SAME, TOO...

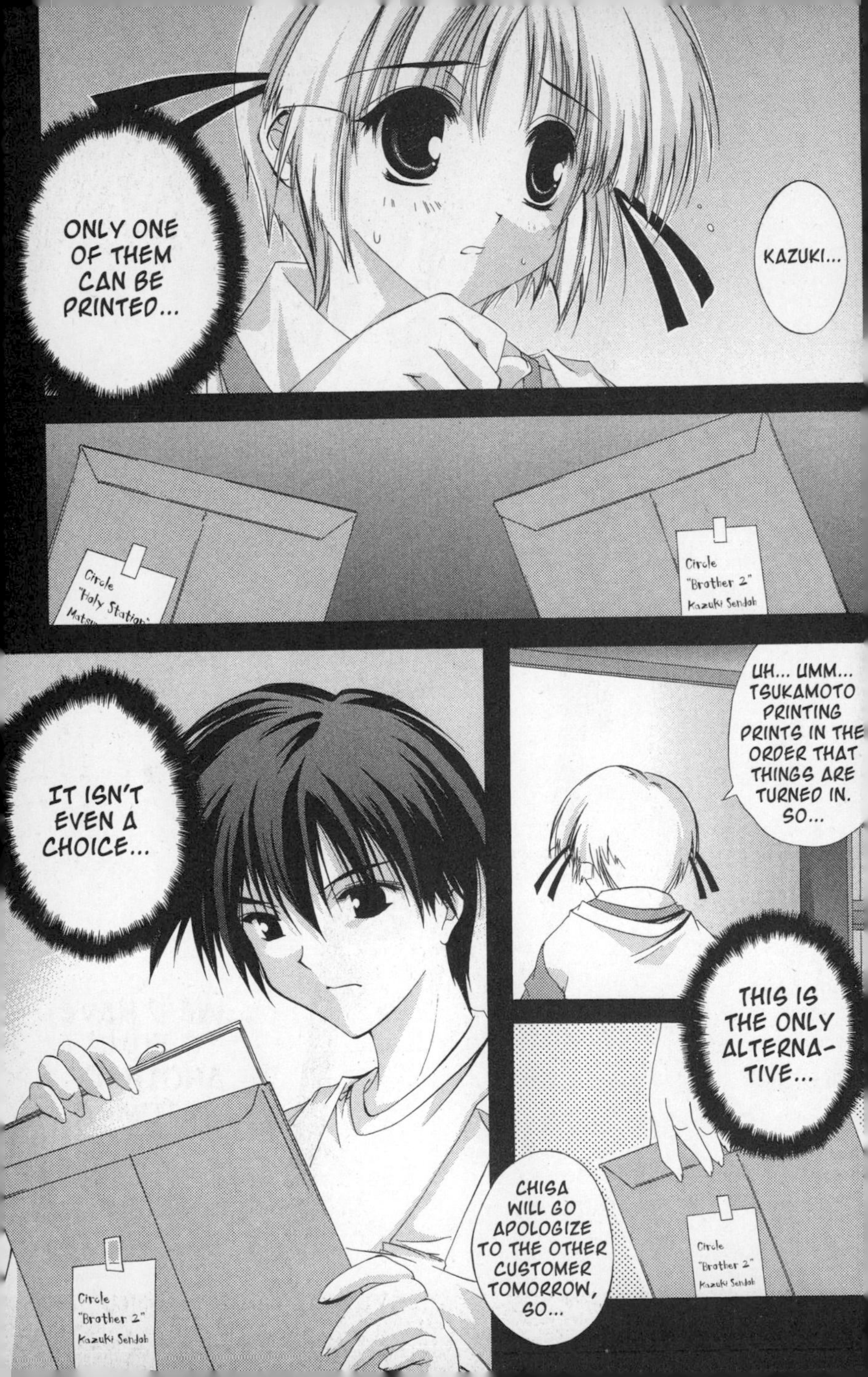
KAZUKI...
ONLY ONE OF THEM CAN BE PRINTED...
Circle "Brother 2" Kazuki Sendoh
Circle "Holy Station"
UH... UMM... TSUKAMOTO PRINTING PRINTS IN THE ORDER THAT THINGS ARE TURNED IN. SO...
THIS IS THE ONLY ALTERNA-TIVE...
CHISA WILL GO APOLOGIZE TO THE OTHER CUSTOMER TOMORROW, SO...
Circle "Brother 2" Kazuki Sendoh
IT ISN'T EVEN A CHOICE...
Circle "Brother 2" Kazuki Sendoh

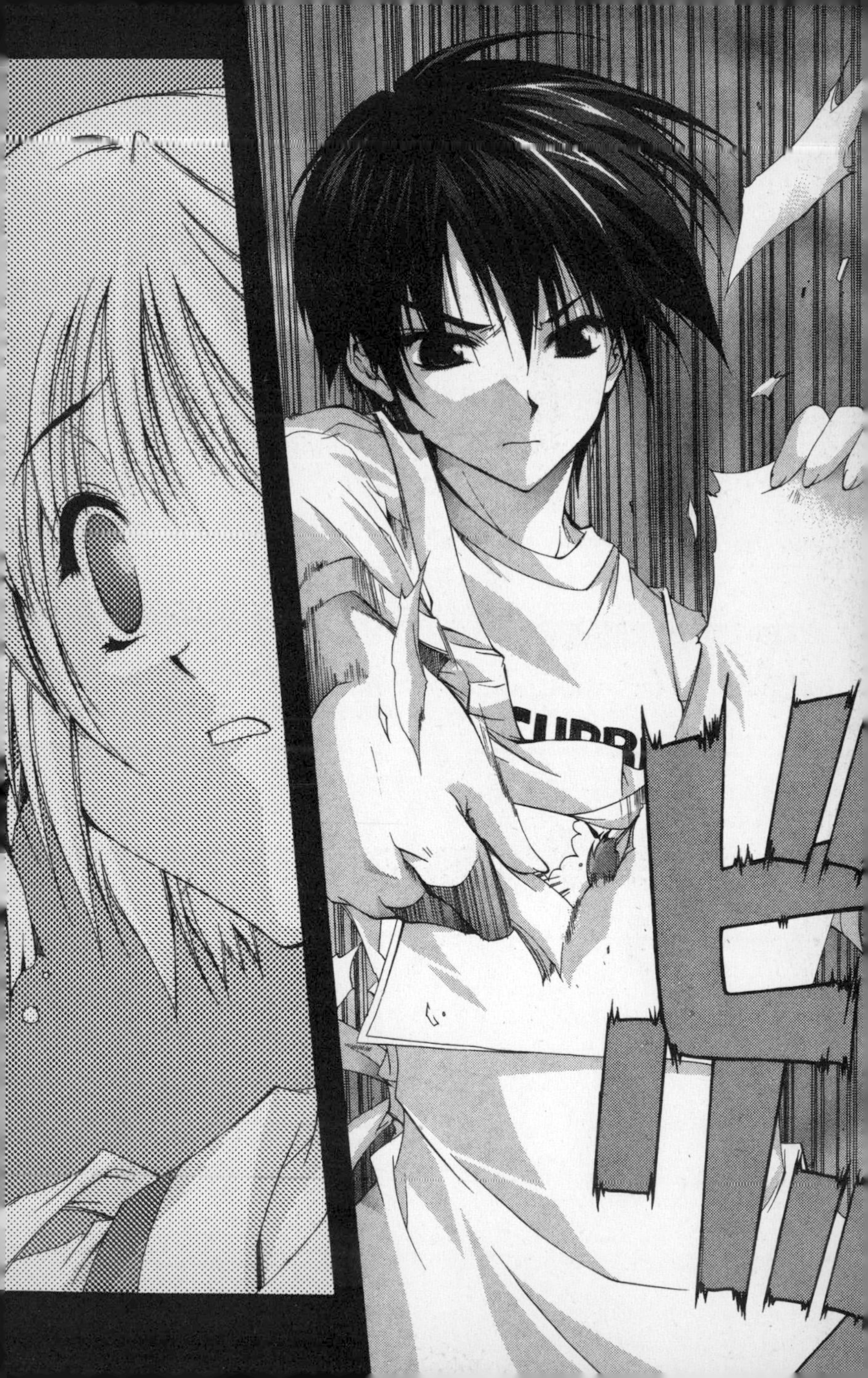

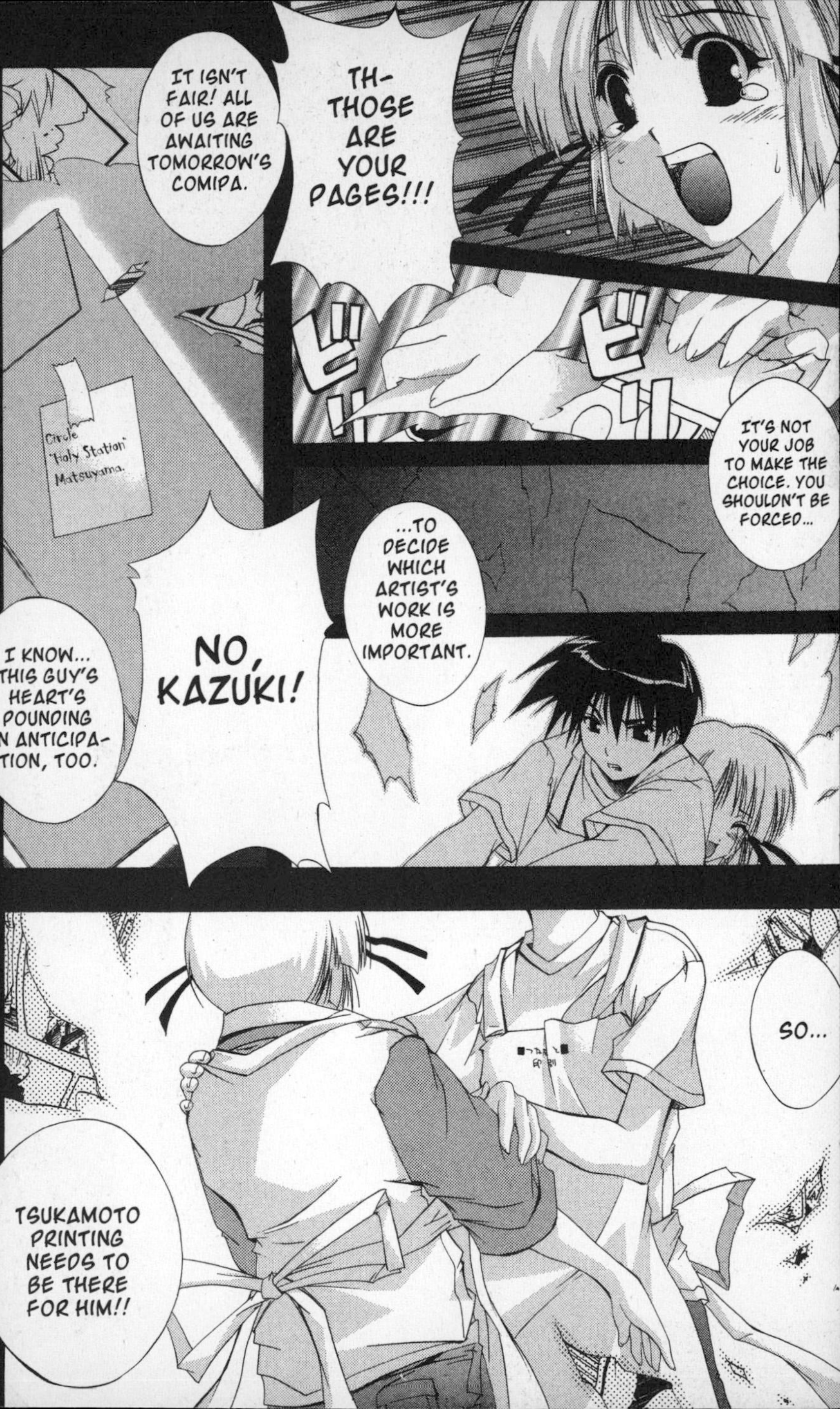
TH- THOSE ARE YOUR PAGES!!!
IT'S NOT YOUR JOB TO MAKE THE CHOICE. YOU SHOULDN'T BE FORCED...
...TO DECIDE WHICH ARTIST'S WORK IS MORE IMPORTANT.
IT ISN'T FAIR! ALL OF US ARE AWAITING TOMORROW'S COMIPA.
Circle "Holy Station" Matsuyama.
I KNOW... THIS GUY'S HEART'S POUNDING IN ANTICIPATION, TOO.
NO, KAZUKI!
SO...
TSUKAMOTO PRINTING NEEDS TO BE THERE FOR HIM!!

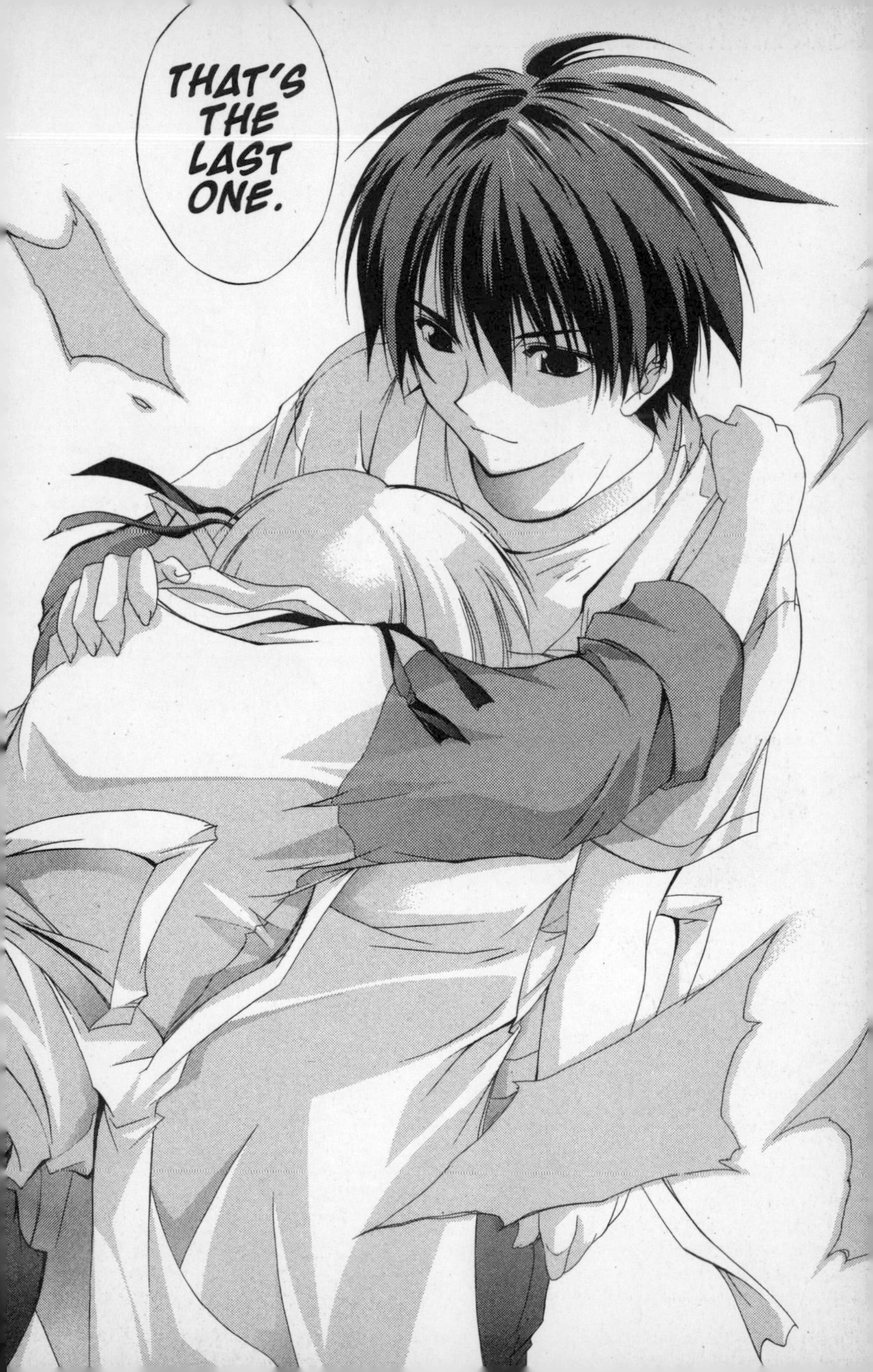
THAT'S THE LAST ONE.

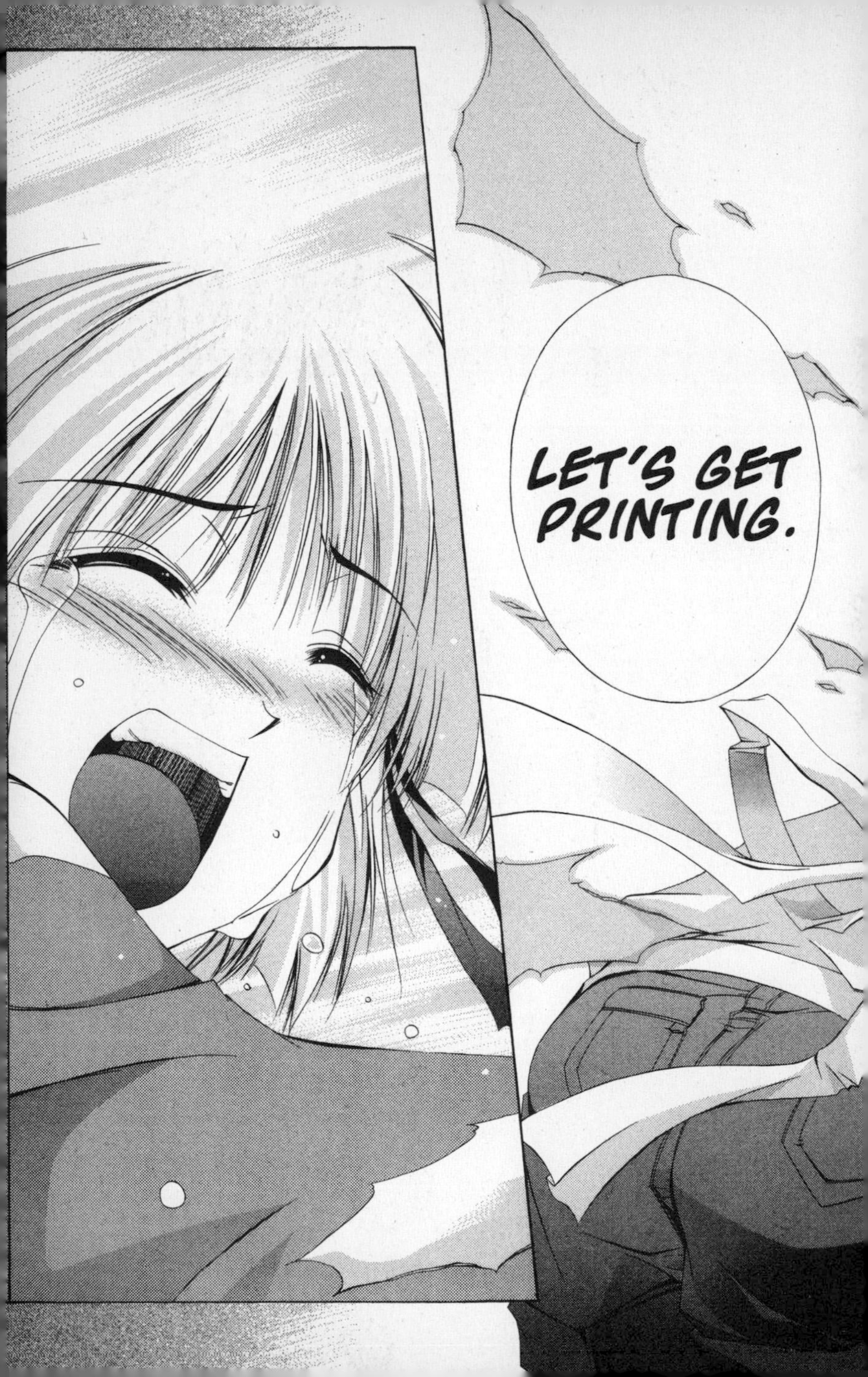
LET'S GET PRINTING.

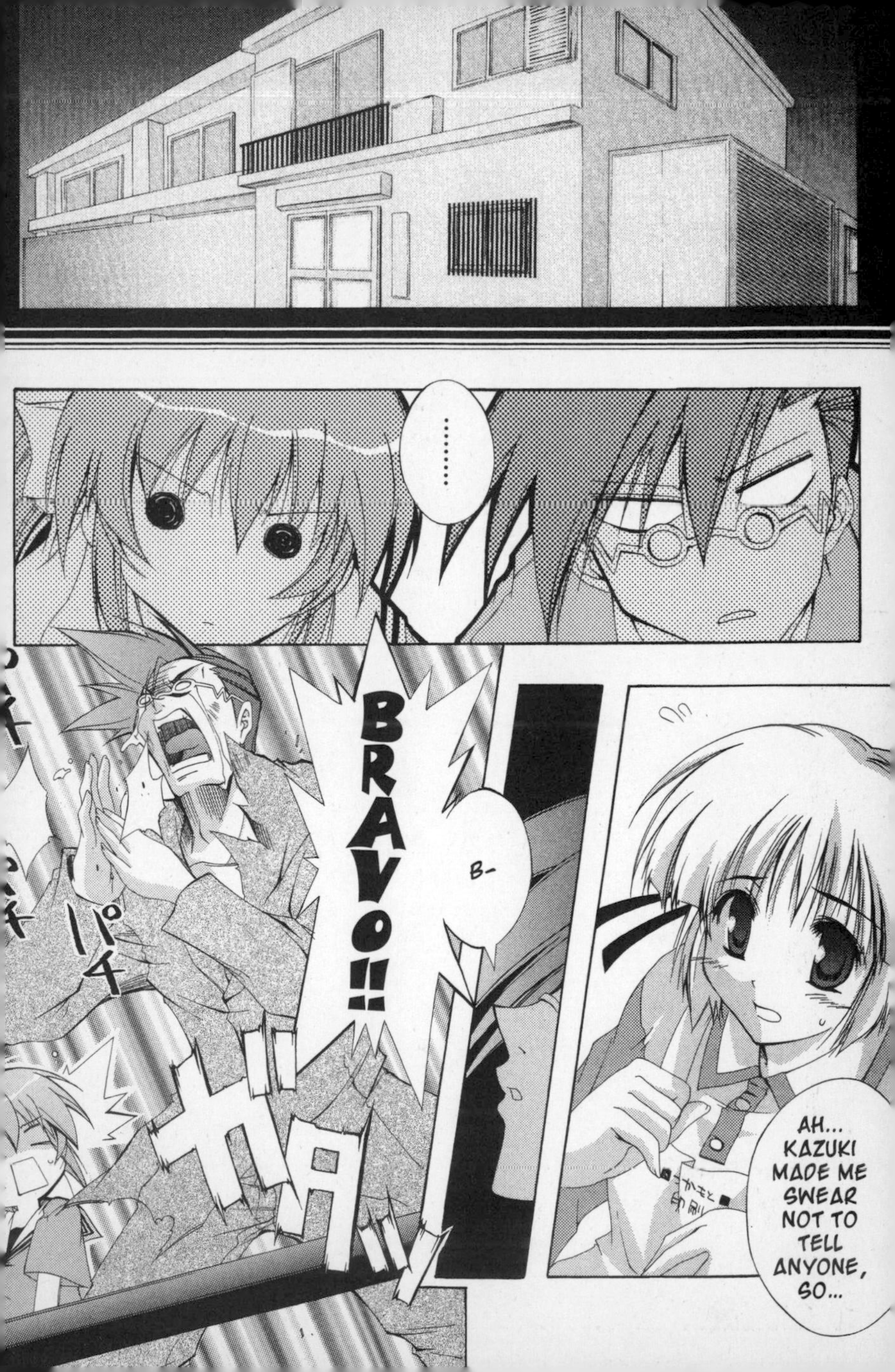

......
AH... KAZUKI MADE ME SWEAR NOT TO TELL ANYONE, SO...
B-
BRAVO!!
パチ

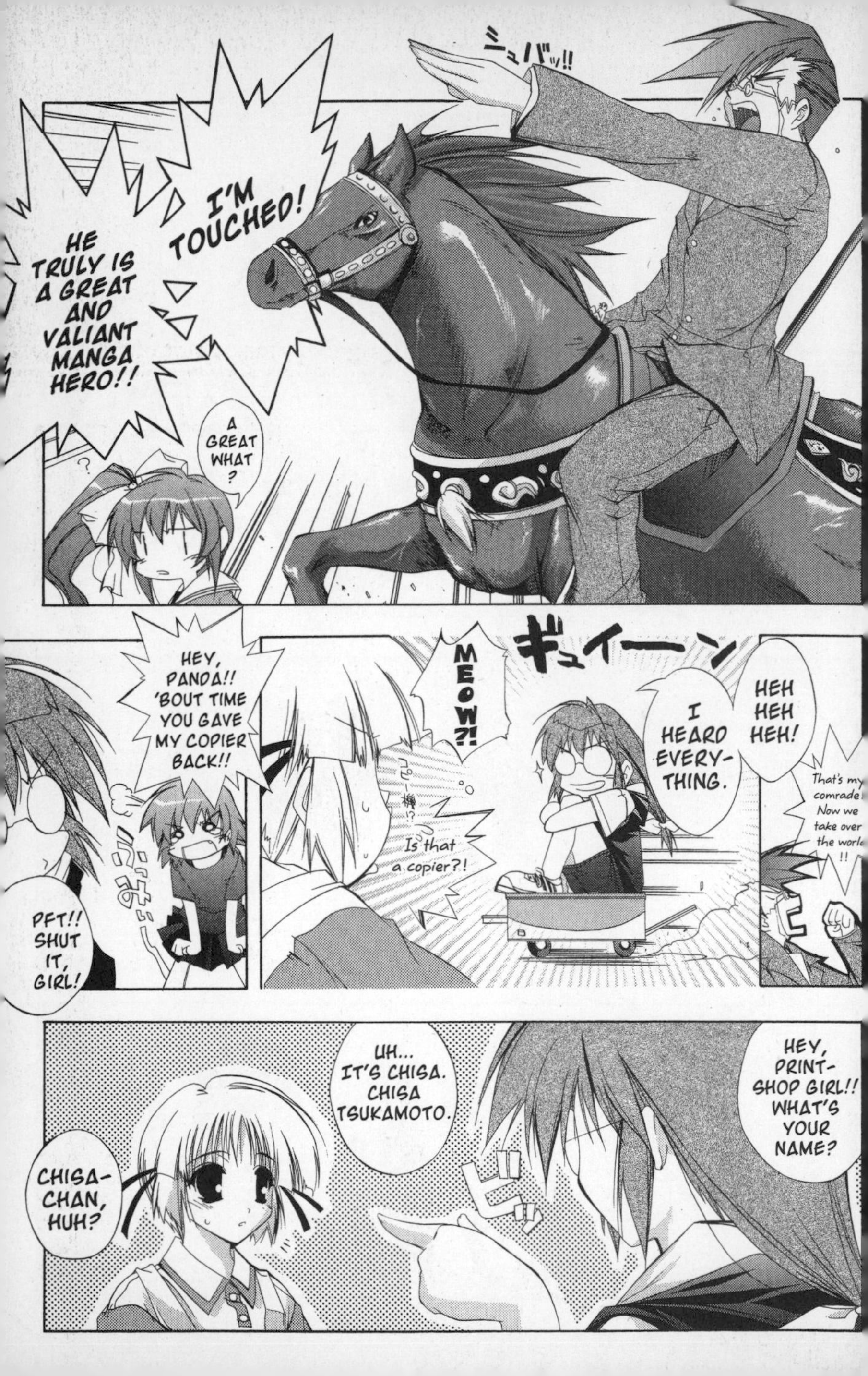
シュバッ!!
I'M TOUCHED!
HE TRULY IS A GREAT AND VALIANT MANGA HERO!!
A GREAT WHAT?
HEH HEH HEH!
That's my comrade! Now we take over the world!!
ギュイーン
I HEARD EVERYTHING.
MEOW?!
コピー機!?
Is that a copier?!
HEY, PANDA!! 'BOUT TIME YOU GAVE MY COPIER BACK!!
PFT!! SHUT IT, GIRL!
HEY, PRINT-SHOP GIRL!! WHAT'S YOUR NAME?
UH... IT'S CHISA. CHISA TSUKAMOTO.
CHISA-CHAN, HUH?

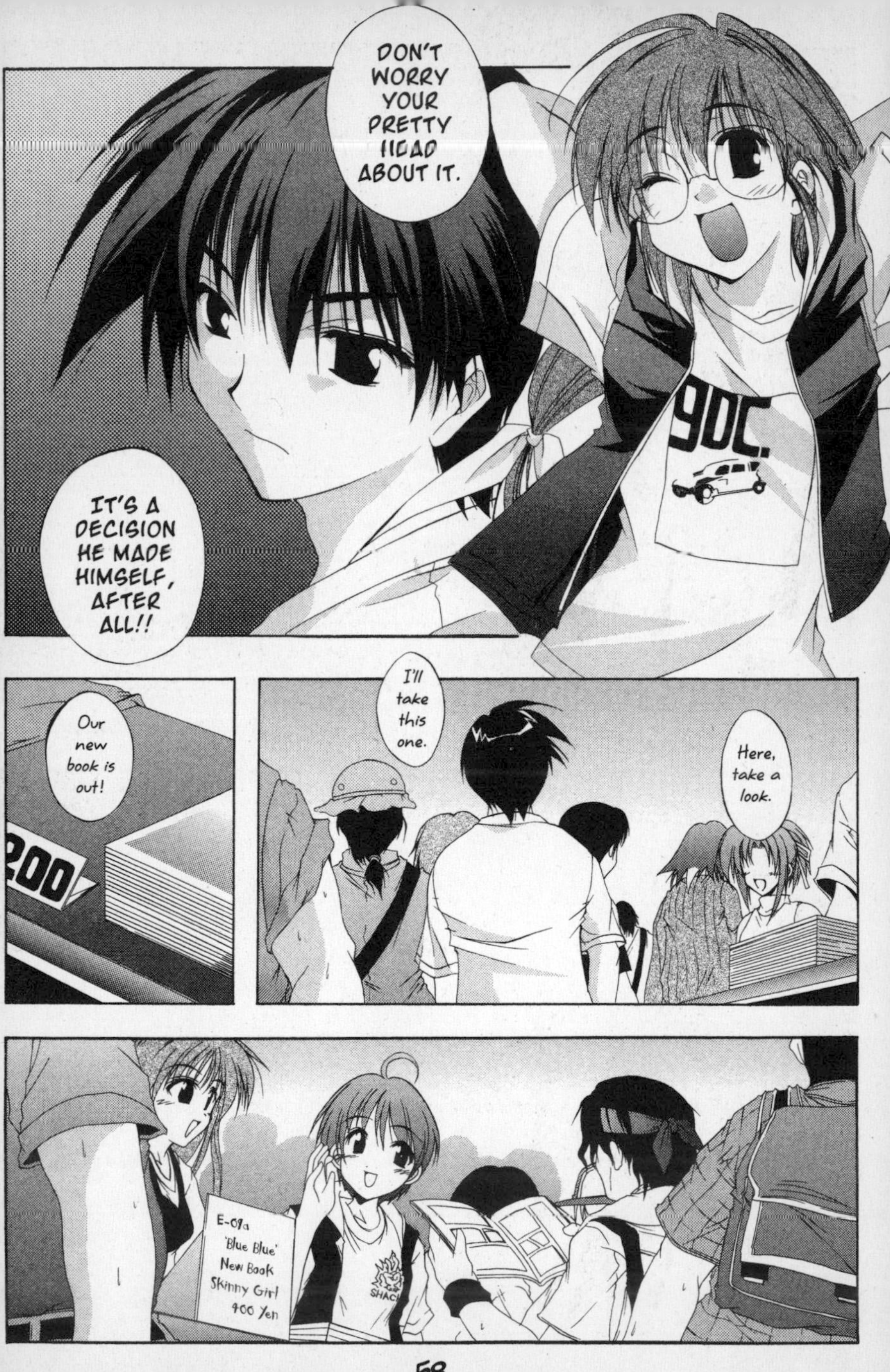
DON'T WORRY YOUR PRETTY HEAD ABOUT IT.
IT'S A DECISION HE MADE HIMSELF, AFTER ALL!!
Here, take a look.
I'll take this one.
Our new book is out!
200
E-09a 'Blue Blue' New Book Skinny Girl 400 Yen

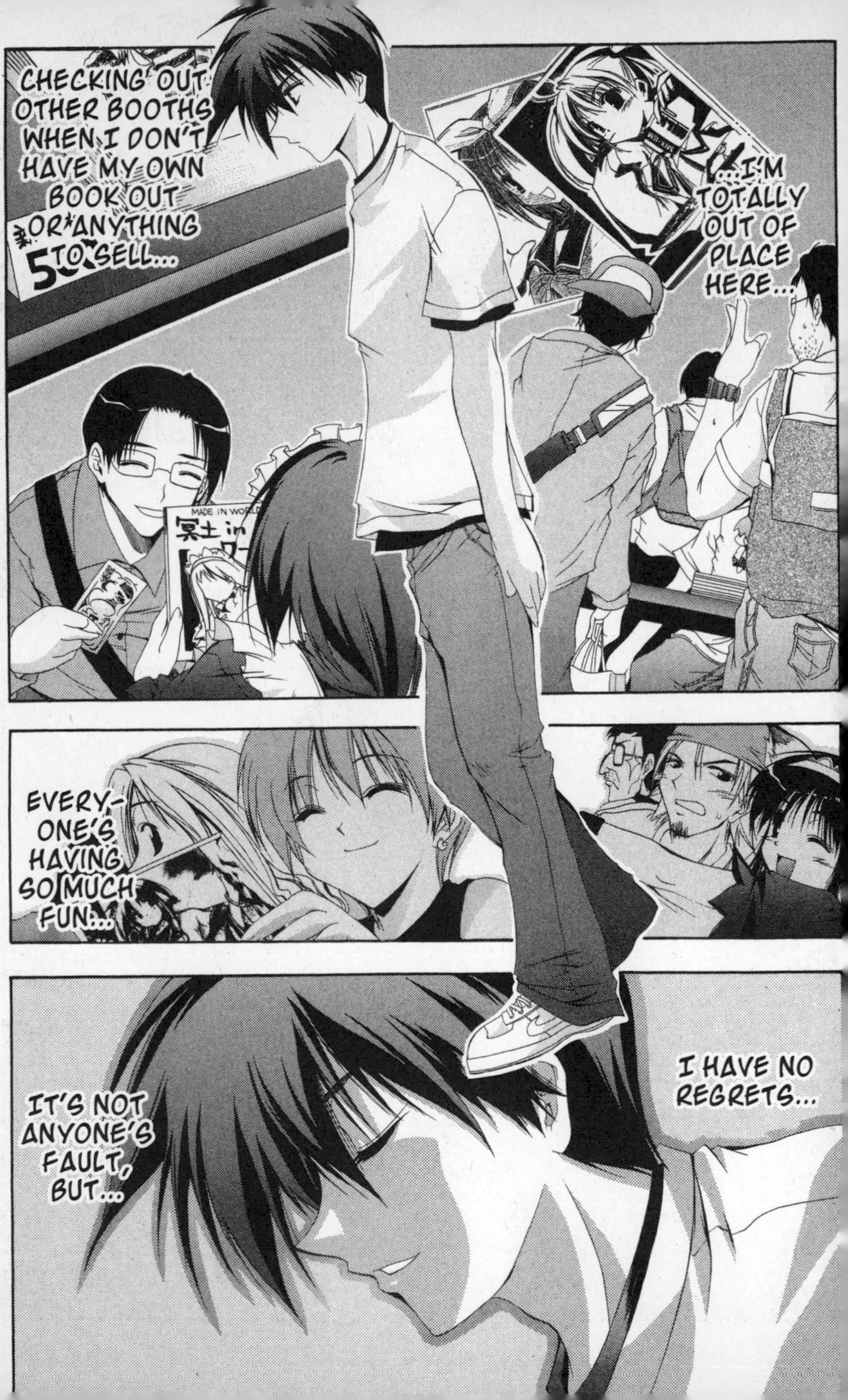
CHECKING OUT OTHER BOOTHS WHEN I DON'T HAVE MY OWN BOOK OUT OR ANYTHING TO SELL...
...I'M TOTALLY OUT OF PLACE HERE...
MADE IN WORLD
EVERYONE'S HAVING SO MUCH FUN...
I HAVE NO REGRETS...
IT'S NOT ANYONE'S FAULT, BUT...

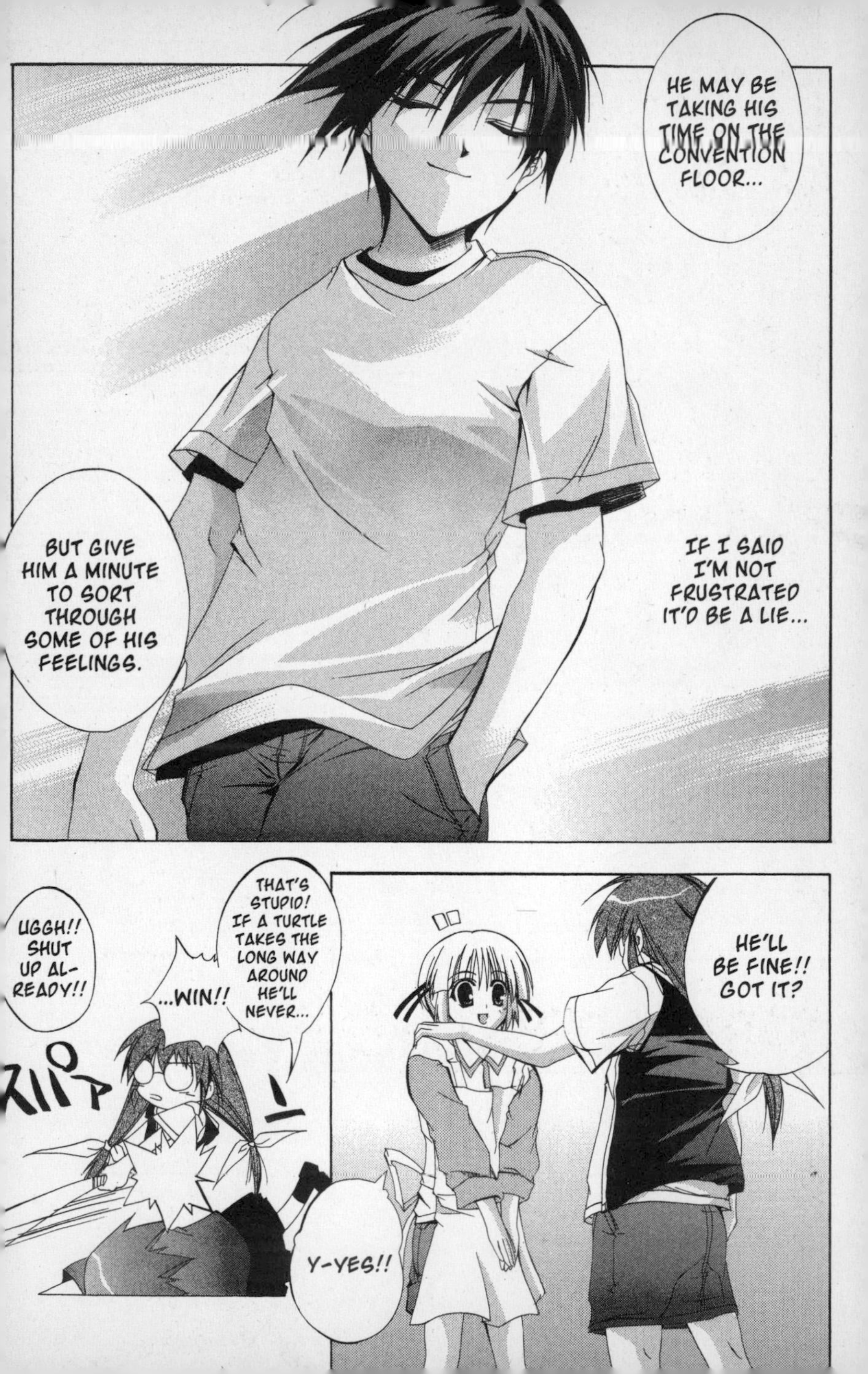
HE MAY BE TAKING HIS TIME ON THE CONVENTION FLOOR...
IF I SAID I'M NOT FRUSTRATED IT'D BE A LIE...
BUT GIVE HIM A MINUTE TO SORT THROUGH SOME OF HIS FEELINGS.
HE'LL BE FINE!! GOT IT?
Y-YES!!
THAT'S STUPID! IF A TURTLE TAKES THE LONG WAY AROUND HE'LL NEVER...
...WIN!!
UGGH!! SHUT UP AL-READY!!

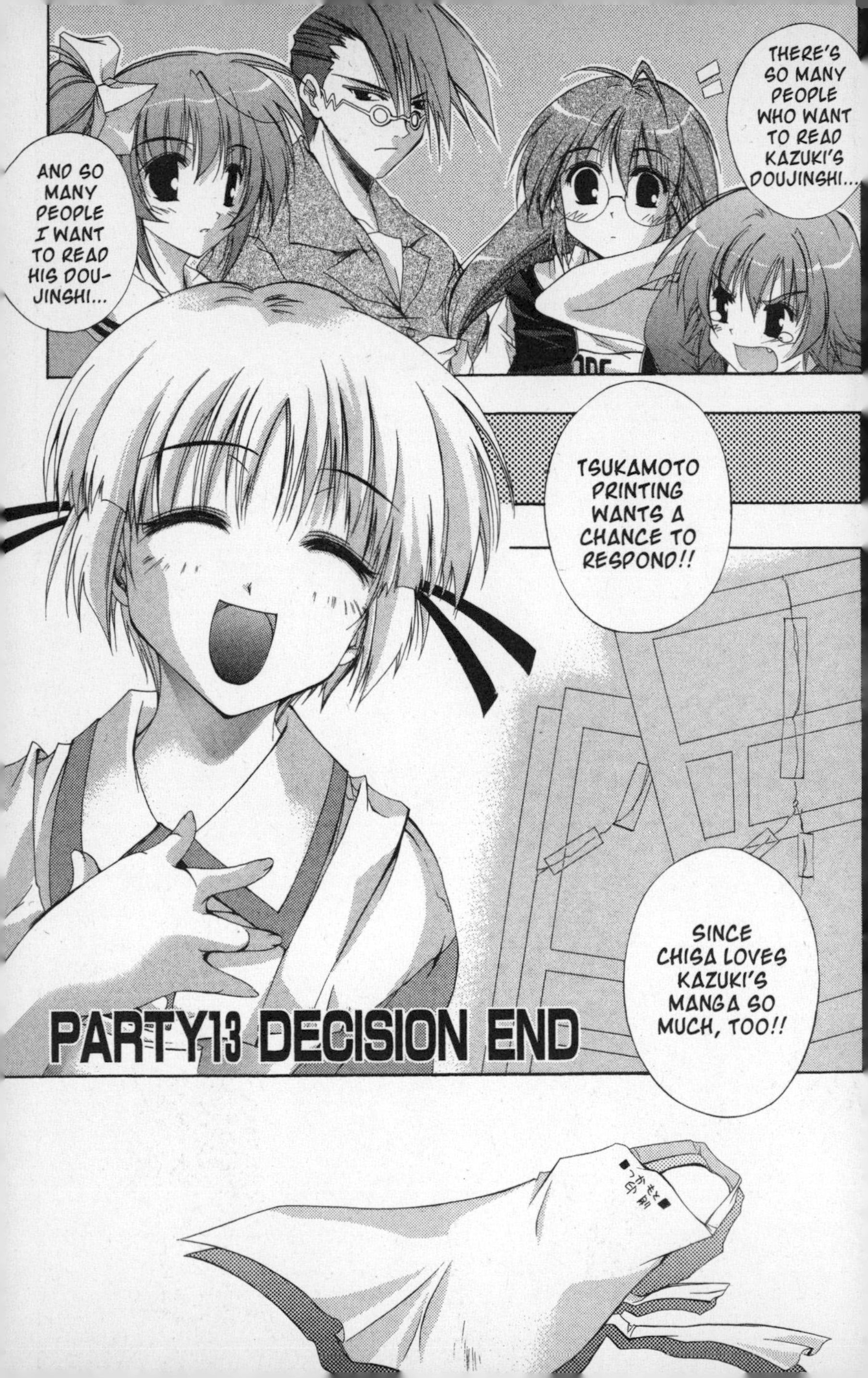
THERE'S SO MANY PEOPLE WHO WANT TO READ KAZUKI'S DOUJINSHI...
AND SO MANY PEOPLE I WANT TO READ HIS DOUJINSHI...
TSUKAMOTO PRINTING WANTS A CHANCE TO RESPOND!!
SINCE CHISA LOVES KAZUKI'S MANGA SO MUCH, TOO!!
PARTY13 DECISION END

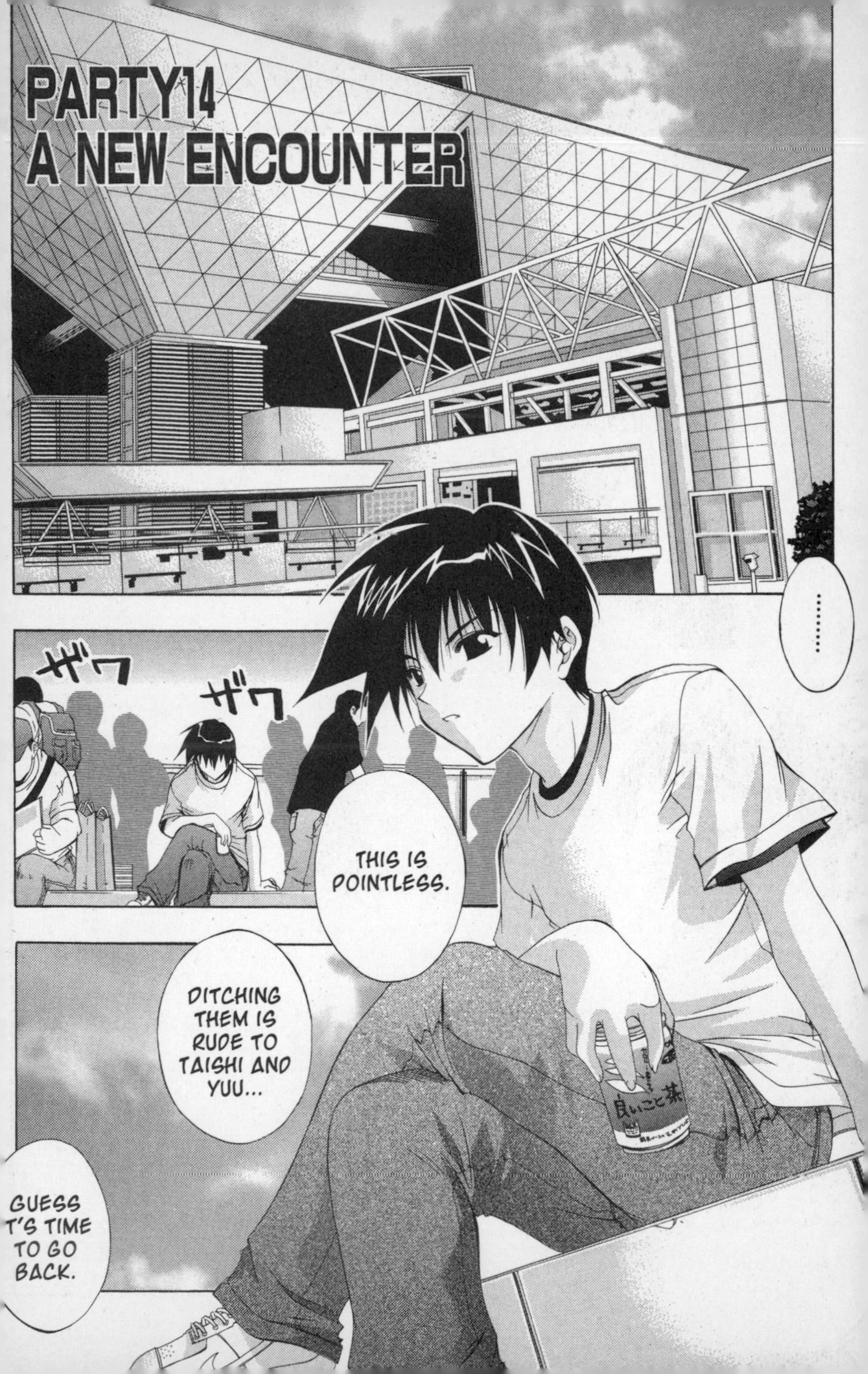
PARTY14
A NEW ENCOUNTER
......
ザワ
ザワ
THIS IS POINTLESS.
DITCHING THEM IS RUDE TO TAISHI AND YUU...
良いこと茶
GUESS T'S TIME TO GO BACK.

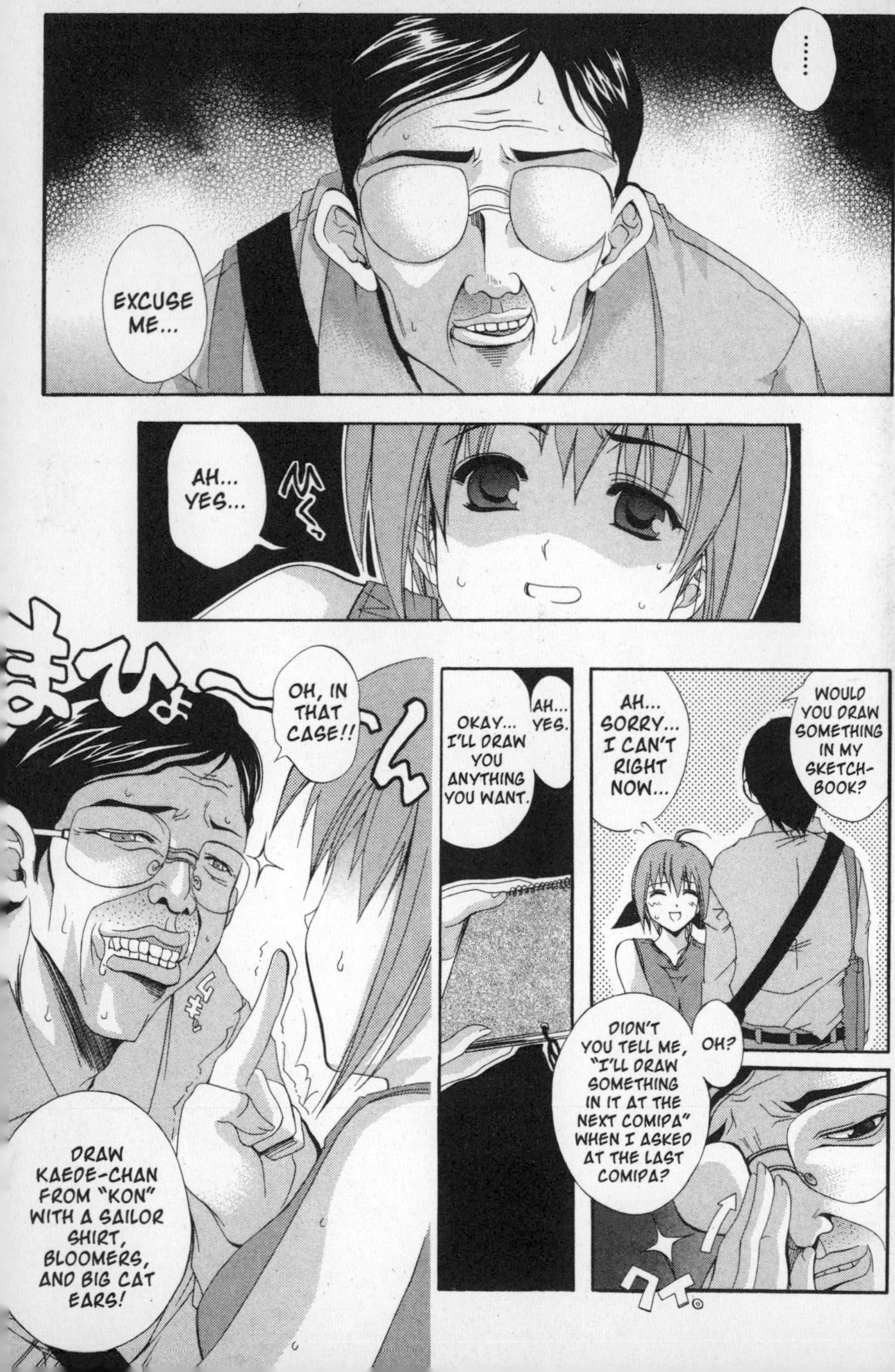
……
EXCUSE ME...
AH... YES...
WOULD YOU DRAW SOMETHING IN MY SKETCH-BOOK?
AH... SORRY... I CAN'T RIGHT NOW...
OH?
DIDN'T YOU TELL ME, "I'LL DRAW SOMETHING IN IT AT THE NEXT COMIPA" WHEN I ASKED AT THE LAST COMIPA?
AH... YES.
OKAY... I'LL DRAW YOU ANYTHING YOU WANT.
OH, IN THAT CASE!!
DRAW KAEDE-CHAN FROM "KON" WITH A SAILOR SHIRT, BLOOMERS, AND BIG CAT EARS!

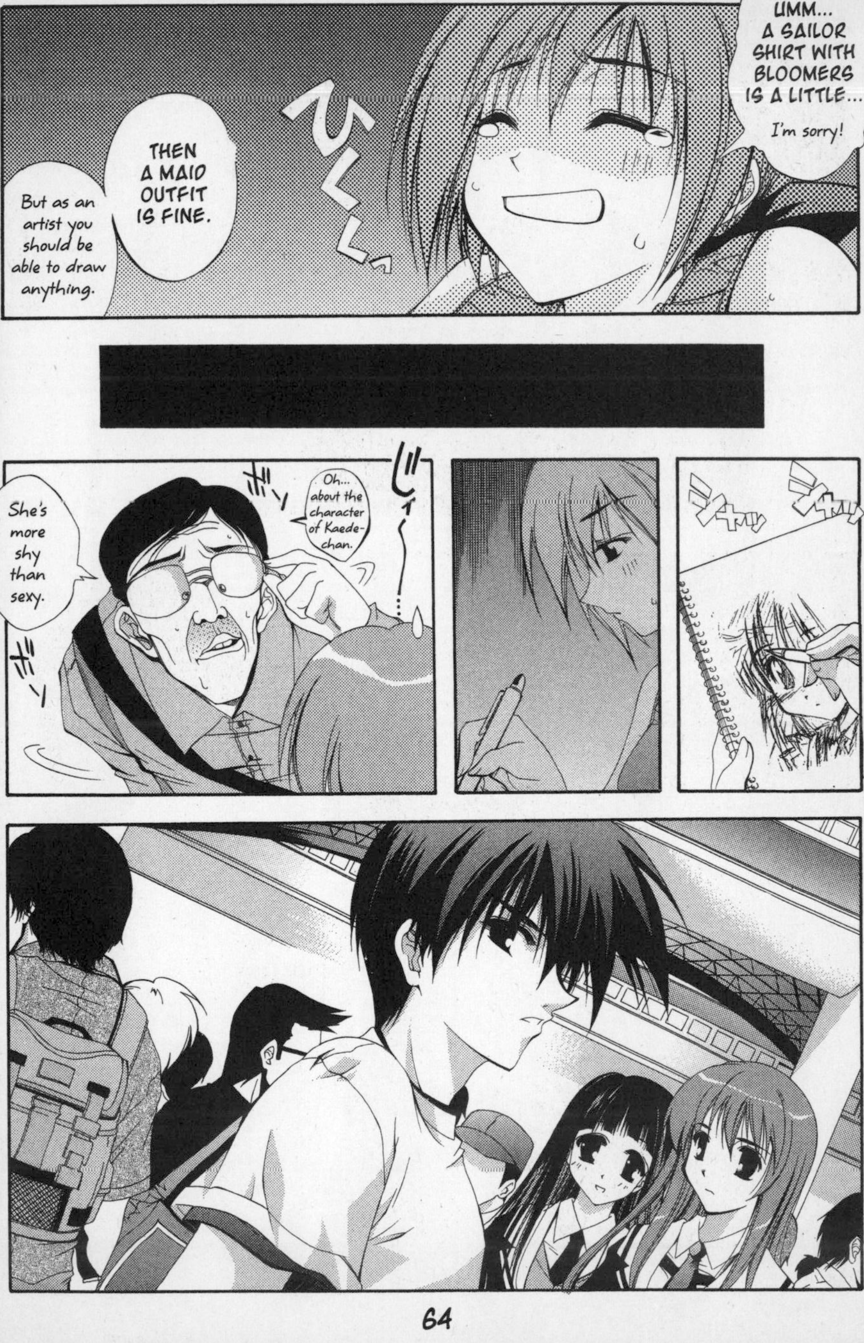
UMM... A SAILOR SHIRT WITH BLOOMERS IS A LITTLE...
I'm sorry!
THEN A MAID OUTFIT IS FINE.
But as an artist you should be able to draw anything.
Oh... about the character of Kaede-chan.
She's more shy than sexy.

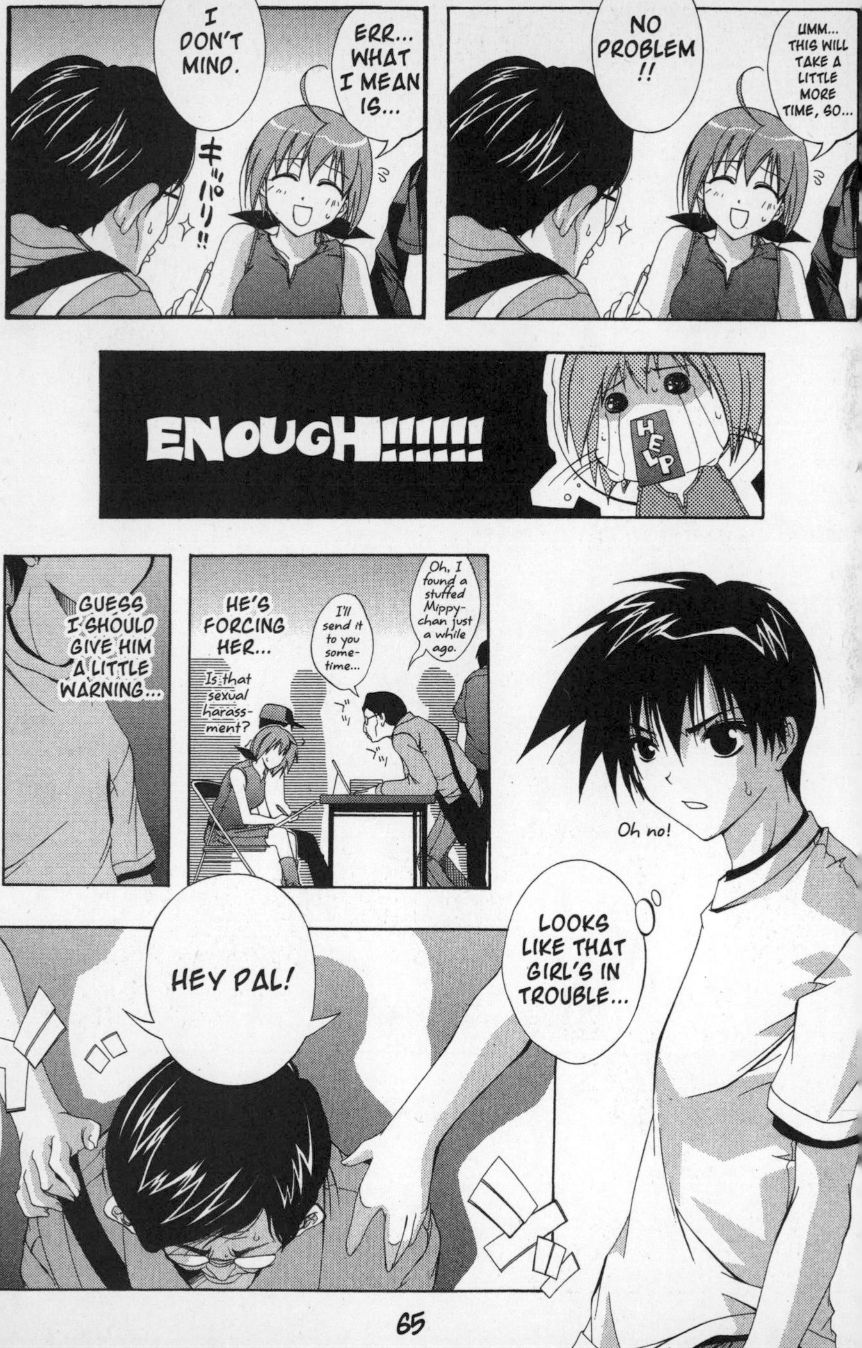
UMM... THIS WILL TAKE A LITTLE MORE TIME, SO...
NO PROBLEM !!
ERR... WHAT I MEAN IS...
I DON'T MIND.
キッパリ!!
HELP
ENOUGH!!!!!!
Oh no!
LOOKS LIKE THAT GIRL'S IN TROUBLE...
Oh, I found a stuffed Mippy-chan just a while ago.
I'll send it to you some-time...
HE'S FORCING HER...
Is that sexual harass-ment?
GUESS I SHOULD GIVE HIM A LITTLE WARNING...
HEY PAL!

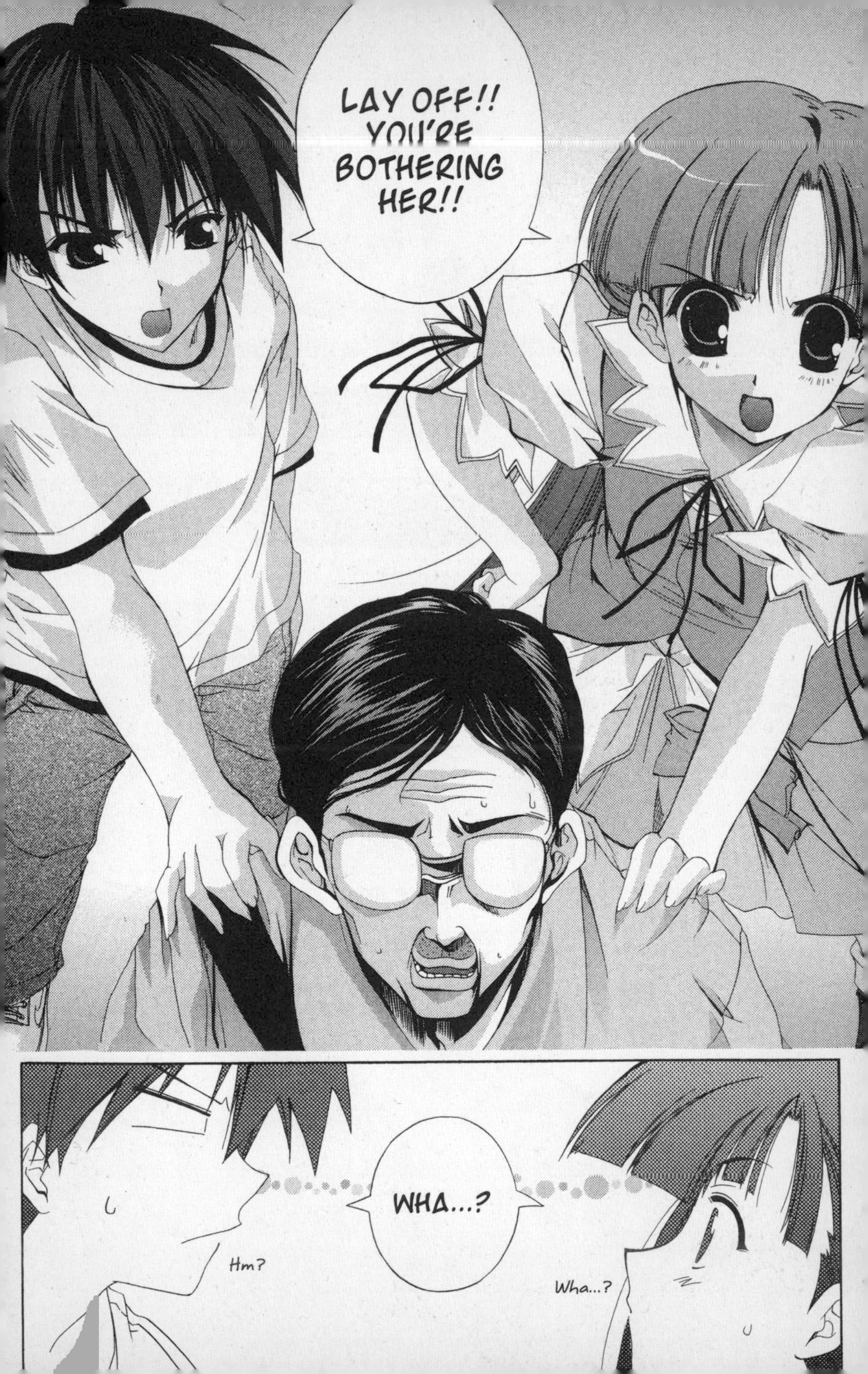
LAY OFF!! YOU'RE BOTHERING HER!!
WHA...?
Wha...?
Hm?

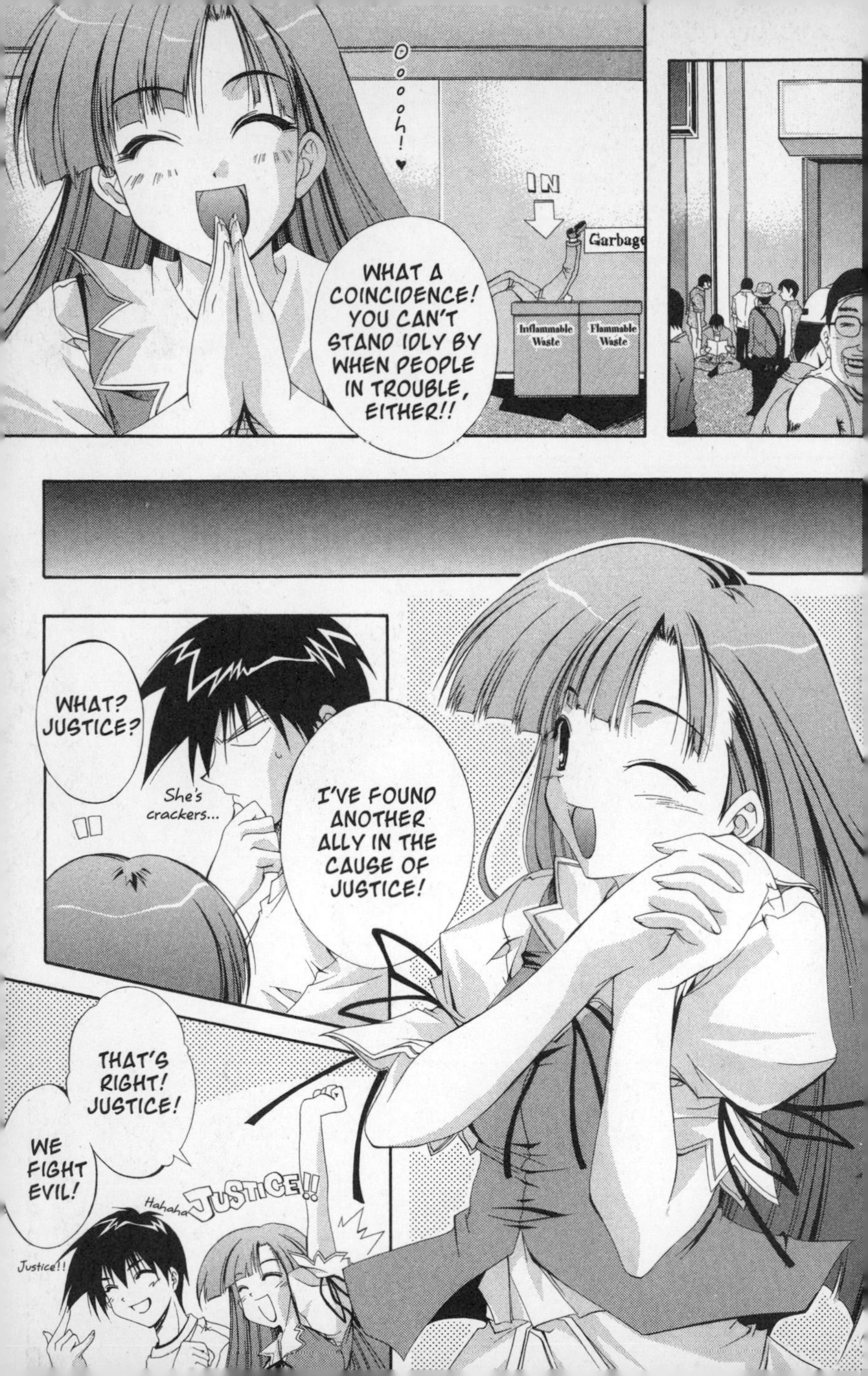
Oooh!♥
IN
Garbage
Inflammable Waste
Flammable Waste
WHAT A COINCIDENCE! YOU CAN'T STAND IDLY BY WHEN PEOPLE IN TROUBLE, EITHER!!
I'VE FOUND ANOTHER ALLY IN THE CAUSE OF JUSTICE!
WHAT? JUSTICE?
She's crackers...
THAT'S RIGHT! JUSTICE!
WE FIGHT EVIL!
Hahaha
JUSTICE!!
Justice!!

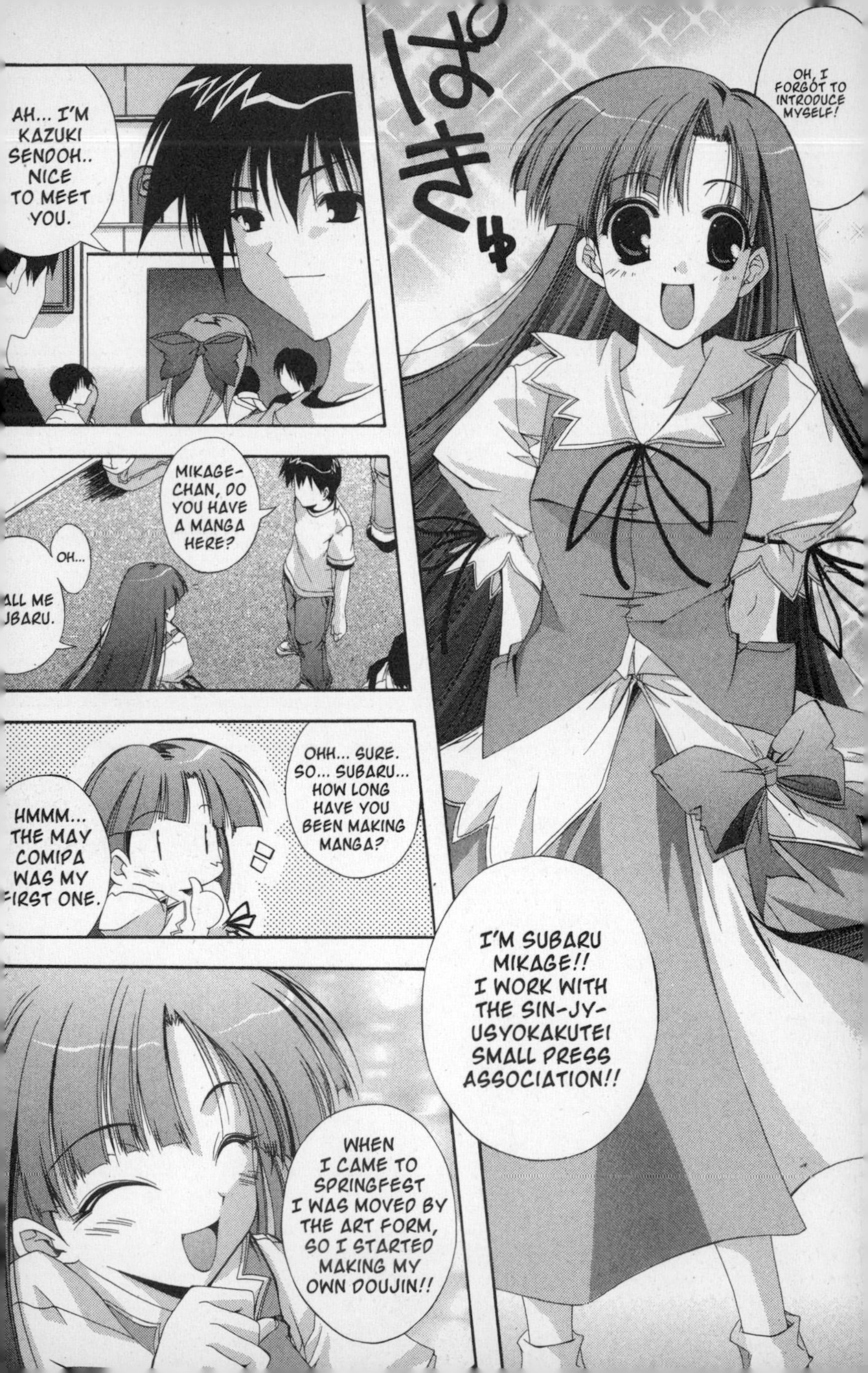
OH, I FORGOT TO INTRODUCE MYSELF!
ぱきゅ
I'M SUBARU MIKAGE!! I WORK WITH THE SIN-JY-USYOKAKUTEI SMALL PRESS ASSOCIATION!!
AH... I'M KAZUKI SENDOH.. NICE TO MEET YOU.
MIKAGE-CHAN, DO YOU HAVE A MANGA HERE?
OH...
ALL ME UBARU.
OHH... SURE. SO... SUBARU... HOW LONG HAVE YOU BEEN MAKING MANGA?
HMMM... THE MAY COMIPA WAS MY FIRST ONE.
WHEN I CAME TO SPRINGFEST I WAS MOVED BY THE ART FORM, SO I STARTED MAKING MY OWN DOUJIN!!

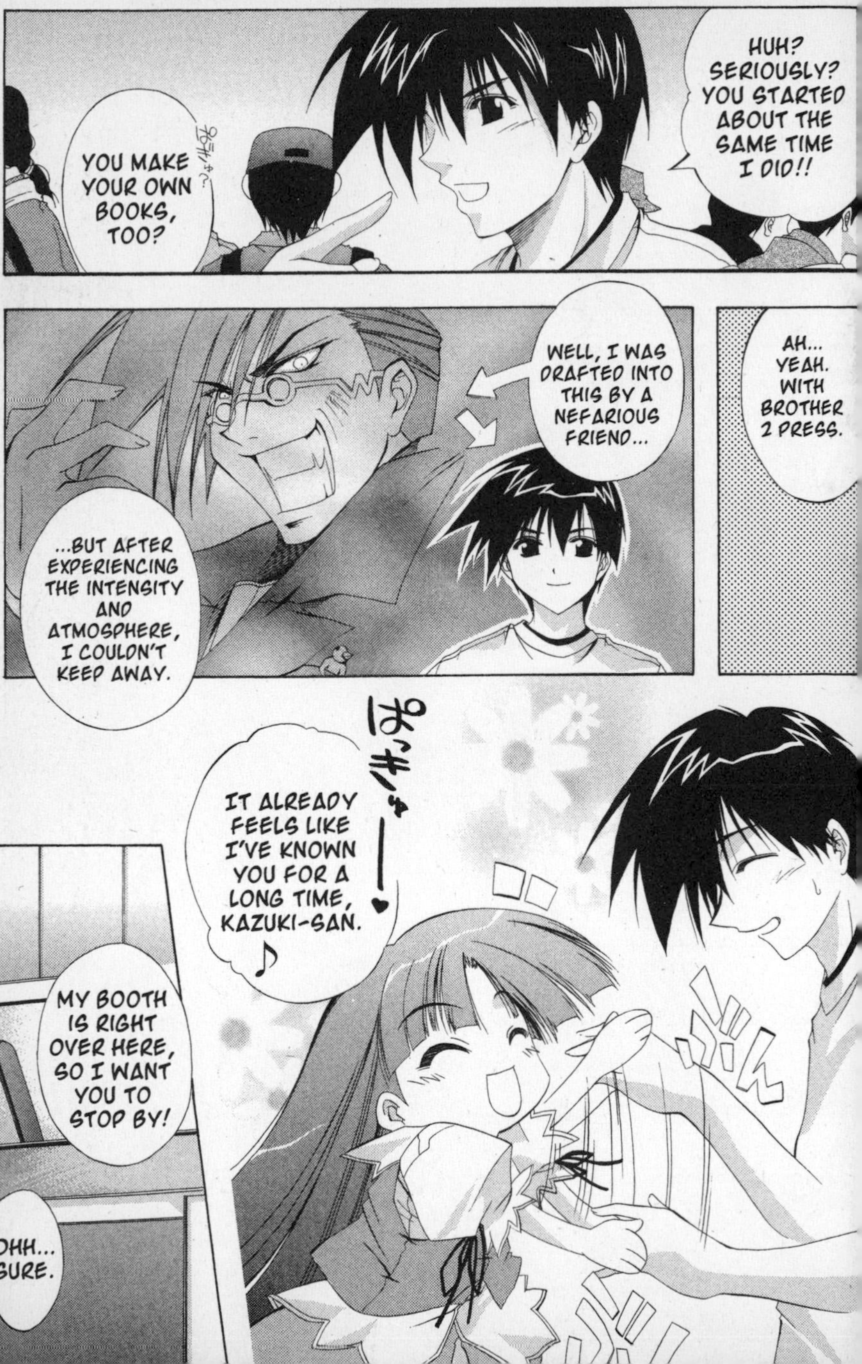
HUH? SERIOUSLY? YOU STARTED ABOUT THE SAME TIME I DID!!
YOU MAKE YOUR OWN BOOKS, TOO?
AH... YEAH. WITH BROTHER 2 PRESS.
WELL, I WAS DRAFTED INTO THIS BY A NEFARIOUS FRIEND...
...BUT AFTER EXPERIENCING THE INTENSITY AND ATMOSPHERE, I COULDN'T KEEP AWAY.
IT ALREADY FEELS LIKE I'VE KNOWN YOU FOR A LONG TIME, KAZUKI-SAN. ♪
MY BOOTH IS RIGHT OVER HERE, SO I WANT YOU TO STOP BY!
OHH... SURE.

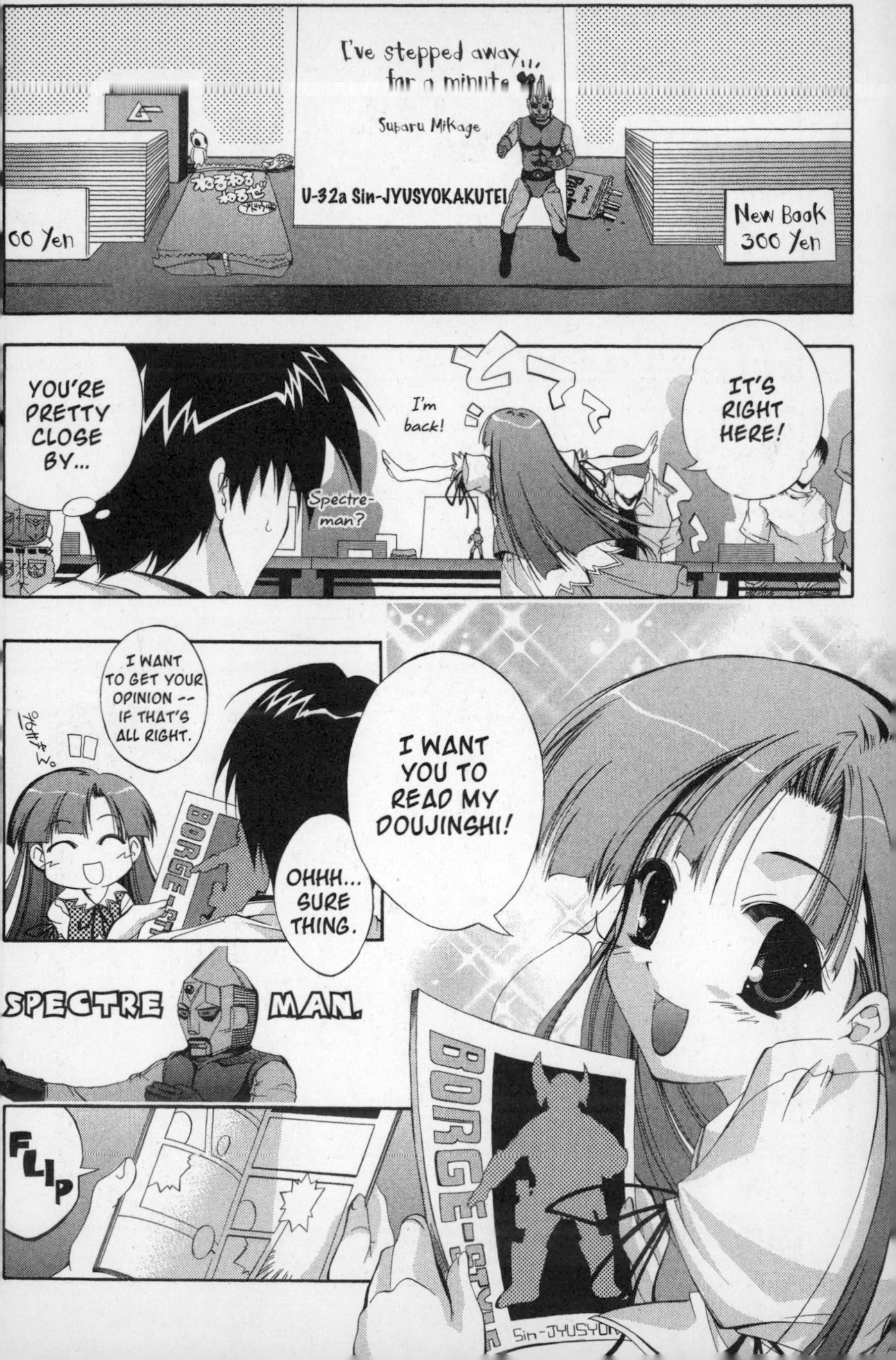
I've stepped away for a minute
Subaru Mikage
U-32a Sin-JYUSYOKAKUTEI
New Book 300 Yen
00 Yen
IT'S RIGHT HERE!
I'm back!
Spectre-man?
YOU'RE PRETTY CLOSE BY...
I WANT YOU TO READ MY DOUJINSHI!
I WANT TO GET YOUR OPINION -- IF THAT'S ALL RIGHT.
OHHH... SURE THING.
SPECTRE MAN.
FLIP

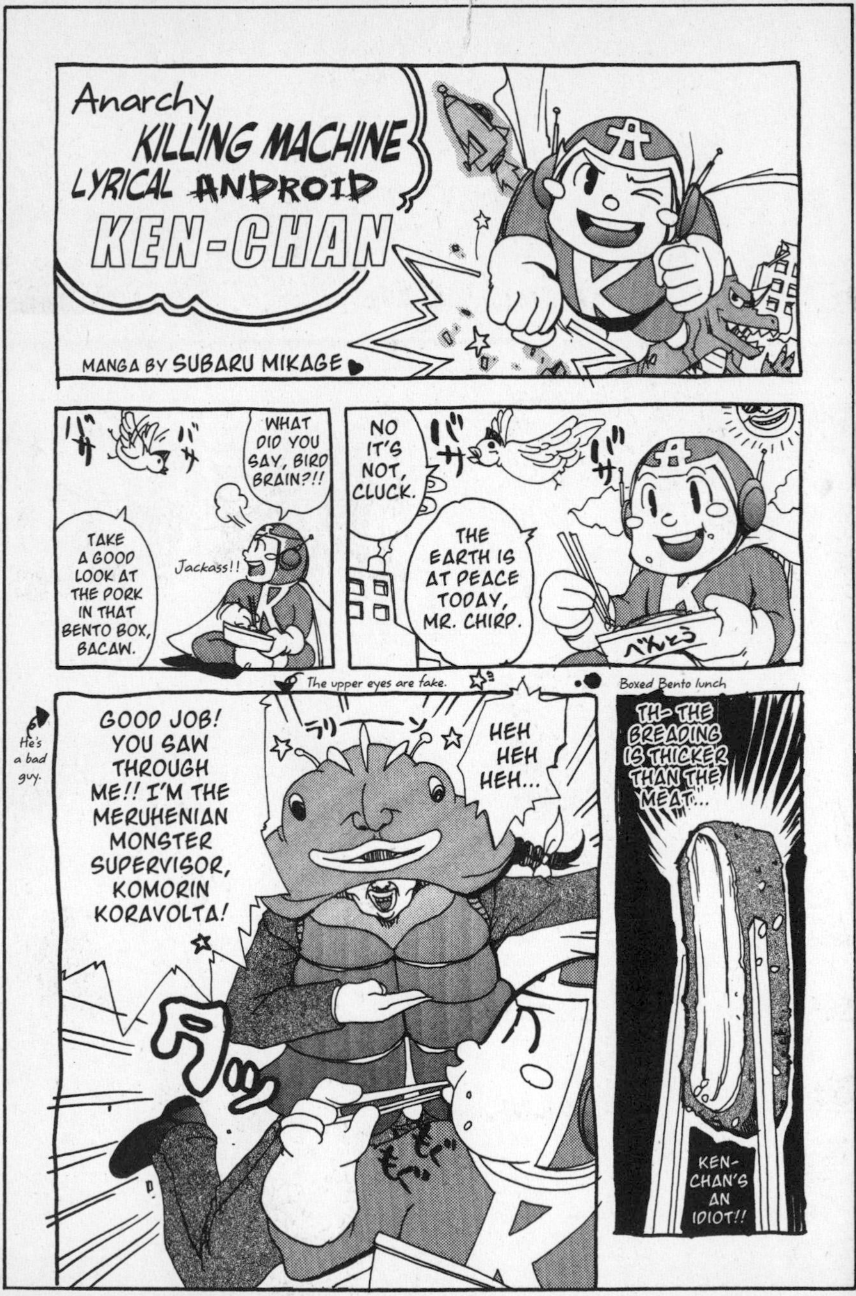
Anarchy
KILLING MACHINE
LYRICAL ANDROID
KEN-CHAN
MANGA BY SUBARU MIKAGE
バサ
バサ
THE EARTH IS AT PEACE TODAY, MR. CHIRP.
NO IT'S NOT, CLUCK.
べんとう
Boxed Bento lunch
バサ
バサ
WHAT DID YOU SAY, BIRD BRAIN?!!
Jackass!!
TAKE A GOOD LOOK AT THE PORK IN THAT BENTO BOX, BACAW.
TH- THE BREADING IS THICKER THAN THE MEAT...
KEN-CHAN'S AN IDIOT!!
HEH HEH HEH...
ラリーン
The upper eyes are fake.
GOOD JOB! YOU SAW THROUGH ME!! I'M THE MERUHENIAN MONSTER SUPERVISOR, KOMORIN KORAVOLTA!
He's a bad guy.
ドッ
もぐもぐ

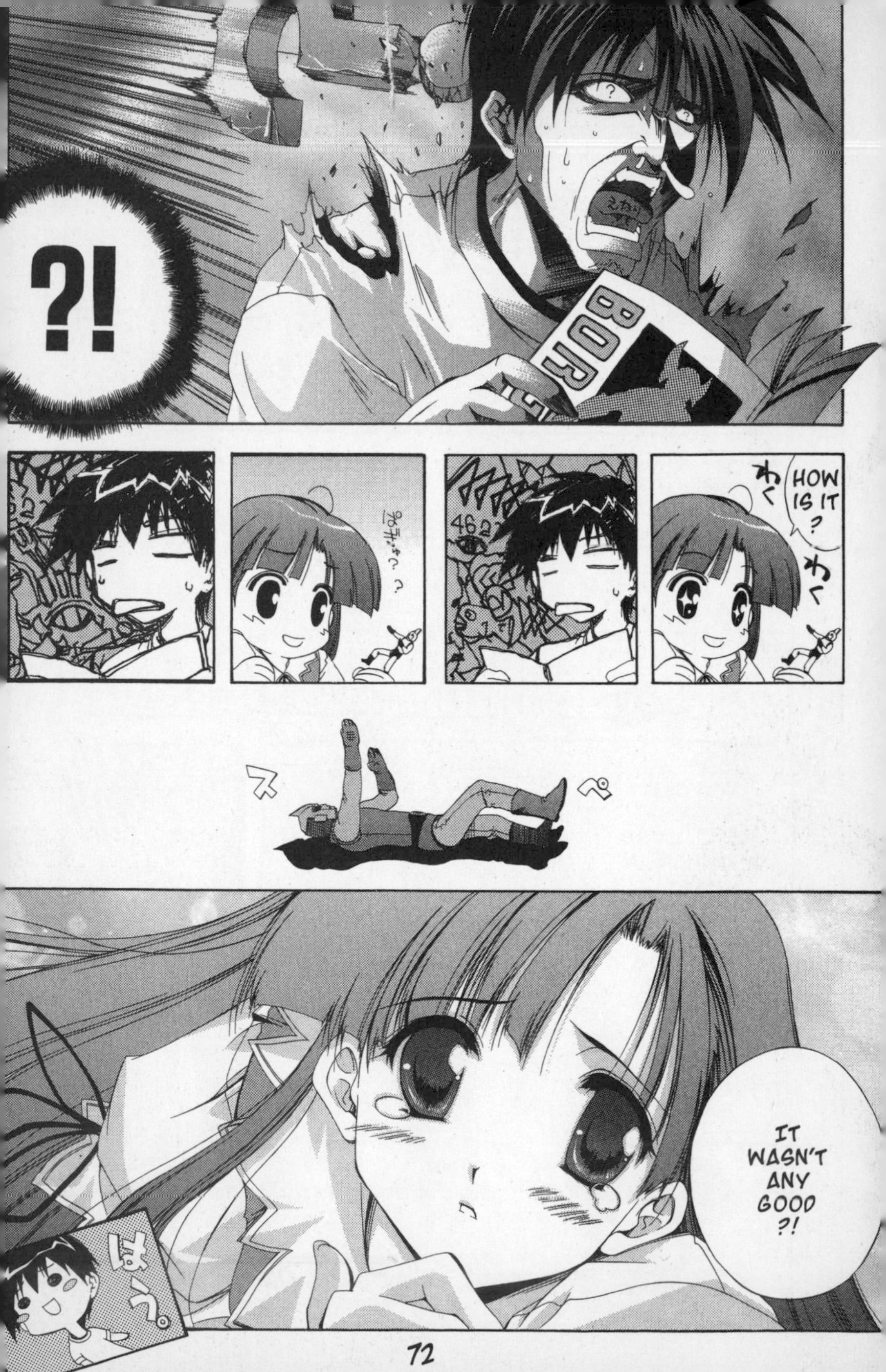
?!
わく
HOW IS IT?
わく
ス
ペ
IT WASN'T ANY GOOD?!
はぅ。

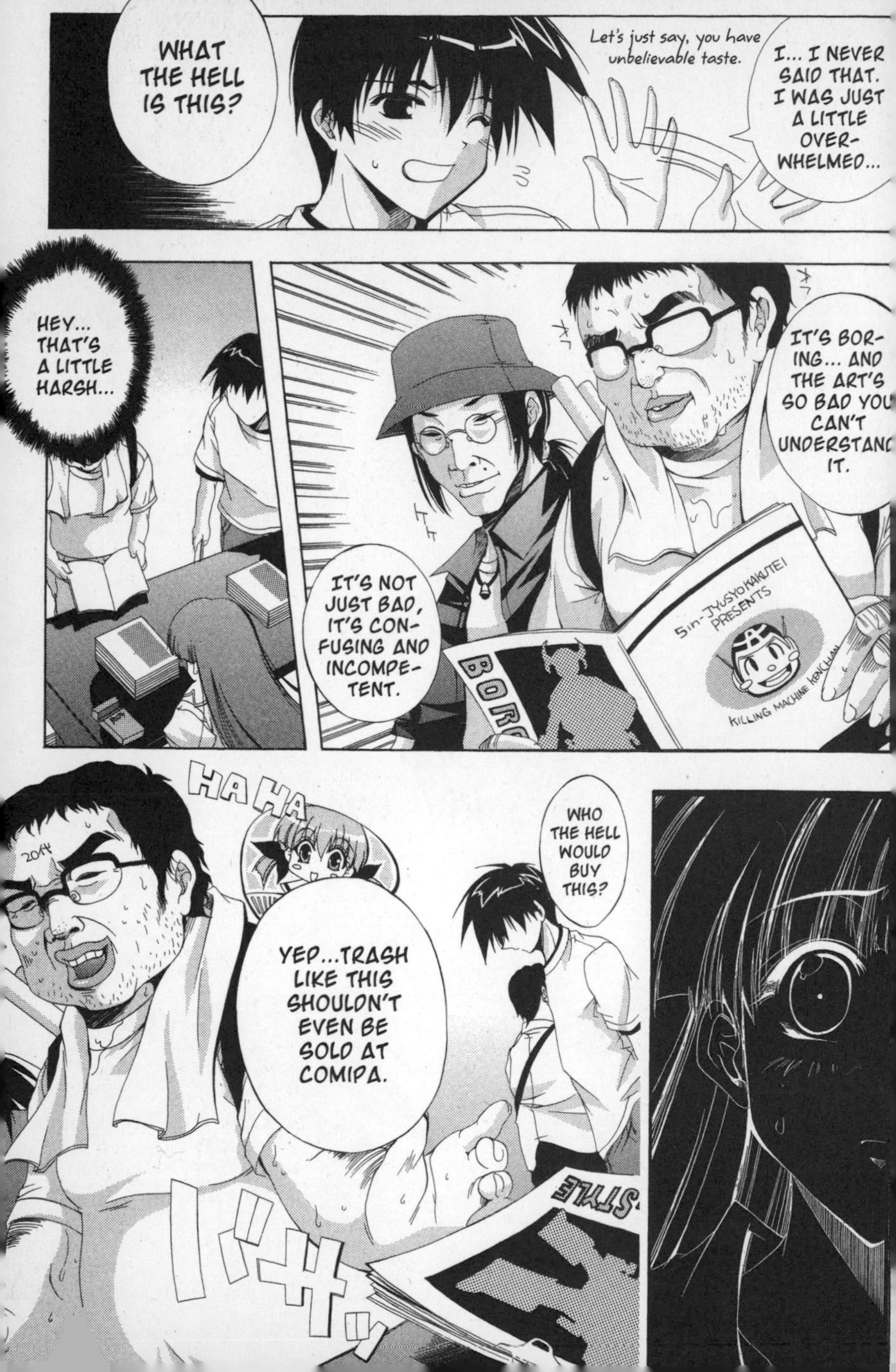
I... I NEVER SAID THAT. I WAS JUST A LITTLE OVER-WHELMED...
Let's just say, you have unbelievable taste.
WHAT THE HELL IS THIS?
IT'S BOR-ING... AND THE ART'S SO BAD YOU CAN'T UNDERSTAND IT.
IT'S NOT JUST BAD, IT'S CON-FUSING AND INCOMPE-TENT.
5in-JYUSYOKAKUTEI PRESENTS
KILLING MACHINE KENCHAN
HEY... THAT'S A LITTLE HARSH...
WHO THE HELL WOULD BUY THIS?
HA HA
YEP...TRASH LIKE THIS SHOULDN'T EVEN BE SOLD AT COMIPA.

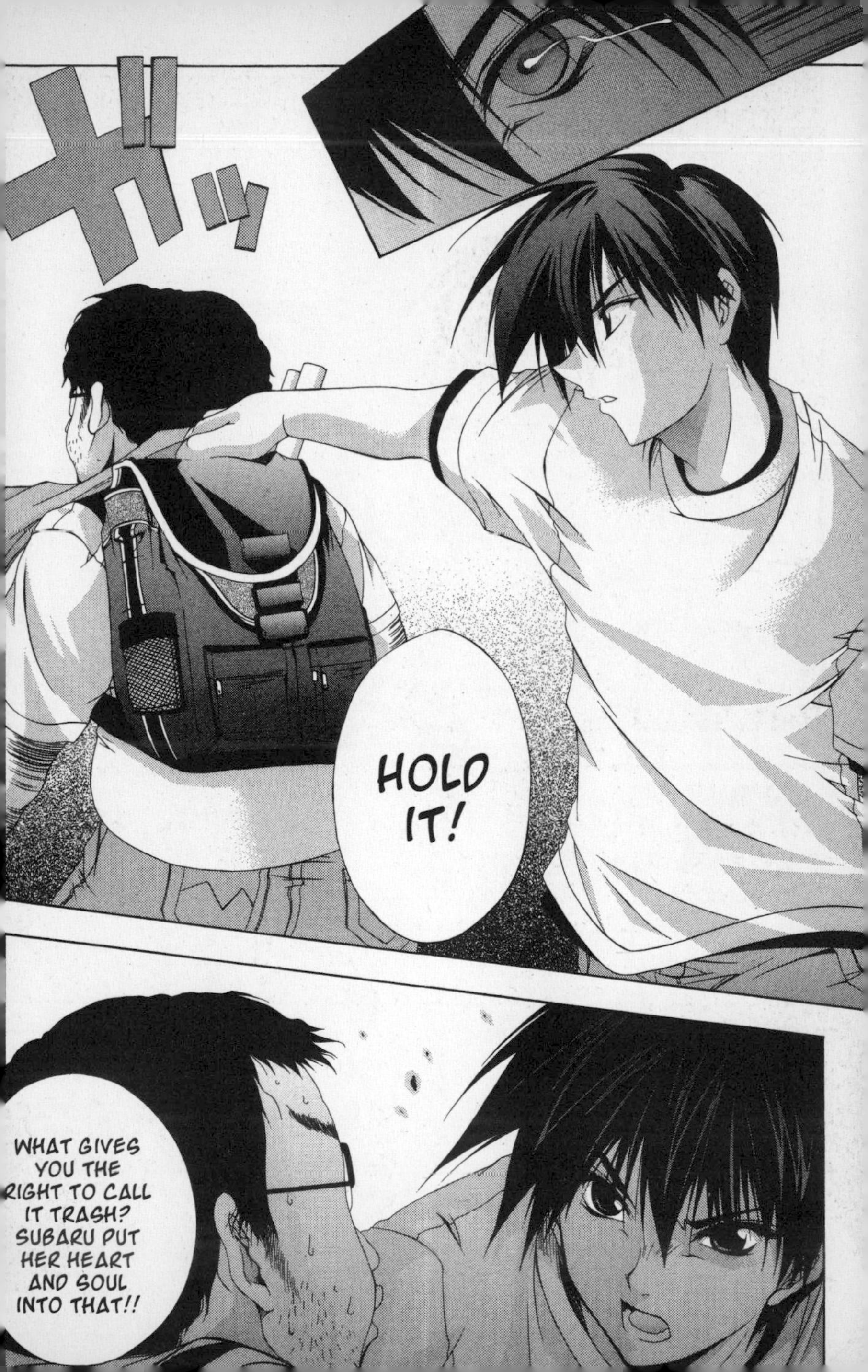
ガッ
HOLD IT!
WHAT GIVES YOU THE RIGHT TO CALL IT TRASH? SUBARU PUT HER HEART AND SOUL INTO THAT!!

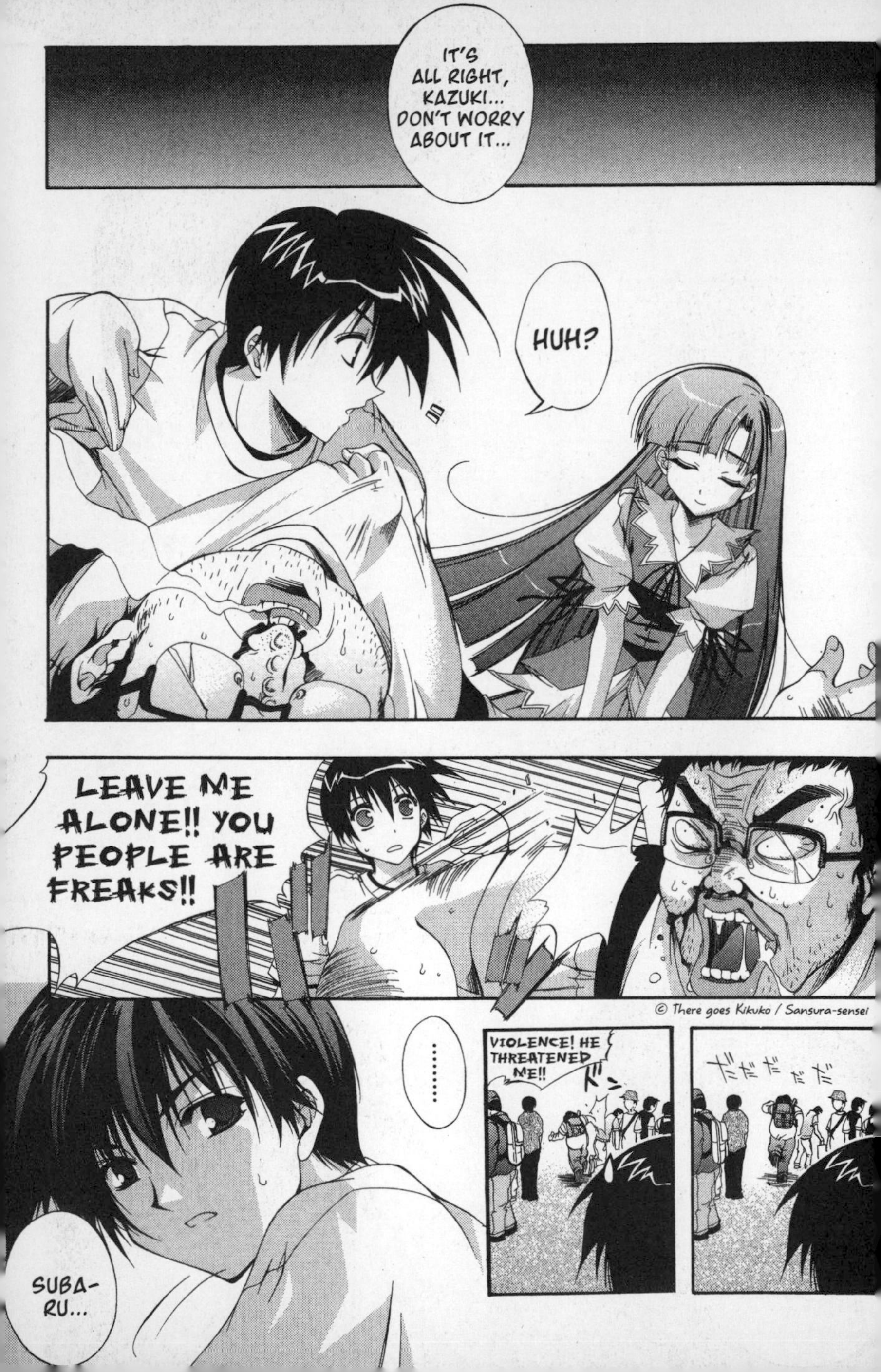
IT'S ALL RIGHT, KAZUKI... DON'T WORRY ABOUT IT...
HUH?
LEAVE ME ALONE!! YOU PEOPLE ARE FREAKS!!
© There goes Kikuko / Sansura-sensei
だだだだだ
VIOLENCE! HE THREATENED ME!!
....
SUBA-RU...

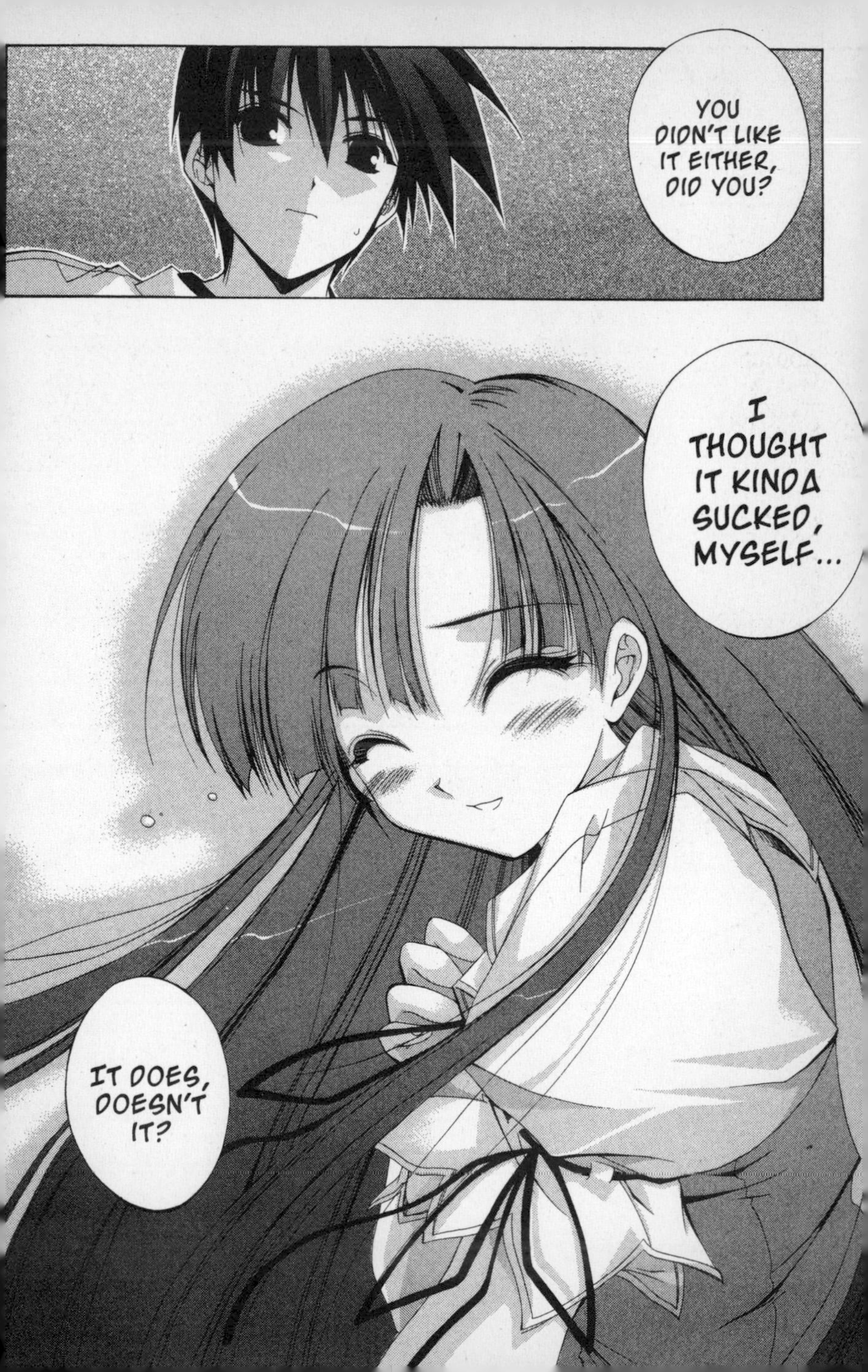
YOU DIDN'T LIKE IT EITHER, DID YOU?
I THOUGHT IT KINDA SUCKED, MYSELF...
IT DOES, DOESN'T IT?

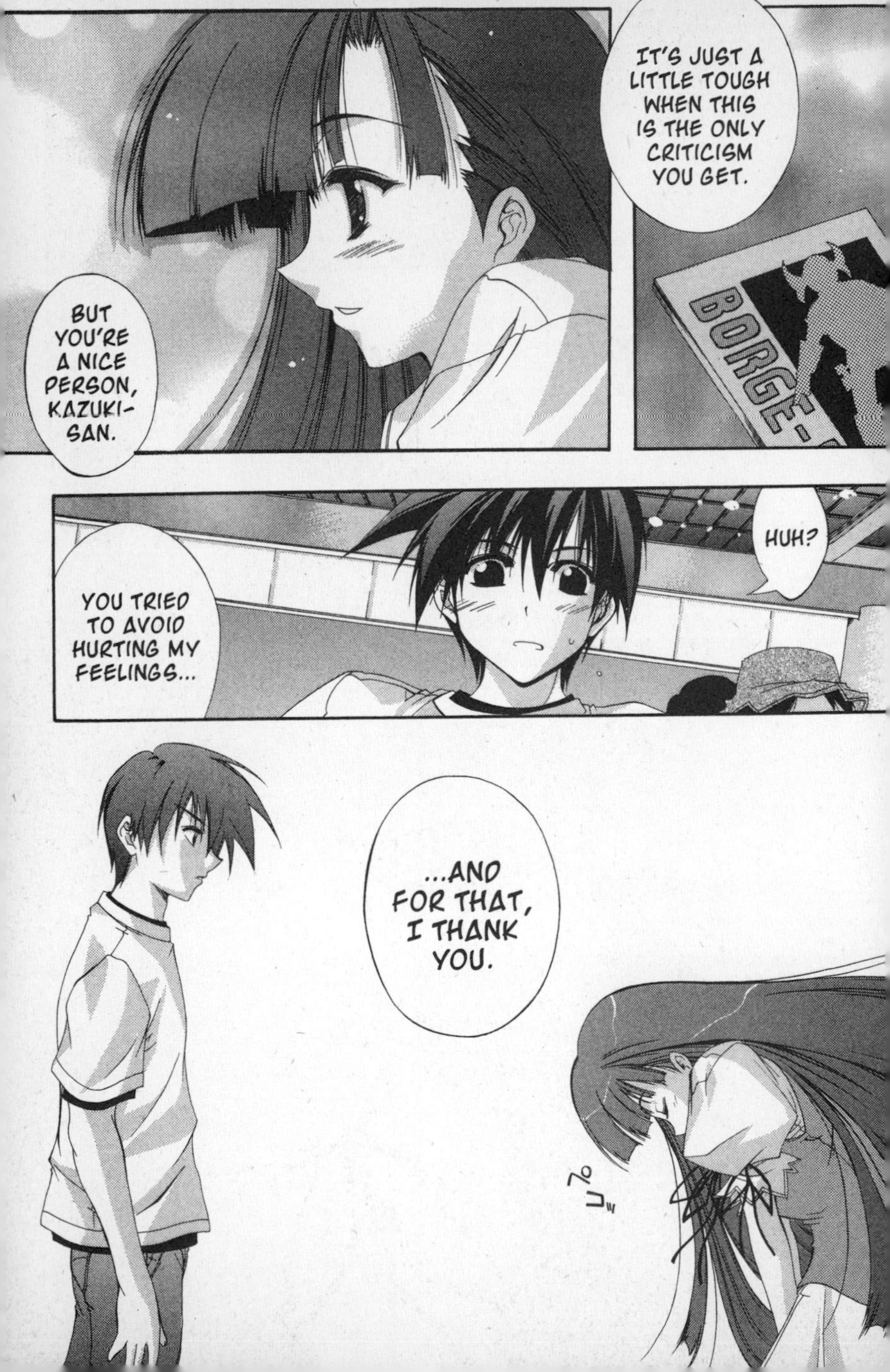
IT'S JUST A LITTLE TOUGH WHEN THIS IS THE ONLY CRITICISM YOU GET.
BORGE-
BUT YOU'RE A NICE PERSON, KAZUKI-SAN.
HUH?
YOU TRIED TO AVOID HURTING MY FEELINGS...
...AND FOR THAT, I THANK YOU.

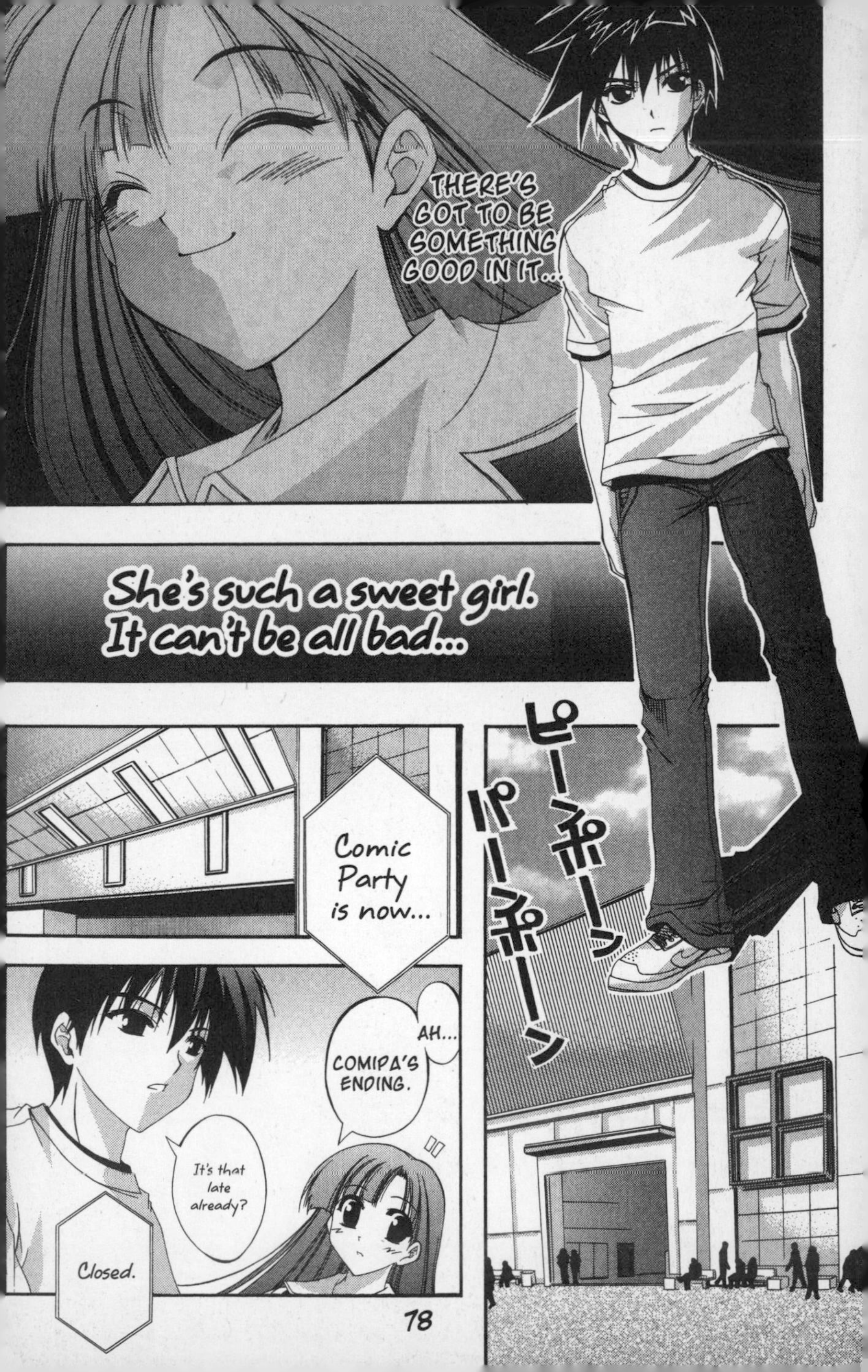
THERE'S GOT TO BE SOMETHING GOOD IN IT...
She's such a sweet girl. It can't be all bad...
ピーンポーン
パーンポーン
Comic Party is now...
AH... COMIPA'S ENDING.
It's that late already?
Closed.

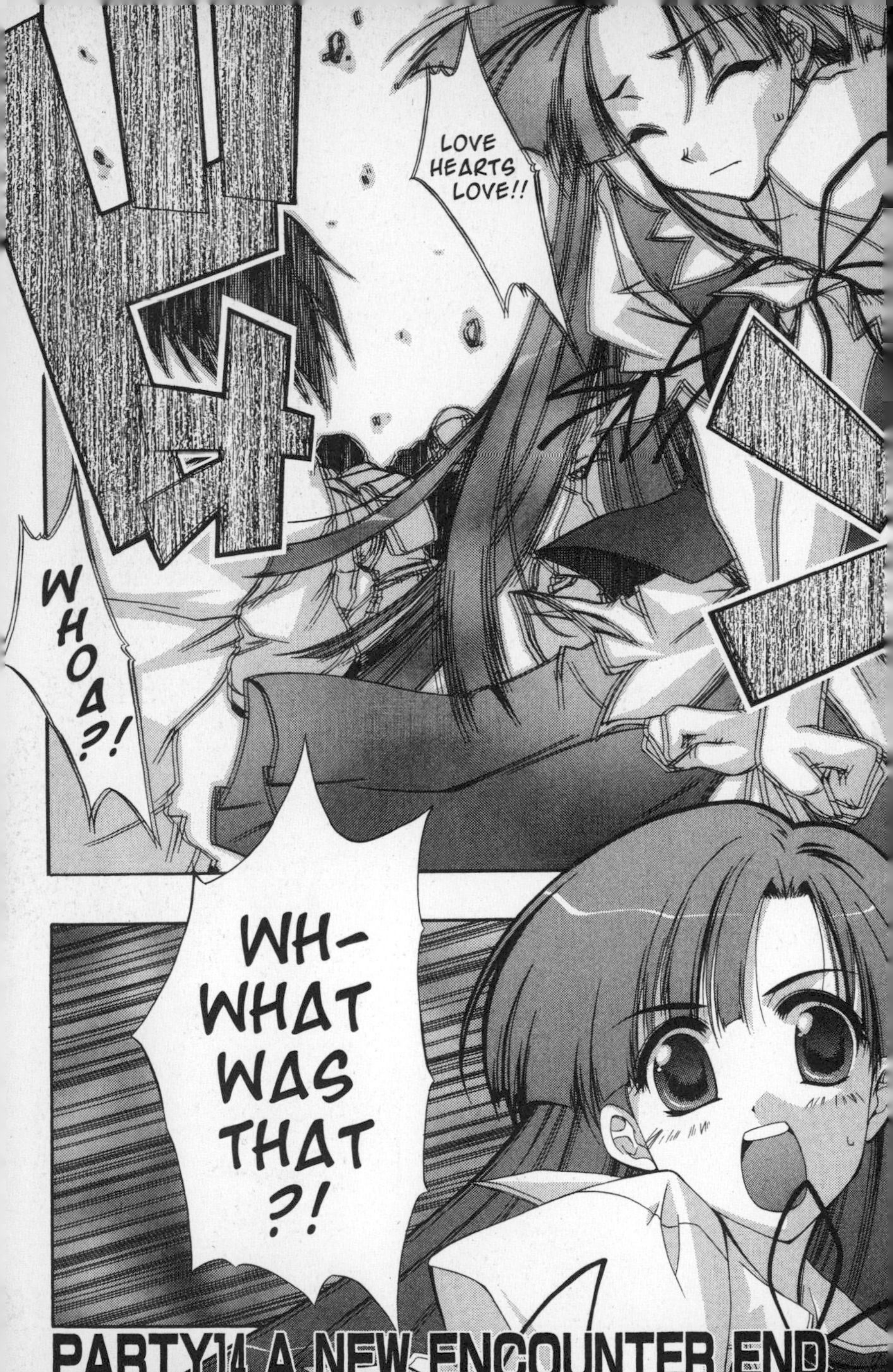
LOVE HEARTS LOVE!!
WHOA?!
WH-WHAT WAS THAT?!

PARTY14 A NEW ENCOUNTER END

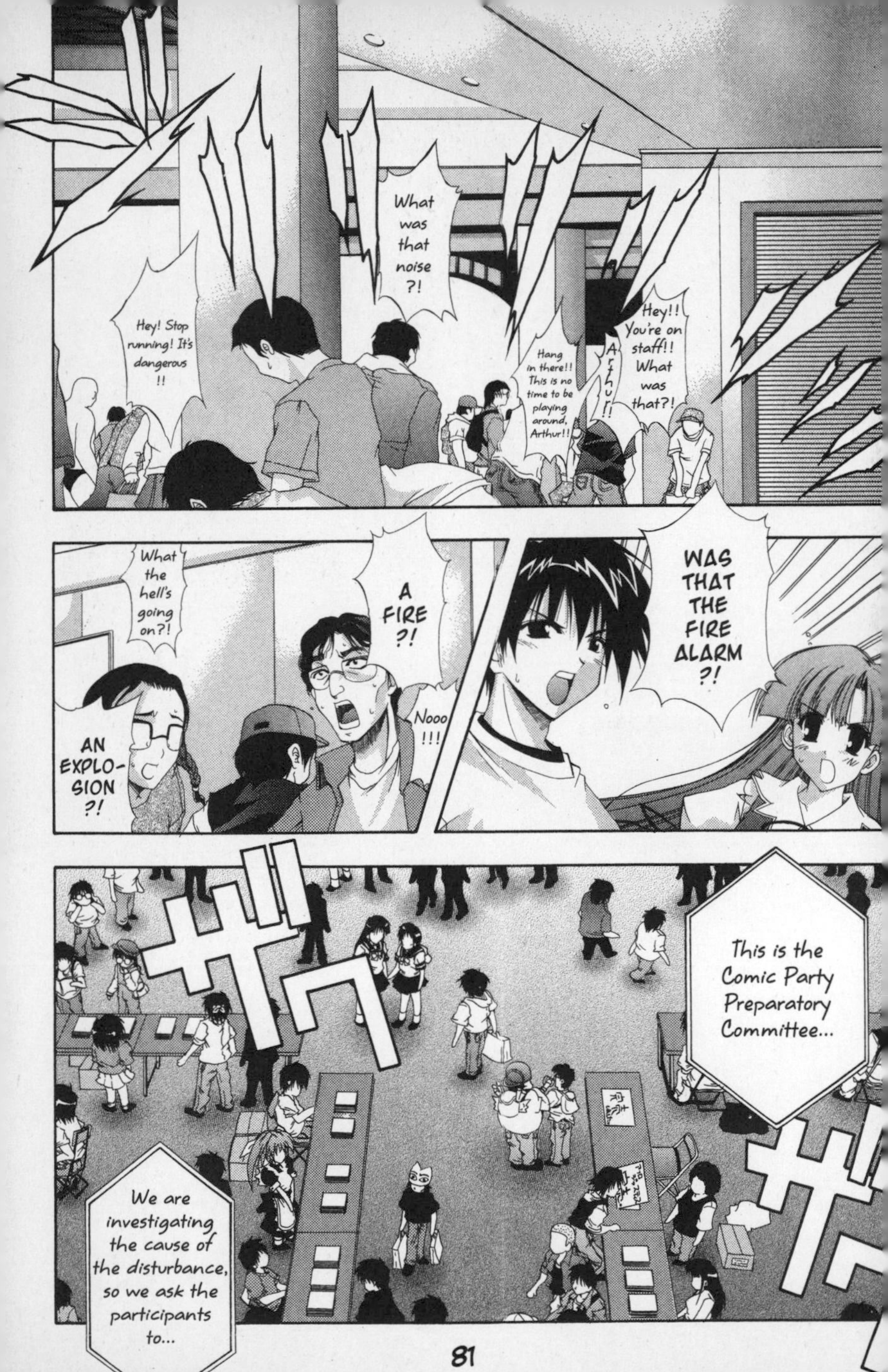
Hey!! You're on staff!! What was that?!
Arthur!!
Hang in there!! This is no time to be playing around, Arthur!!
What was that noise?!
Hey! Stop running! It's dangerous!!
WAS THAT THE FIRE ALARM?!
A FIRE?!
What the hell's going on?!
Nooo!!!
AN EXPLOSION?!
This is the Comic Party Preparatory Committee...
We are investigating the cause of the disturbance, so we ask the participants to...

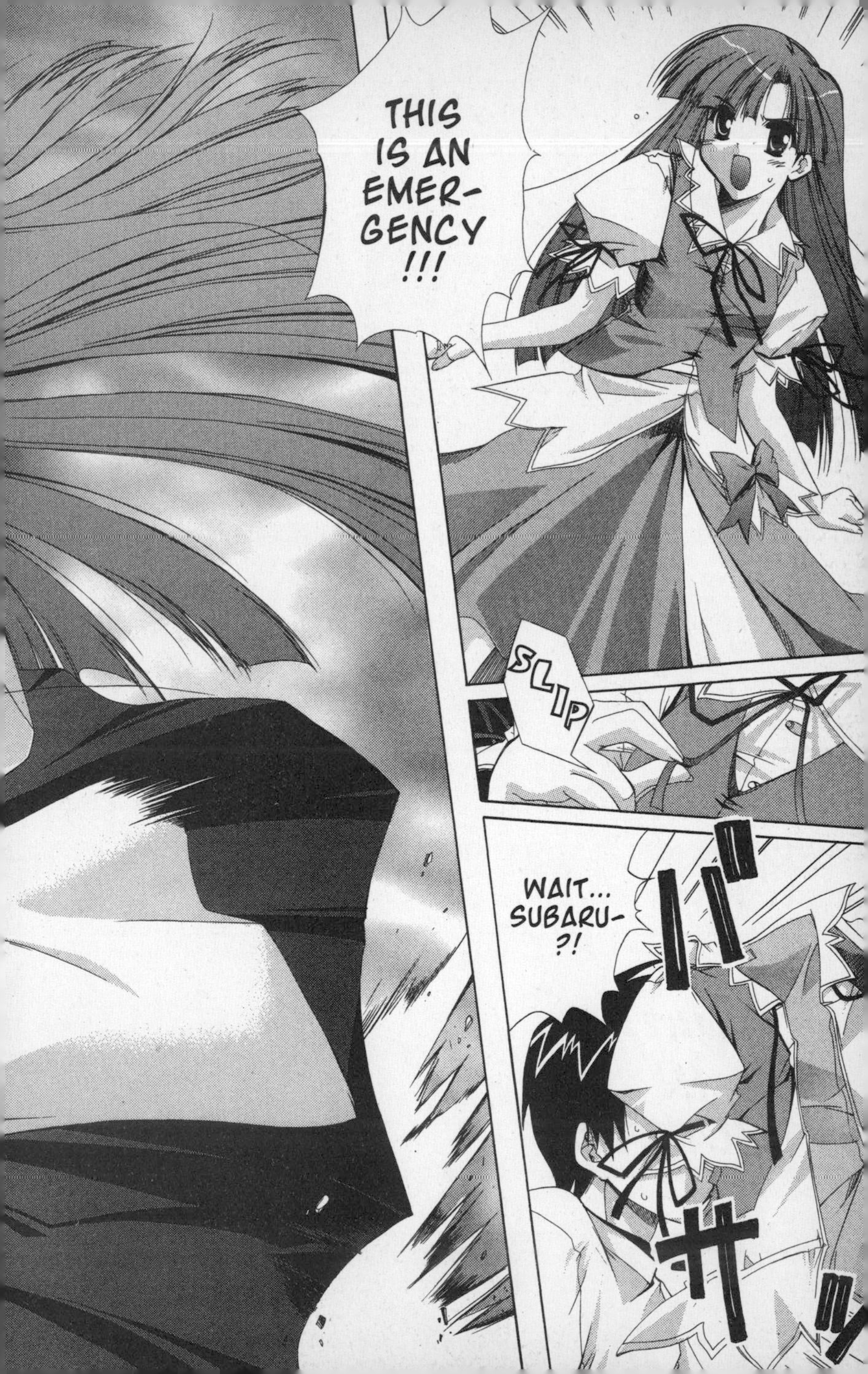
THIS IS AN EMER-GENCY !!!
SLIP
WAIT... SUBARU-?!

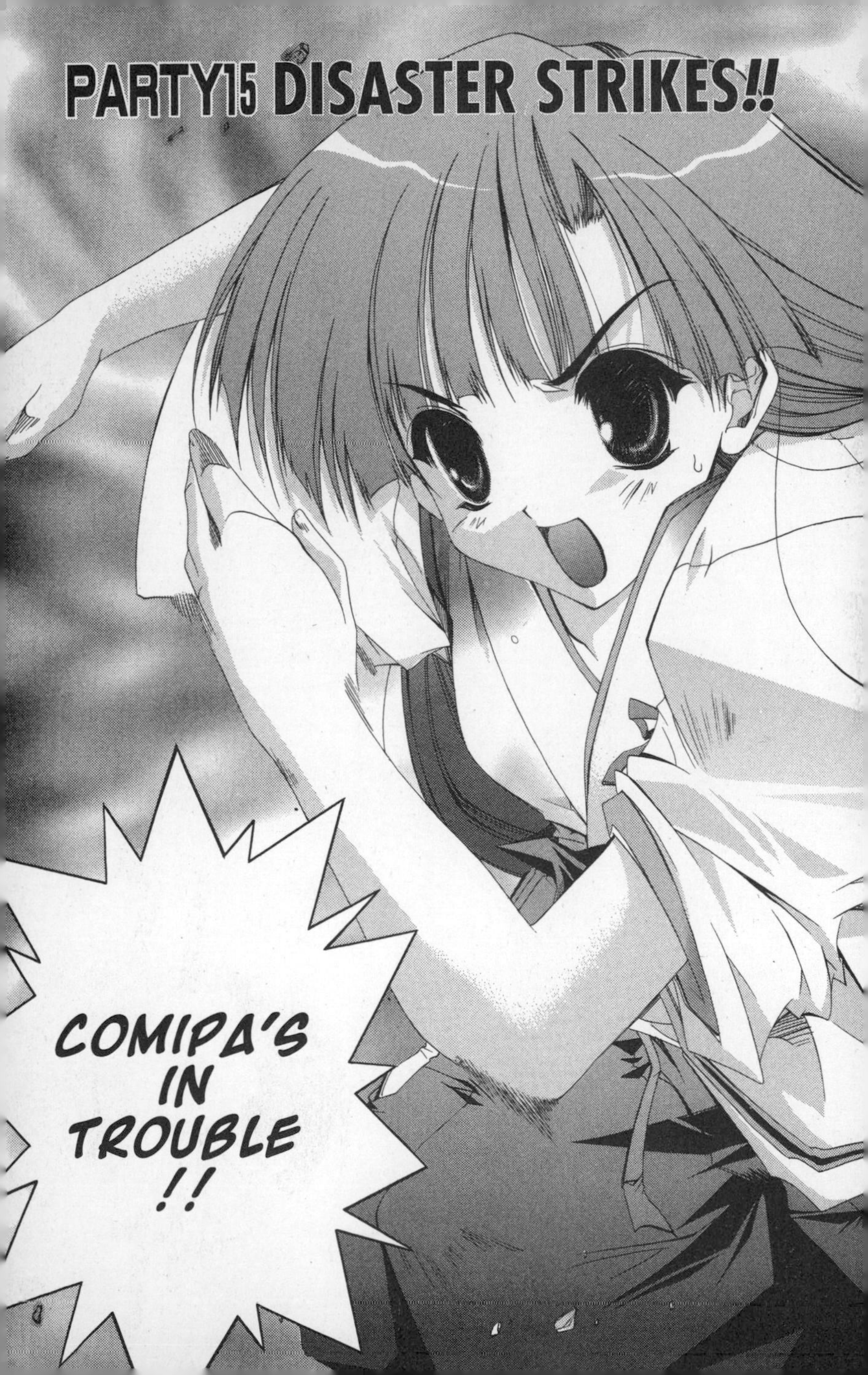
PARTY15 DISASTER STRIKES!!
COMIPA'S IN TROUBLE !!

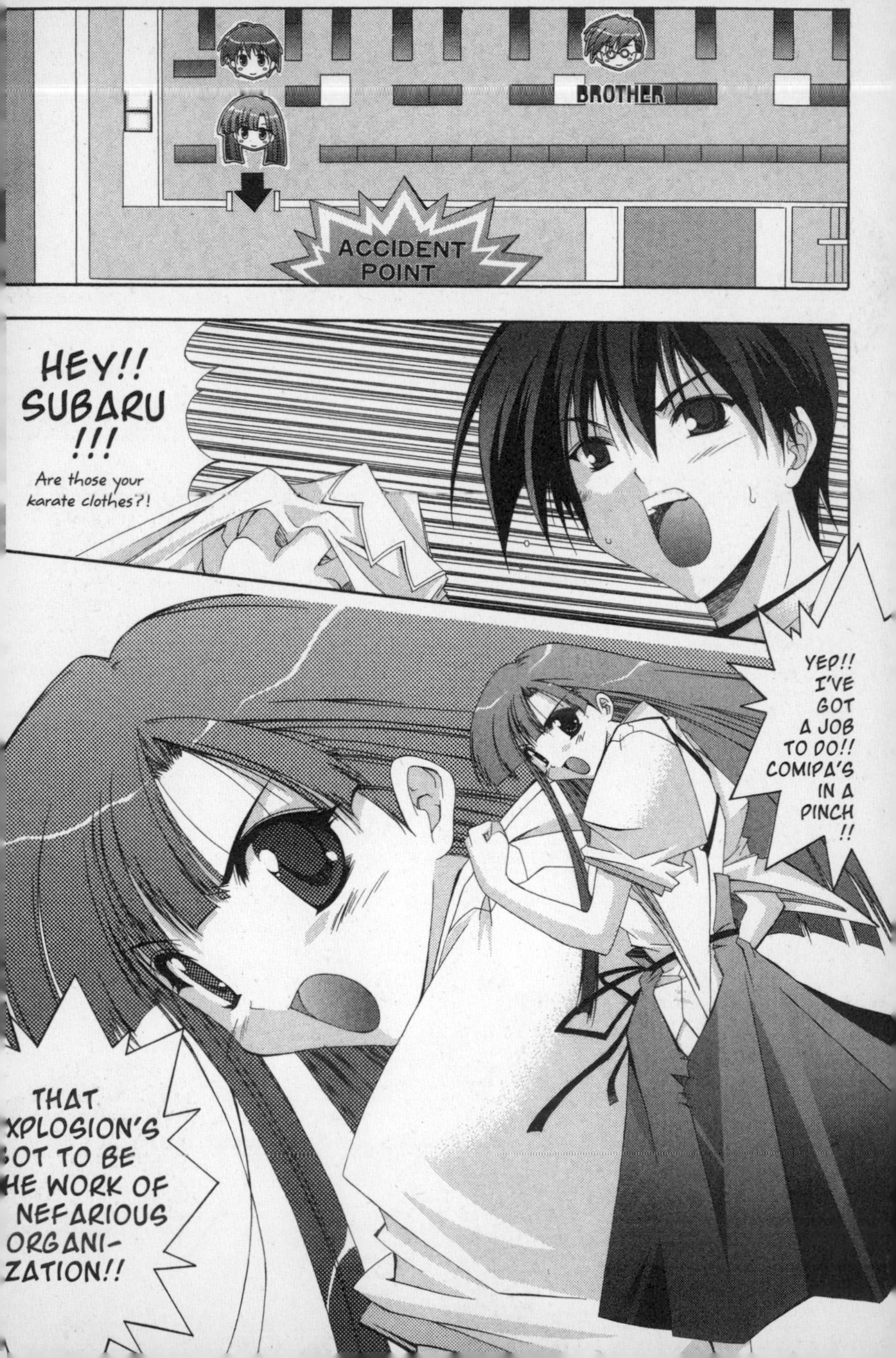
BROTHER
ACCIDENT POINT
HEY!! SUBARU !!!
Are those your karate clothes?!
YEP!! I'VE GOT A JOB TO DO!! COMIPA'S IN A PINCH !!
THAT XPLOSION'S OT TO BE HE WORK OF NEFARIOUS ORGANI- ZATION!!

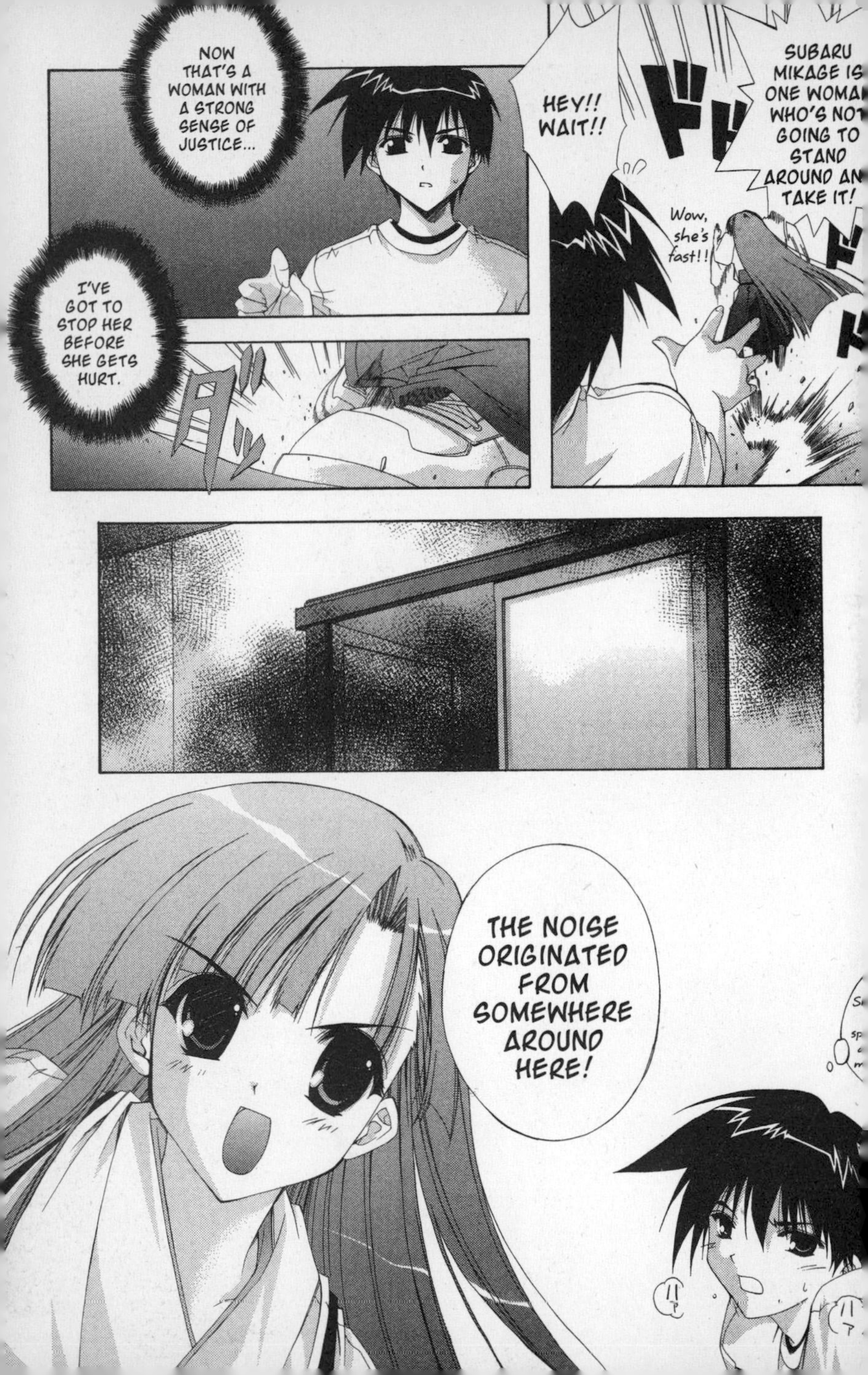
SUBARU MIKAGE IS ONE WOMA WHO'S NO GOING TO STAND AROUND AN TAKE IT!
HEY!! WAIT!!
Wow, she's fast!!
NOW THAT'S A WOMAN WITH A STRONG SENSE OF JUSTICE...
I'VE GOT TO STOP HER BEFORE SHE GETS HURT.
THE NOISE ORIGINATED FROM SOMEWHERE AROUND HERE!

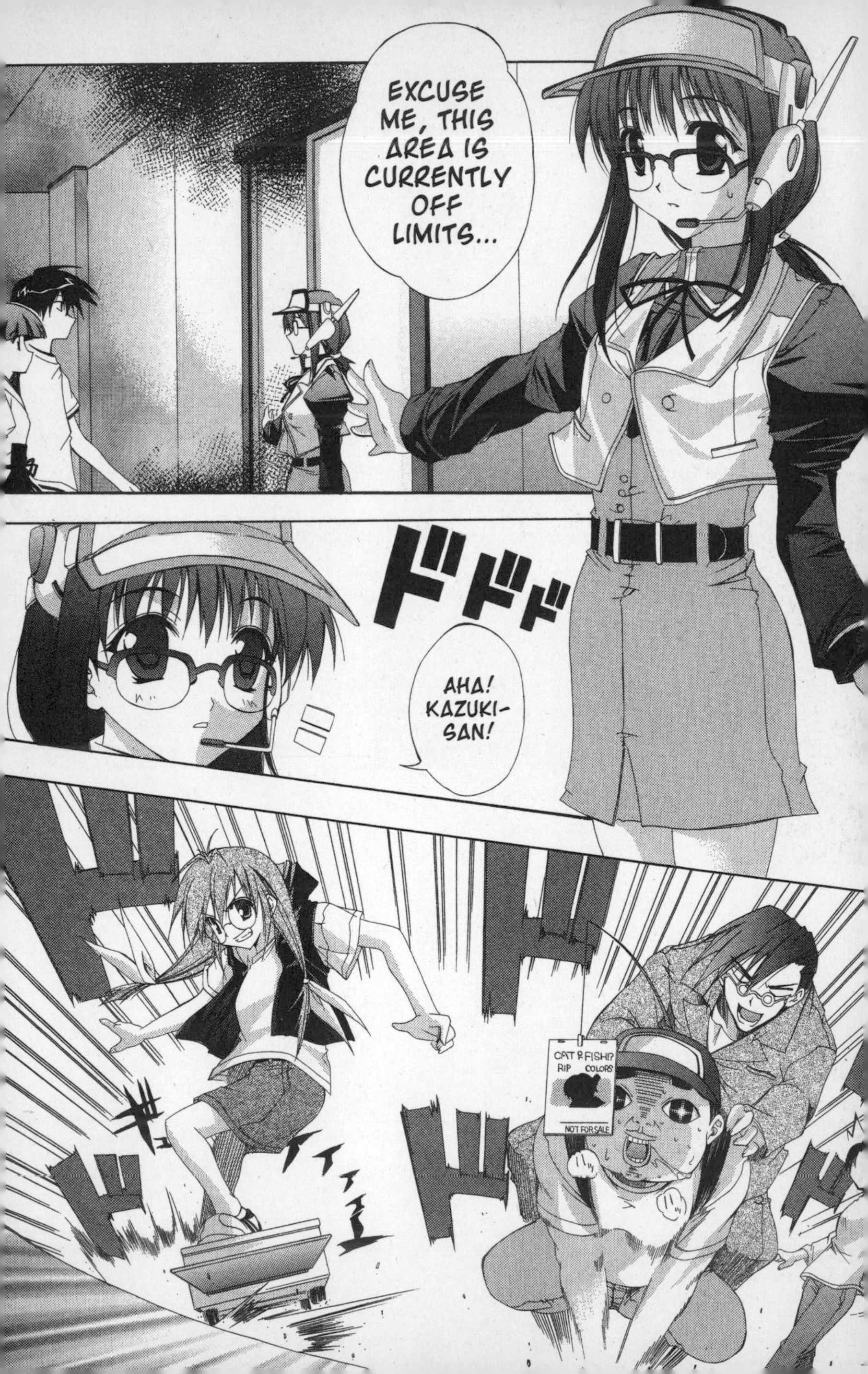
EXCUSE ME, THIS AREA IS CURRENTLY OFF LIMITS...
ドドド
AHA! KAZUKI-SAN!
CAT OR FISH!? RIP COLORS
NOT FOR SALE

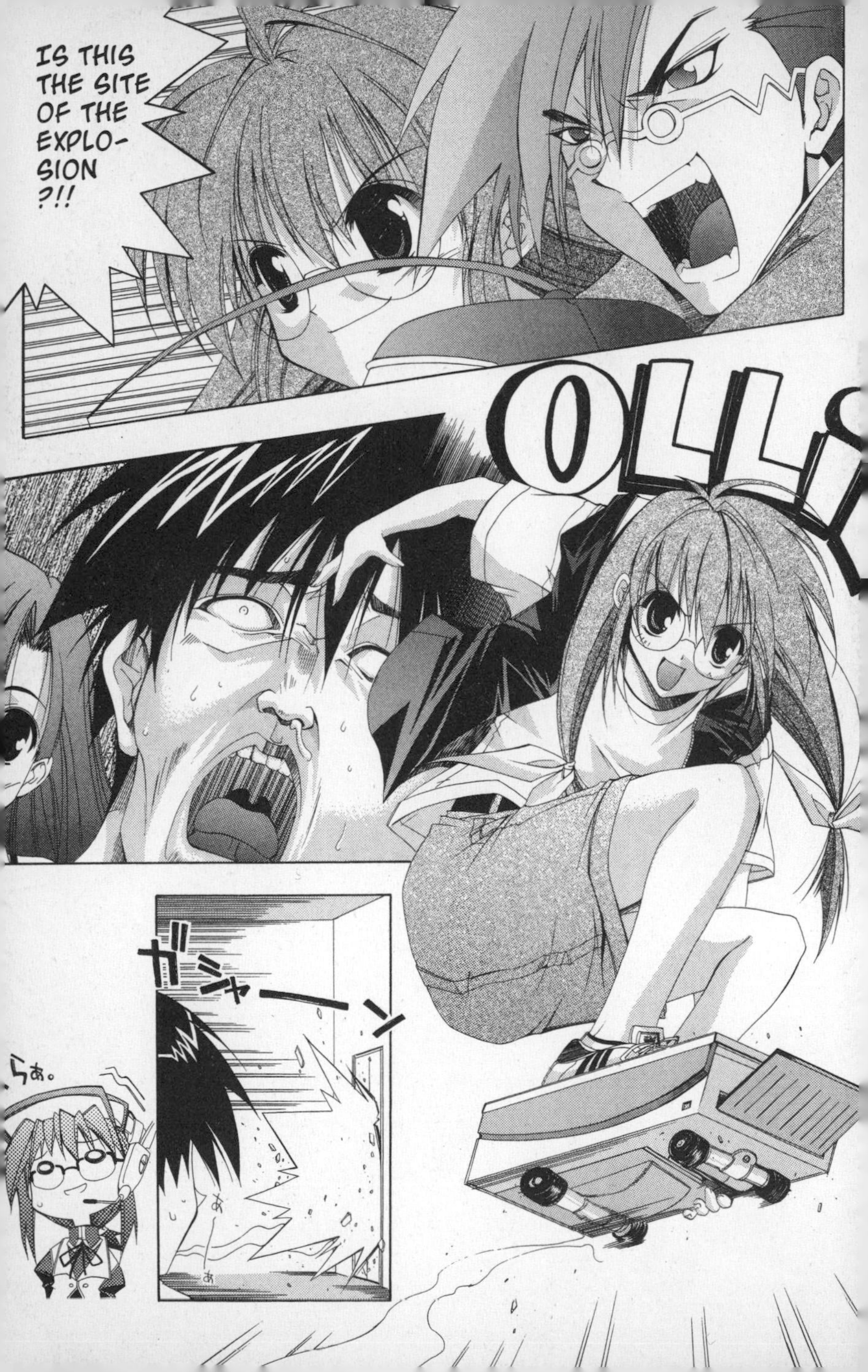
IS THIS THE SITE OF THE EXPLOSION ?!!
OLLI
ガシャーーン
らあ。

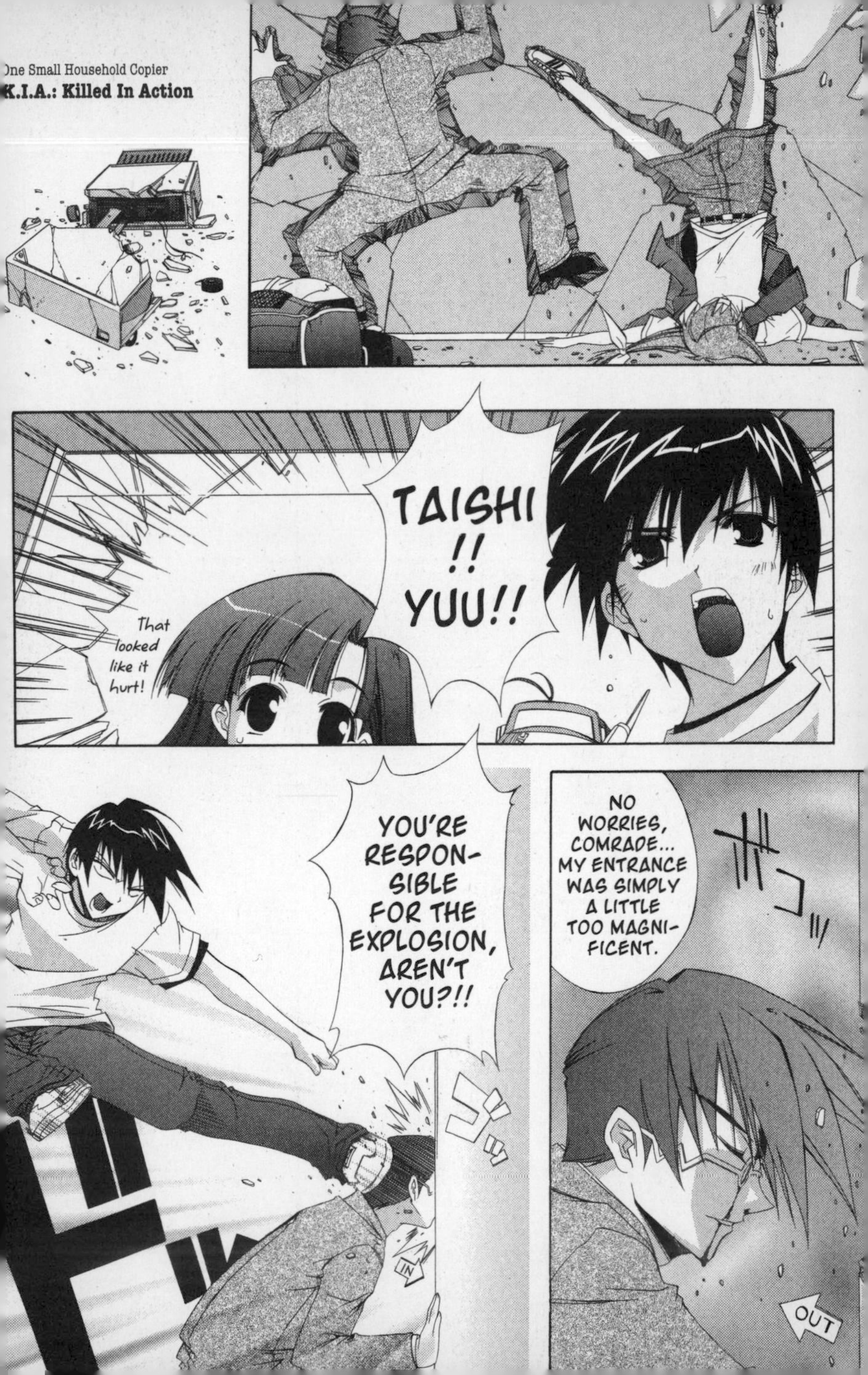
One Small Household Copier
K.I.A.: Killed In Action
TAISHI!! YUU!!
That looked like it hurt!
NO WORRIES, COMRADE... MY ENTRANCE WAS SIMPLY A LITTLE TOO MAGNIFICENT.
OUT
YOU'RE RESPONSIBLE FOR THE EXPLOSION, AREN'T YOU?!!
IN

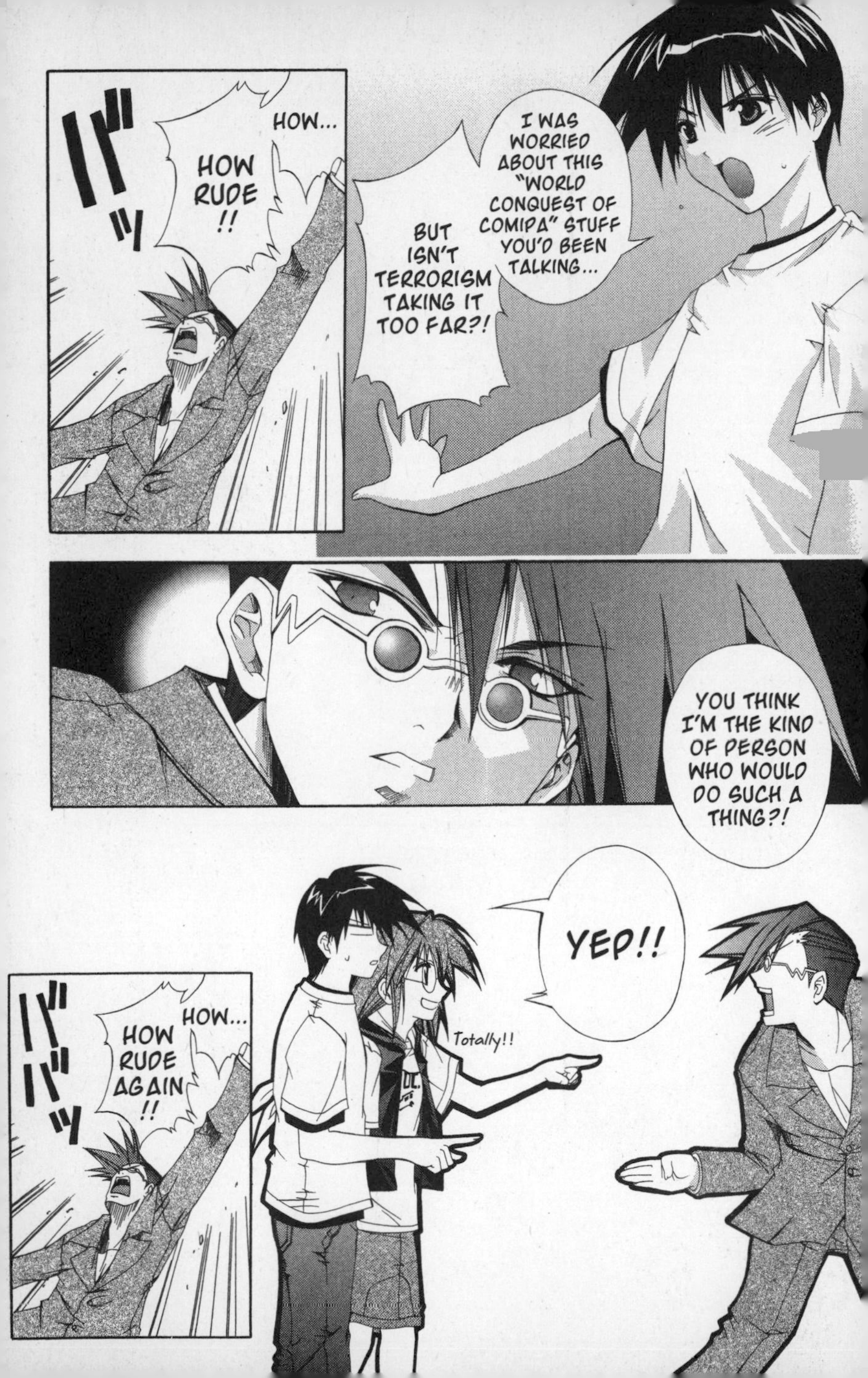
I WAS WORRIED ABOUT THIS "WORLD CONQUEST OF COMIPA" STUFF YOU'D BEEN TALKING...
BUT ISN'T TERRORISM TAKING IT TOO FAR?!
HOW...
HOW RUDE !!
バッ
YOU THINK I'M THE KIND OF PERSON WHO WOULD DO SUCH A THING?!
YEP!!
Totally!!
HOW...
HOW RUDE AGAIN !!
ババッ

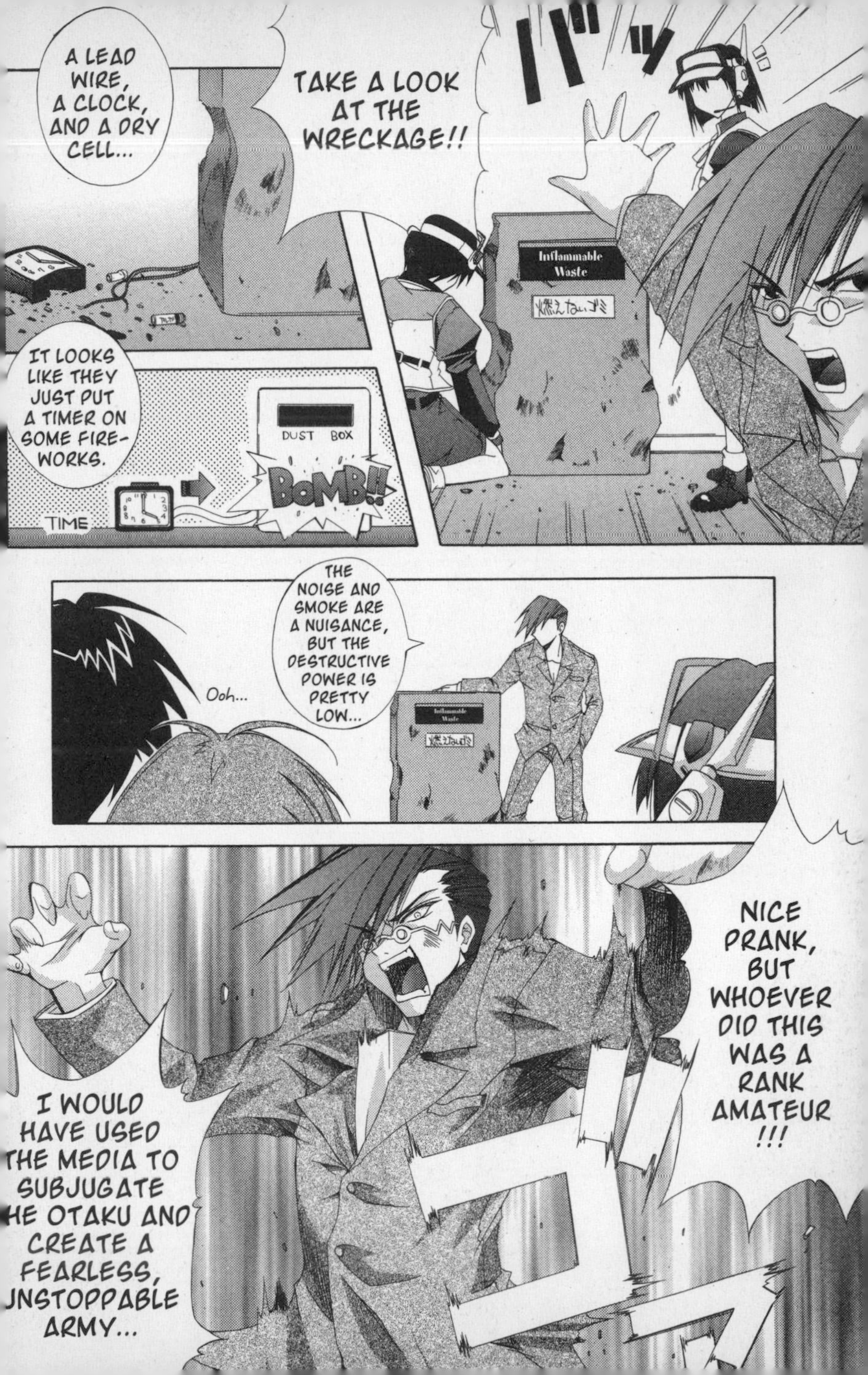
バッ
TAKE A LOOK AT THE WRECKAGE!!
Inflammable Waste
燃えないゴミ
A LEAD WIRE, A CLOCK, AND A DRY CELL...
IT LOOKS LIKE THEY JUST PUT A TIMER ON SOME FIRE-WORKS.
DUST BOX
BOMB!!
TIME
THE NOISE AND SMOKE ARE A NUISANCE, BUT THE DESTRUCTIVE POWER IS PRETTY LOW...
Ooh...
NICE PRANK, BUT WHOEVER DID THIS WAS A RANK AMATEUR!!!
I WOULD HAVE USED THE MEDIA TO SUBJUGATE THE OTAKU AND CREATE A FEARLESS, UNSTOPPABLE ARMY...

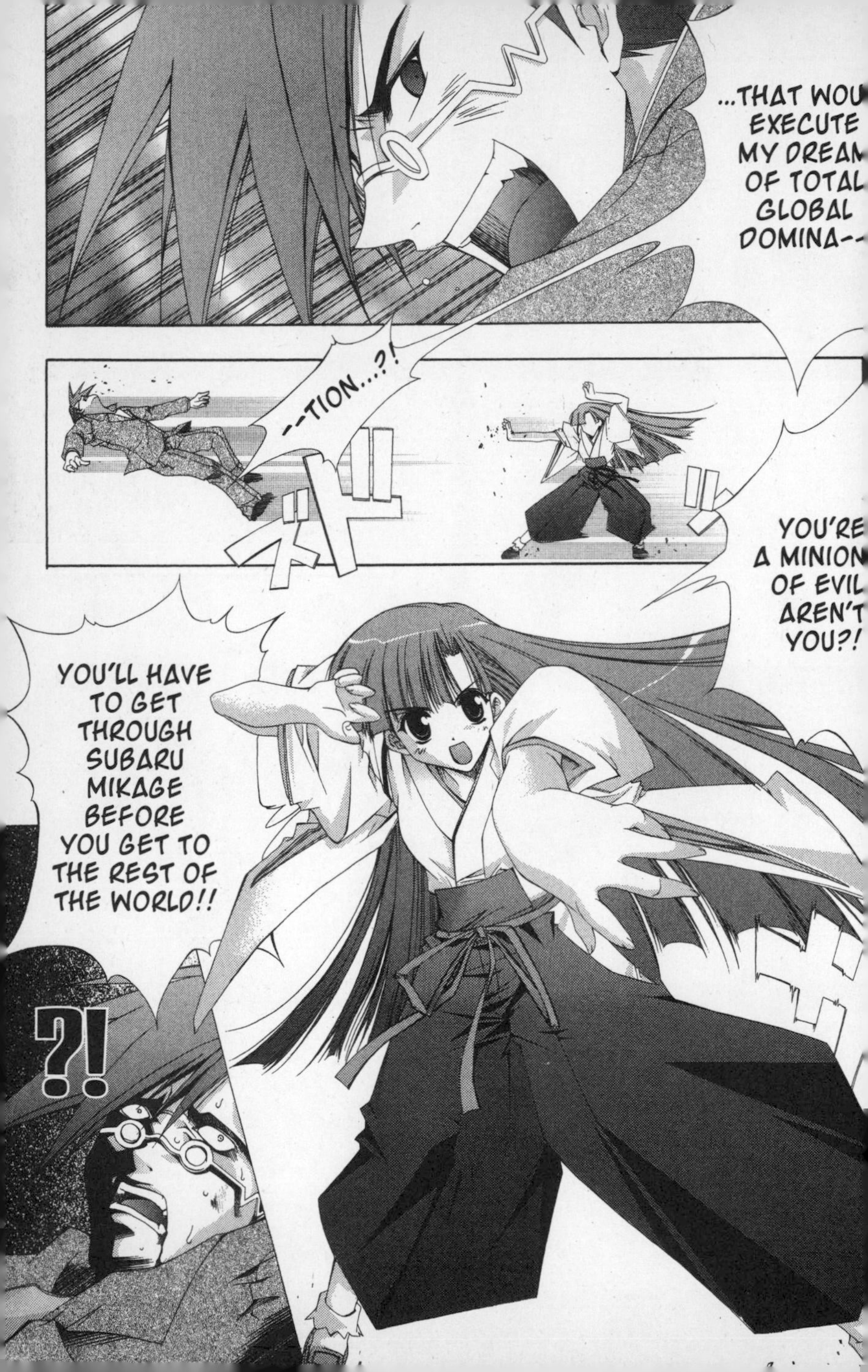
...THAT WOU EXECUTE MY DREAM OF TOTAL GLOBAL DOMINA--
--TION...?!
YOU'RE A MINION OF EVIL AREN'T YOU?!
YOU'LL HAVE TO GET THROUGH SUBARU MIKAGE BEFORE YOU GET TO THE REST OF THE WORLD!!
?!

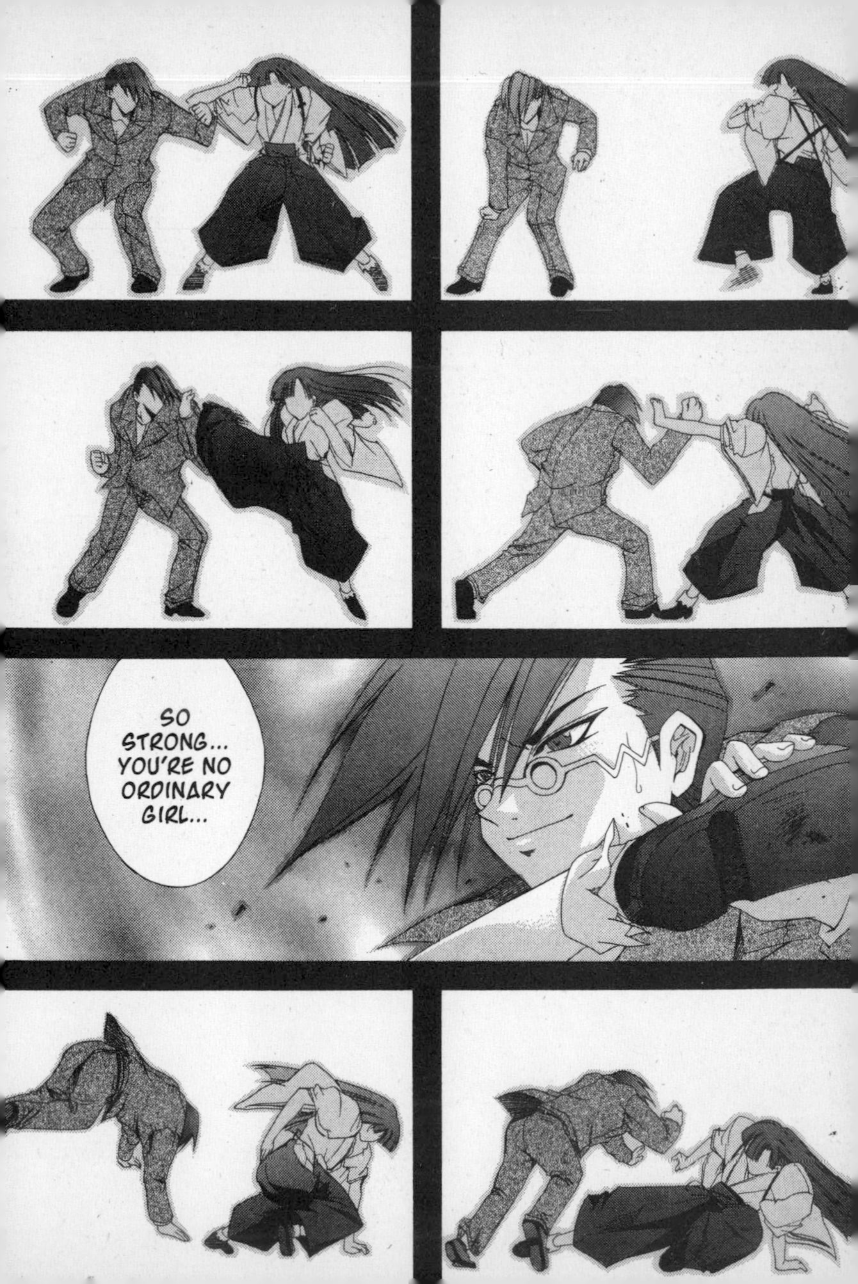
SO STRONG... YOU'RE NO ORDINARY GIRL...

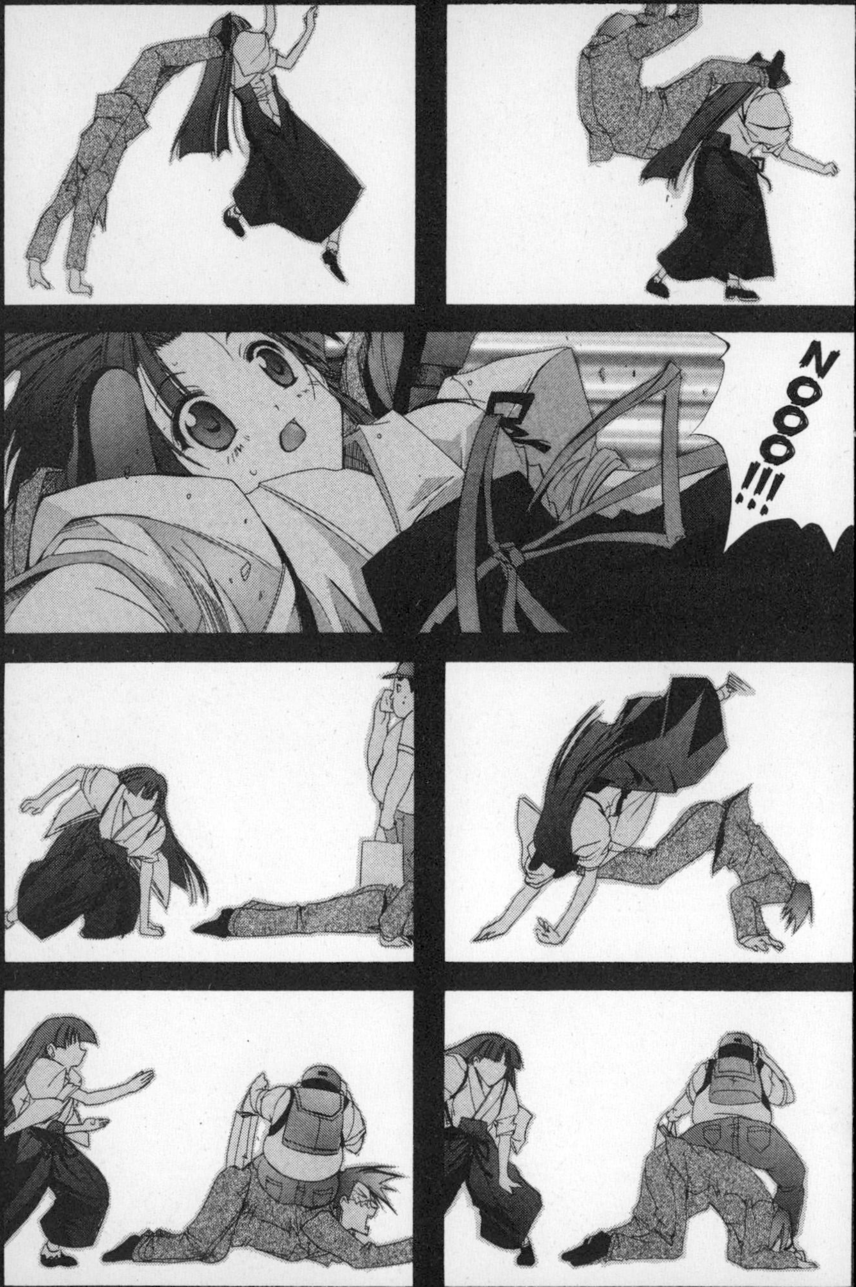
NOOOO!!!!

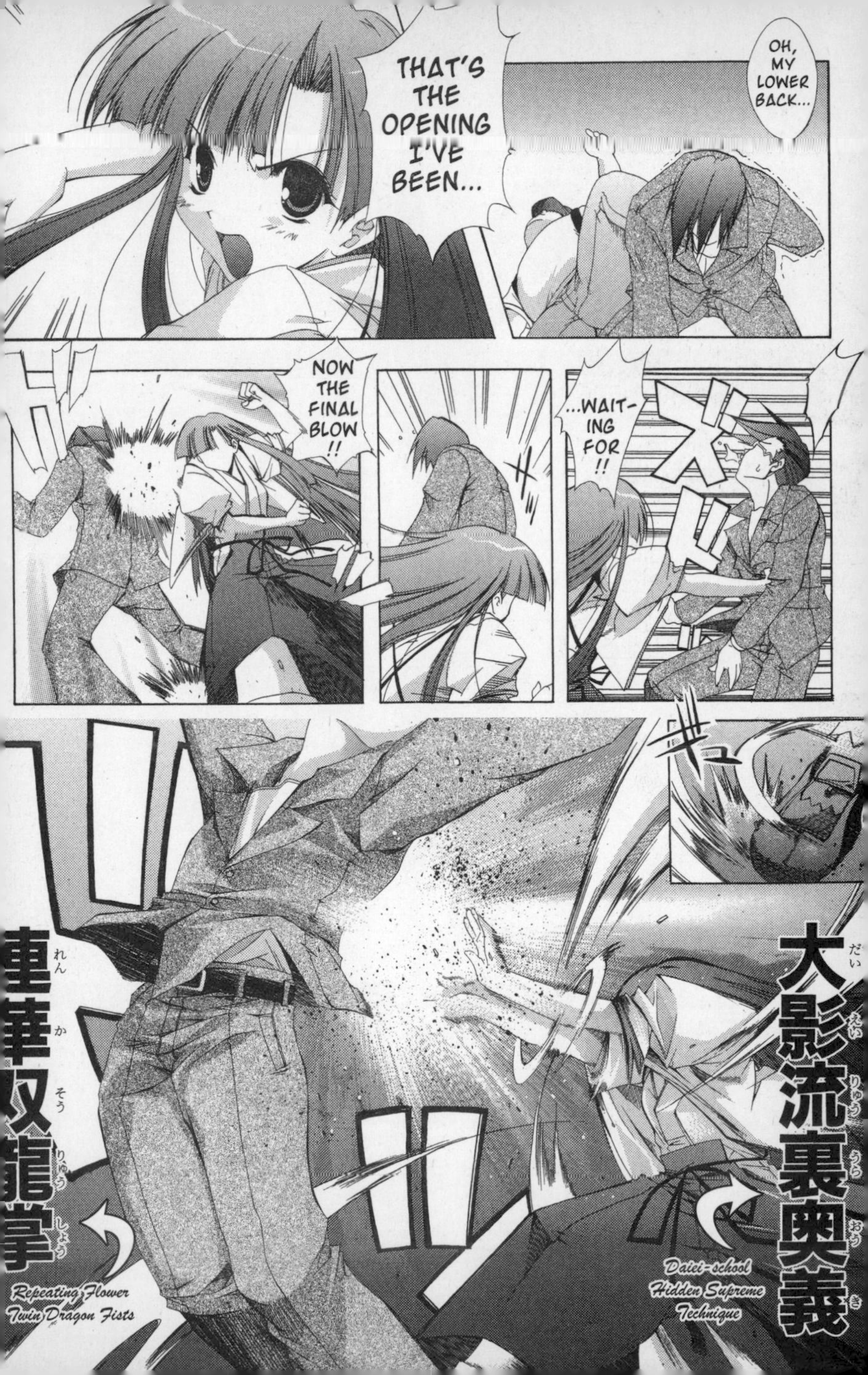
OH, MY LOWER BACK...
THAT'S THE OPENING I'VE BEEN...
...WAIT-ING FOR!!
NOW THE FINAL BLOW!!
大影流裏奥義
Daiei-school Hidden Supreme Technique
連華双龍掌
Repeating Flower Twin Dragon Fists

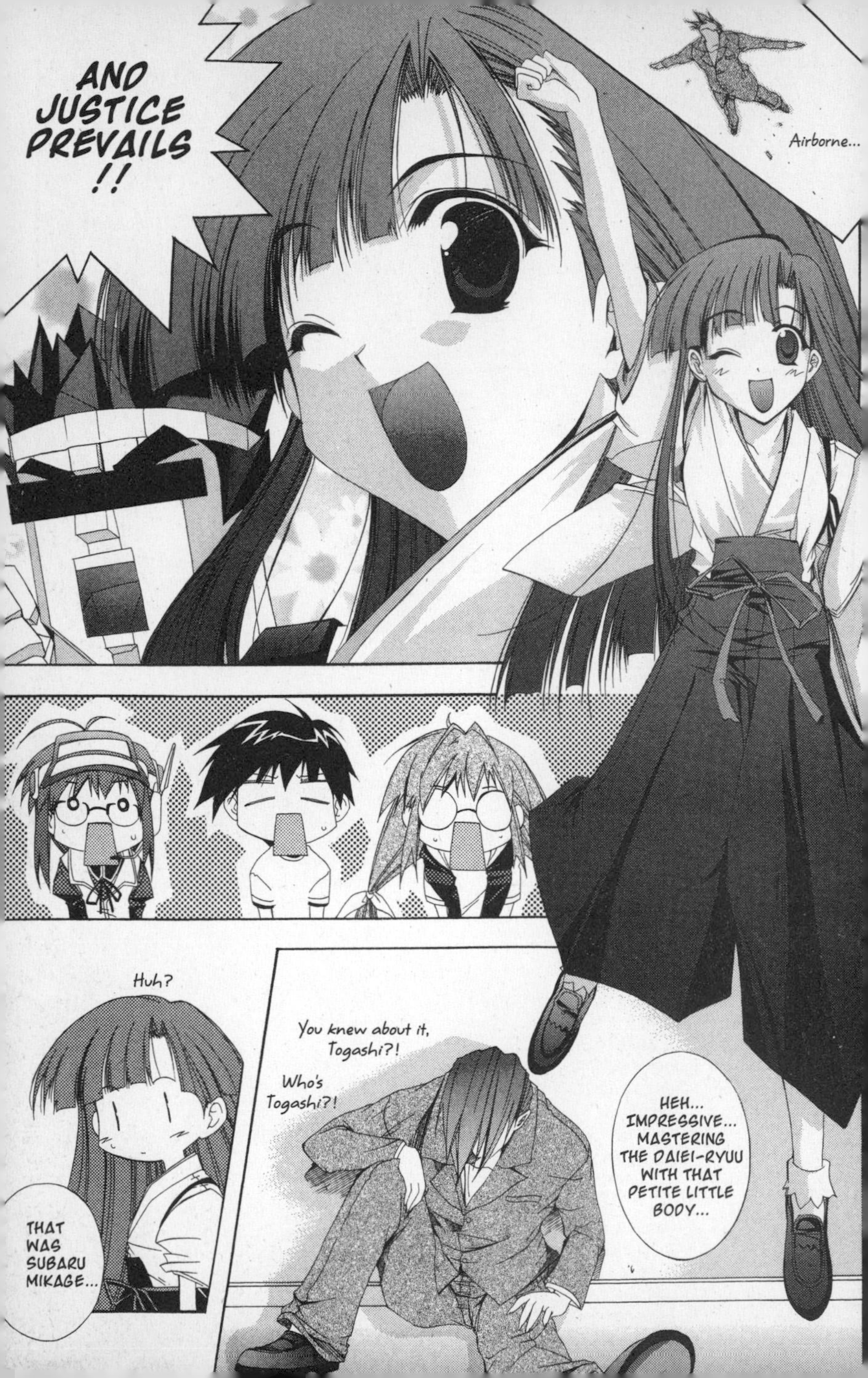
Airborne...
AND JUSTICE PREVAILS !!
HEH... IMPRESSIVE... MASTERING THE DAIEI-RYUU WITH THAT PETITE LITTLE BODY...
You knew about it, Togashi?!
Who's Togashi?!
Huh?
THAT WAS SUBARU MIKAGE...

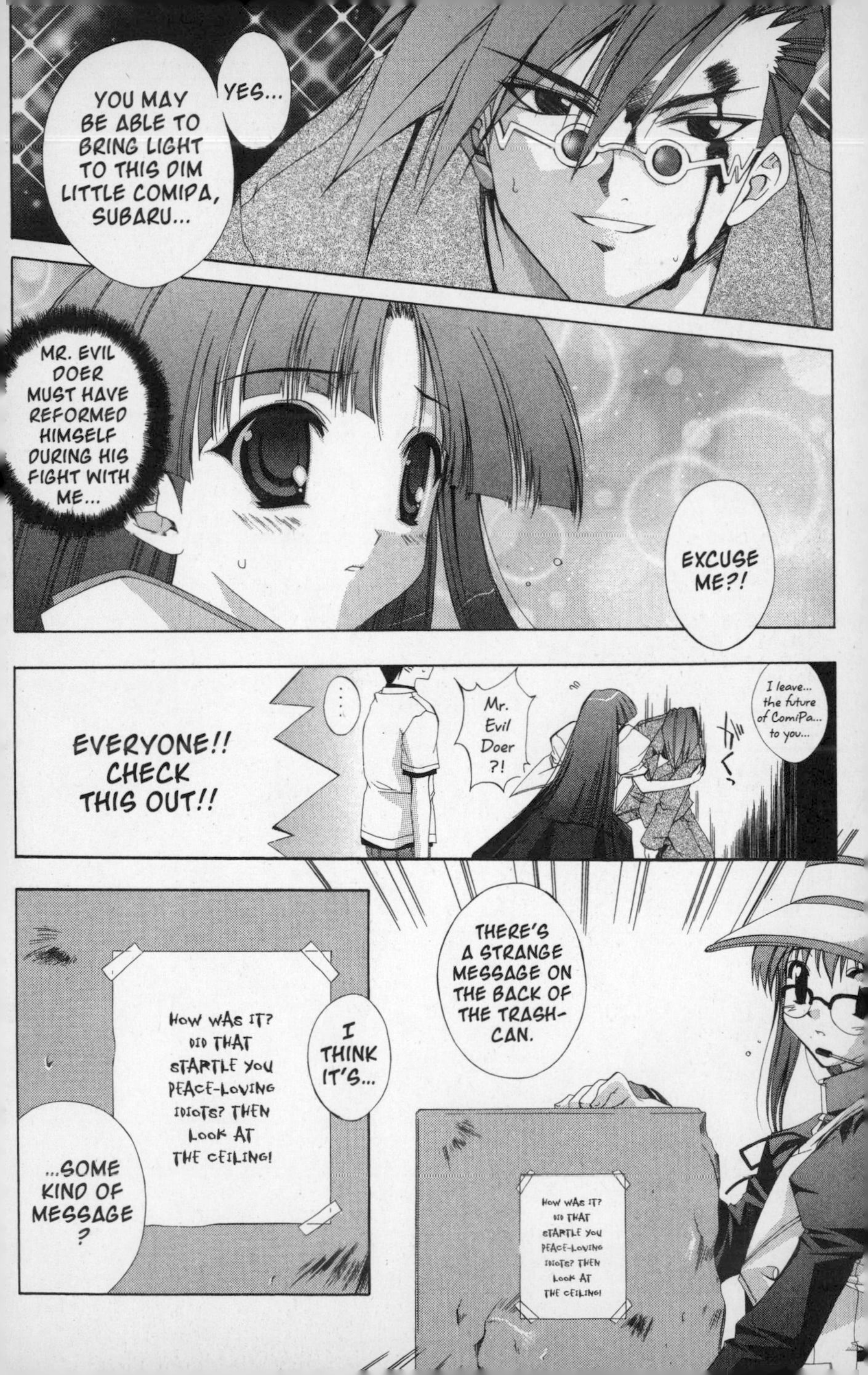
YES...
YOU MAY BE ABLE TO BRING LIGHT TO THIS DIM LITTLE COMIPA, SUBARU...
EXCUSE ME?!
MR. EVIL DOER MUST HAVE REFORMED HIMSELF DURING HIS FIGHT WITH ME...
I leave... the future of ComiPa... to you...
Mr. Evil Doer ?!
...
EVERYONE!! CHECK THIS OUT!!
THERE'S A STRANGE MESSAGE ON THE BACK OF THE TRASH-CAN.
HOW WAS IT? DID THAT STARTLE YOU PEACE-LOVING IDIOTS? THEN LOOK AT THE CEILING!
I THINK IT'S...
HOW WAS IT? DID THAT STARTLE YOU PEACE-LOVING IDIOTS? THEN LOOK AT THE CEILING!
...SOME KIND OF MESSAGE?

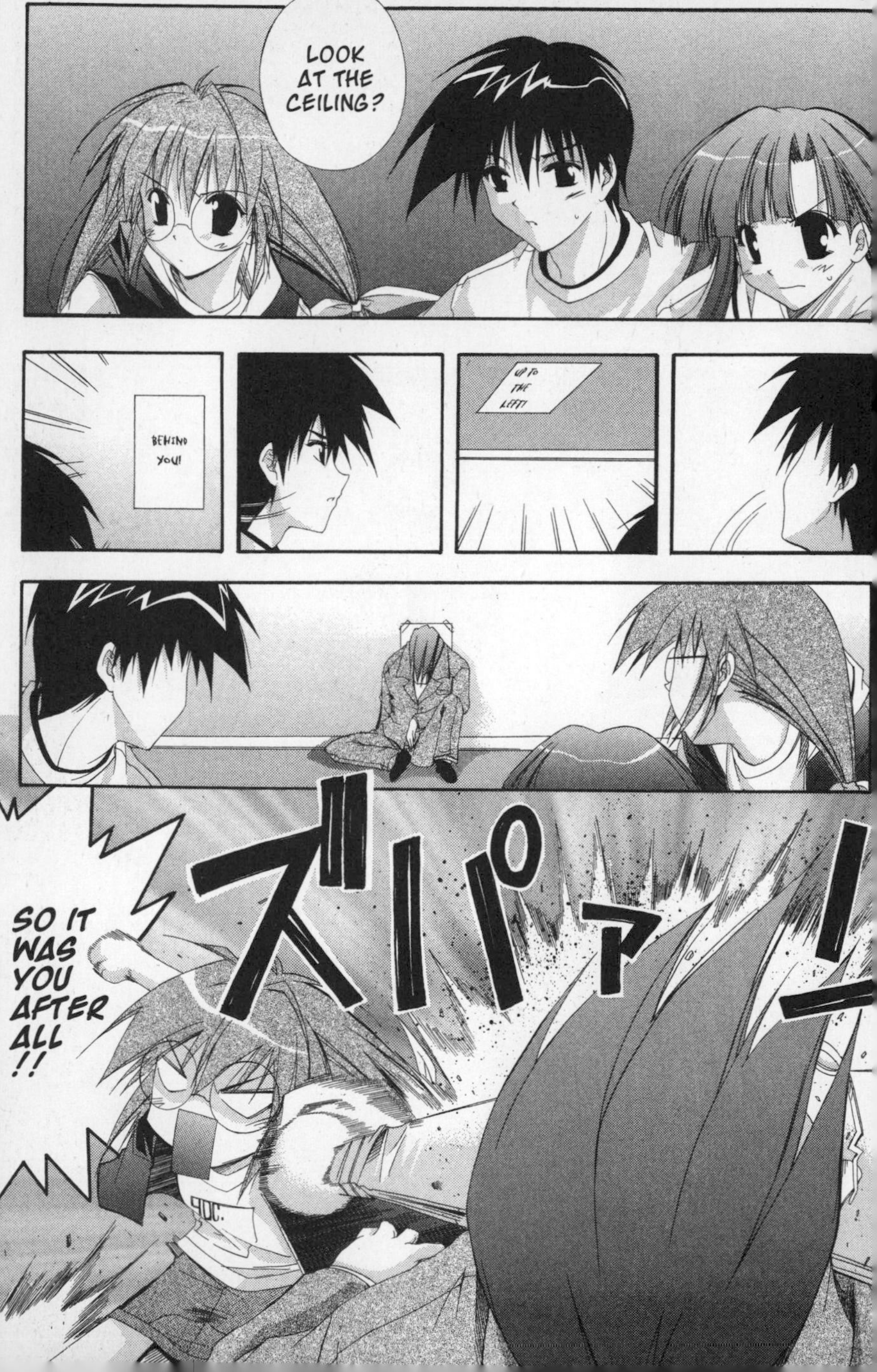
LOOK AT THE CEILING?
UP TO THE LEFT!
BEHIND YOU!
ズパァー
SO IT WAS YOU AFTER ALL!!

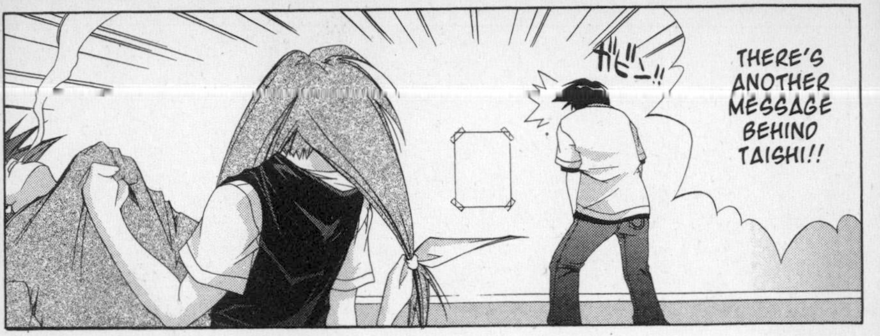
THERE'S ANOTHER MESSAGE BEHIND TAISHI!!
ガビーン!!

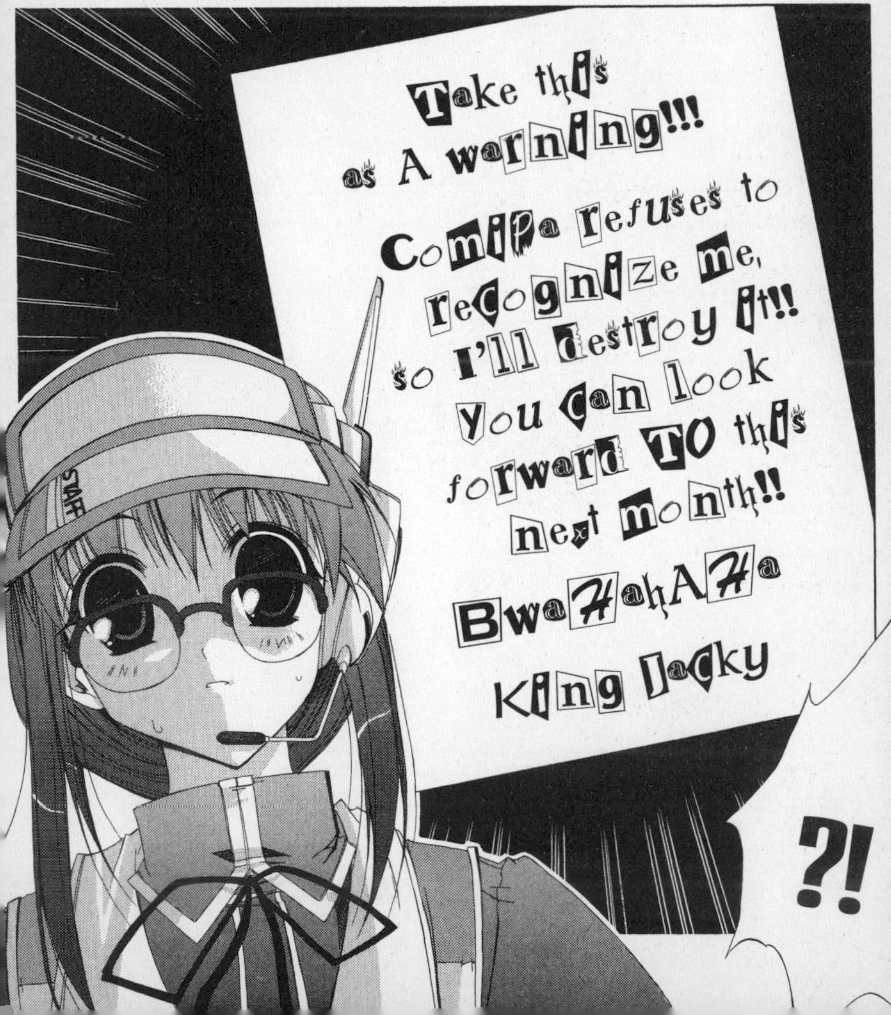
Take this as A warning!!!
Comipa refuses to recognize me,
so I'll destroy it!!
You can look forward TO this next month!!
BwaHahAHa
King Jacky
?!

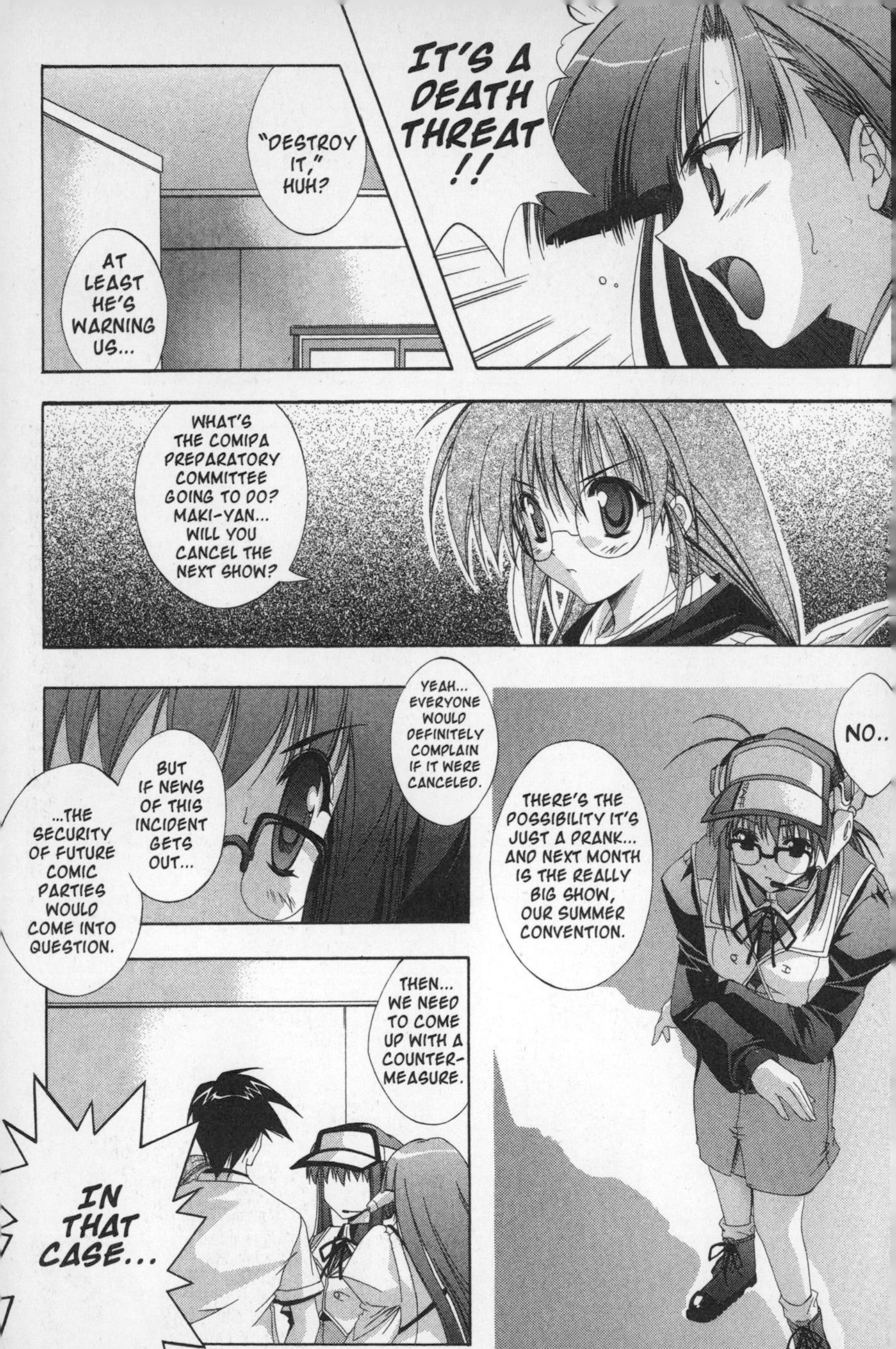
IT'S A DEATH THREAT!!
"DESTROY IT," HUH?
AT LEAST HE'S WARNING US...
WHAT'S THE COMIPA PREPARATORY COMMITTEE GOING TO DO? MAKI-YAN... WILL YOU CANCEL THE NEXT SHOW?
NO..
THERE'S THE POSSIBILITY IT'S JUST A PRANK... AND NEXT MONTH IS THE REALLY BIG SHOW, OUR SUMMER CONVENTION.
YEAH... EVERYONE WOULD DEFINITELY COMPLAIN IF IT WERE CANCELED.
BUT IF NEWS OF THIS INCIDENT GETS OUT...
...THE SECURITY OF FUTURE COMIC PARTIES WOULD COME INTO QUESTION.
THEN... WE NEED TO COME UP WITH A COUNTER-MEASURE.
IN THAT CASE...

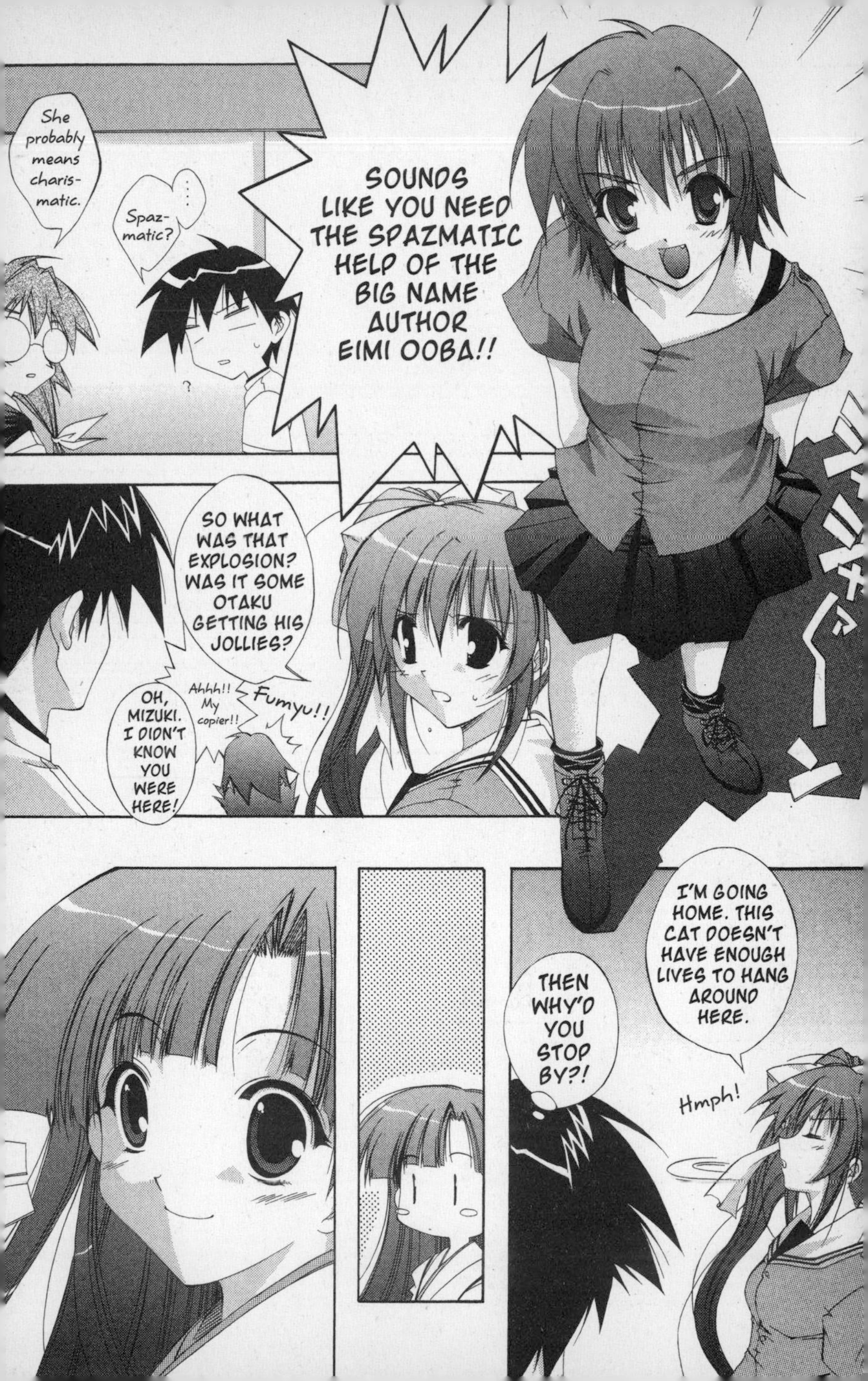
SOUNDS LIKE YOU NEED THE SPAZMATIC HELP OF THE BIG NAME AUTHOR EIMI OOBA!!
...
Spaz-matic?
She probably means charis-matic.
SO WHAT WAS THAT EXPLOSION? WAS IT SOME OTAKU GETTING HIS JOLLIES?
Fumyu!!
Ahhh!! My copier!!
OH, MIZUKI. I DIDN'T KNOW YOU WERE HERE!
I'M GOING HOME. THIS CAT DOESN'T HAVE ENOUGH LIVES TO HANG AROUND HERE.
Hmph!
THEN WHY'D YOU STOP BY?!

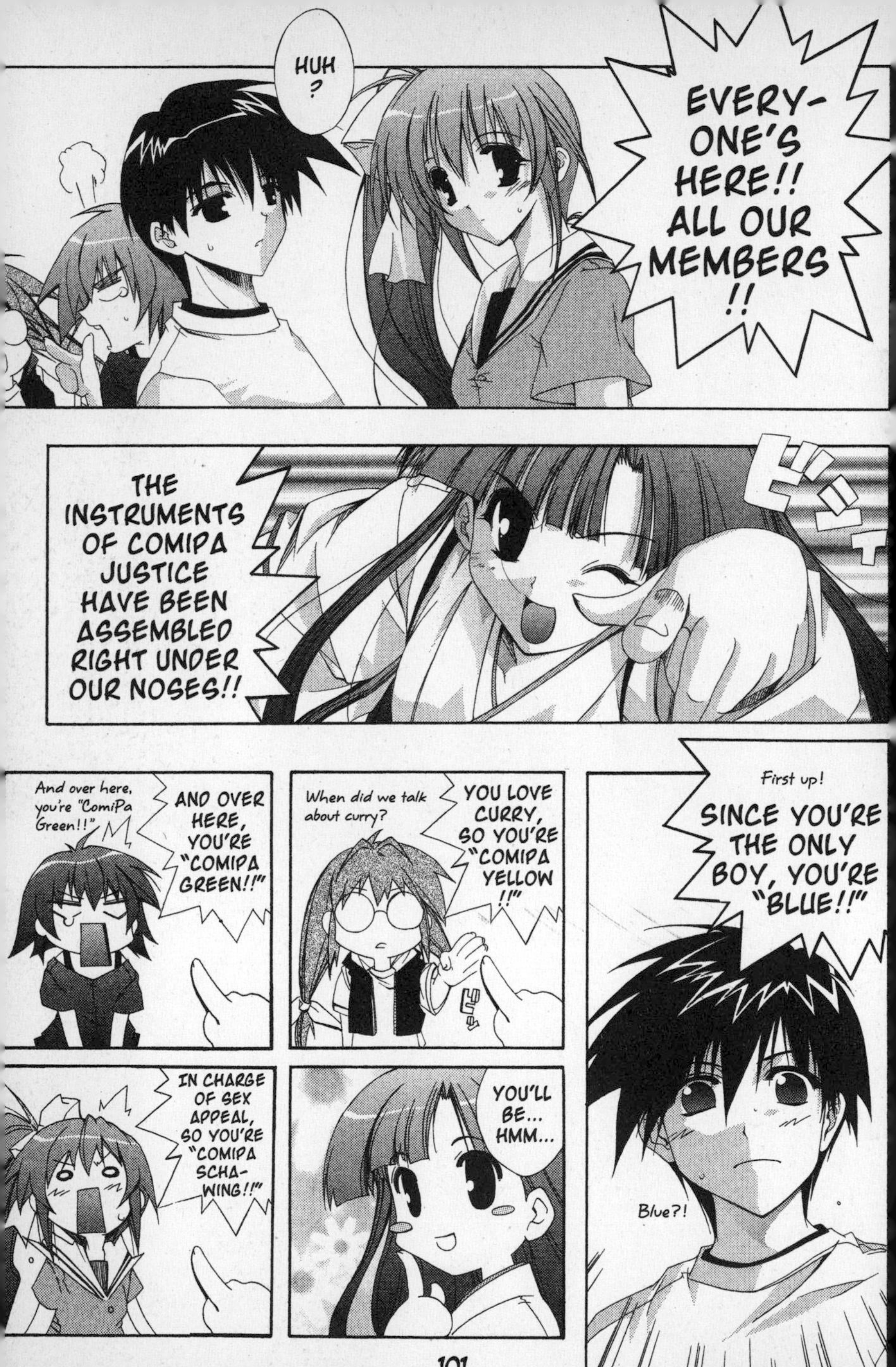
EVERY-ONE'S HERE!! ALL OUR MEMBERS!!
HUH?
THE INSTRUMENTS OF COMIPA JUSTICE HAVE BEEN ASSEMBLED RIGHT UNDER OUR NOSES!!
First up!
SINCE YOU'RE THE ONLY BOY, YOU'RE "BLUE!!"
Blue?!
YOU LOVE CURRY, SO YOU'RE "COMIPA YELLOW!!"
When did we talk about curry?
AND OVER HERE, YOU'RE "COMIPA GREEN!!"
And over here, you're "ComiPa Green!!"
YOU'LL BE... HMM...
IN CHARGE OF SEX APPEAL, SO YOU'RE "COMIPA SCHA-WING!!"

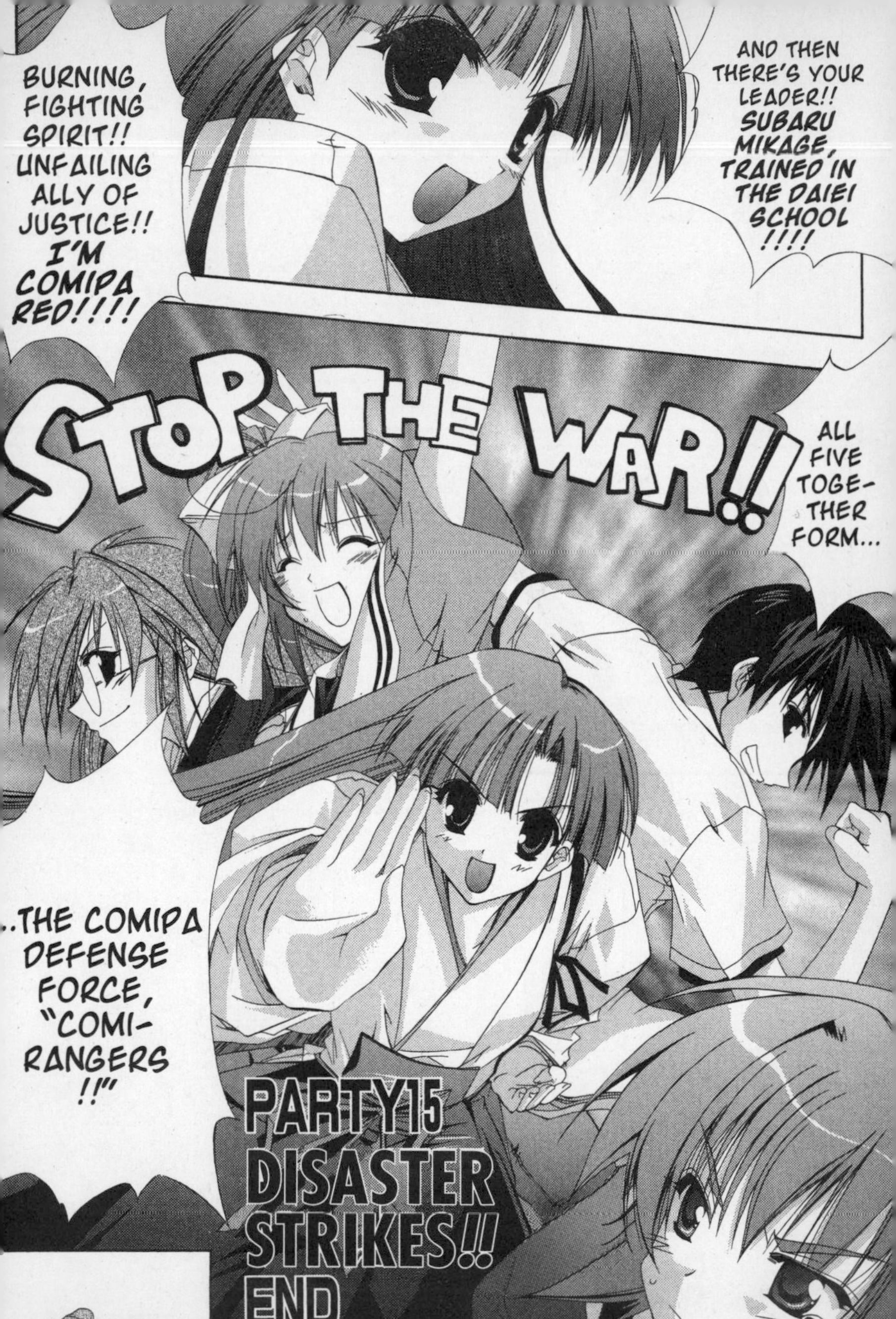
AND THEN THERE'S YOUR LEADER!! SUBARU MIKAGE, TRAINED IN THE DAIEI SCHOOL !!!!
BURNING, FIGHTING SPIRIT!! UNFAILING ALLY OF JUSTICE!! I'M COMIPA RED!!!!!
STOP THE WAR!!
ALL FIVE TOGE-THER FORM...
..THE COMIPA DEFENSE FORCE, "COMI-RANGERS !!"
PARTY15 DISASTER STRIKES!! END

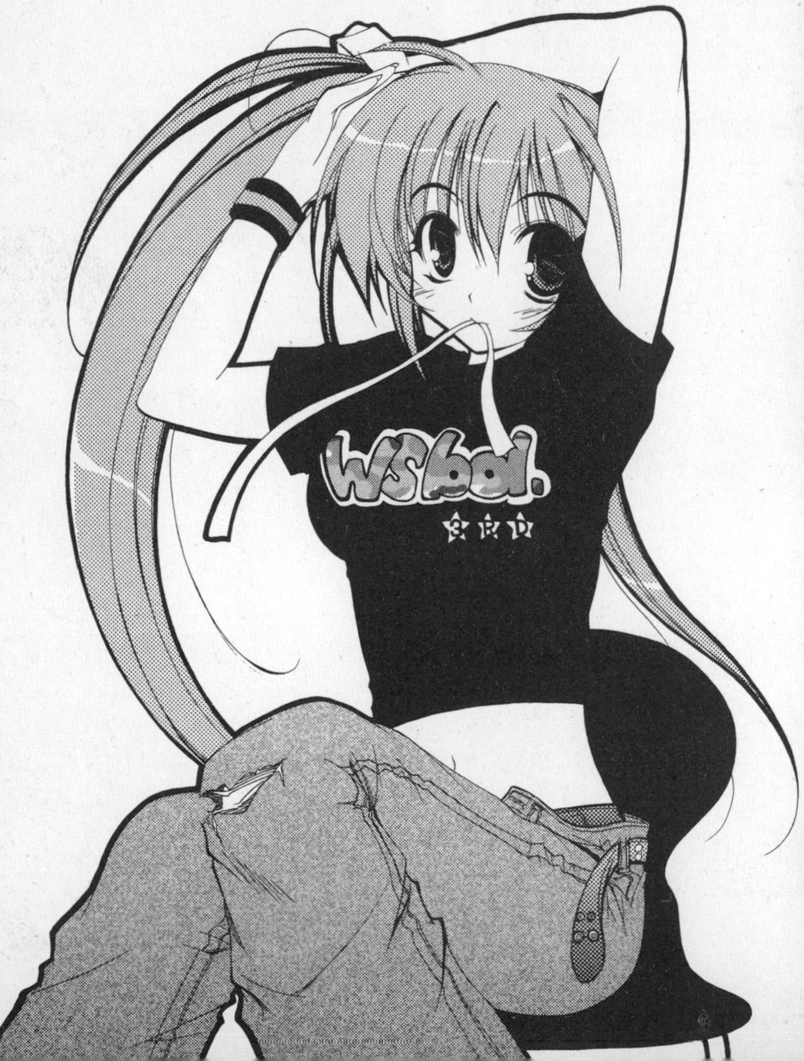

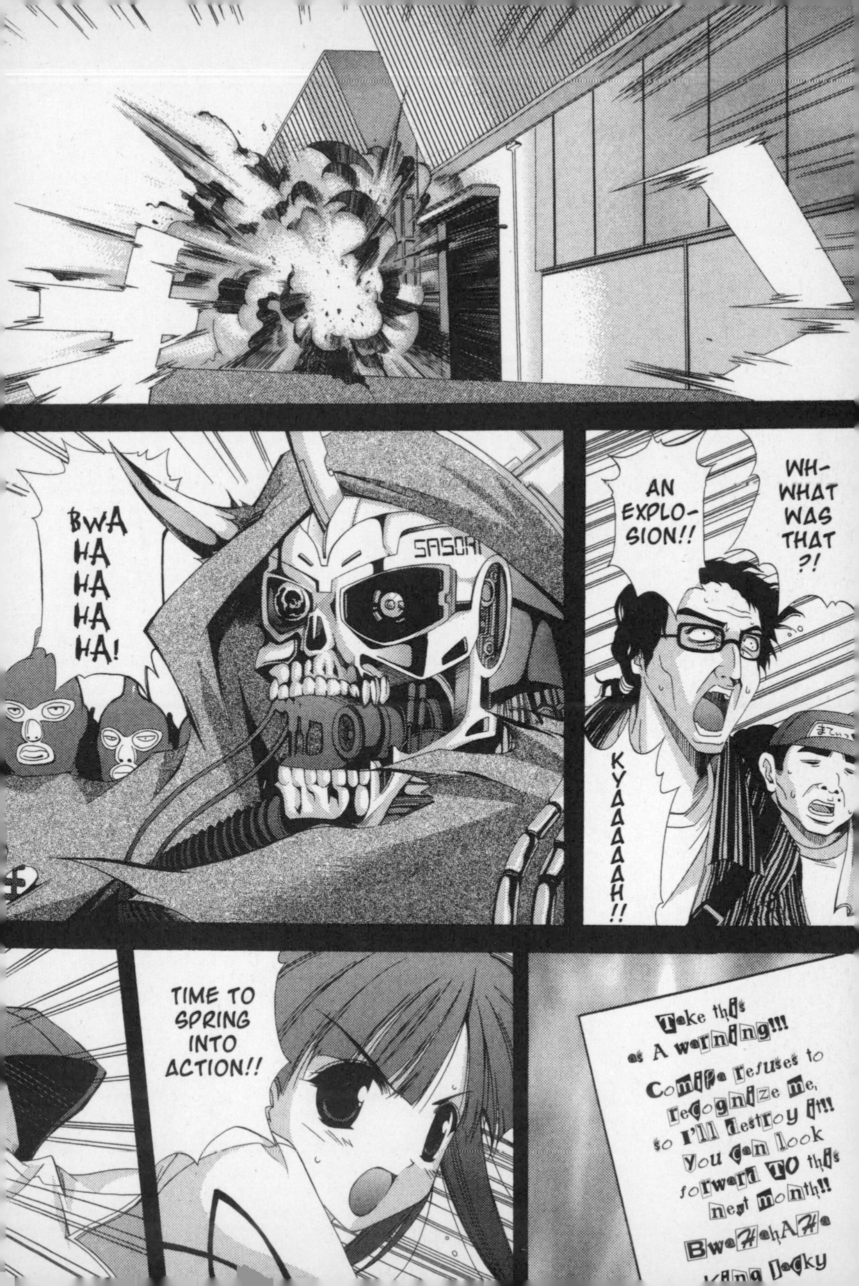
WH-WHAT WAS THAT?!
AN EXPLOSION!!
KYAAAAAAH!!
SASORI
BWA HA HA HA HA HA!
Take this as A warning!!! as Comipa refuses to recognize me, so I'll destroy it!! You can look forward TO this next month!! BwaHahAHa
King Jocky
TIME TO SPRING INTO ACTION!!

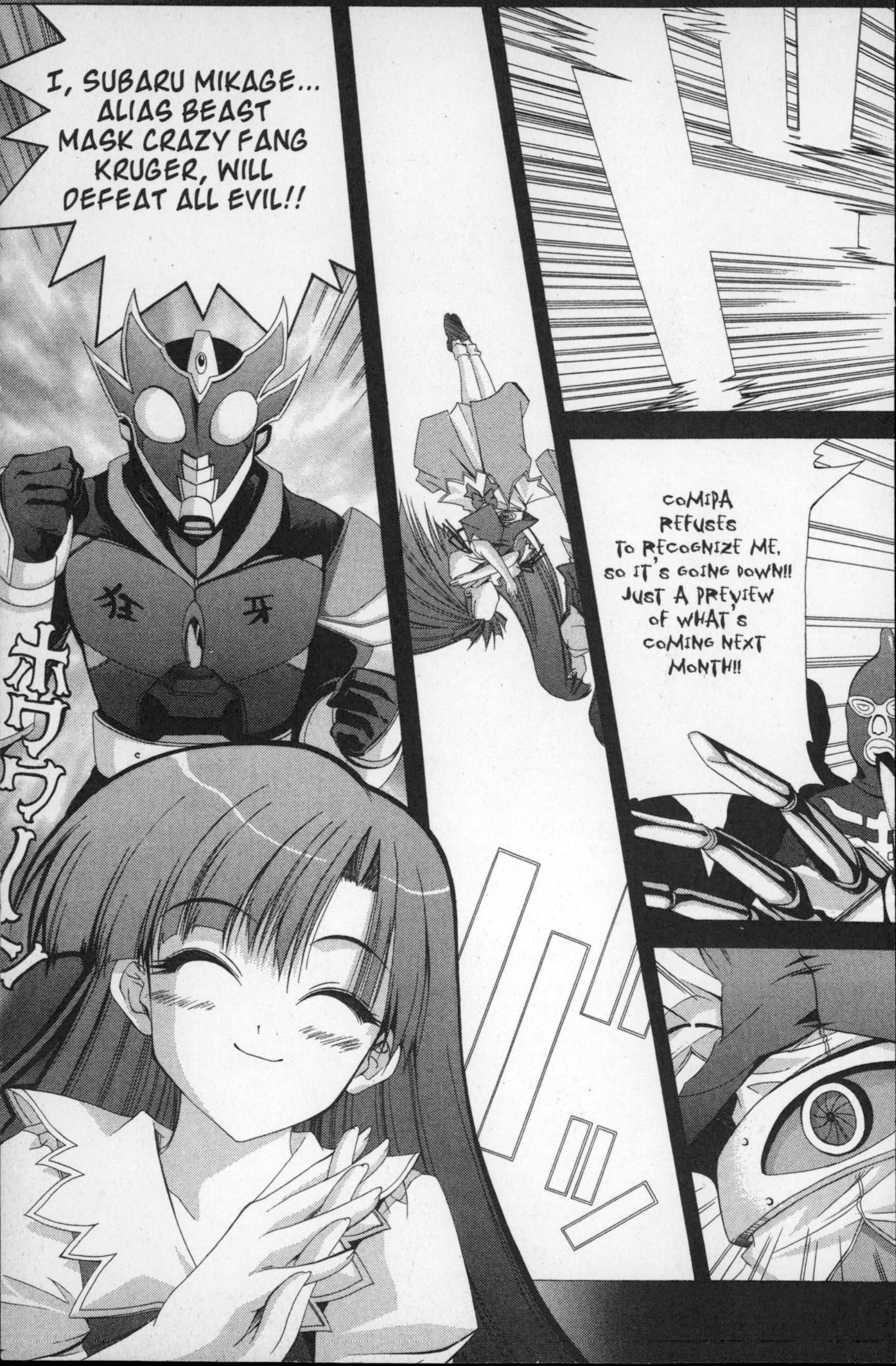
COMIPA REFUSES TO RECOGNIZE ME, SO IT'S GOING DOWN!! JUST A PREVIEW OF WHAT'S COMING NEXT MONTH!!
I, SUBARU MIKAGE... ALIAS BEAST MASK CRAZY FANG KRUGER, WILL DEFEAT ALL EVIL!!

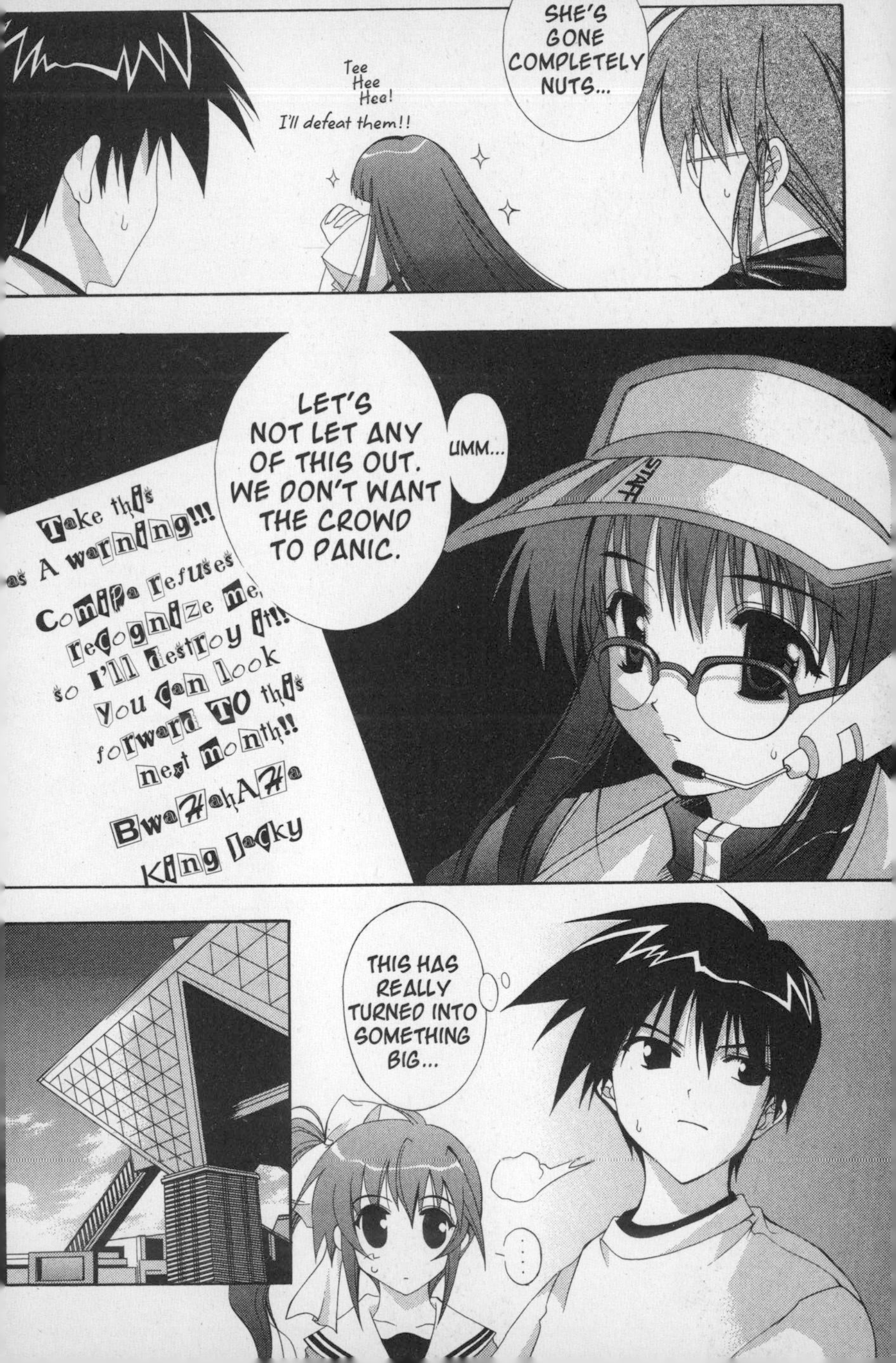
SHE'S GONE COMPLETELY NUTS...
Tee Hee Hee!
I'll defeat them!!
UMM...
LET'S NOT LET ANY OF THIS OUT. WE DON'T WANT THE CROWD TO PANIC.
STAFF
Take this as A warning!!! Comipa refuses recognize me, so I'll destroy it!! You can look forward TO this next month!! BwaHahAHa King Jacky
THIS HAS REALLY TURNED INTO SOMETHING BIG...
...

PARTY16 PRAY FOR PEACE

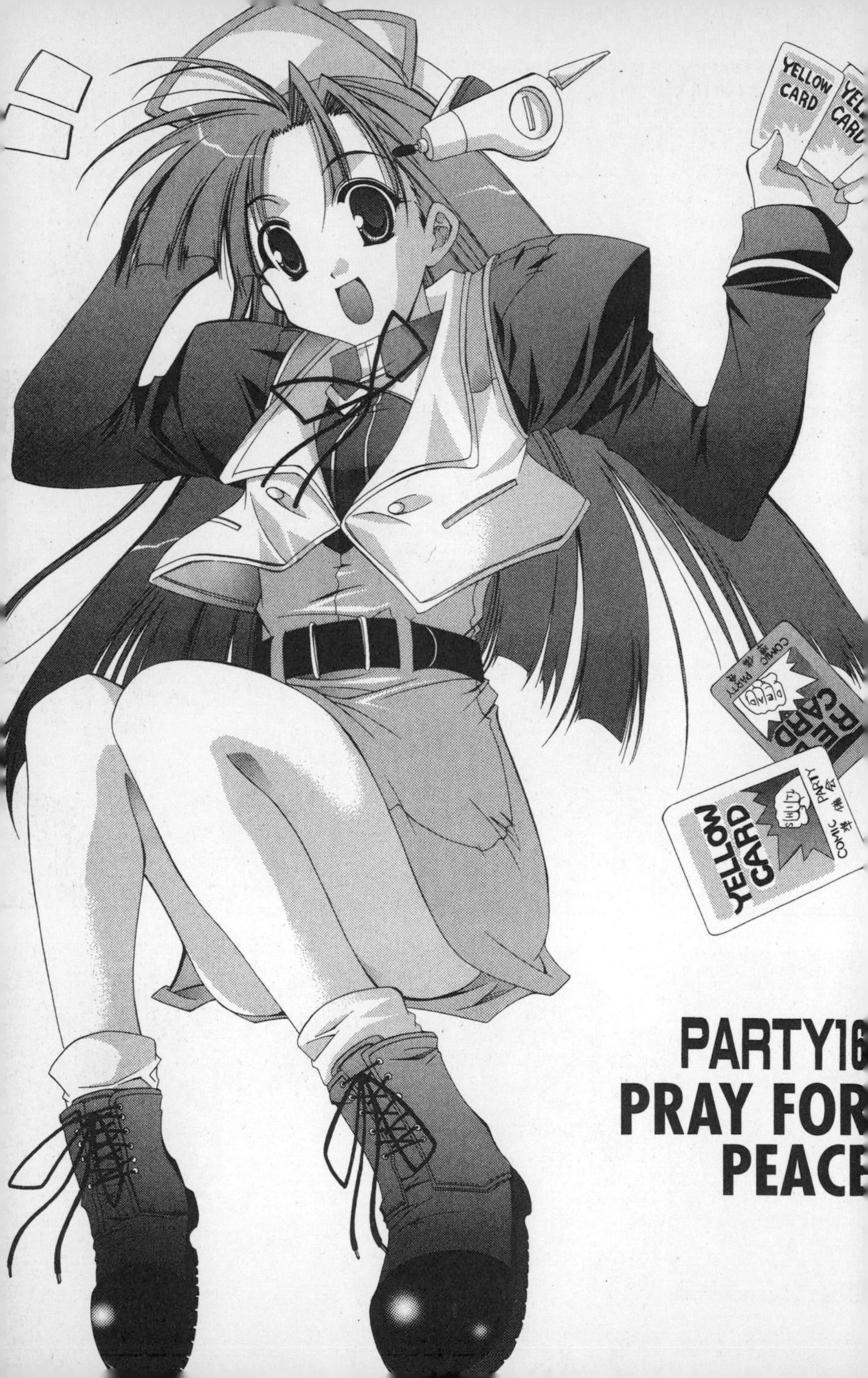
YELLOW CARD
YELLOW CARD
YELLOW CARD
COMIC PARTY 準備会

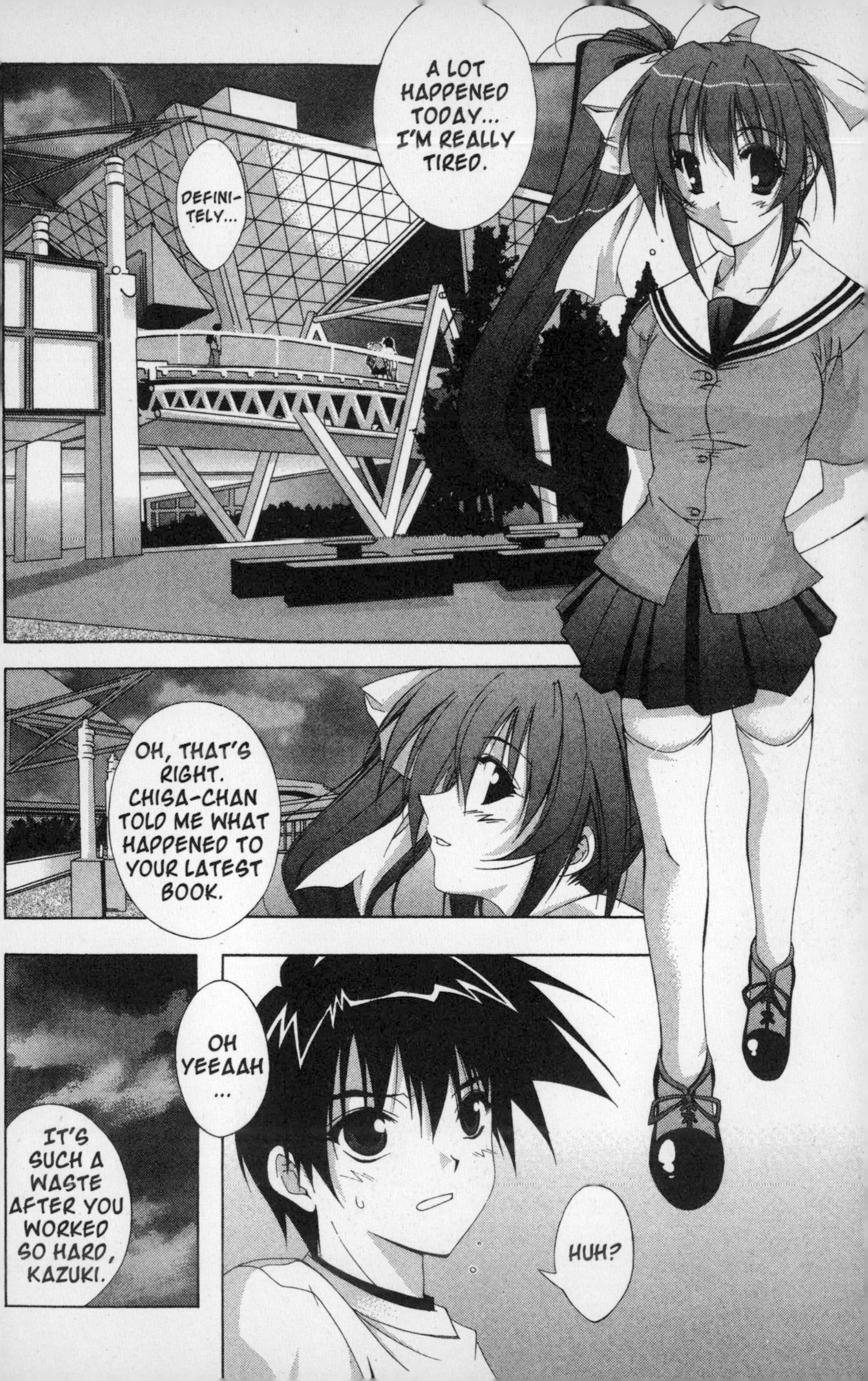

A LOT HAPPENED TODAY... I'M REALLY TIRED.
DEFINI-TELY...
OH, THAT'S RIGHT. CHISA-CHAN TOLD ME WHAT HAPPENED TO YOUR LATEST BOOK.
OH YEEAAH ...
HUH?
IT'S SUCH A WASTE AFTER YOU WORKED SO HARD, KAZUKI.

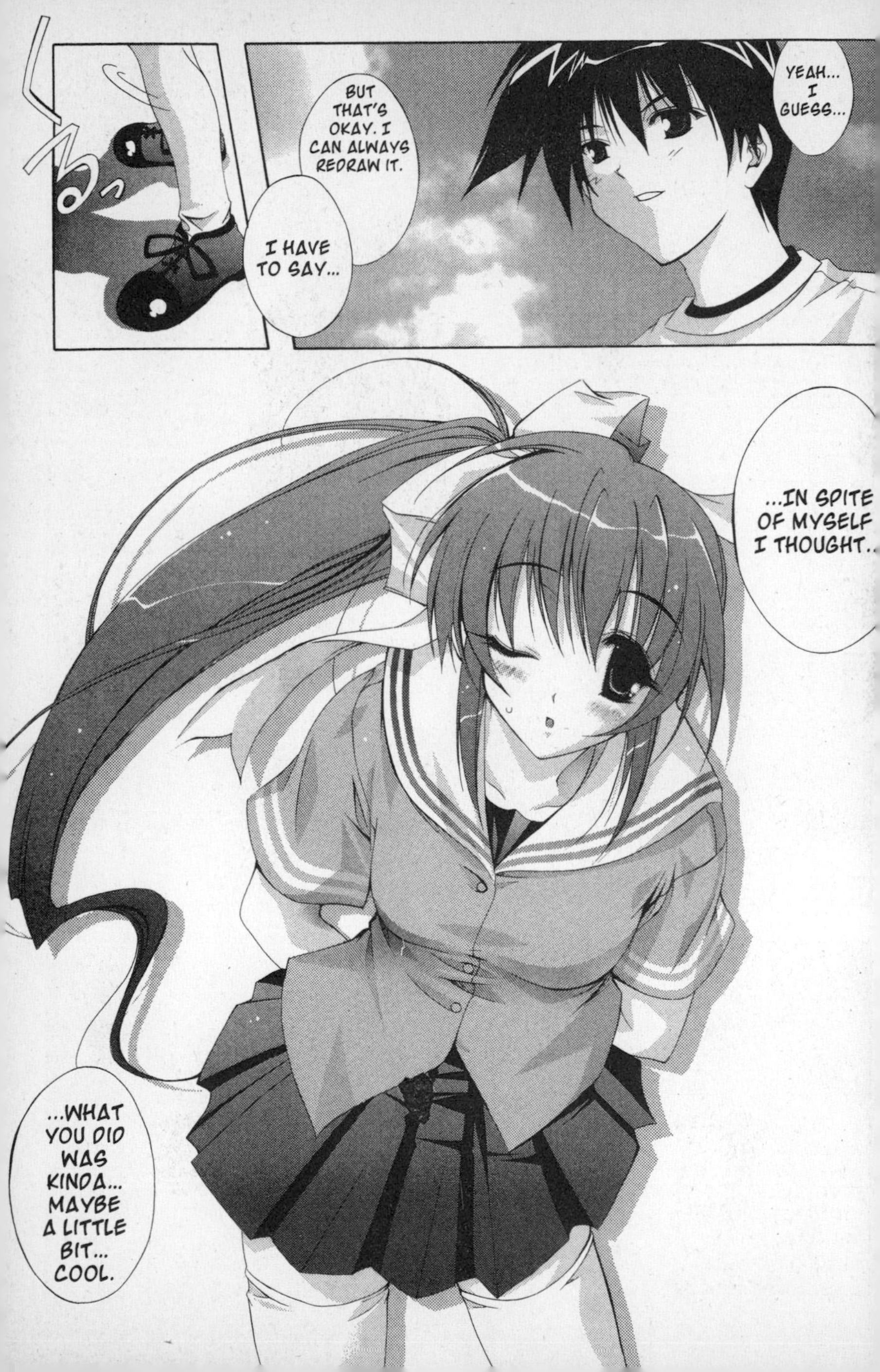
YEAH... I GUESS...
BUT THAT'S OKAY. I CAN ALWAYS REDRAW IT.
I HAVE TO SAY...
くるっ
...IN SPITE OF MYSELF I THOUGHT..
...WHAT YOU DID WAS KINDA... MAYBE A LITTLE BIT... COOL.

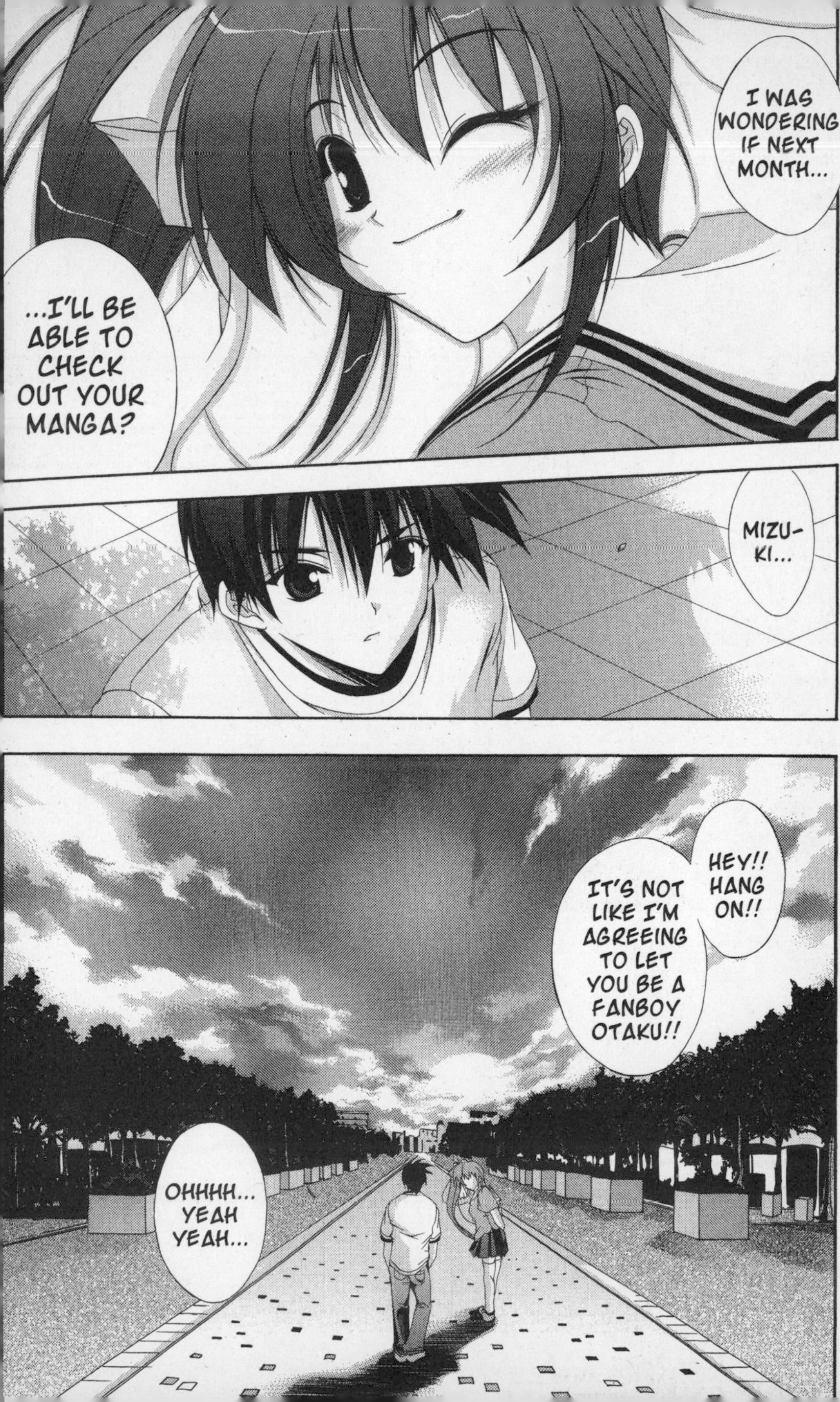
I WAS WONDERING IF NEXT MONTH...
...I'LL BE ABLE TO CHECK OUT YOUR MANGA?
MIZU-KI...
HEY!! HANG ON!!
IT'S NOT LIKE I'M AGREEING TO LET YOU BE A FANBOY OTAKU!!
OHHHH... YEAH YEAH...

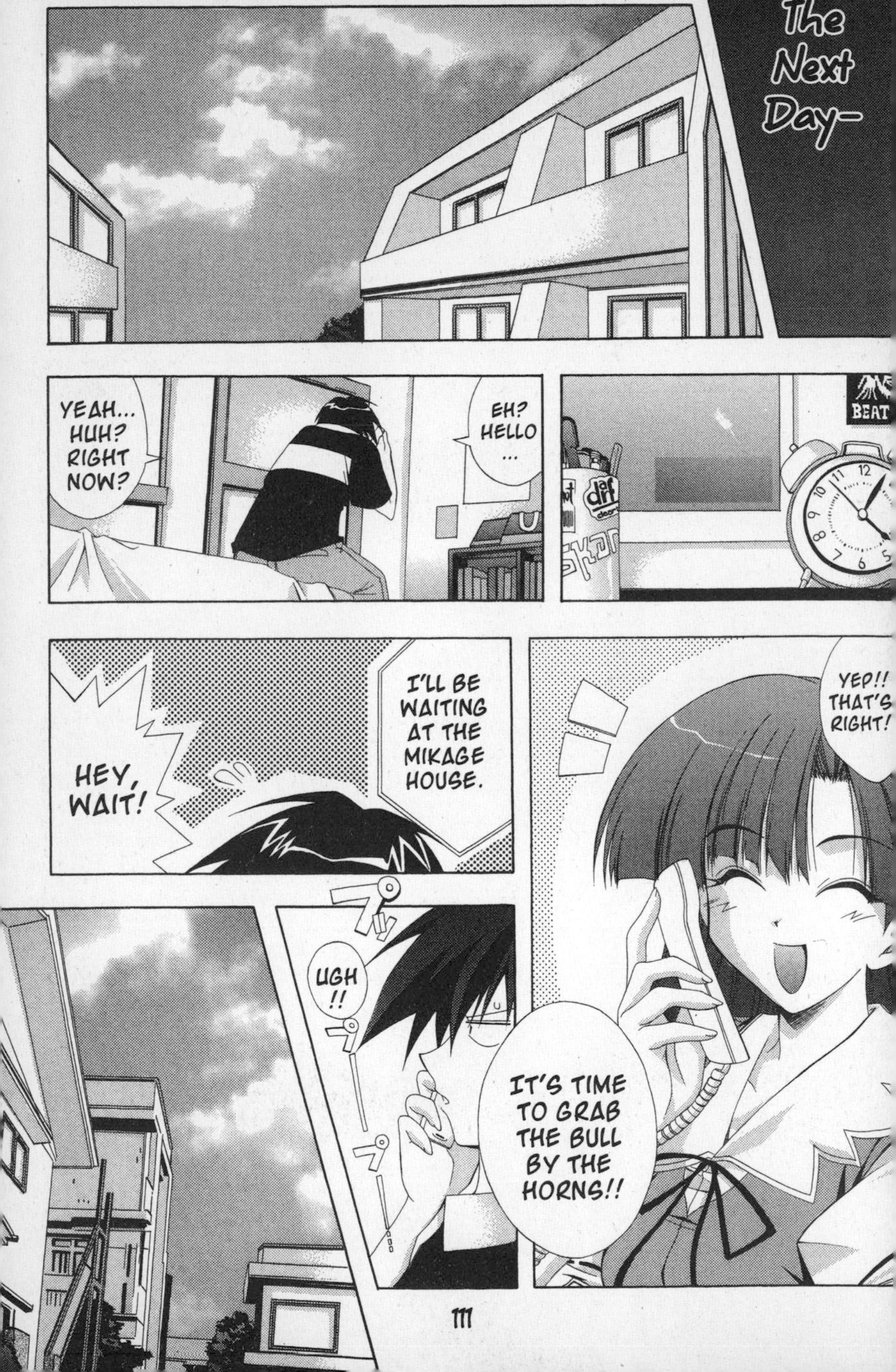
The Next Day-
EH? HELLO ...
YEAH... HUH? RIGHT NOW?
BEAT
YEP!! THAT'S RIGHT!
IT'S TIME TO GRAB THE BULL BY THE HORNS!!
I'LL BE WAITING AT THE MIKAGE HOUSE.
HEY, WAIT!
UGH !!

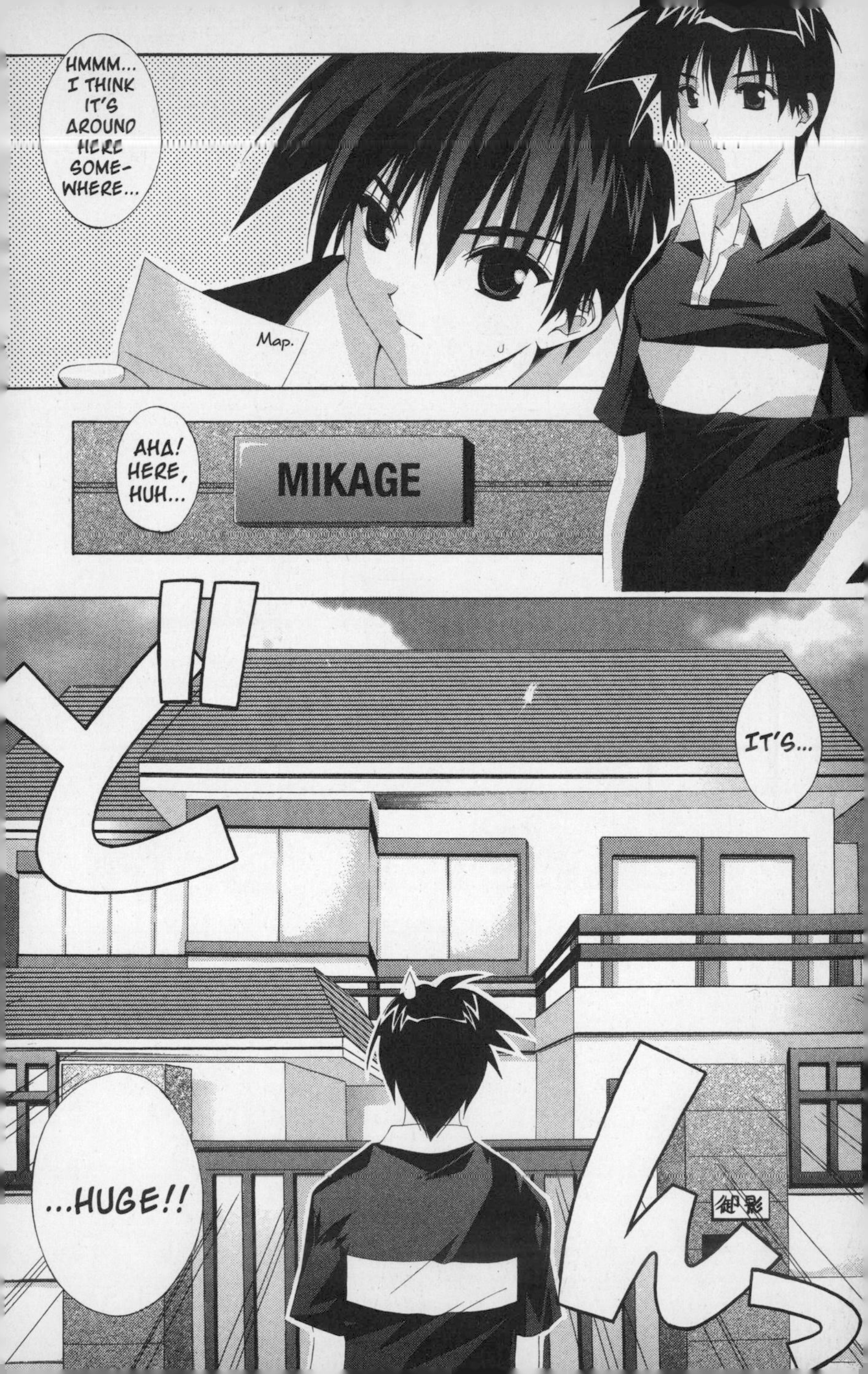
HMMM... I THINK IT'S AROUND HERE SOME-WHERE...
Map.
AHA! HERE, HUH...
MIKAGE
IT'S...
どんっ
御影
...HUGE!!

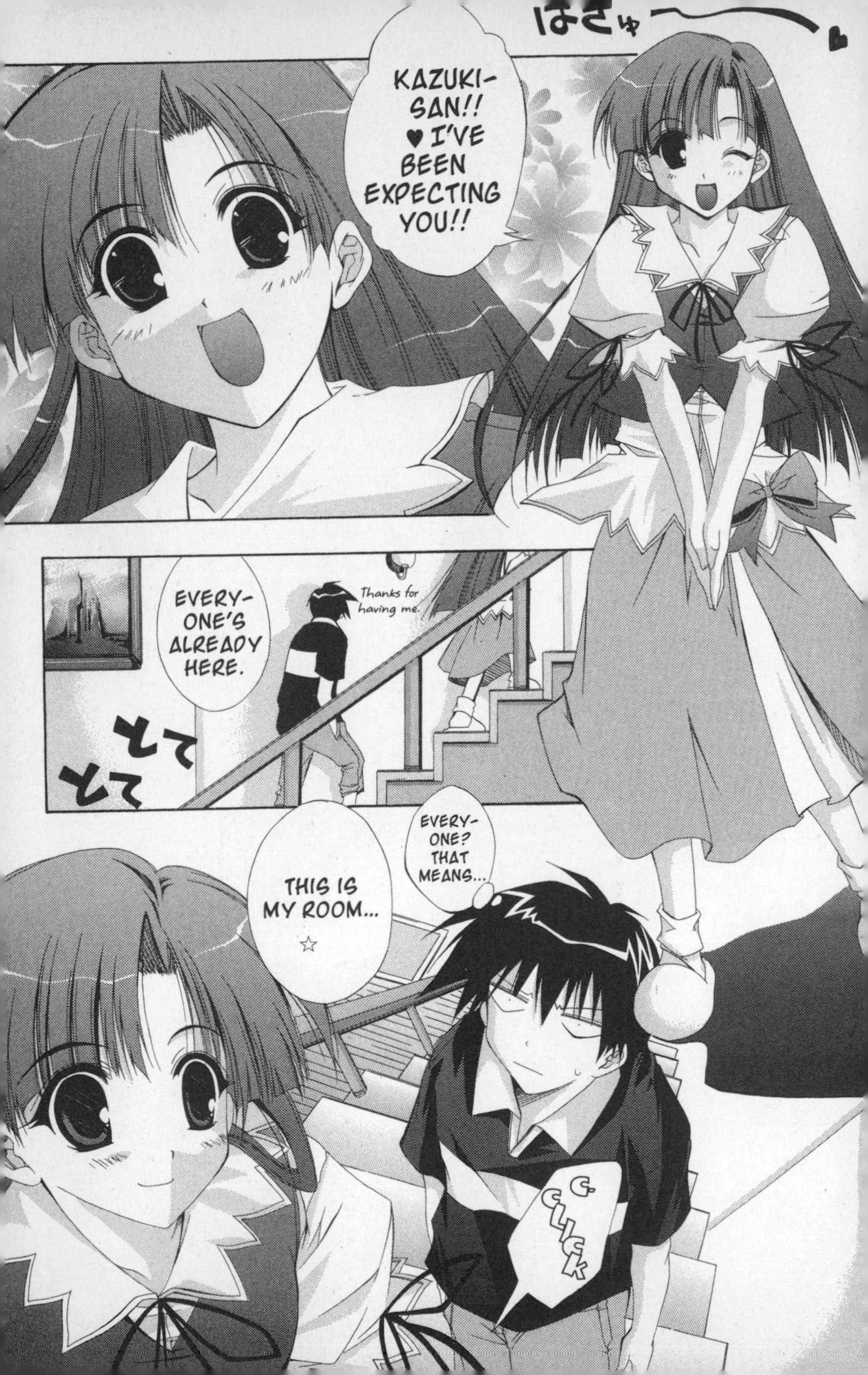
はさゅ～♥
KAZUKI-SAN!! ♥ I'VE BEEN EXPECTING YOU!!
Thanks for having me.
EVERY-ONE'S ALREADY HERE.
とてとて
EVERY-ONE? THAT MEANS...
THIS IS MY ROOM... ☆
G-CLICK

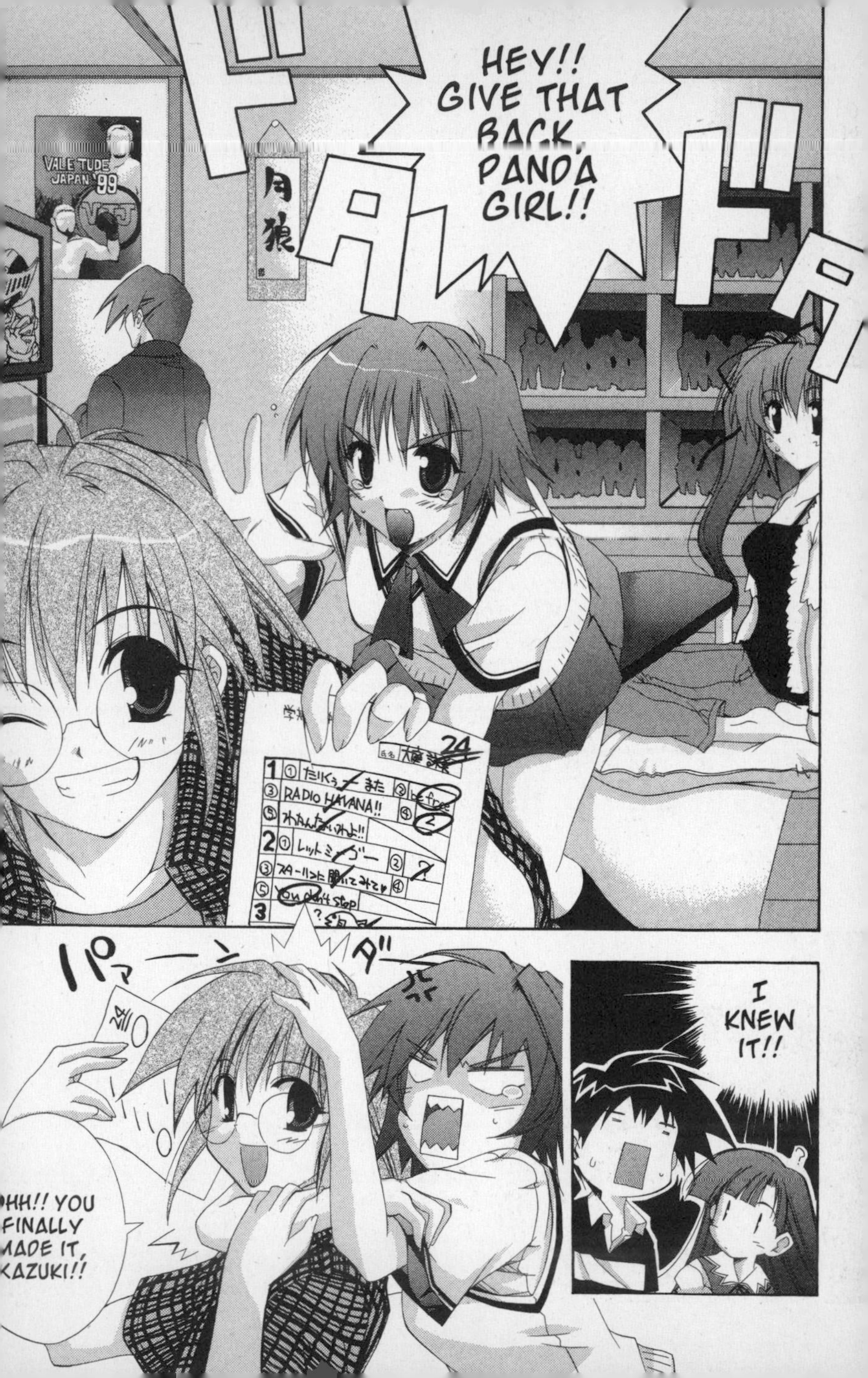
ドタ
HEY!! GIVE THAT BACK, PANDA GIRL!!
ドタ
パァーーン
ダーー
I KNEW IT!!
OHH!! YOU FINALLY MADE IT, KAZUKI!!

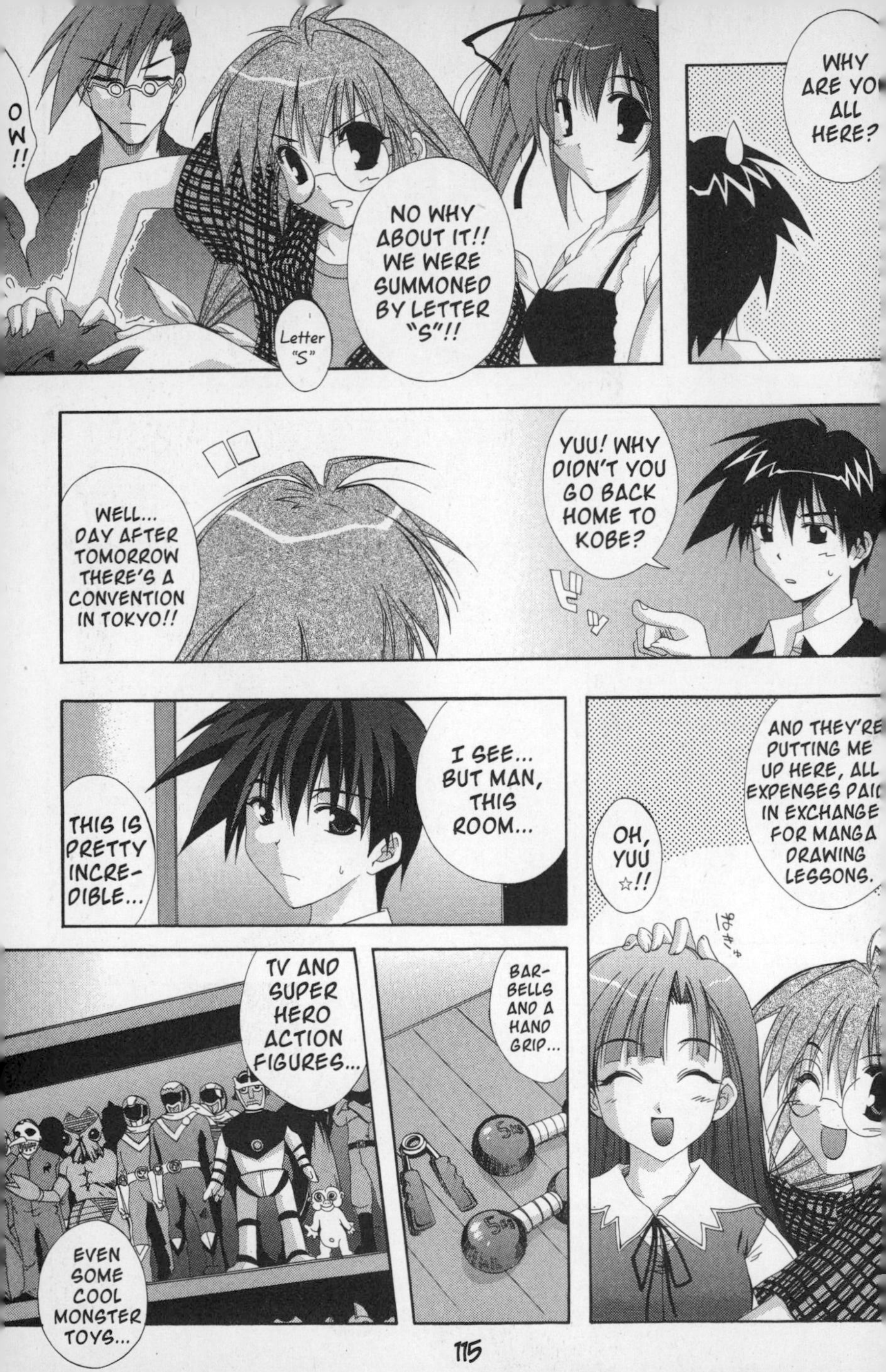
WHY ARE YO ALL HERE?
NO WHY ABOUT IT!! WE WERE SUMMONED BY LETTER "S"!!
Letter "S"
OW!!
YUU! WHY DIDN'T YOU GO BACK HOME TO KOBE?
WELL... DAY AFTER TOMORROW THERE'S A CONVENTION IN TOKYO!!
AND THEY'RE PUTTING ME UP HERE, ALL EXPENSES PAI IN EXCHANGE FOR MANGA DRAWING LESSONS.
OH, YUU☆!!
I SEE... BUT MAN, THIS ROOM...
THIS IS PRETTY INCRE-DIBLE...
BAR-BELLS AND A HAND GRIP...
TV AND SUPER HERO ACTION FIGURES...
EVEN SOME COOL MONSTER TOYS...

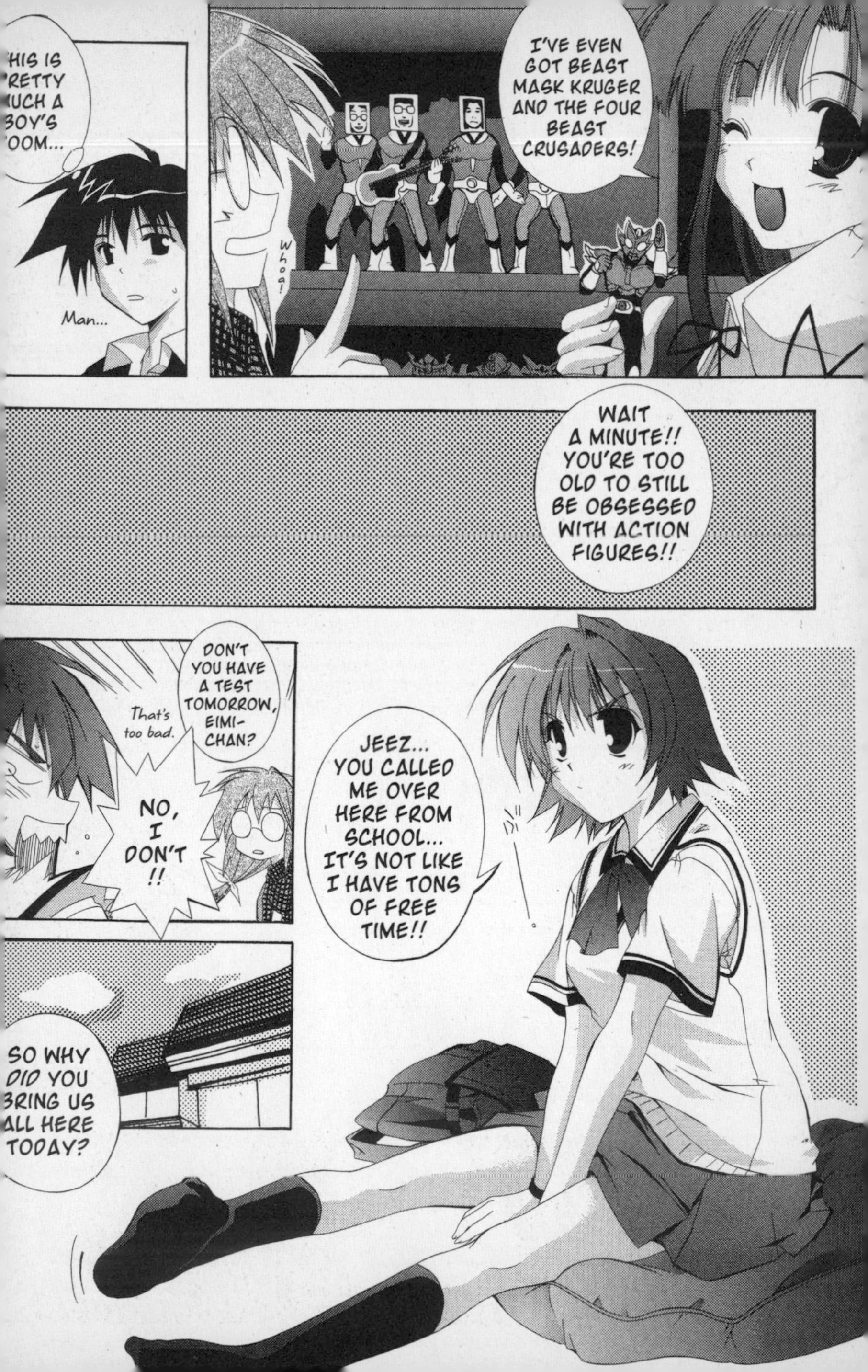
I'VE EVEN GOT BEAST MASK KRUGER AND THE FOUR BEAST CRUSADERS!
Whoa!
HIS IS RETTY UCH A BOY'S OOM...
Man...
WAIT A MINUTE!! YOU'RE TOO OLD TO STILL BE OBSESSED WITH ACTION FIGURES!!
JEEZ... YOU CALLED ME OVER HERE FROM SCHOOL... IT'S NOT LIKE I HAVE TONS OF FREE TIME!!
DON'T YOU HAVE A TEST TOMORROW, EIMI-CHAN?
That's too bad.
NO, I DON'T!!
SO WHY DID YOU BRING US ALL HERE TODAY?

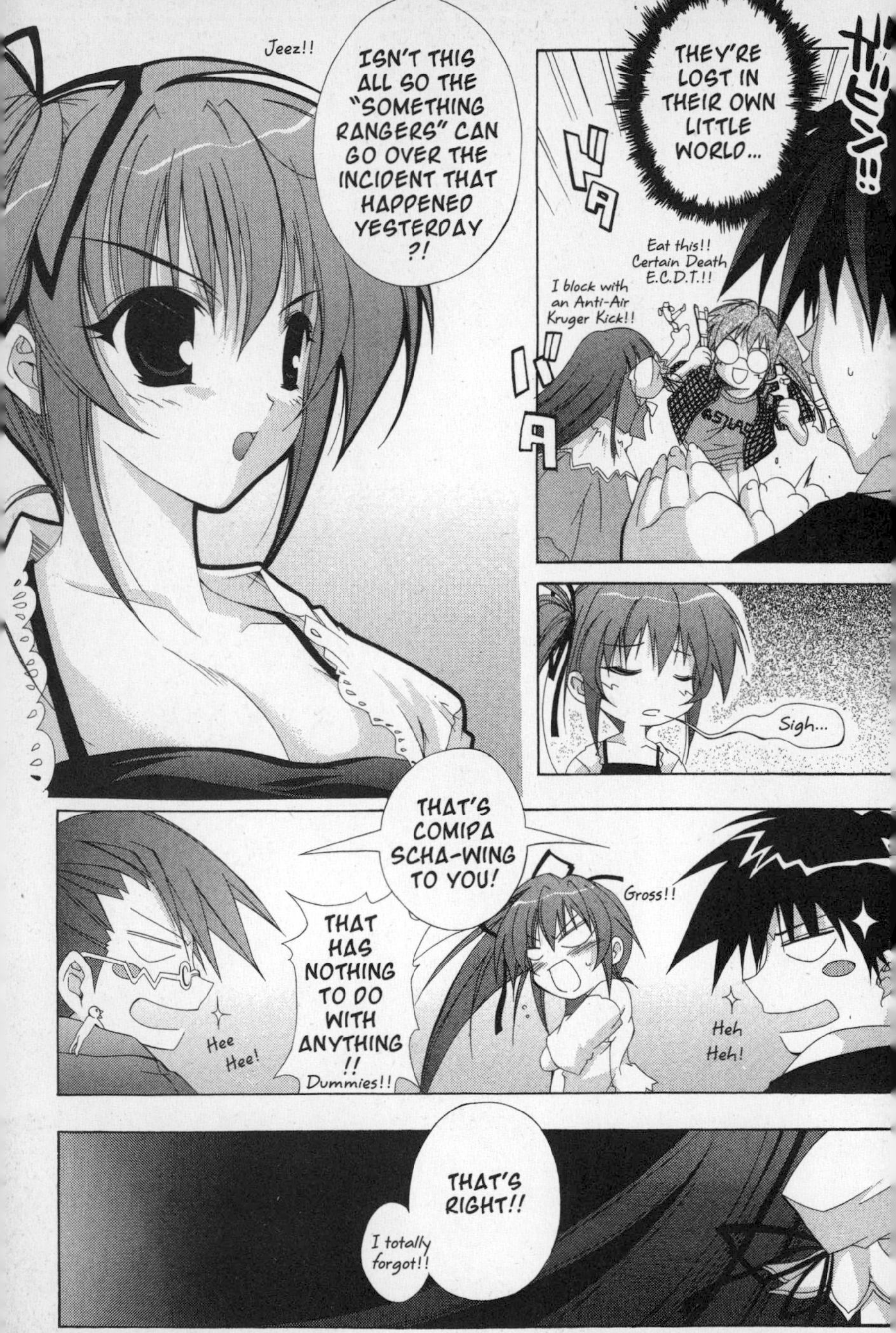
THEY'RE LOST IN THEIR OWN LITTLE WORLD...
Eat this!! Certain Death E.C.D.T.!!
I block with an Anti-Air Kruger Kick!!
Sigh...
Jeez!!
ISN'T THIS ALL SO THE "SOMETHING RANGERS" CAN GO OVER THE INCIDENT THAT HAPPENED YESTERDAY ?!
THAT'S COMIPA SCHA-WING TO YOU!
Gross!!
Heh Heh!
THAT HAS NOTHING TO DO WITH ANYTHING !!
Dummies!!
Hee Hee!
THAT'S RIGHT!!
I totally forgot!!

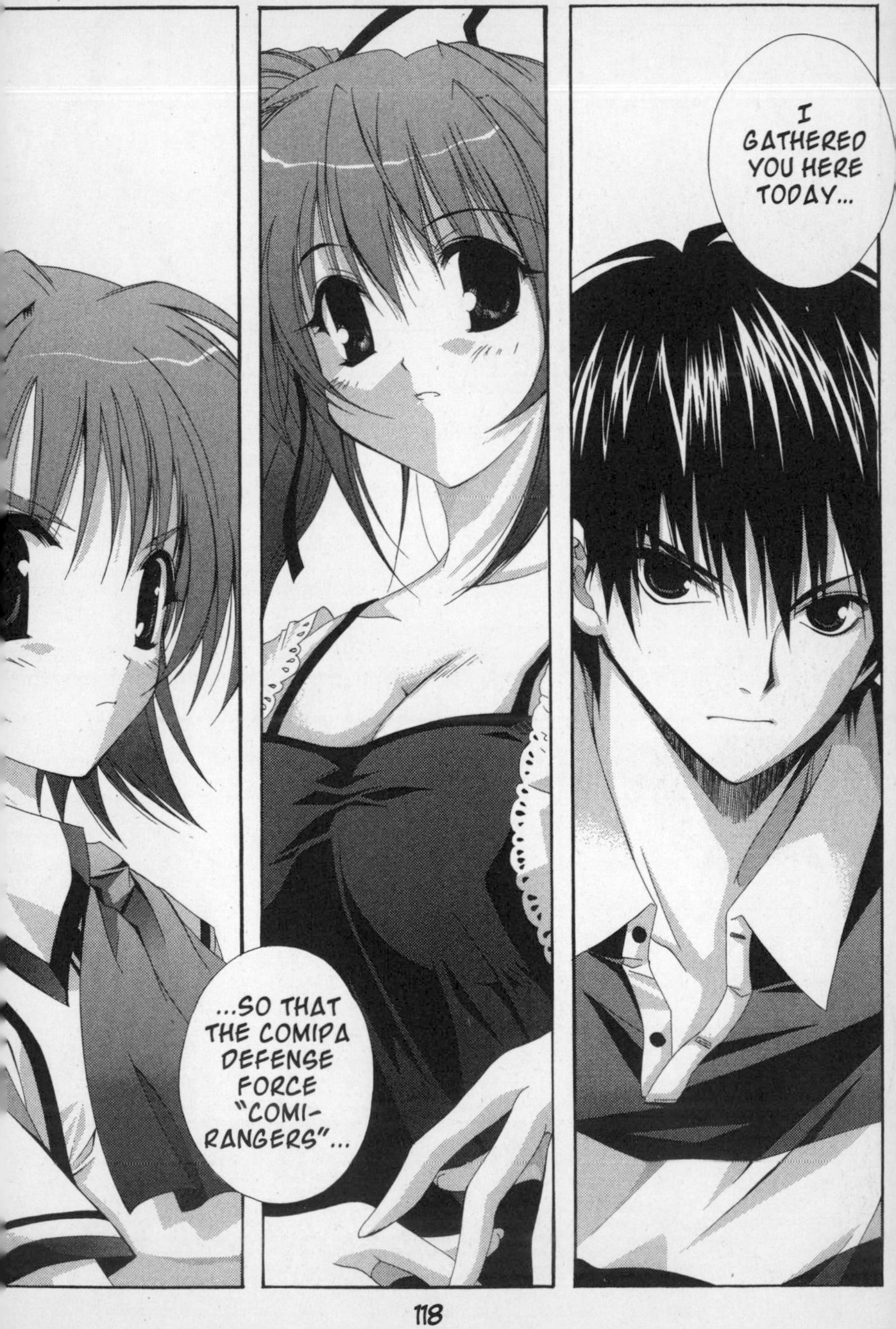
I GATHERED YOU HERE TODAY...
...SO THAT THE COMIPA DEFENSE FORCE "COMI-RANGERS"...

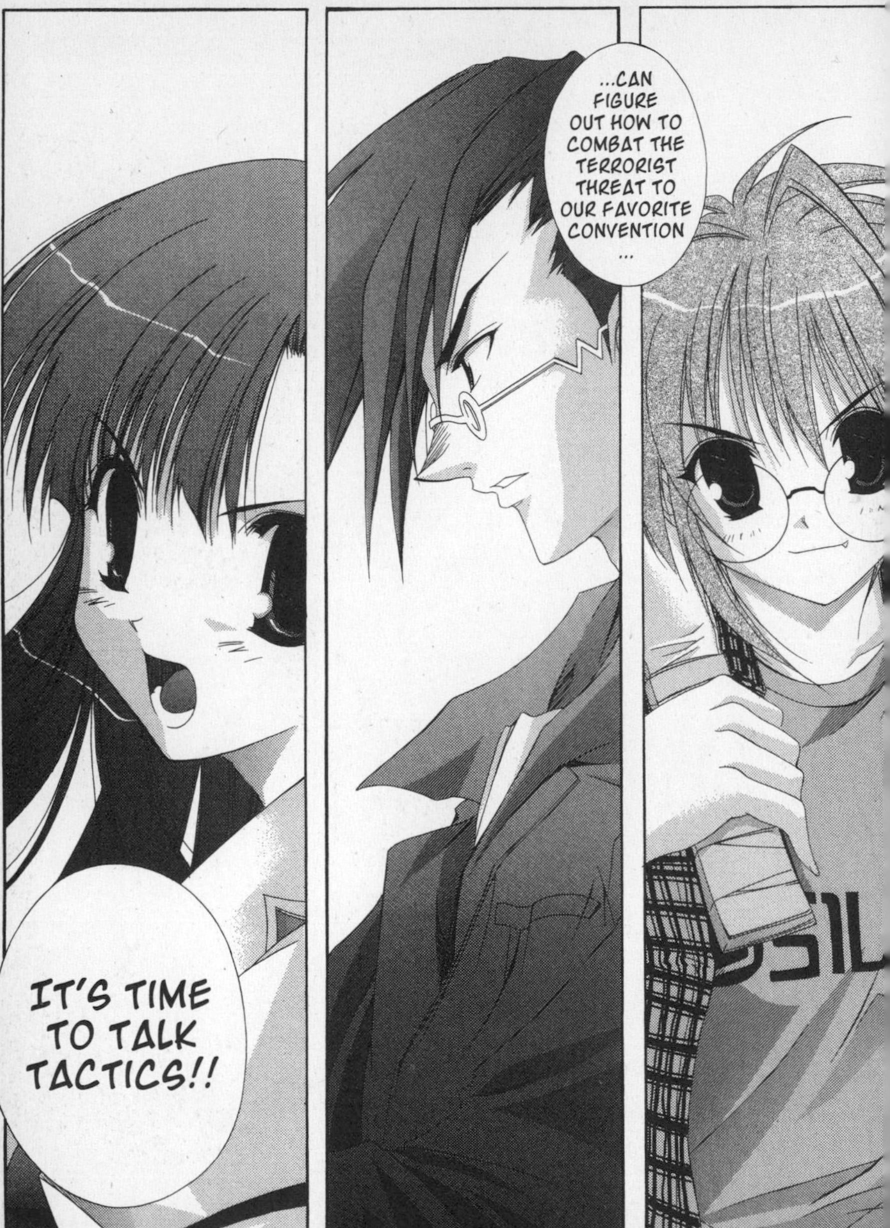
...CAN FIGURE OUT HOW TO COMBAT THE TERRORIST THREAT TO OUR FAVORITE CONVENTION ...
IT'S TIME TO TALK TACTICS!!

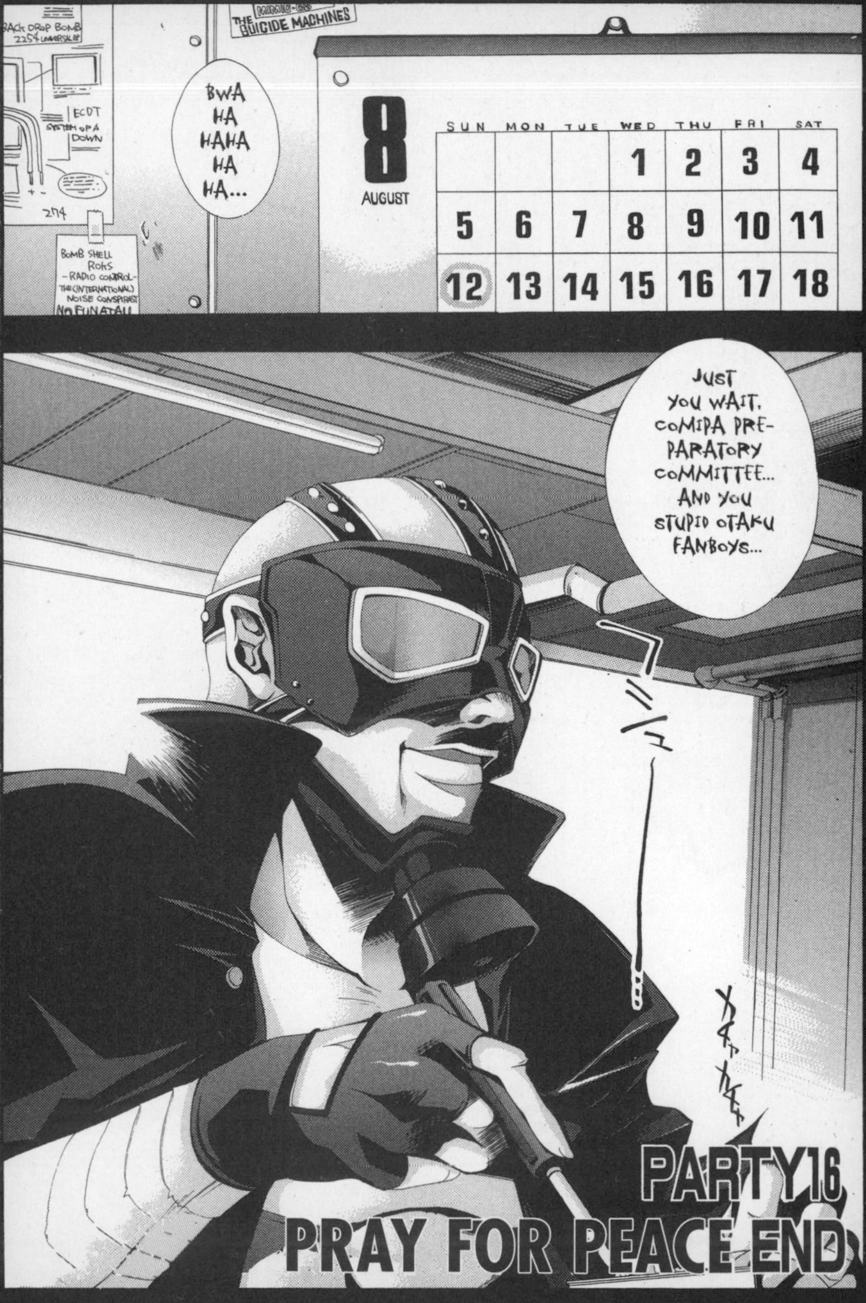
THE SUICIDE MACHINES
SYSTEM OF A DOWN
BWA HA HAHA HA HA...
8 AUGUST
SUN MON TUE WED THU FRI SAT
1 2 3 4
5 6 7 8 9 10 11
12 13 14 15 16 17 18
JUST YOU WAIT, COMIPA PRE-PARATORY COMMITTEE... AND YOU STUPID OTAKU FANBOYS...
PARTY16
PRAY FOR PEACE END

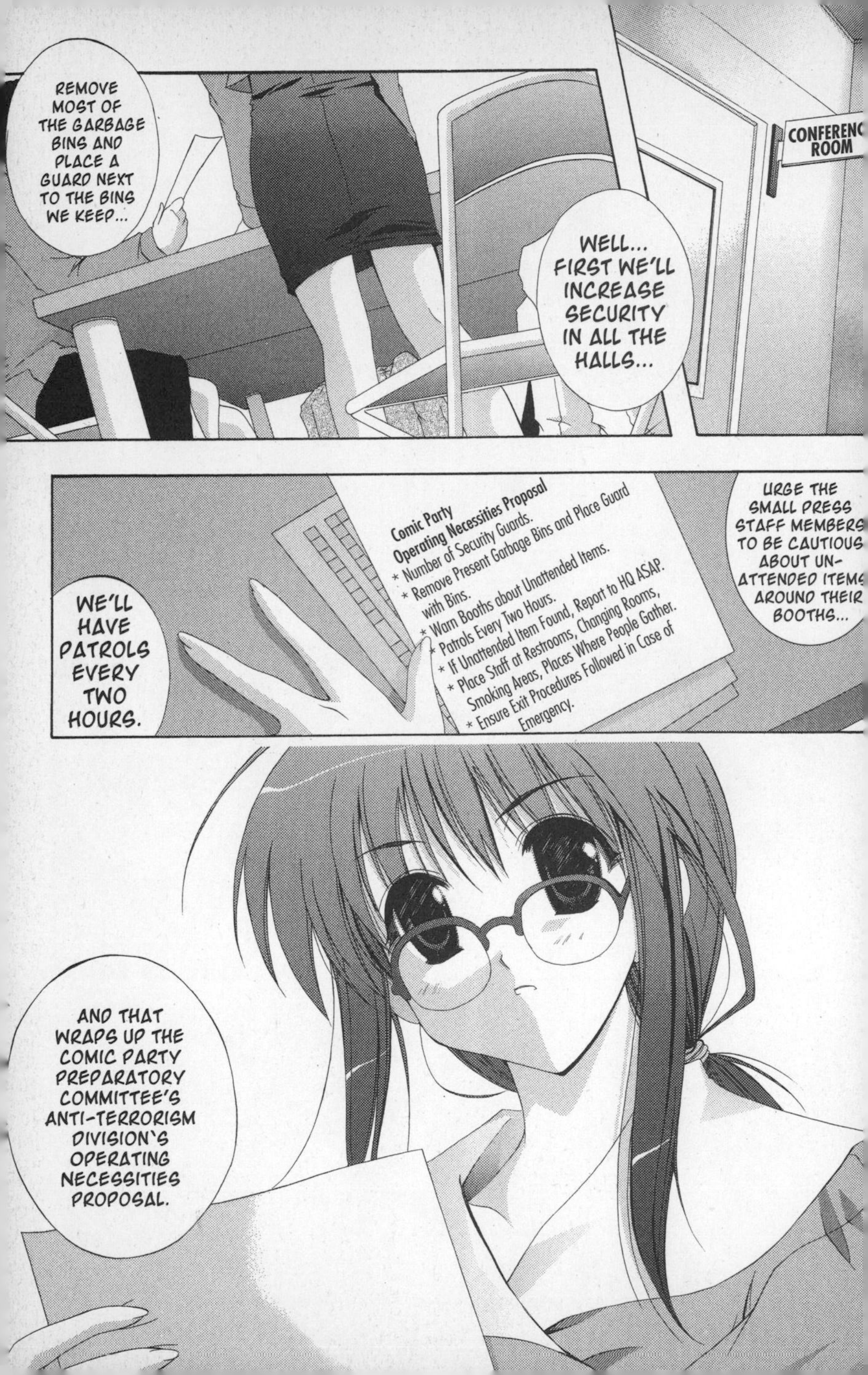
CONFERENC ROOM
WELL... FIRST WE'LL INCREASE SECURITY IN ALL THE HALLS...
REMOVE MOST OF THE GARBAGE BINS AND PLACE A GUARD NEXT TO THE BINS WE KEEP...
URGE THE SMALL PRESS STAFF MEMBERS TO BE CAUTIOUS ABOUT UN-ATTENDED ITEMS AROUND THEIR BOOTHS...
Comic Party
Operating Necessities Proposal
* Number of Security Guards.
* Remove Present Garbage Bins and Place Guard with Bins.
* Warn Booths about Unattended Items.
* Patrols Every Two Hours.
* If Unattended Item Found, Report to HQ ASAP.
* Place Staff at Restrooms, Changing Rooms, Smoking Areas, Places Where People Gather.
* Ensure Exit Procedures Followed in Case of Emergency.
WE'LL HAVE PATROLS EVERY TWO HOURS.
AND THAT WRAPS UP THE COMIC PARTY PREPARATORY COMMITTEE'S ANTI-TERRORISM DIVISION`S OPERATING NECESSITIES PROPOSAL.

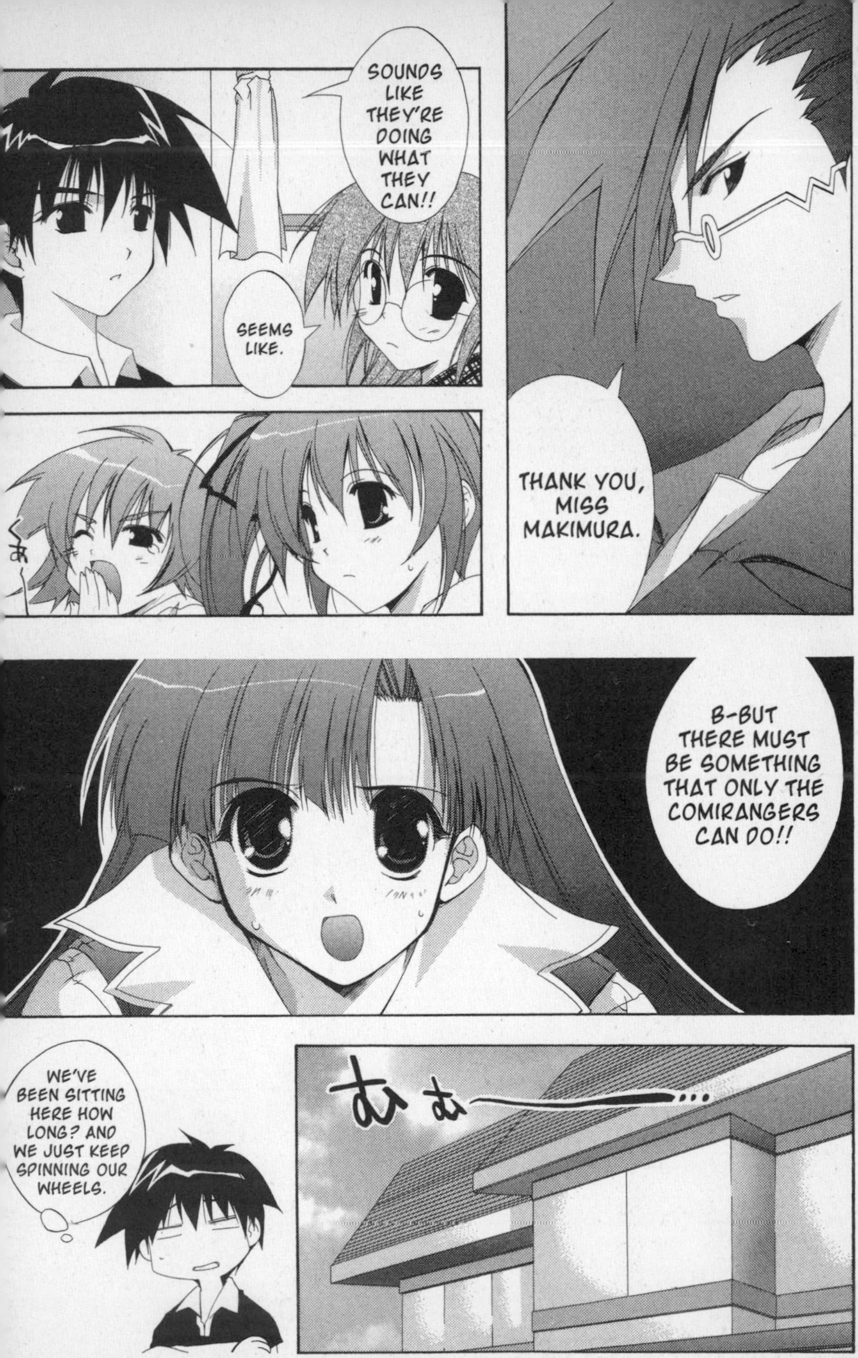
THANK YOU, MISS MAKIMURA.
SOUNDS LIKE THEY'RE DOING WHAT THEY CAN!!
SEEMS LIKE.
B-BUT THERE MUST BE SOMETHING THAT ONLY THE COMIRANGERS CAN DO!!
むむ――…
WE'VE BEEN SITTING HERE HOW LONG? AND WE JUST KEEP SPINNING OUR WHEELS.

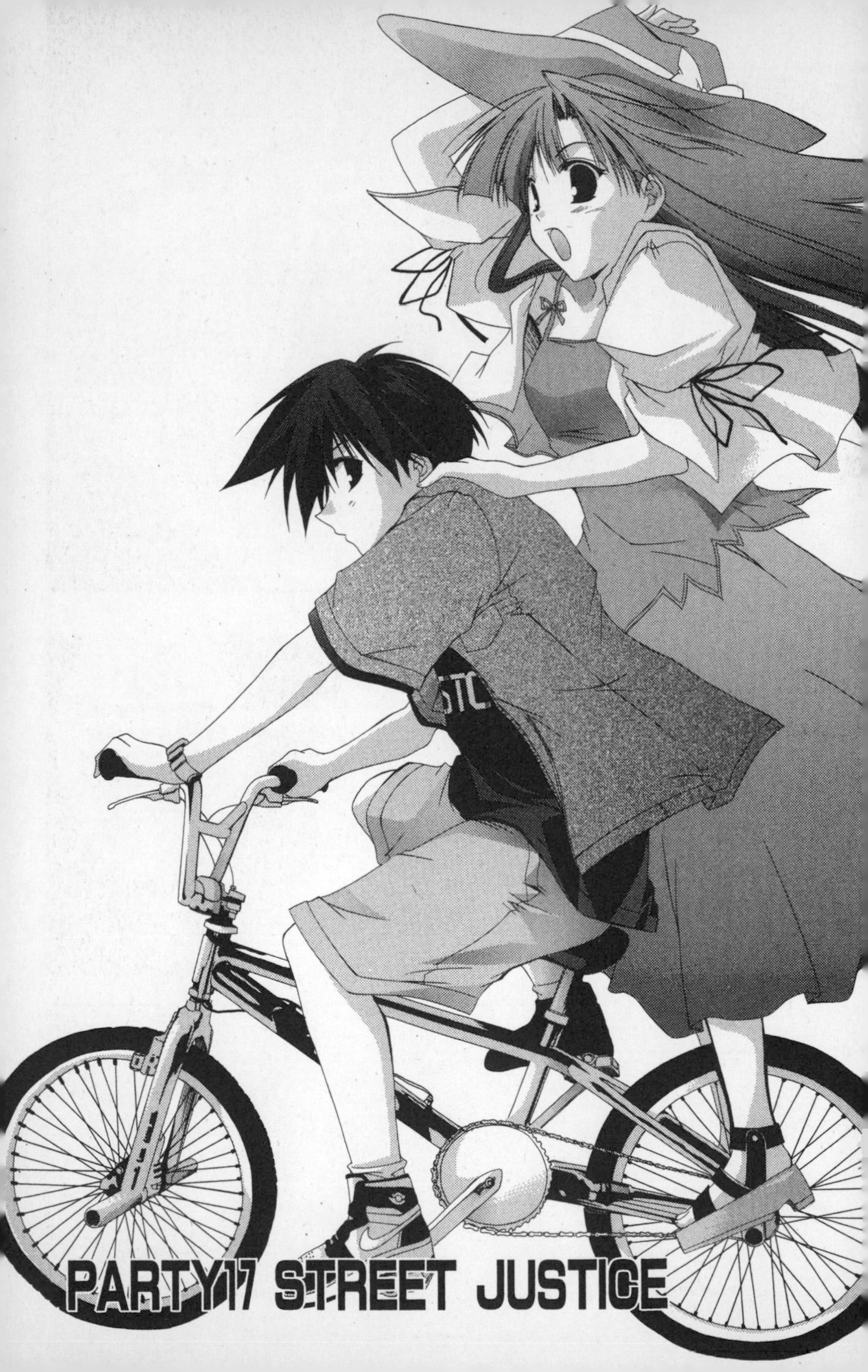

PARTY17 STREET JUSTICE

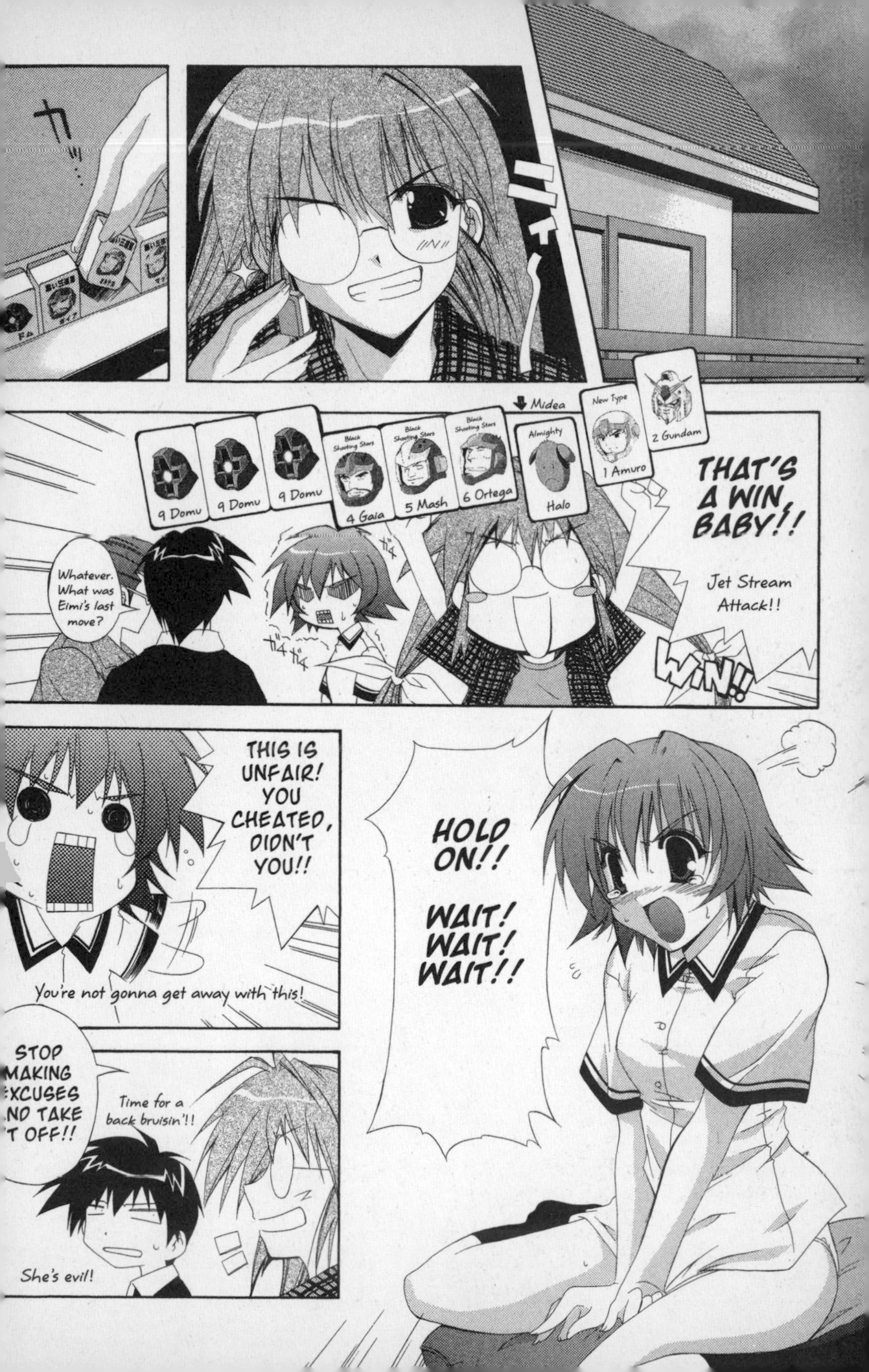
2 Gundam
New Type
1 Amuro
Midea
Almighty
Halo
Black Shooting Stars
6 Ortega
Black Shooting Stars
5 Mash
Black Shooting Stars
4 Gaia
9 Domu
9 Domu
9 Domu
THAT'S A WIN, BABY!!
Jet Stream Attack!!
WIN!!
Whatever. What was Eimi's last move?
HOLD ON!!
WAIT! WAIT! WAIT!!
THIS IS UNFAIR! YOU CHEATED, DIDN'T YOU!!
You're not gonna get away with this!
Time for a back bruisin'!!
STOP MAKING XCUSES ND TAKE T OFF!!
She's evil!

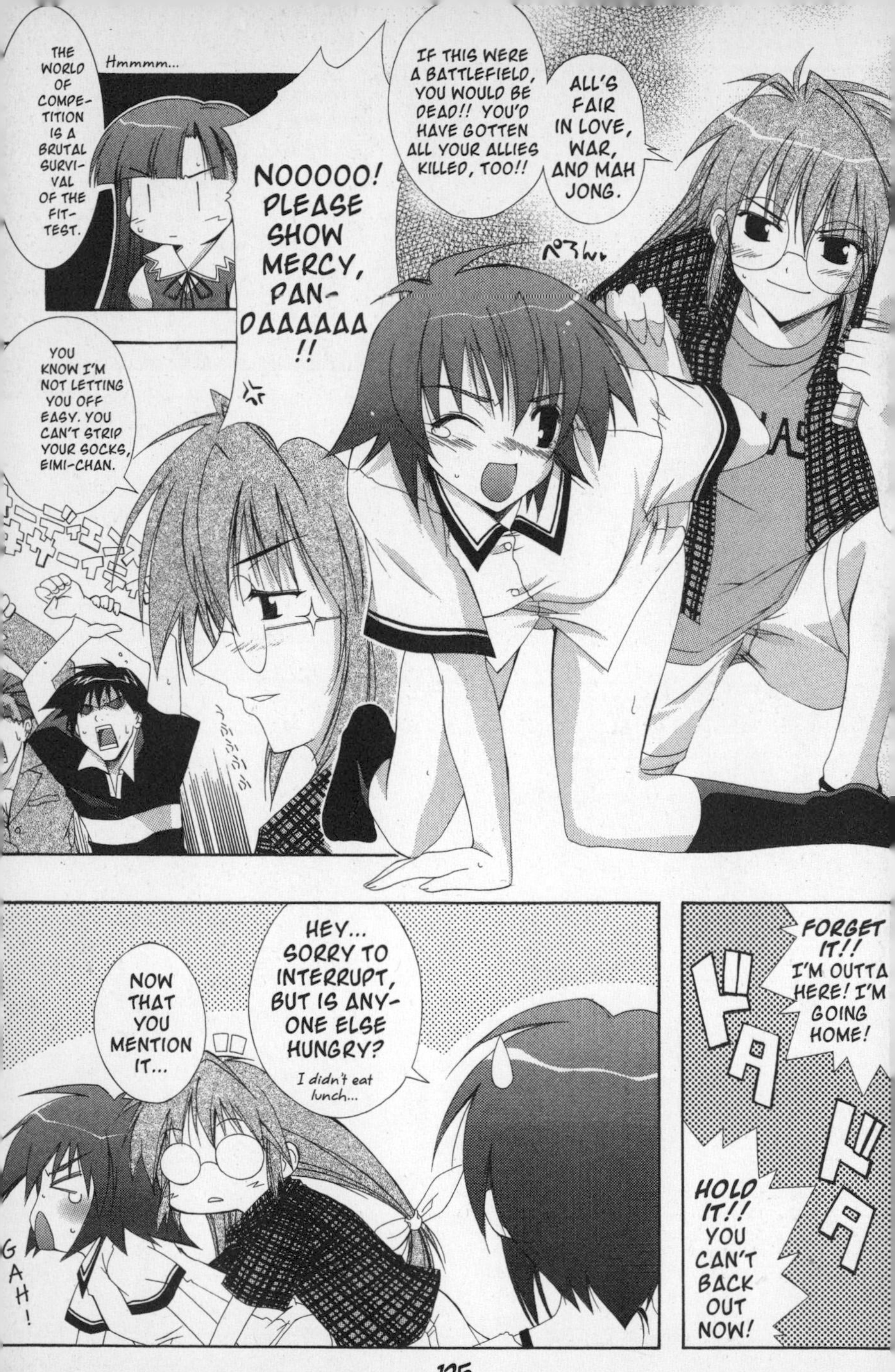
ALL'S FAIR IN LOVE, WAR, AND MAH JONG.
IF THIS WERE A BATTLEFIELD, YOU WOULD BE DEAD!! YOU'D HAVE GOTTEN ALL YOUR ALLIES KILLED, TOO!!
NOOOOO! PLEASE SHOW MERCY, PAN-DAAAAAAA!!
THE WORLD OF COMPETITION IS A BRUTAL SURVIVAL OF THE FITTEST.
Hmmmm...
YOU KNOW I'M NOT LETTING YOU OFF EASY. YOU CAN'T STRIP YOUR SOCKS, EIMI-CHAN.
FORGET IT!! I'M OUTTA HERE! I'M GOING HOME!
HOLD IT!! YOU CAN'T BACK OUT NOW!
HEY... SORRY TO INTERRUPT, BUT IS ANYONE ELSE HUNGRY?
I didn't eat lunch...
NOW THAT YOU MENTION IT...
GAH!

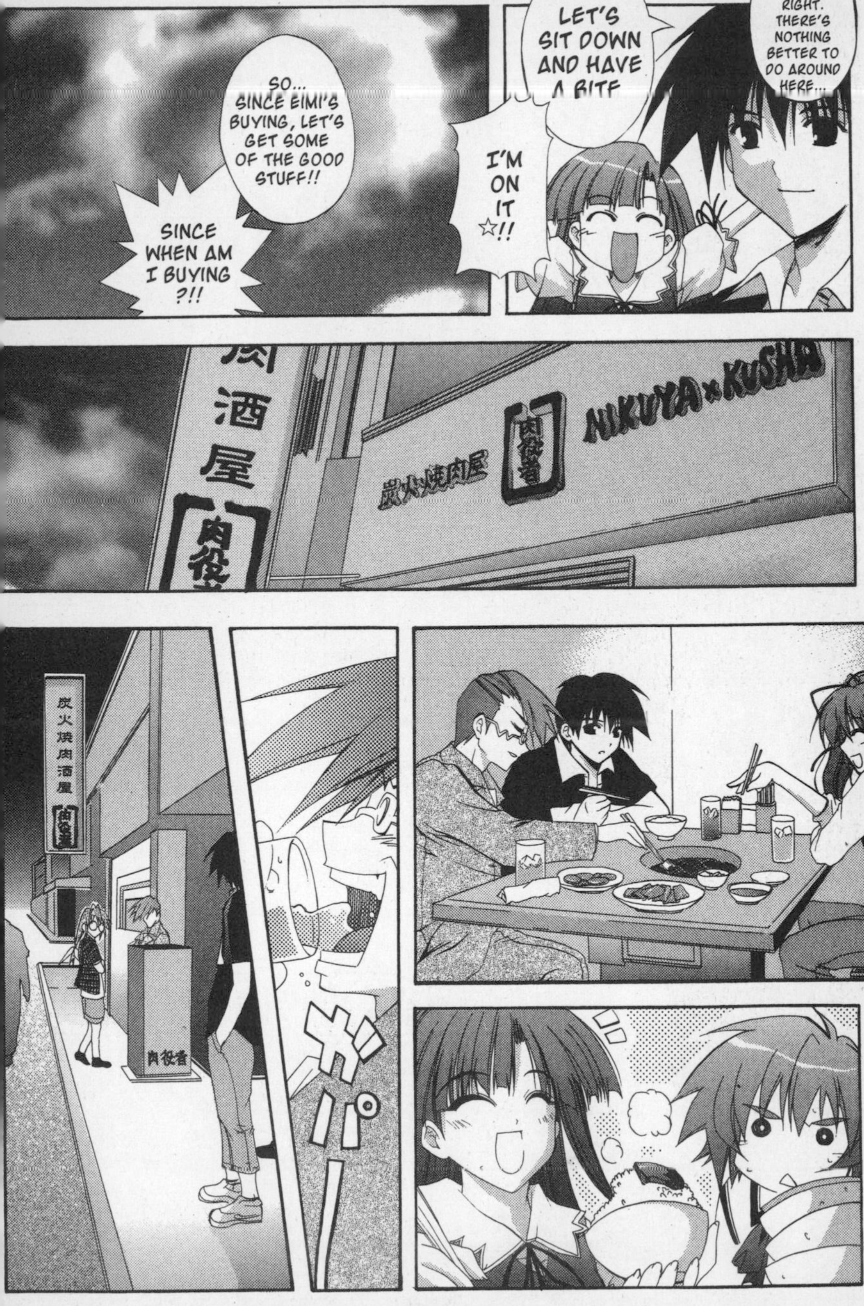
YOU'RE RIGHT. THERE'S NOTHING BETTER TO DO AROUND HERE...
LET'S SIT DOWN AND HAVE A BITE
I'M ON IT ☆!!
SO... SINCE EIMI'S BUYING, LET'S GET SOME OF THE GOOD STUFF!!
SINCE WHEN AM I BUYING ?!!
NIKUYA×KUSHA
肉役者
炭火焼肉屋
炭火焼肉酒屋
肉役者

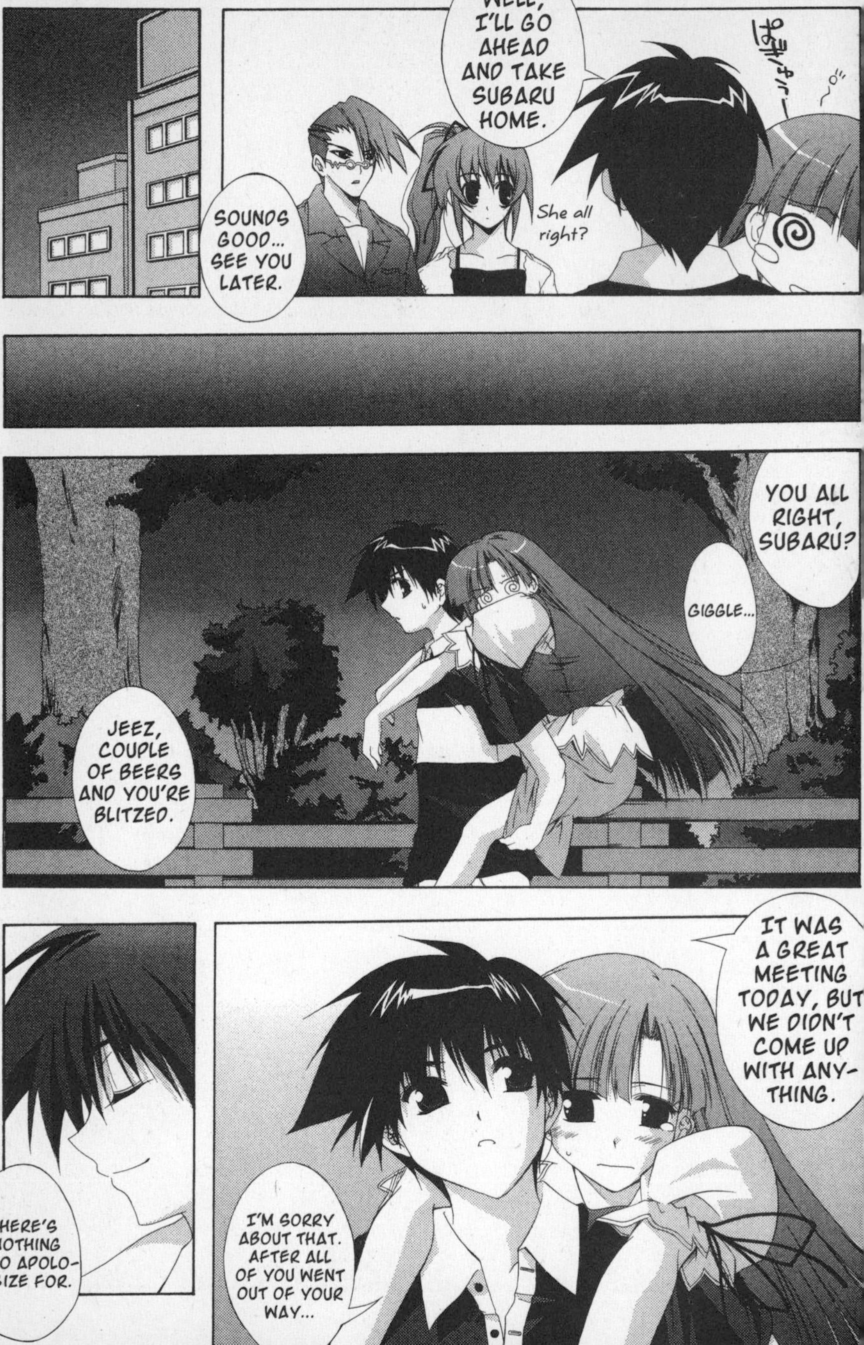
WELL, I'LL GO AHEAD AND TAKE SUBARU HOME.
She all right?
SOUNDS GOOD... SEE YOU LATER.
YOU ALL RIGHT, SUBARU?
GIGGLE...
JEEZ, COUPLE OF BEERS AND YOU'RE BLITZED.
IT WAS A GREAT MEETING TODAY, BUT WE DIDN'T COME UP WITH ANY-THING.
I'M SORRY ABOUT THAT. AFTER ALL OF YOU WENT OUT OF YOUR WAY...
THERE'S NOTHING TO APOLO-GIZE FOR.

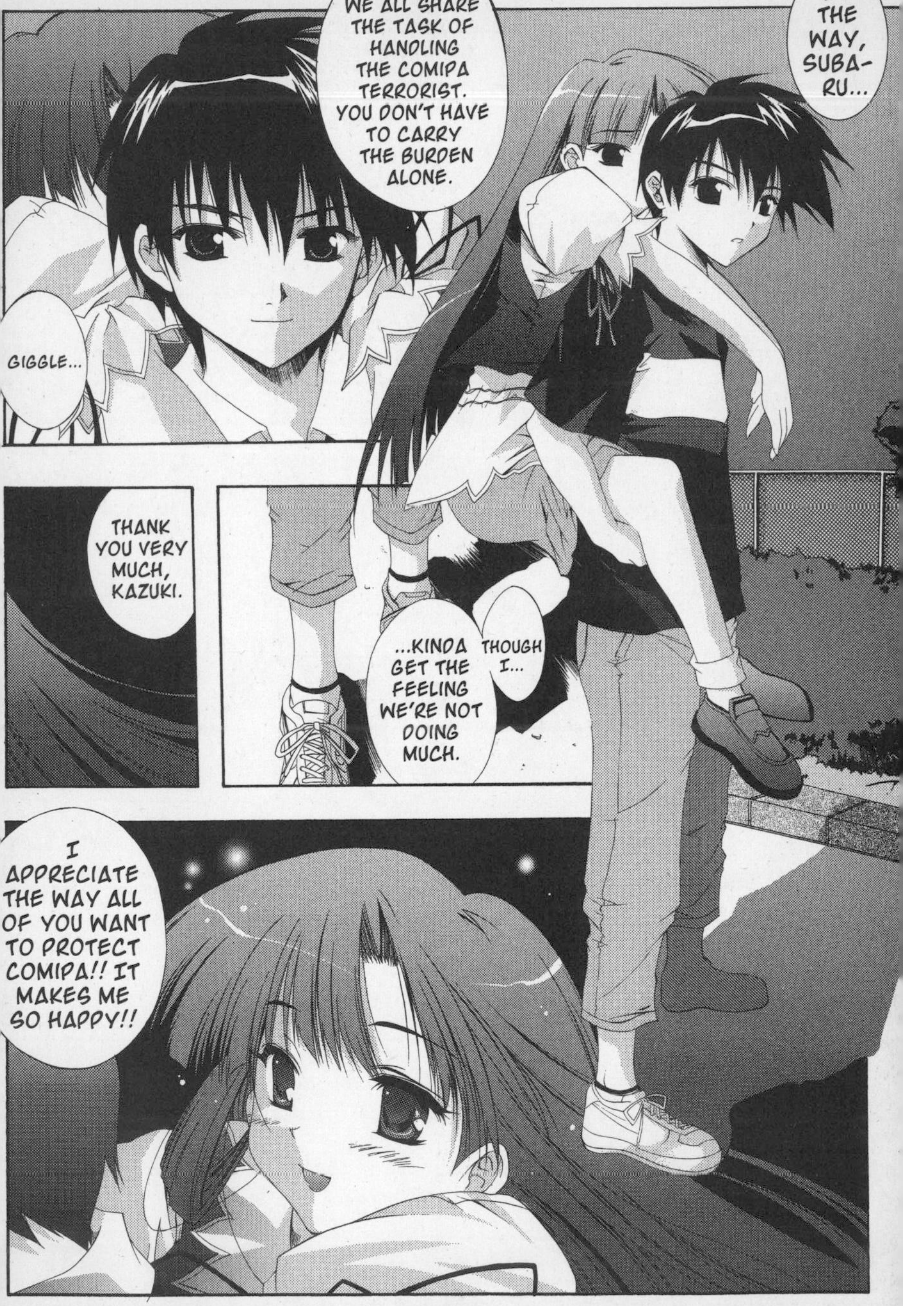

BY THE WAY, SUBA-RU...
THOUGH I...
...KINDA GET THE FEELING WE'RE NOT DOING MUCH.
WE ALL SHARE THE TASK OF HANDLING THE COMIPA TERRORIST. YOU DON'T HAVE TO CARRY THE BURDEN ALONE.
GIGGLE...
THANK YOU VERY MUCH, KAZUKI.
I APPRECIATE THE WAY ALL OF YOU WANT TO PROTECT COMIPA!! IT MAKES ME SO HAPPY!!

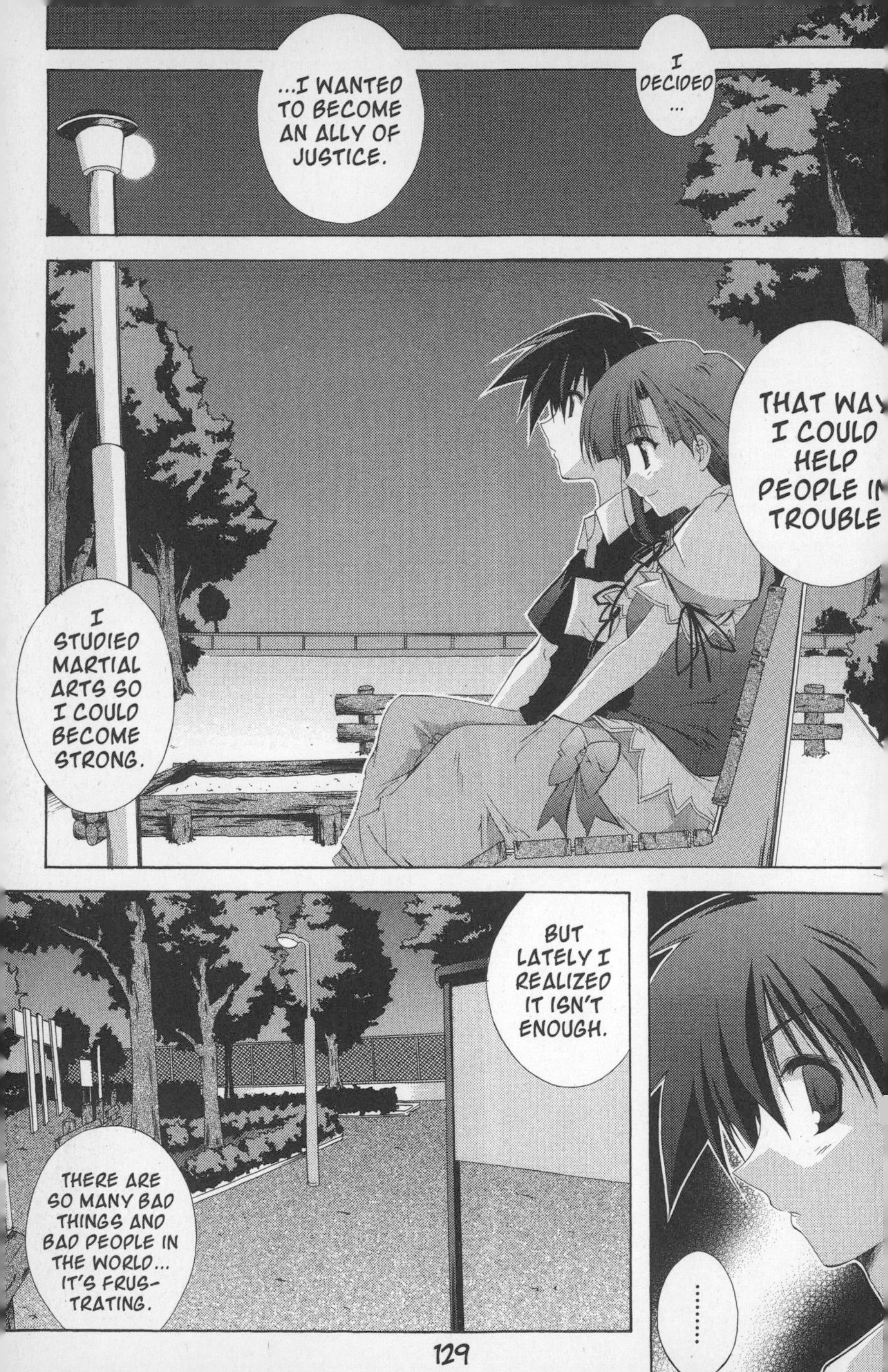
I DECIDED ...
...I WANTED TO BECOME AN ALLY OF JUSTICE.
THAT WAY I COULD HELP PEOPLE IN TROUBLE
I STUDIED MARTIAL ARTS SO I COULD BECOME STRONG.
....
BUT LATELY I REALIZED IT ISN'T ENOUGH.
THERE ARE SO MANY BAD THINGS AND BAD PEOPLE IN THE WORLD... IT'S FRUS-TRATING.

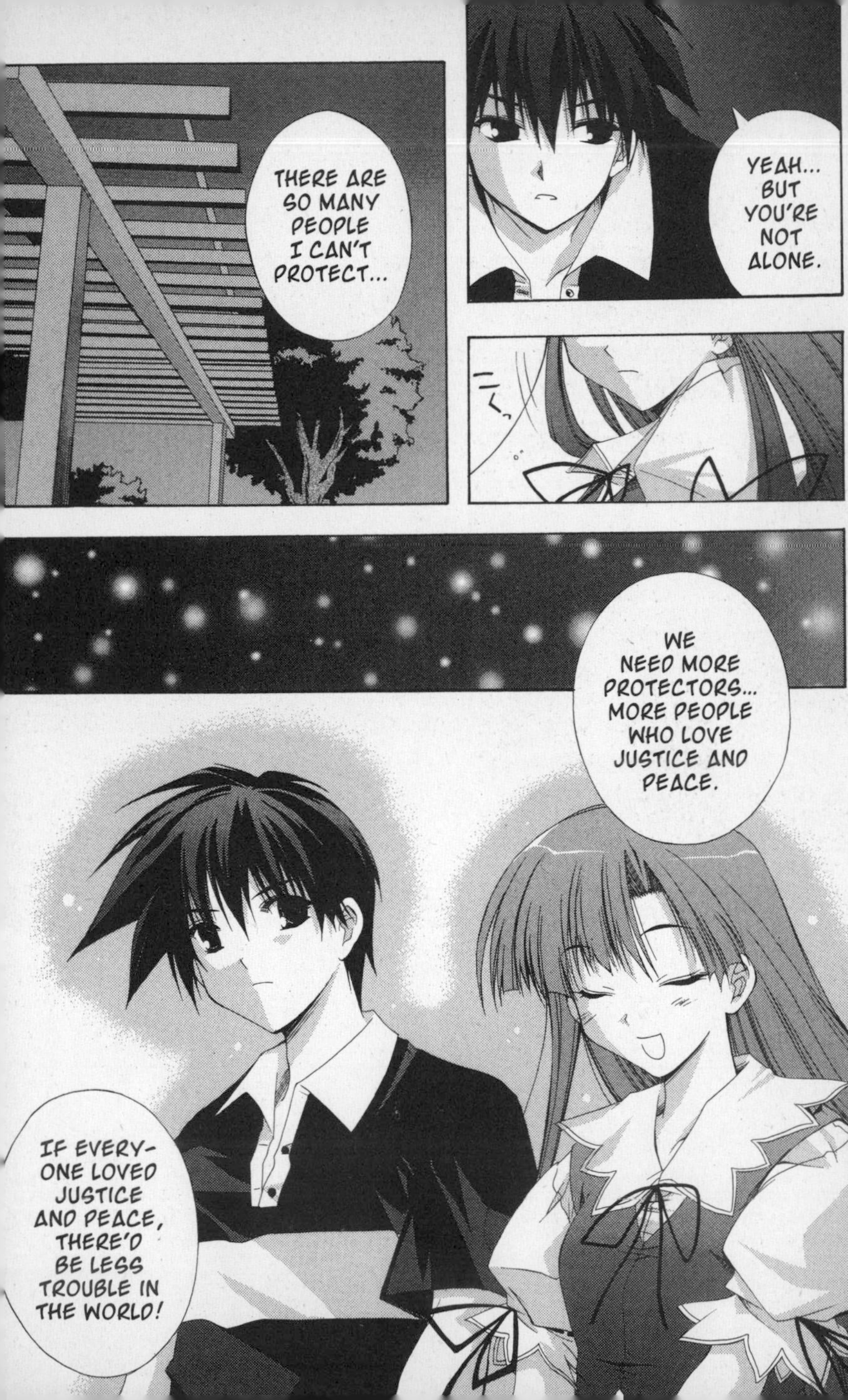
YEAH... BUT YOU'RE NOT ALONE.
THERE ARE SO MANY PEOPLE I CAN'T PROTECT...
WE NEED MORE PROTECTORS... MORE PEOPLE WHO LOVE JUSTICE AND PEACE.
IF EVERY-ONE LOVED JUSTICE AND PEACE, THERE'D BE LESS TROUBLE IN THE WORLD!

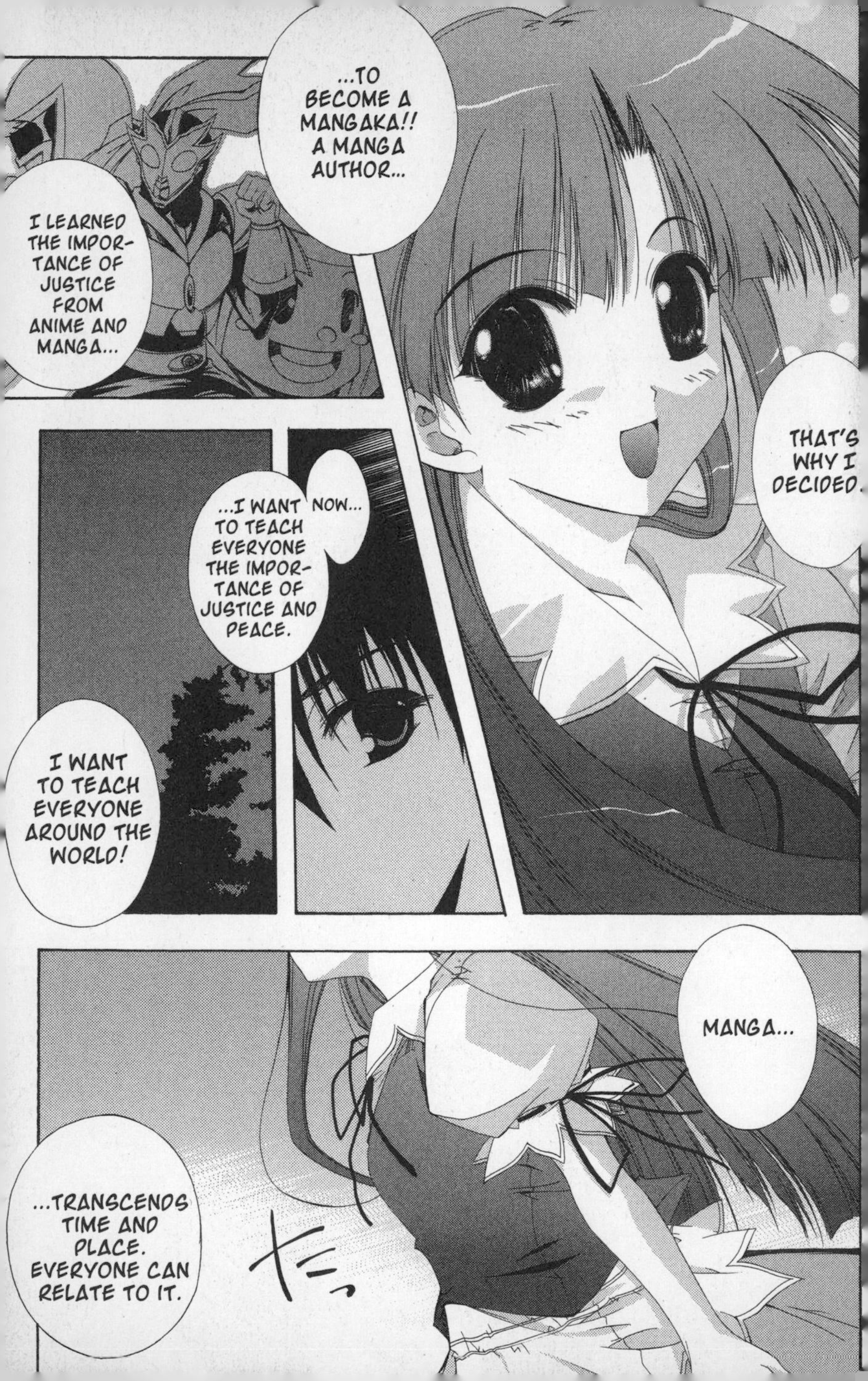
I LEARNED THE IMPORTANCE OF JUSTICE FROM ANIME AND MANGA...
THAT'S WHY I DECIDED...
...TO BECOME A MANGAKA!! A MANGA AUTHOR...
NOW...
...I WANT TO TEACH EVERYONE THE IMPORTANCE OF JUSTICE AND PEACE.
I WANT TO TEACH EVERYONE AROUND THE WORLD!
MANGA...
...TRANSCENDS TIME AND PLACE. EVERYONE CAN RELATE TO IT.

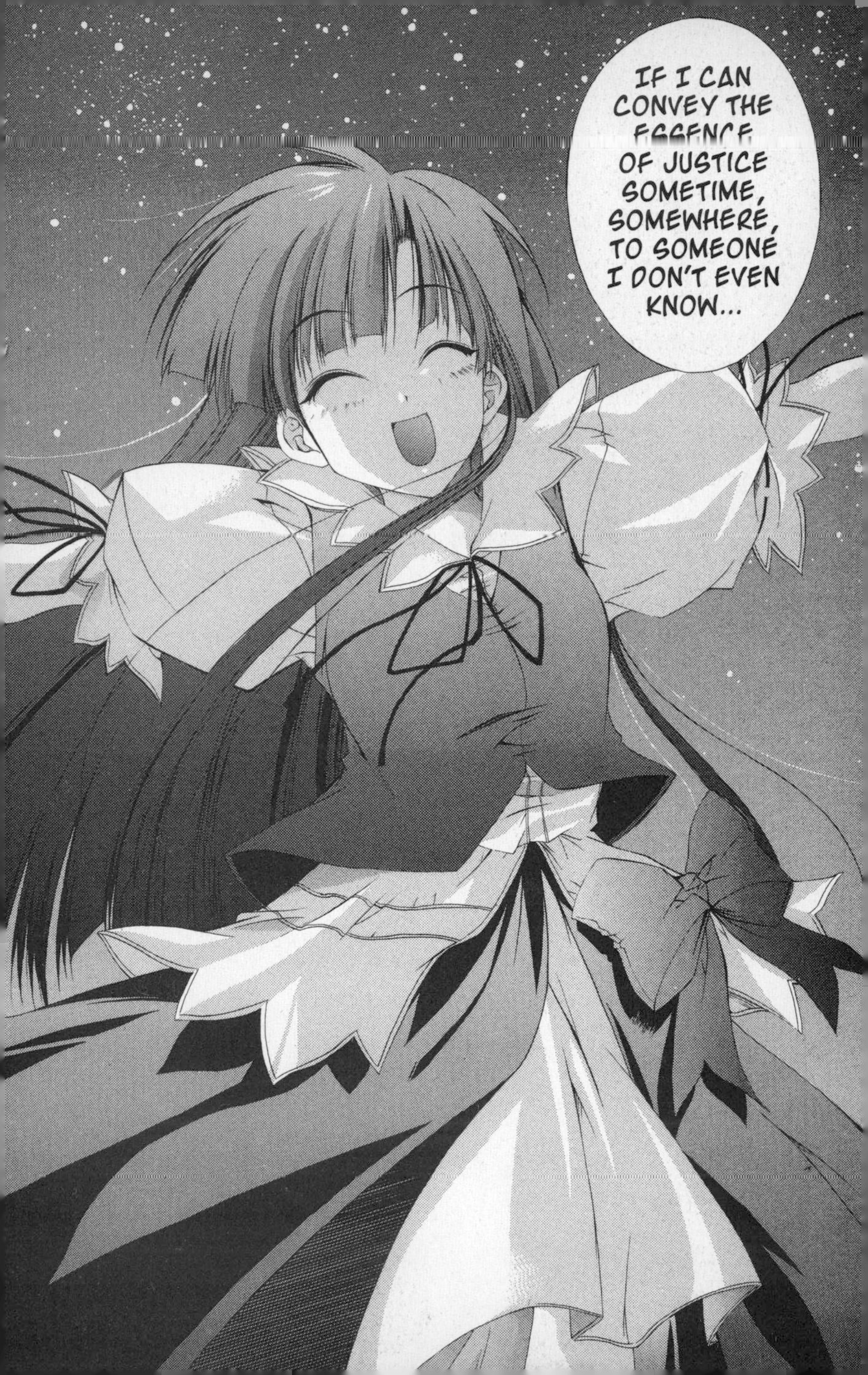
IF I CAN CONVEY THE ESSENCE OF JUSTICE SOMETIME, SOMEWHERE, TO SOMEONE I DON'T EVEN KNOW...

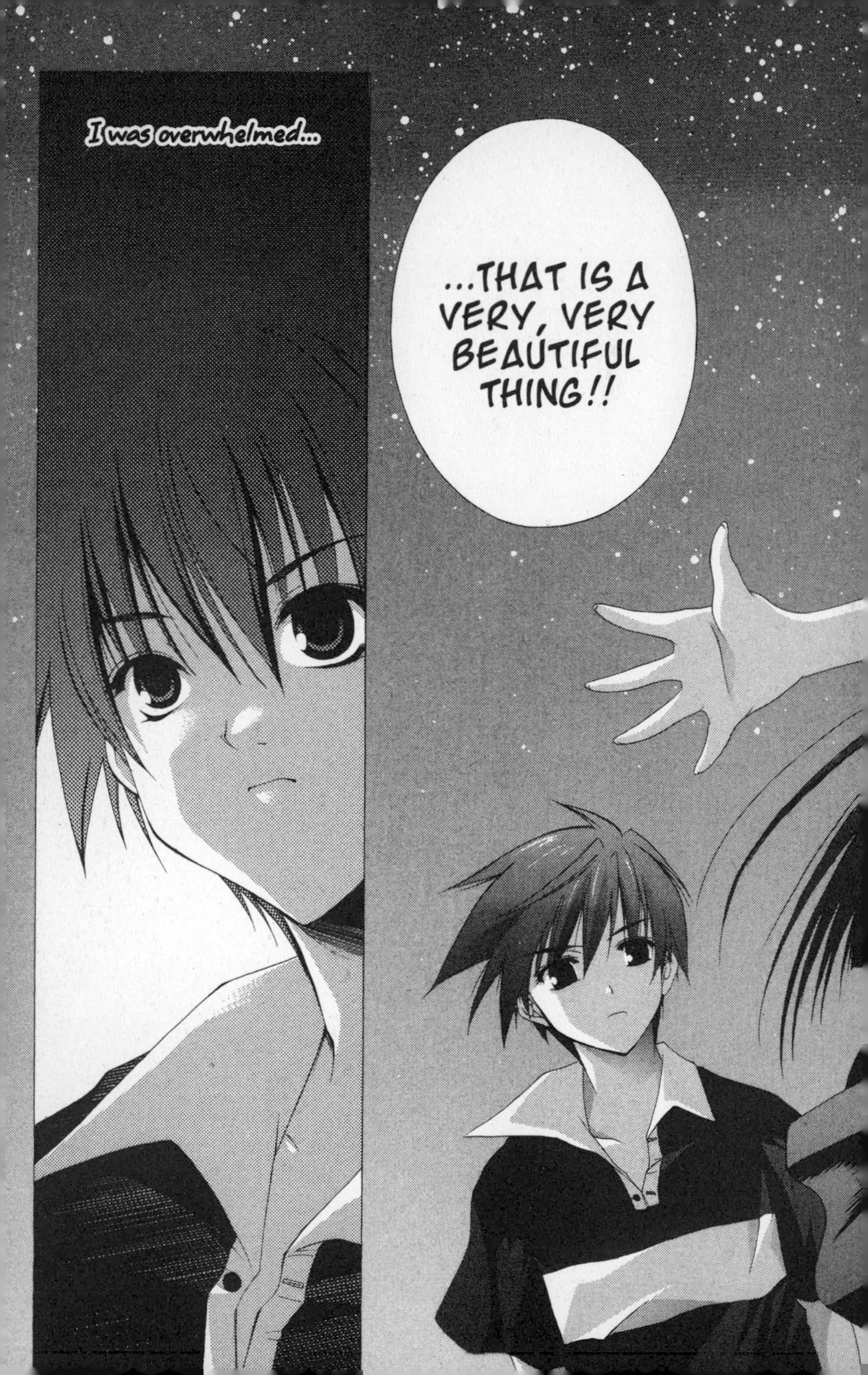
...THAT IS A VERY, VERY BEAUTIFUL THING!!
I was overwhelmed...

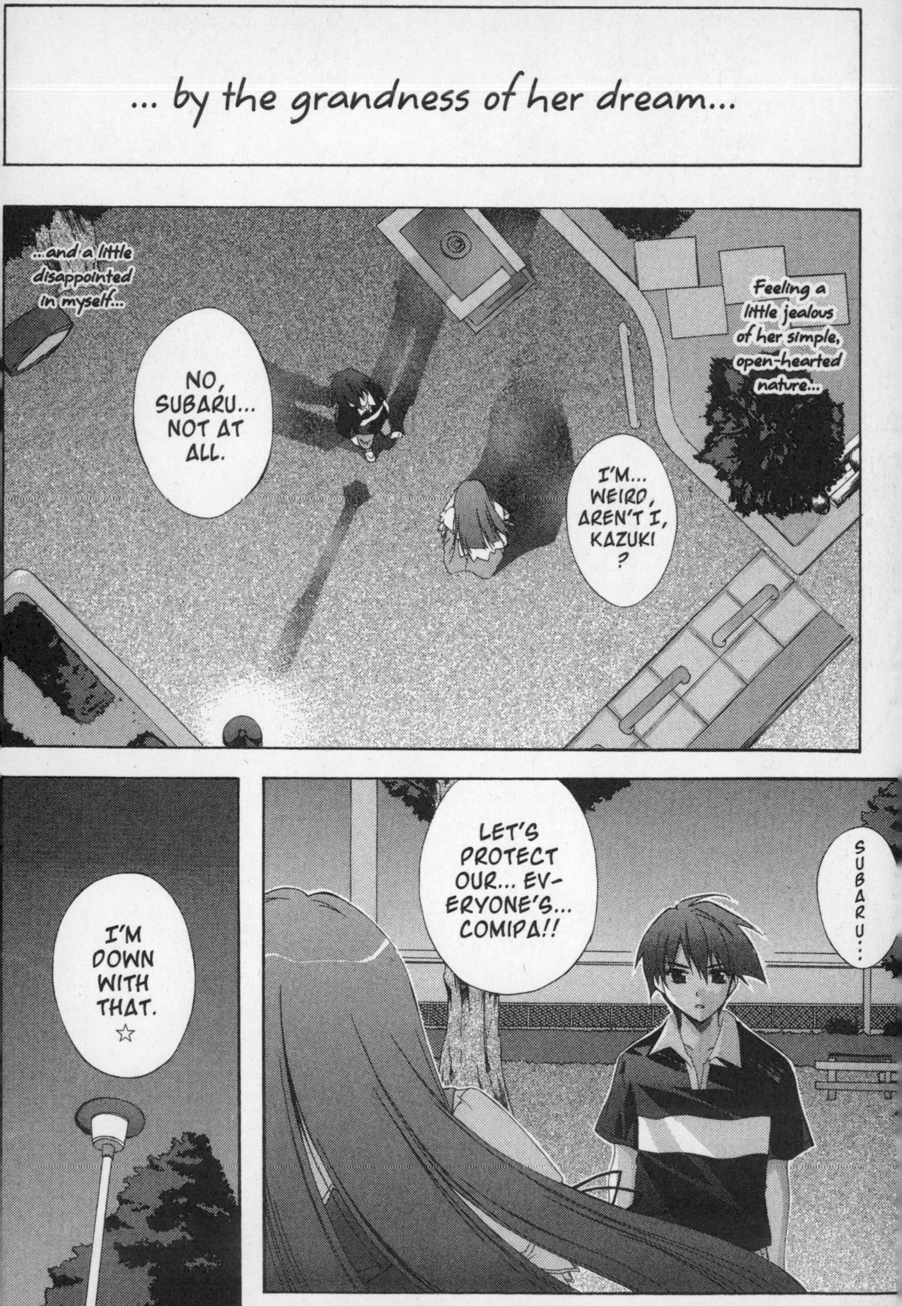
... by the grandness of her dream...
Feeling a little jealous of her simple, open-hearted nature...
...and a little disappointed in myself...
I'M... WEIRD, AREN'T I, KAZUKI?
NO, SUBARU... NOT AT ALL.
SUBARU...
LET'S PROTECT OUR... EV-ERYONE'S... COMIPA!!
I'M DOWN WITH THAT. ☆

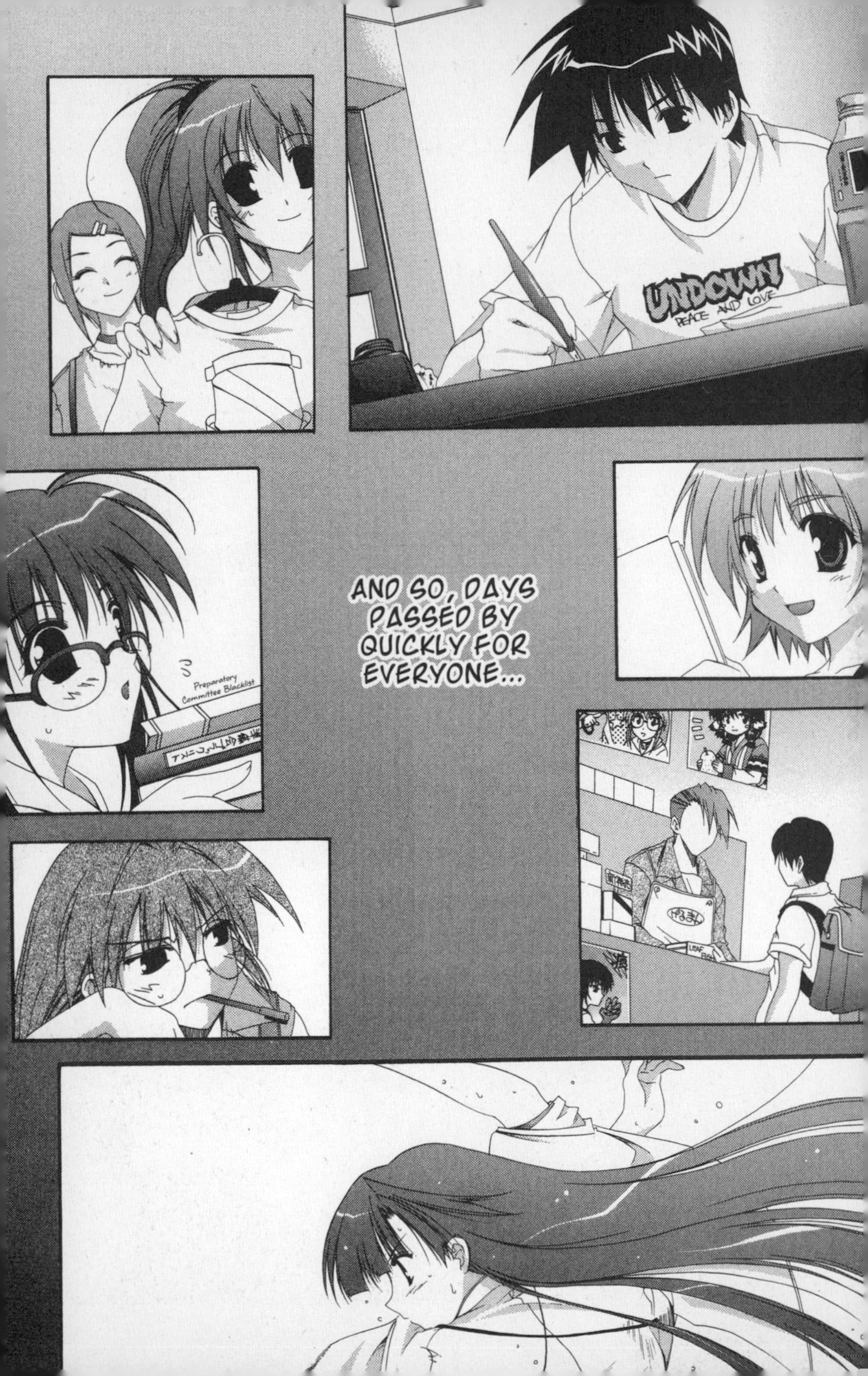
UNDOWN
PEACE AND LOVE
AND SO, DAYS PASSED BY QUICKLY FOR EVERYONE...
Preparatory Committee Blacklist

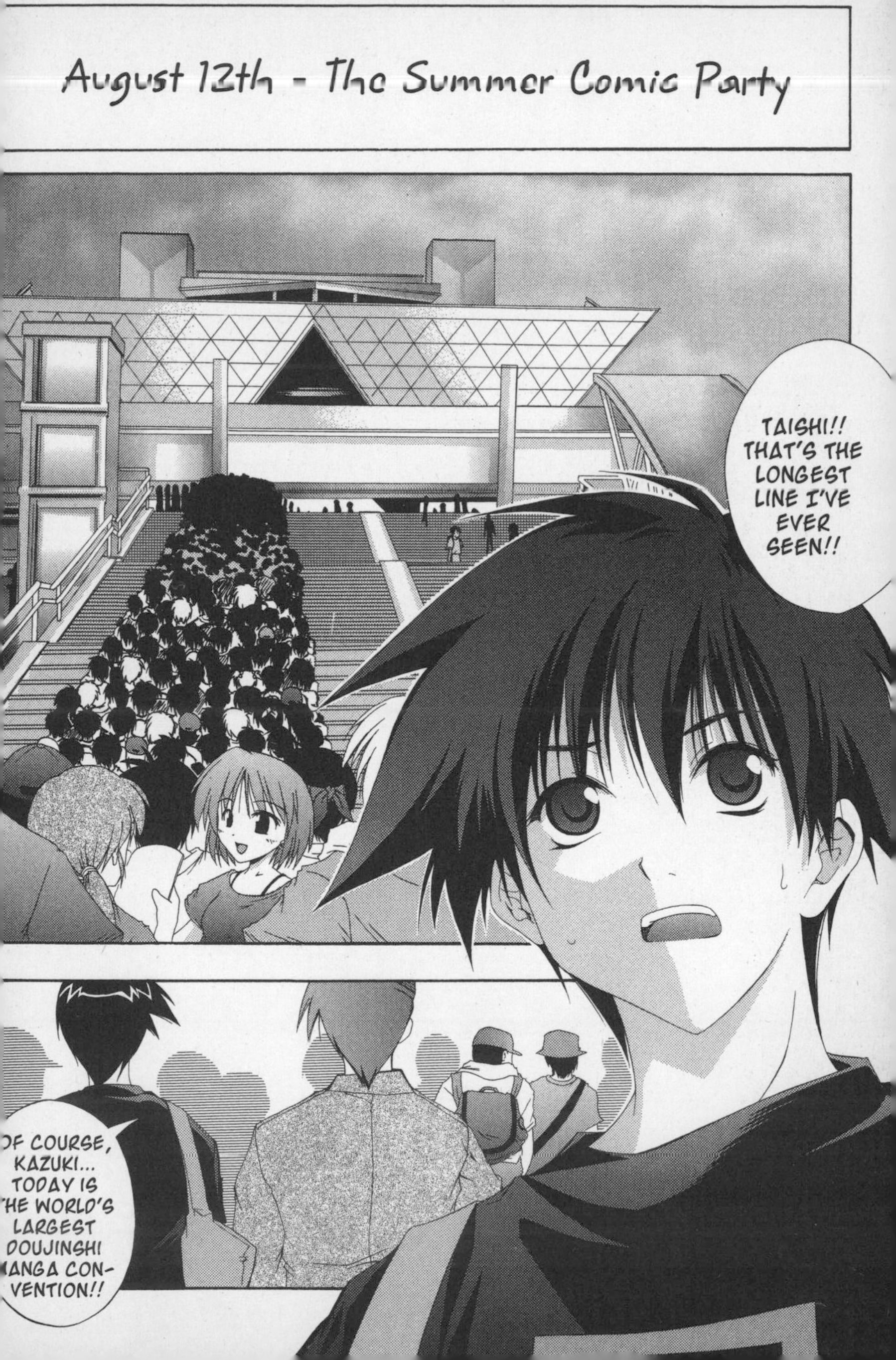
August 12th - The Summer Comic Party
TAISHI!! THAT'S THE LONGEST LINE I'VE EVER SEEN!!
OF COURSE, KAZUKI... TODAY IS THE WORLD'S LARGEST DOUJINSHI MANGA CON-VENTION!!

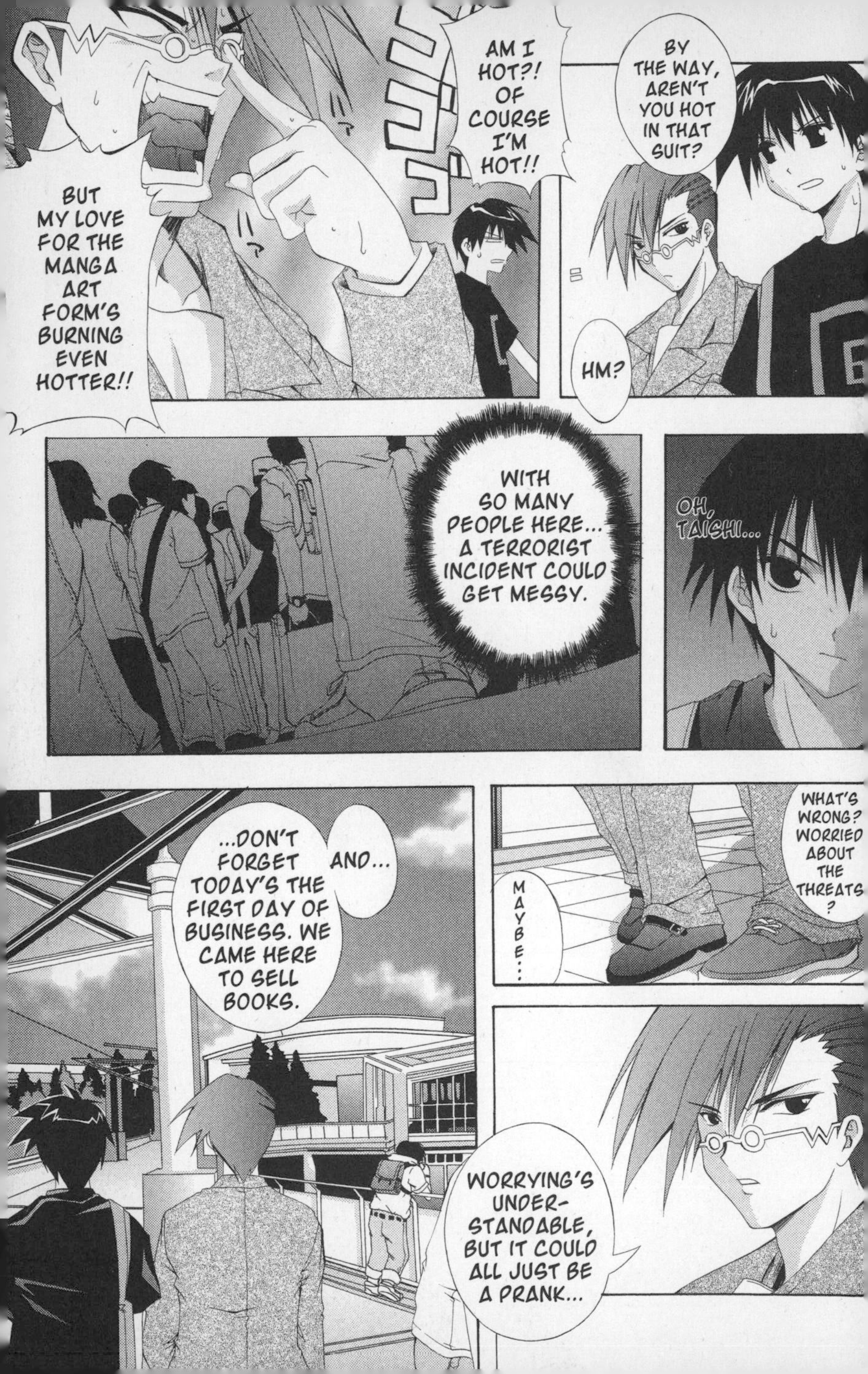
BY THE WAY, AREN'T YOU HOT IN THAT SUIT?
HM?
AM I HOT?! OF COURSE I'M HOT!!
BUT MY LOVE FOR THE MANGA ART FORM'S BURNING EVEN HOTTER!!
OH, TAISHI...
WITH SO MANY PEOPLE HERE... A TERRORIST INCIDENT COULD GET MESSY.
WHAT'S WRONG? WORRIED ABOUT THE THREATS?
MAYBE...
WORRYING'S UNDER-STANDABLE, BUT IT COULD ALL JUST BE A PRANK...
AND...
...DON'T FORGET TODAY'S THE FIRST DAY OF BUSINESS. WE CAME HERE TO SELL BOOKS.

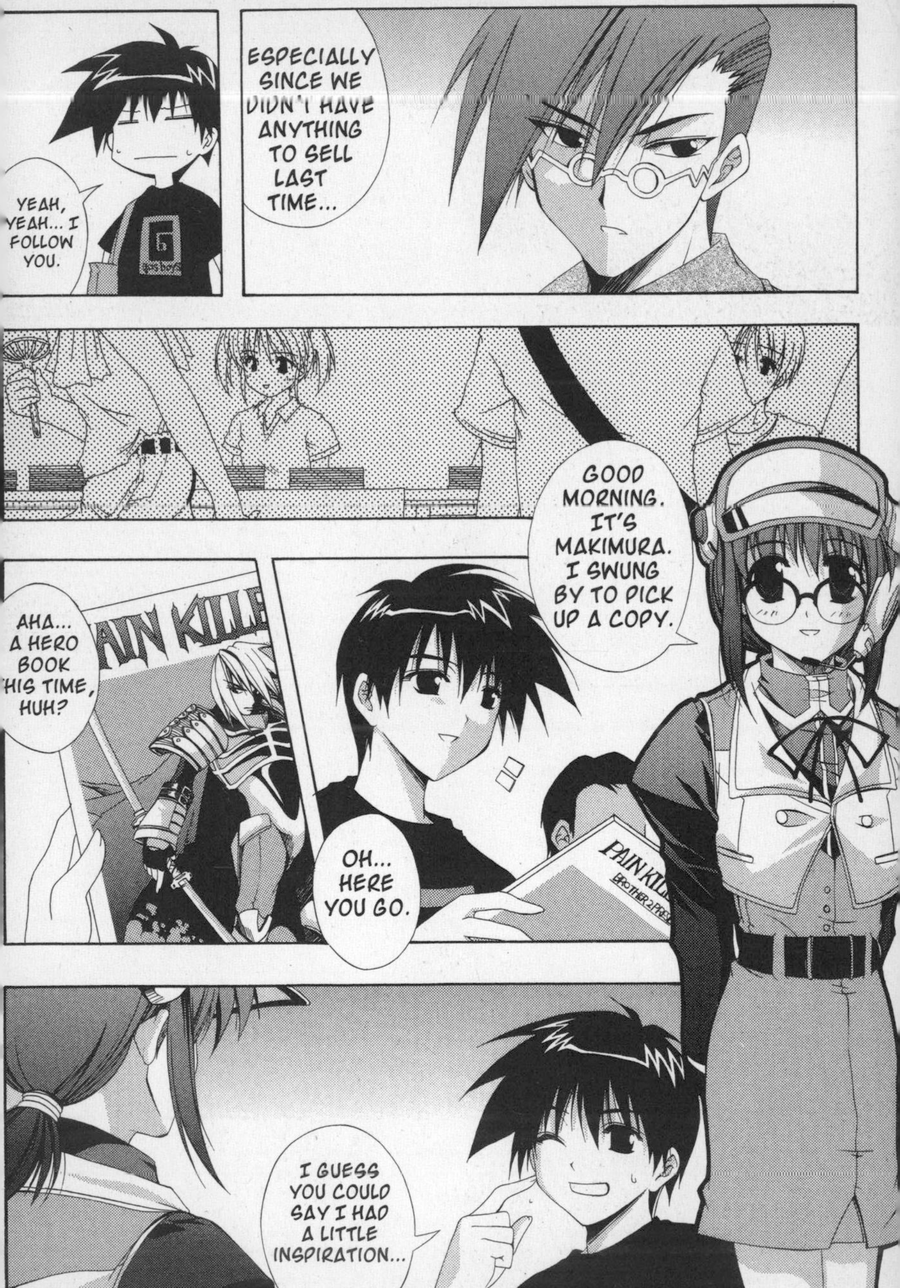
ESPECIALLY SINCE WE DIDN'T HAVE ANYTHING TO SELL LAST TIME...
YEAH, YEAH... I FOLLOW YOU.
GOOD MORNING. IT'S MAKIMURA. I SWUNG BY TO PICK UP A COPY.
OH... HERE YOU GO.
AHA... A HERO BOOK THIS TIME, HUH?
I GUESS YOU COULD SAY I HAD A LITTLE INSPIRATION...

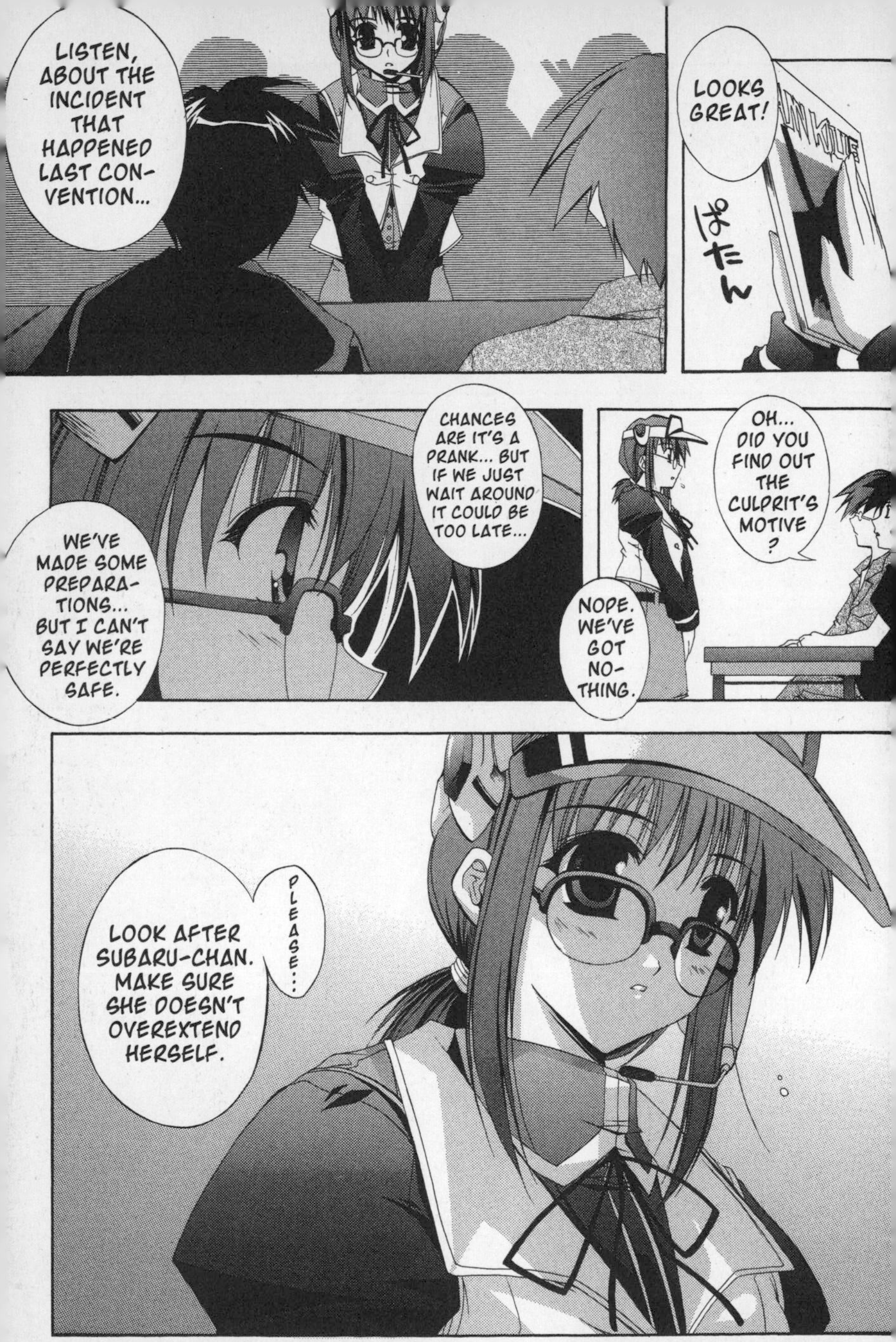
LOOKS GREAT!
ぱたん
LISTEN, ABOUT THE INCIDENT THAT HAPPENED LAST CON-VENTION...
OH... DID YOU FIND OUT THE CULPRIT'S MOTIVE?
NOPE. WE'VE GOT NO-THING.
CHANCES ARE IT'S A PRANK... BUT IF WE JUST WAIT AROUND IT COULD BE TOO LATE...
WE'VE MADE SOME PREPARA-TIONS... BUT I CAN'T SAY WE'RE PERFECTLY SAFE.
PLEASE...
LOOK AFTER SUBARU-CHAN. MAKE SURE SHE DOESN'T OVEREXTEND HERSELF.

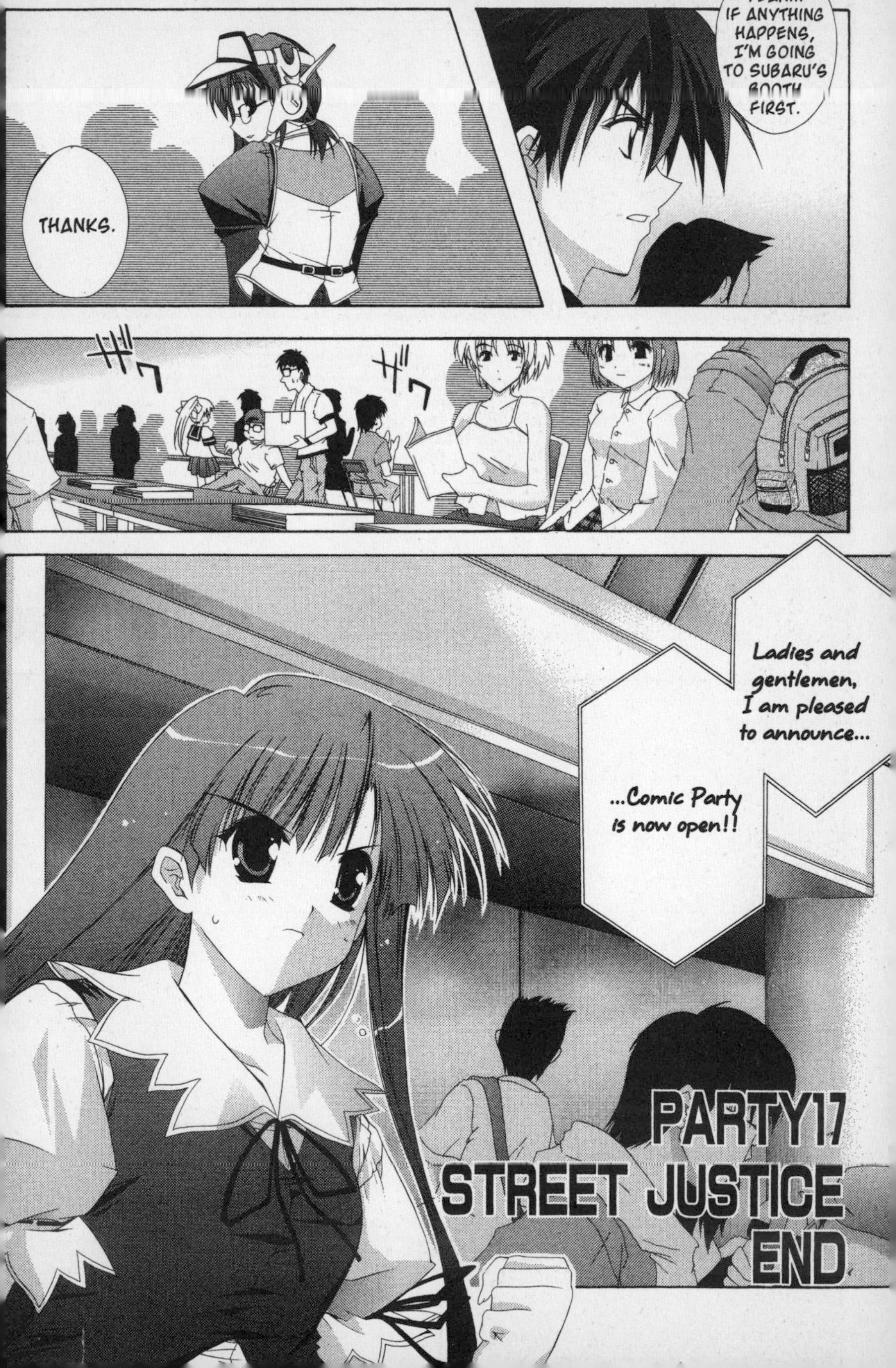
YEAH... IF ANYTHING HAPPENS, I'M GOING TO SUBARU'S BOOTH FIRST.
THANKS.
ザワ
ザワ
Ladies and gentlemen, I am pleased to announce...
...Comic Party is now open!!
PARTY17 STREET JUSTICE END

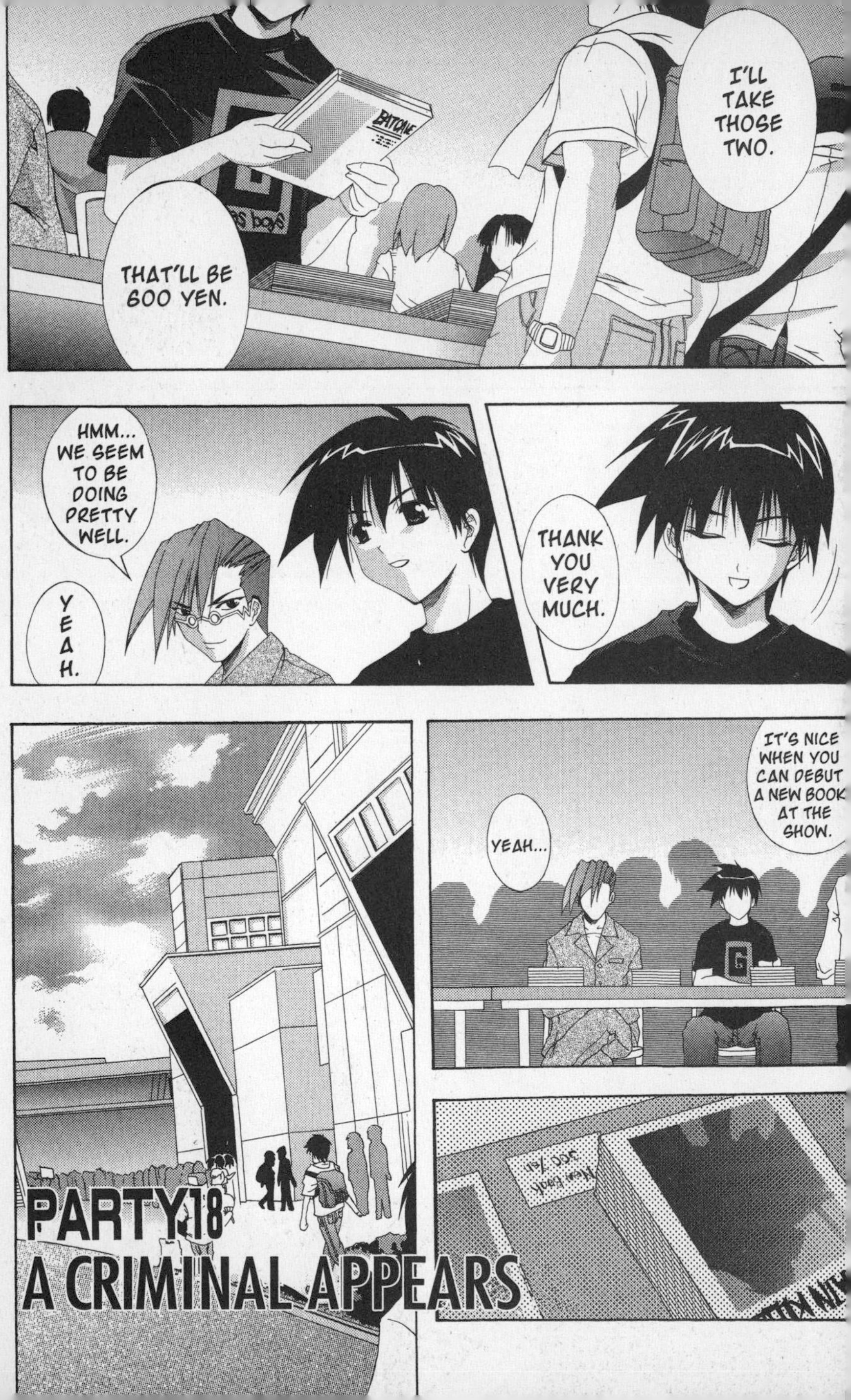
I'LL TAKE THOSE TWO.
THAT'LL BE 600 YEN.
THANK YOU VERY MUCH.
HMM... WE SEEM TO BE DOING PRETTY WELL.
YEAH.
IT'S NICE WHEN YOU CAN DEBUT A NEW BOOK AT THE SHOW.
YEAH...
PARTY 18
A CRIMINAL APPEARS

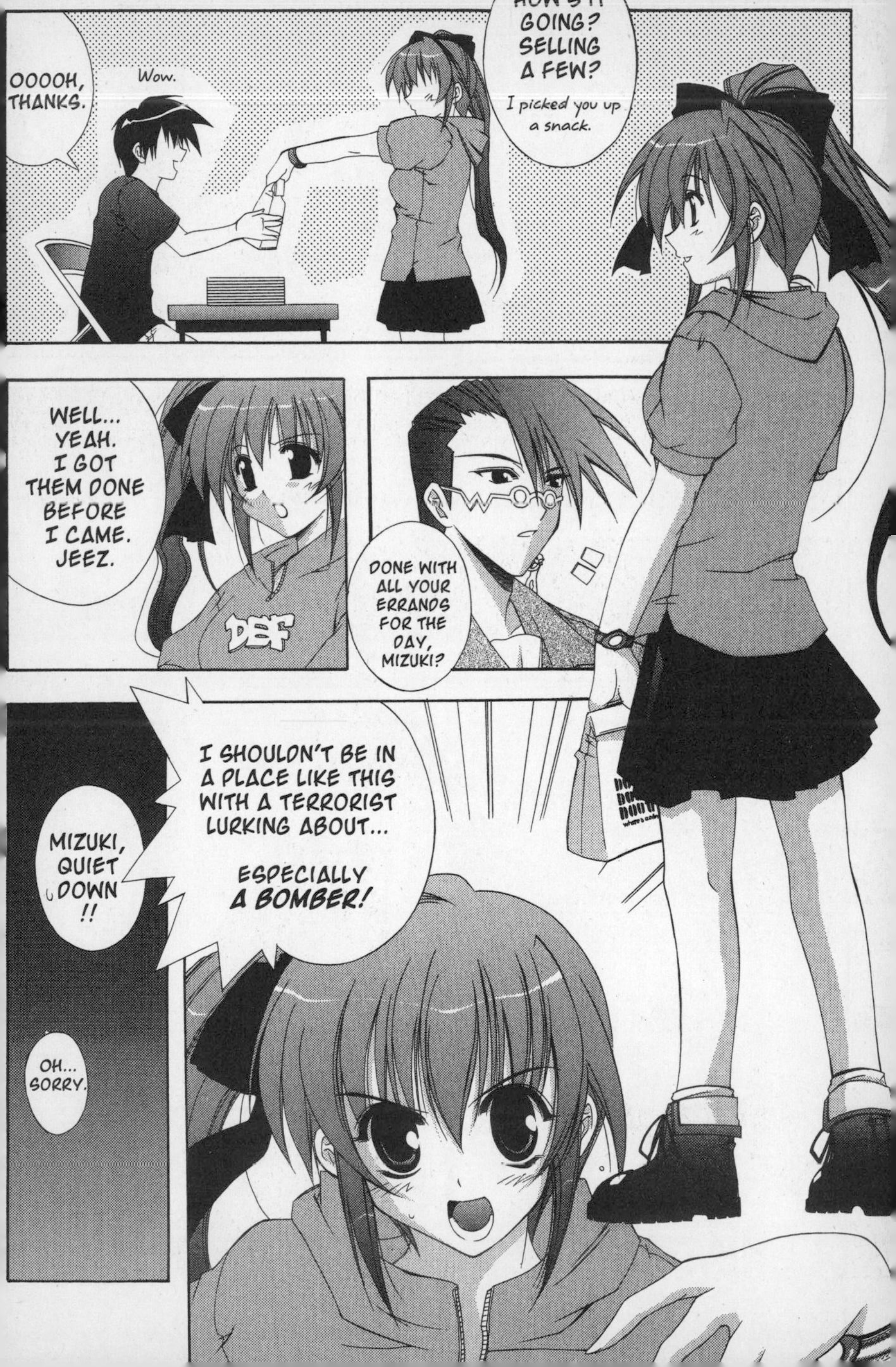
HOW'S IT GOING? SELLING A FEW?
I picked you up a snack.
Wow.
OOOOH, THANKS.
DONE WITH ALL YOUR ERRANDS FOR THE DAY, MIZUKI?
WELL... YEAH. I GOT THEM DONE BEFORE I CAME. JEEZ.
DEF
I SHOULDN'T BE IN A PLACE LIKE THIS WITH A TERRORIST LURKING ABOUT...
ESPECIALLY A BOMBER!
MIZUKI, QUIET DOWN!!
OH... SORRY.

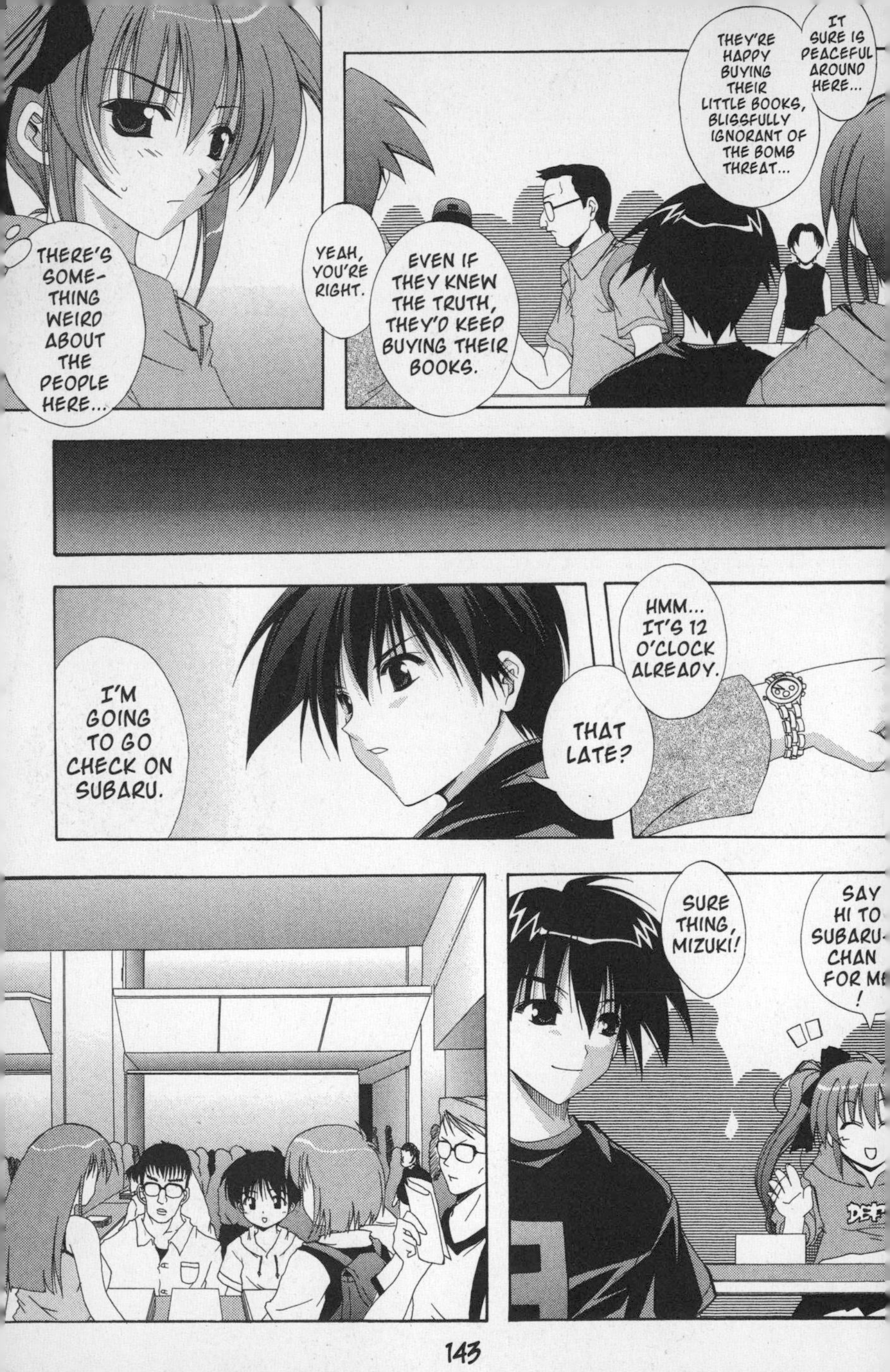
IT SURE IS PEACEFUL AROUND HERE...
THEY'RE HAPPY BUYING THEIR LITTLE BOOKS, BLISSFULLY IGNORANT OF THE BOMB THREAT...
EVEN IF THEY KNEW THE TRUTH, THEY'D KEEP BUYING THEIR BOOKS.
YEAH, YOU'RE RIGHT.
THERE'S SOME-THING WEIRD ABOUT THE PEOPLE HERE...
HMM... IT'S 12 O'CLOCK ALREADY.
THAT LATE?
I'M GOING TO GO CHECK ON SUBARU.
SAY HI TO SUBARU-CHAN FOR ME!
SURE THING, MIZUKI!

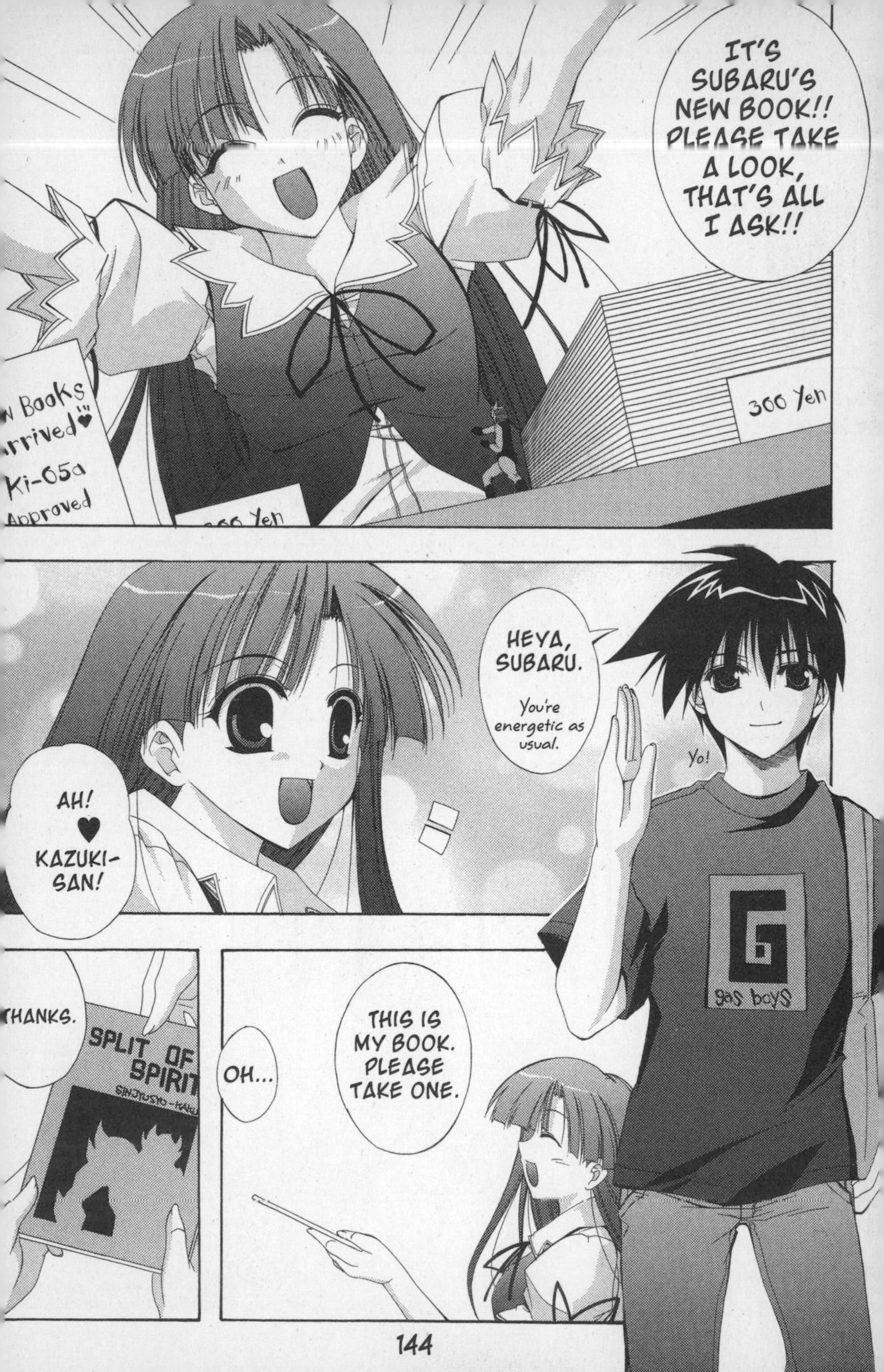
IT'S SUBARU'S NEW BOOK!! PLEASE TAKE A LOOK, THAT'S ALL I ASK!!
300 Yen
Ki-05a
Approved
HEYA, SUBARU.
You're energetic as usual.
Yo!
gas boys
AH! ♥ KAZUKI-SAN!
THIS IS MY BOOK. PLEASE TAKE ONE.
OH...
THANKS.
SPLIT OF SPIRIT

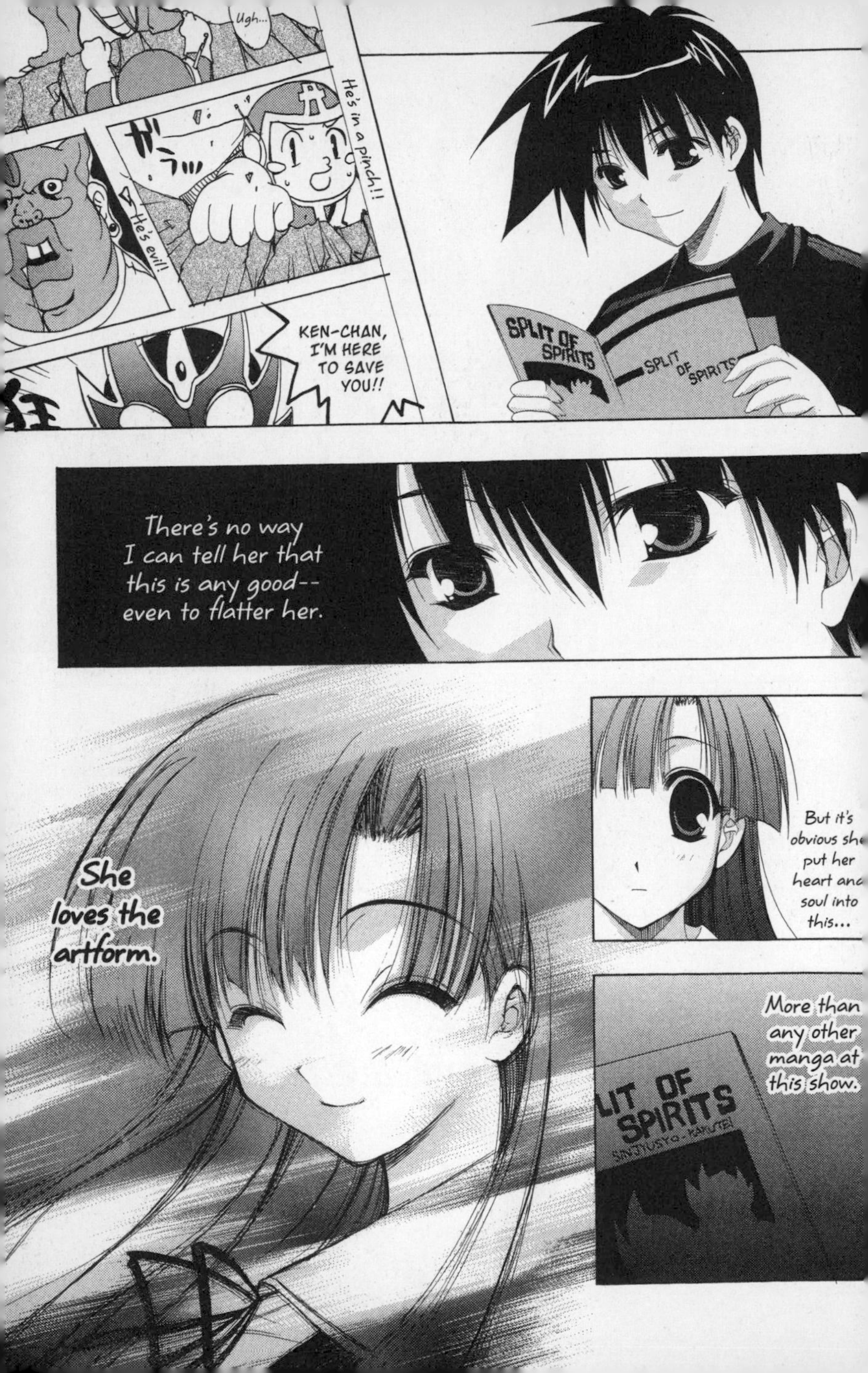
SPLIT OF SPIRITS
SPLIT OF SPIRITS
Ugh...
He's in a pinch!!
He's evil!
KEN-CHAN, I'M HERE TO SAVE YOU!!
There's no way I can tell her that this is any good-- even to flatter her.
But it's obvious sh put her heart an soul into this...
LIT OF SPIRITS
More than any other manga at this show.
She loves the artform.

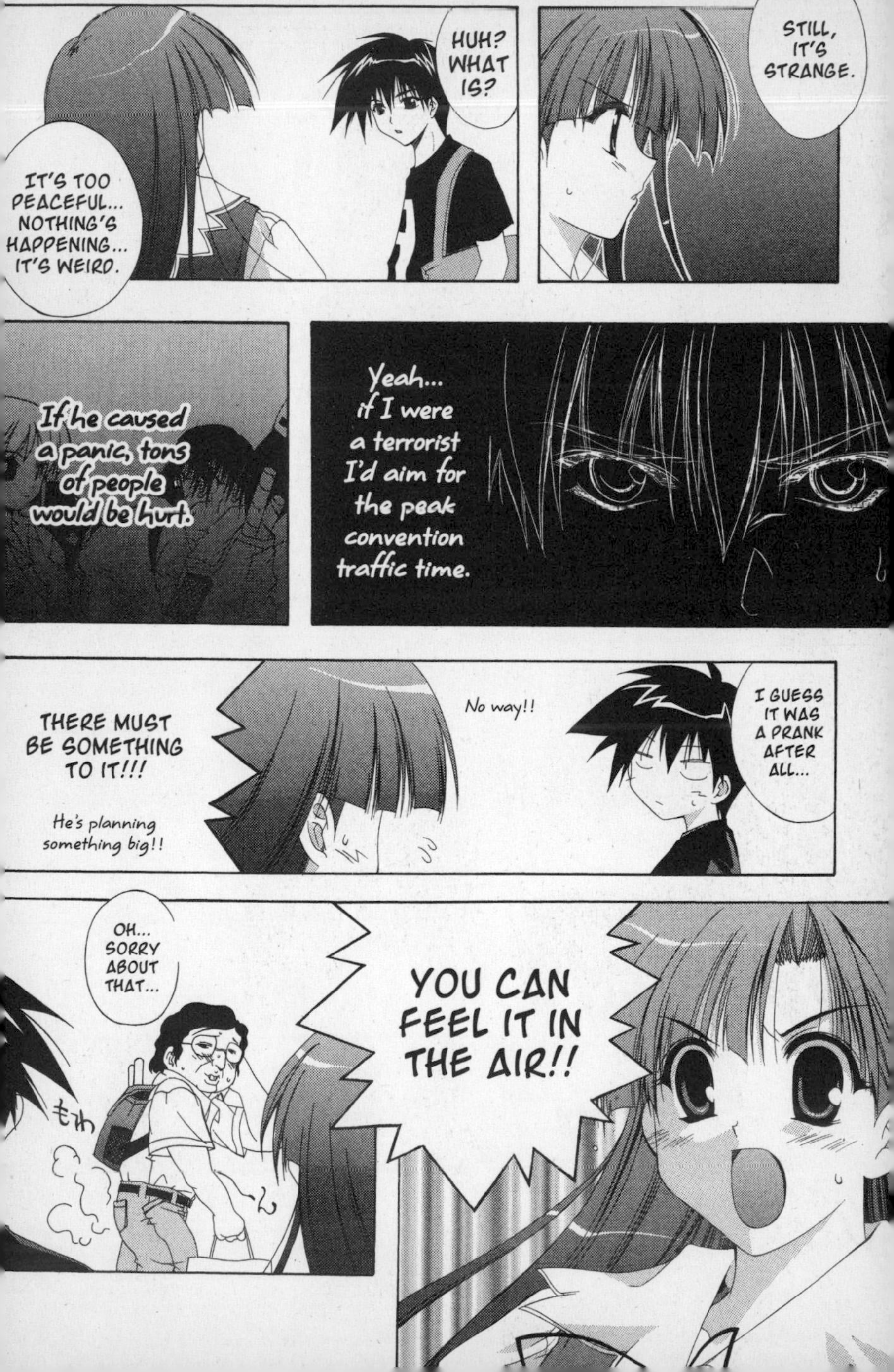
STILL, IT'S STRANGE.
HUH? WHAT IS?
IT'S TOO PEACEFUL... NOTHING'S HAPPENING... IT'S WEIRD.
Yeah... if I were a terrorist I'd aim for the peak convention traffic time.
If he caused a panic, tons of people would be hurt.
I GUESS IT WAS A PRANK AFTER ALL...
No way!!
THERE MUST BE SOMETHING TO IT!!!
He's planning something big!!
YOU CAN FEEL IT IN THE AIR!!
OH... SORRY ABOUT THAT...
もわ

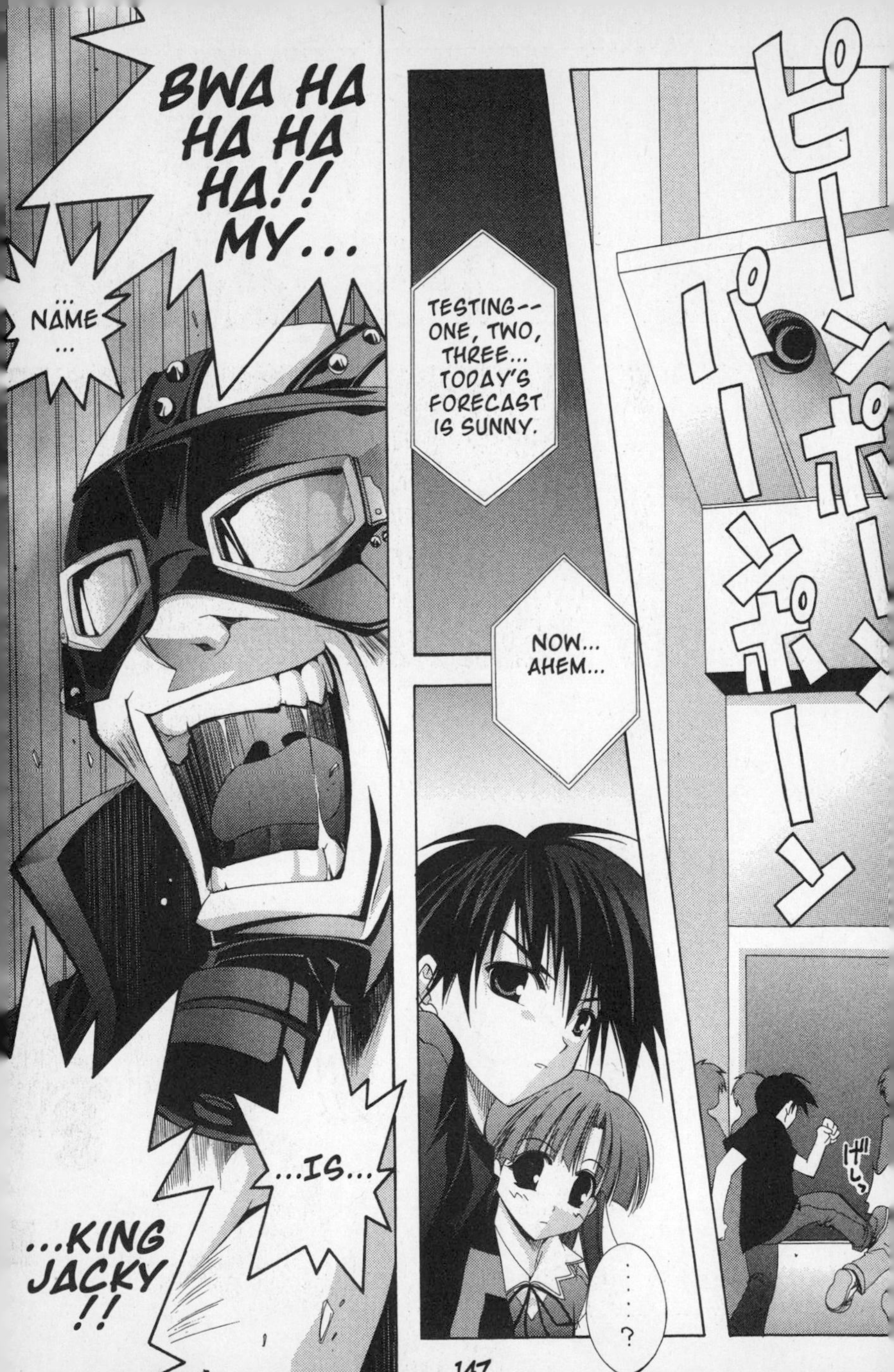
ピーンポーン
パーンポーン
TESTING--ONE, TWO, THREE... TODAY'S FORECAST IS SUNNY.
NOW... AHEM...
......?
BWA HA HA HA HA!! MY...
...NAME...
...IS...
...KING JACKY!!

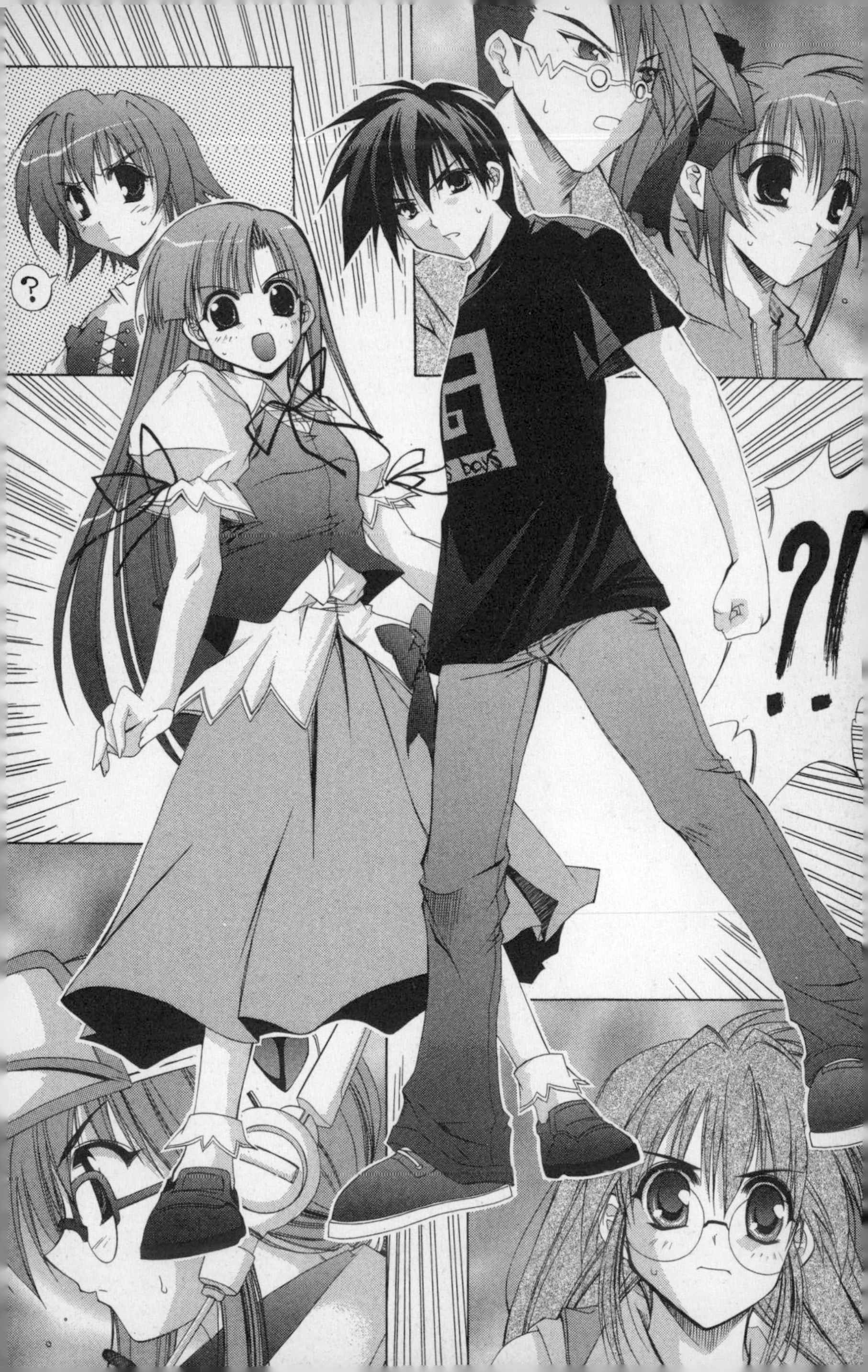
?!
?

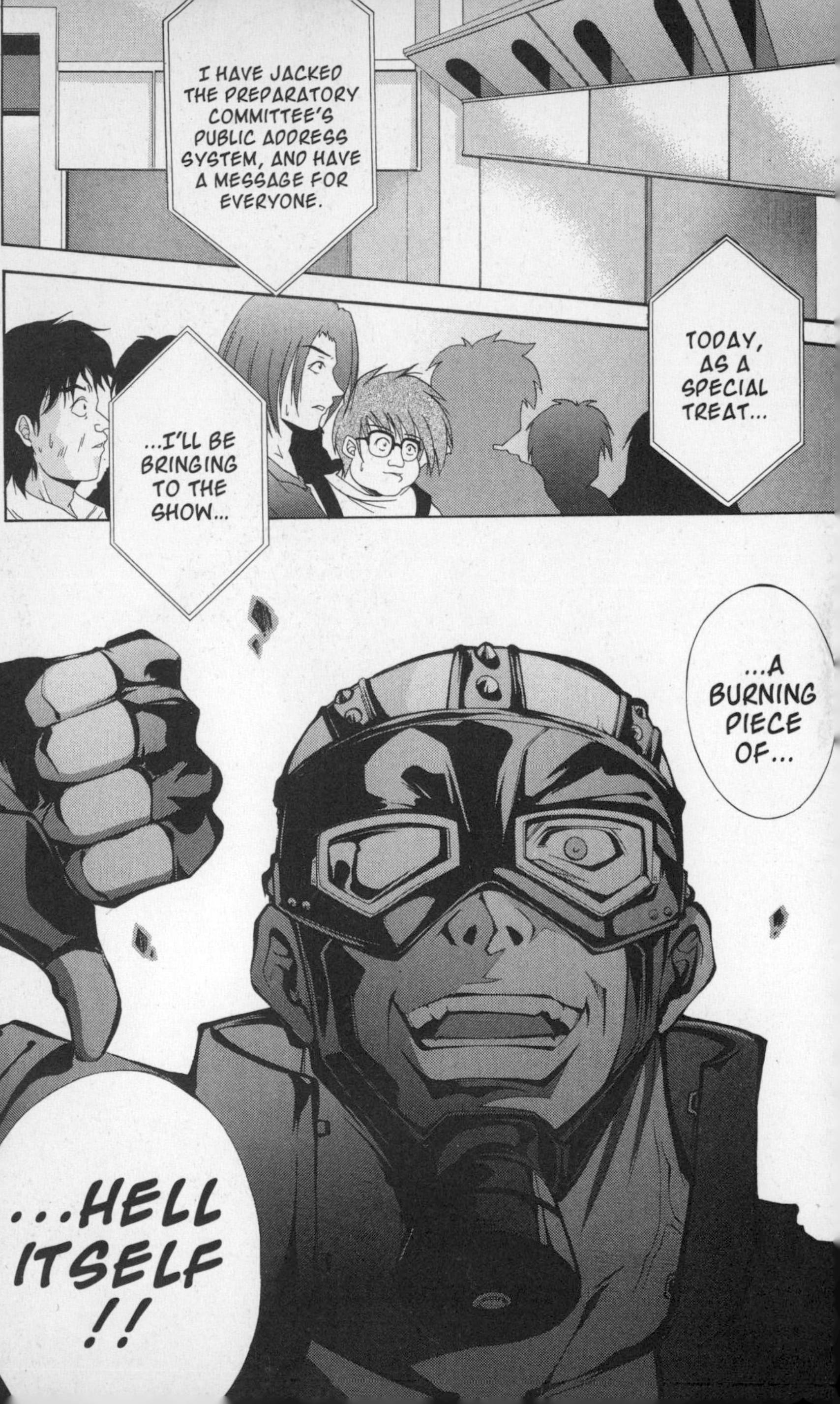
I HAVE JACKED THE PREPARATORY COMMITTEE'S PUBLIC ADDRESS SYSTEM, AND HAVE A MESSAGE FOR EVERYONE.
TODAY, AS A SPECIAL TREAT...
...I'LL BE BRINGING TO THE SHOW...
...A BURNING PIECE OF...
...HELL ITSELF!!

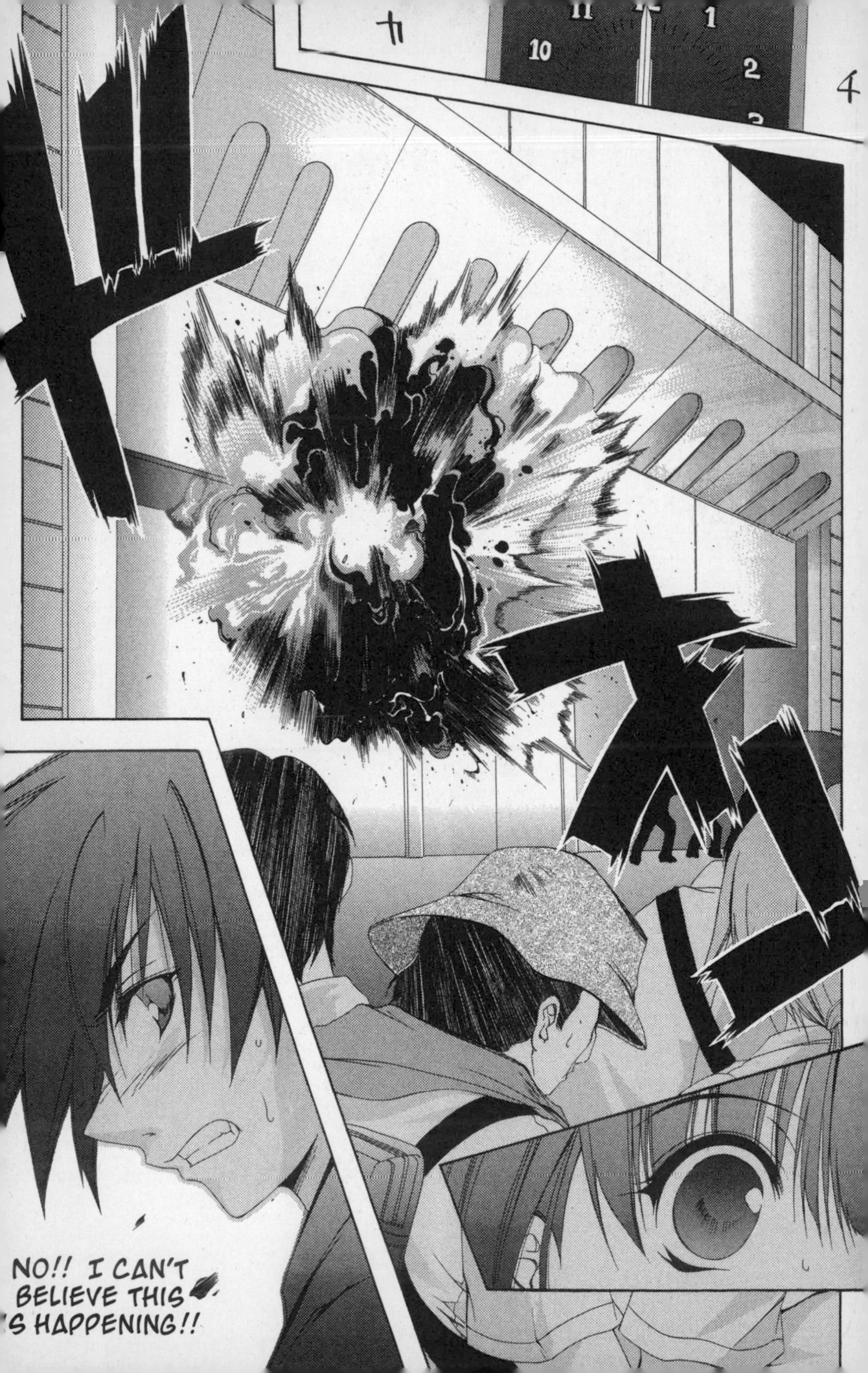

NO!! I CAN'T BELIEVE THIS 'S HAPPENING!!

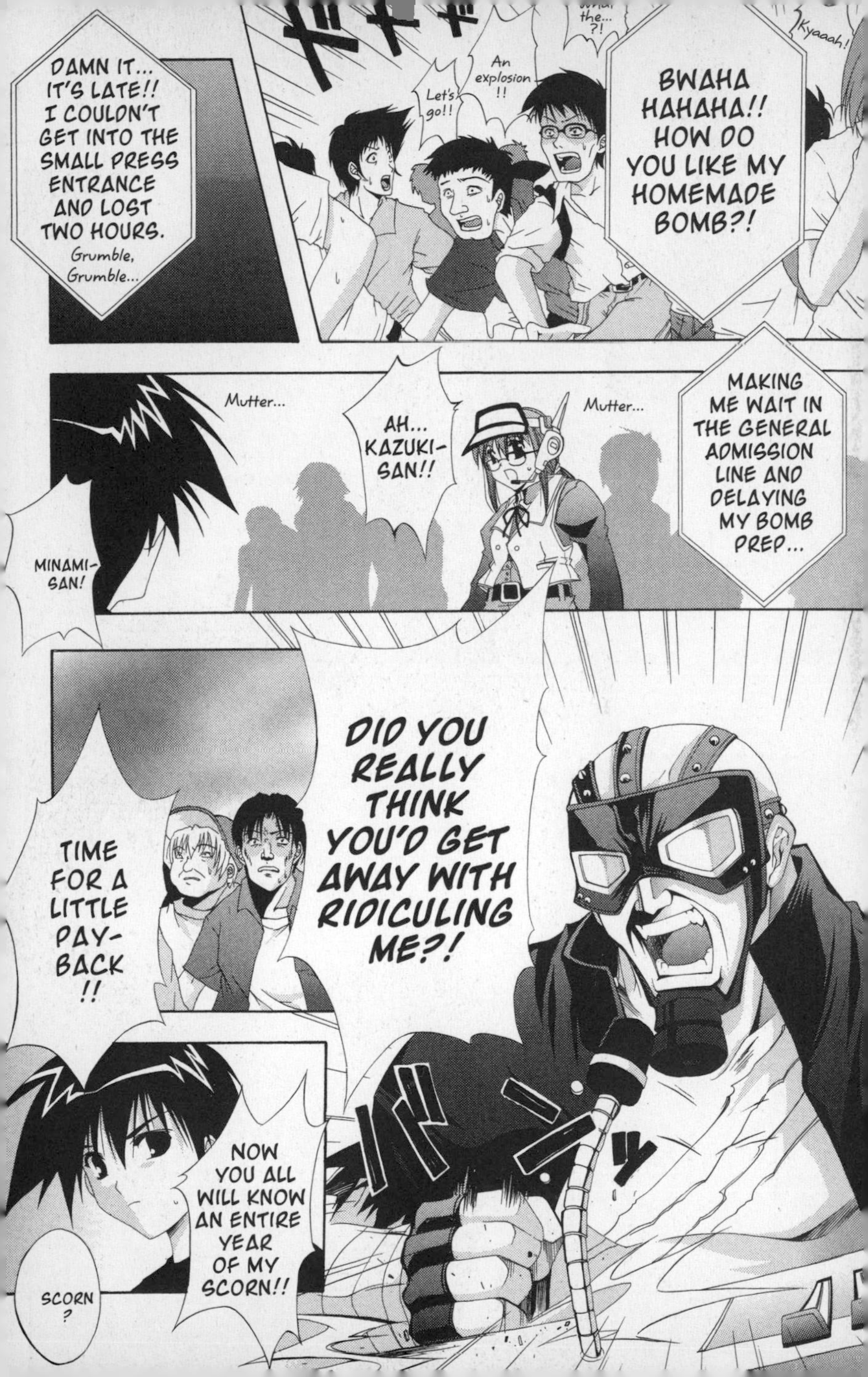
Kyaaah!
the...?!
BWAHA HAHAHA!! HOW DO YOU LIKE MY HOMEMADE BOMB?!
An explosion!!
Let's go!!
DAMN IT... IT'S LATE!! I COULDN'T GET INTO THE SMALL PRESS ENTRANCE AND LOST TWO HOURS.
Grumble, Grumble...
MAKING ME WAIT IN THE GENERAL ADMISSION LINE AND DELAYING MY BOMB PREP...
Mutter...
AH... KAZUKI-SAN!!
Mutter...
MINAMI-SAN!
DID YOU REALLY THINK YOU'D GET AWAY WITH RIDICULING ME?!
TIME FOR A LITTLE PAY-BACK!!
NOW YOU ALL WILL KNOW AN ENTIRE YEAR OF MY SCORN!!
SCORN?

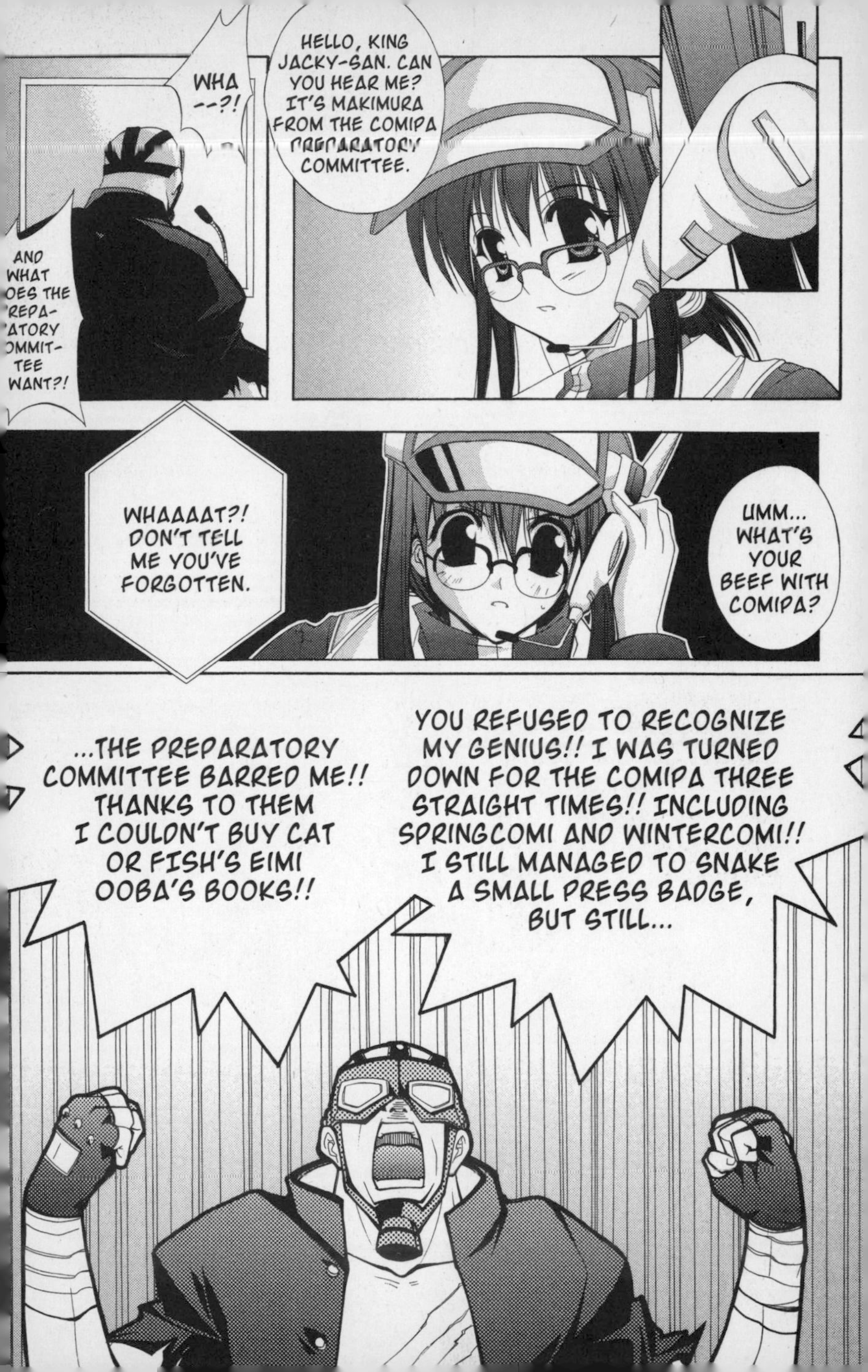
HELLO, KING JACKY-SAN. CAN YOU HEAR ME? IT'S MAKIMURA FROM THE COMIPA PREPARATORY COMMITTEE.
WHA --?!
AND WHAT DOES THE PREPA-RATORY COMMIT-TEE WANT?!
UMM... WHAT'S YOUR BEEF WITH COMIPA?
WHAAAAT?! DON'T TELL ME YOU'VE FORGOTTEN.
YOU REFUSED TO RECOGNIZE MY GENIUS!! I WAS TURNED DOWN FOR THE COMIPA THREE STRAIGHT TIMES!! INCLUDING SPRINGCOMI AND WINTERCOMI!! I STILL MANAGED TO SNAKE A SMALL PRESS BADGE, BUT STILL...
...THE PREPARATORY COMMITTEE BARRED ME!! THANKS TO THEM I COULDN'T BUY CAT OR FISH'S EIMI OOBA'S BOOKS!!

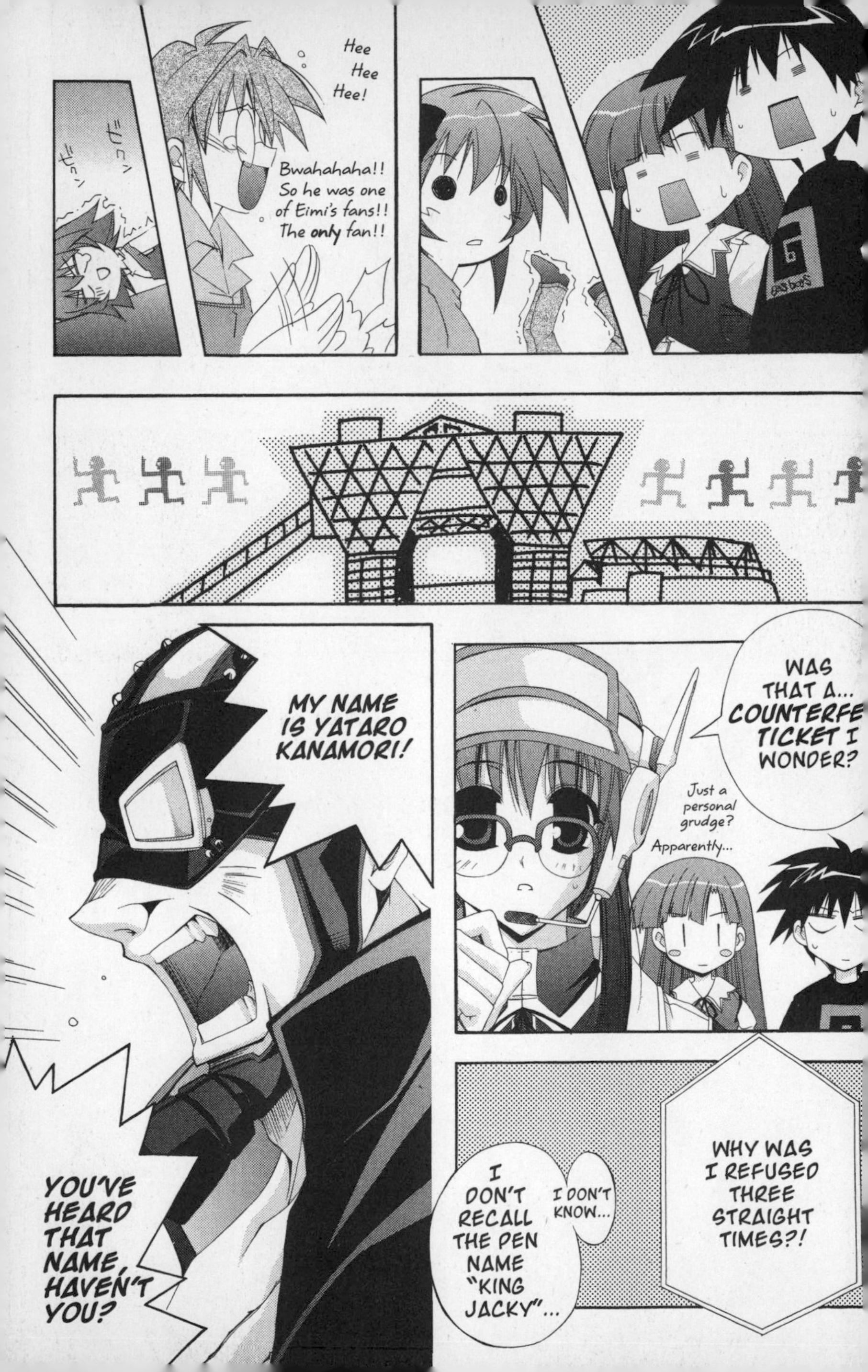
Hee Hee Hee!
Bwahahaha!! So he was one of Eimi's fans!! The only fan!!
WAS THAT A... COUNTERFE TICKET I WONDER?
Just a personal grudge?
Apparently...
WHY WAS I REFUSED THREE STRAIGHT TIMES?!
I DON'T KNOW...
I DON'T RECALL THE PEN NAME "KING JACKY"...
MY NAME IS YATARO KANAMORI!
YOU'VE HEARD THAT NAME, HAVEN'T YOU?

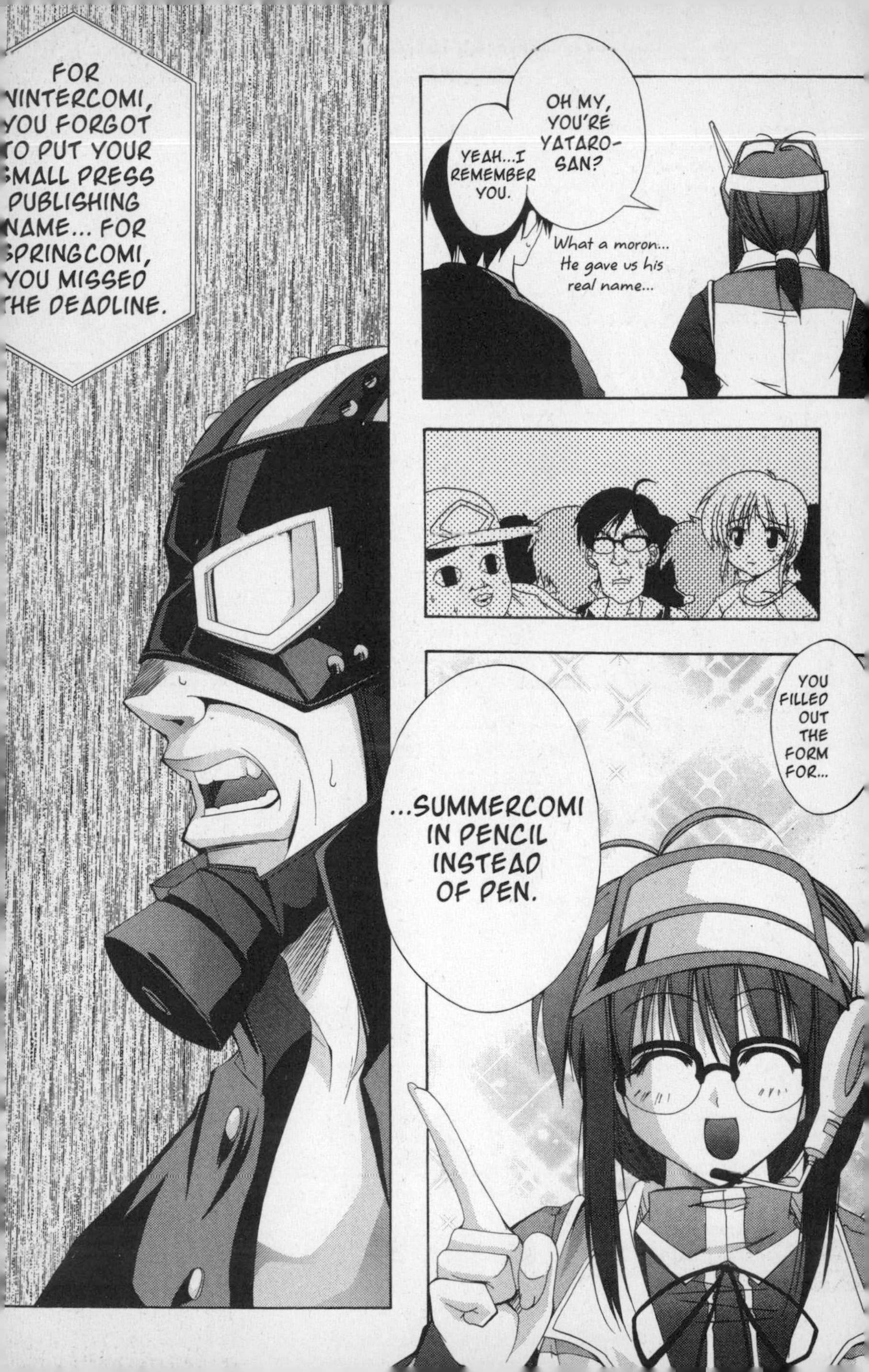
OH MY, YOU'RE YATARO-SAN?
YEAH...I REMEMBER YOU.
What a moron... He gave us his real name...
YOU FILLED OUT THE FORM FOR...
...SUMMERCOMI IN PENCIL INSTEAD OF PEN.
FOR WINTERCOMI, YOU FORGOT TO PUT YOUR SMALL PRESS PUBLISHING NAME... FOR SPRINGCOMI, YOU MISSED THE DEADLINE.

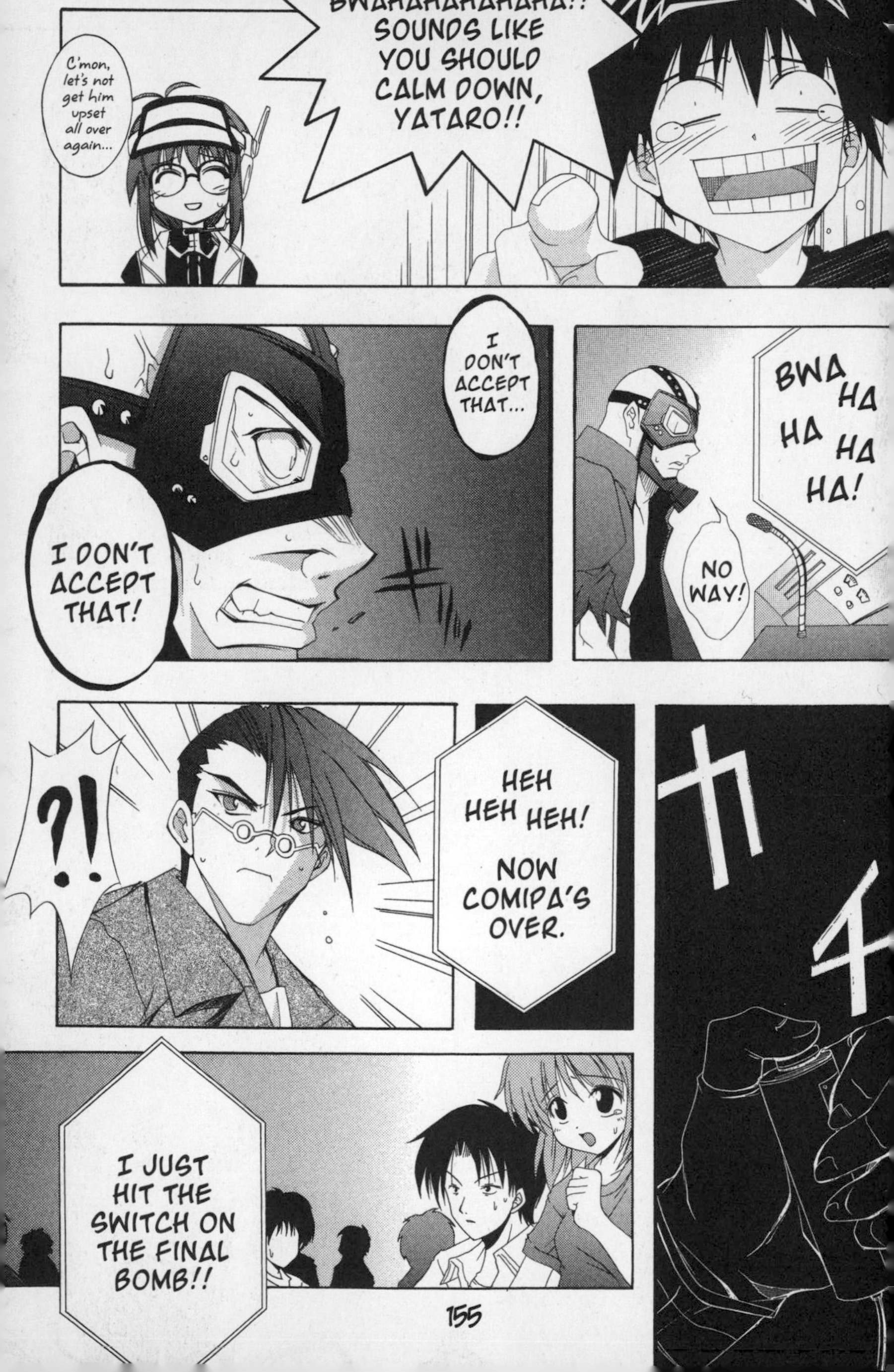
BWAHAHAHAHAHA!! SOUNDS LIKE YOU SHOULD CALM DOWN, YATARO!!
C'mon, let's not get him upset all over again...
BWA HA HA HA HA HA!
NO WAY!
I DON'T ACCEPT THAT...
I DON'T ACCEPT THAT!
HEH HEH HEH!
NOW COMIPA'S OVER.
?!
I JUST HIT THE SWITCH ON THE FINAL BOMB!!

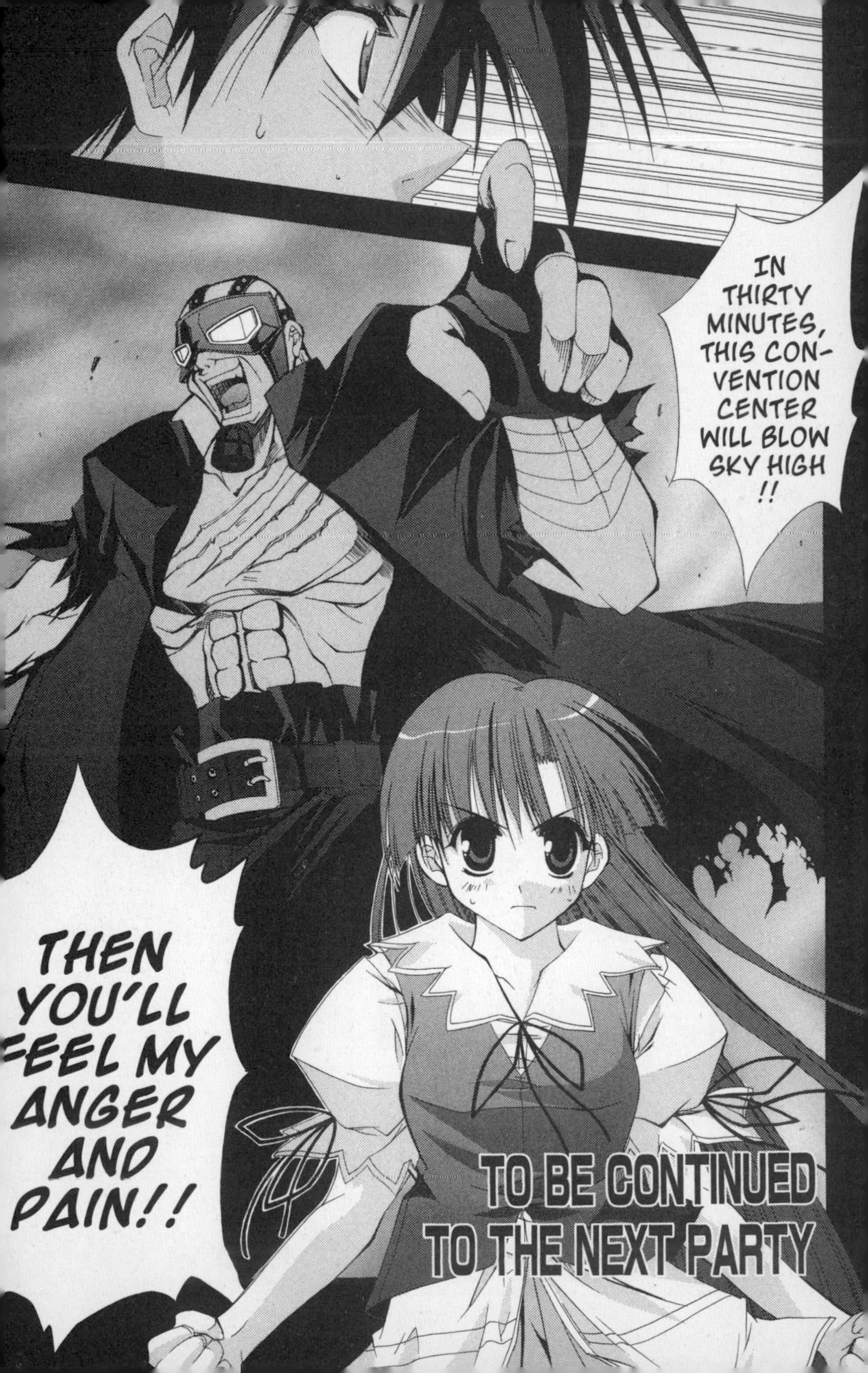
IN THIRTY MINUTES, THIS CON-VENTION CENTER WILL BLOW SKY HIGH !!
THEN YOU'LL FEEL MY ANGER AND PAIN!!
TO BE CONTINUED TO THE NEXT PARTY

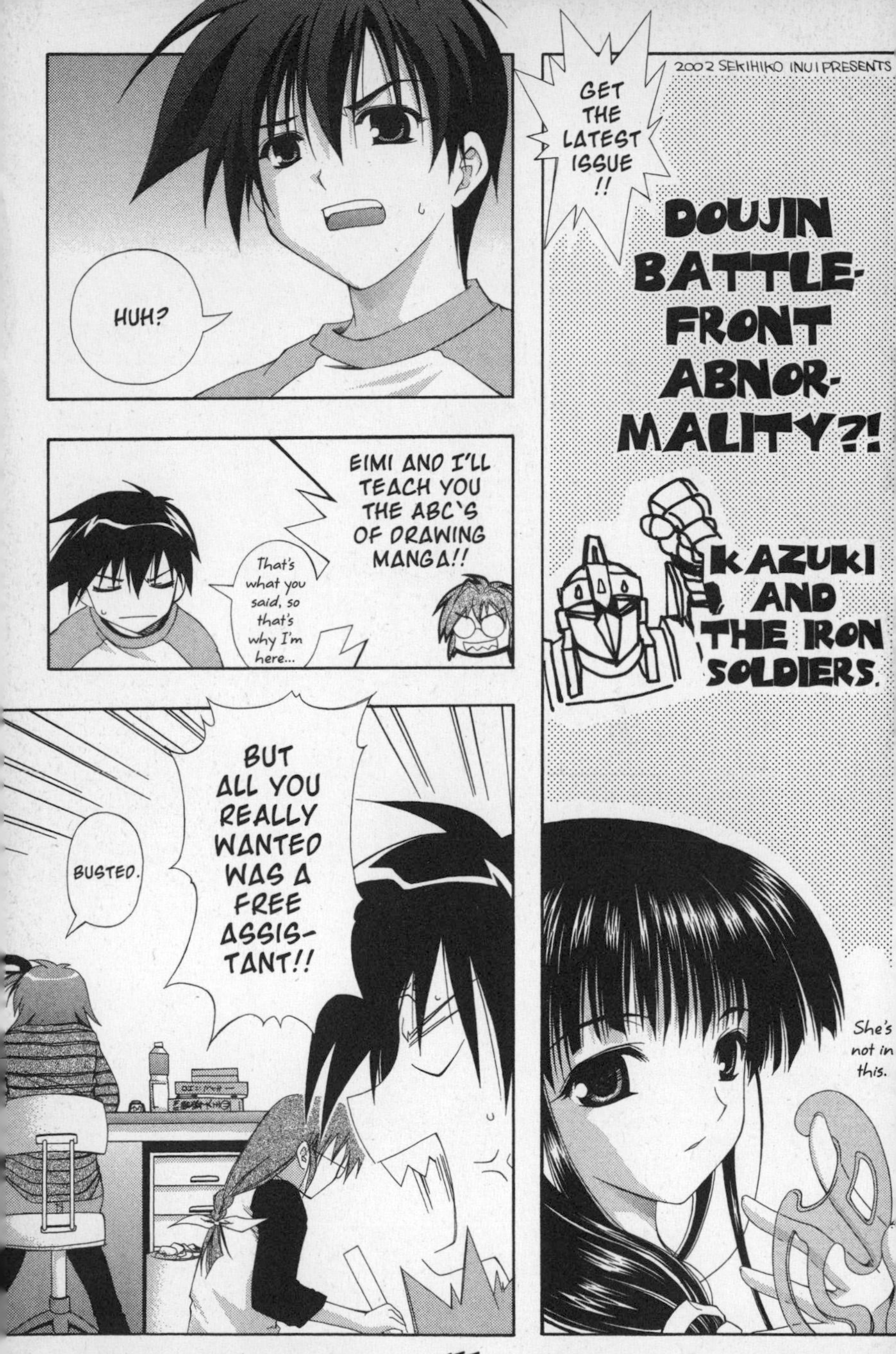
2002 SEKIHIKO INUI PRESENTS
GET THE LATEST ISSUE !!
DOUJIN BATTLE-FRONT ABNORMALITY?!
KAZUKI AND THE IRON SOLDIERS.
She's not in this.
HUH?
EIMI AND I'LL TEACH YOU THE ABC'S OF DRAWING MANGA!!
That's what you said, so that's why I'm here...
BUT ALL YOU REALLY WANTED WAS A FREE ASSISTANT!!
BUSTED.

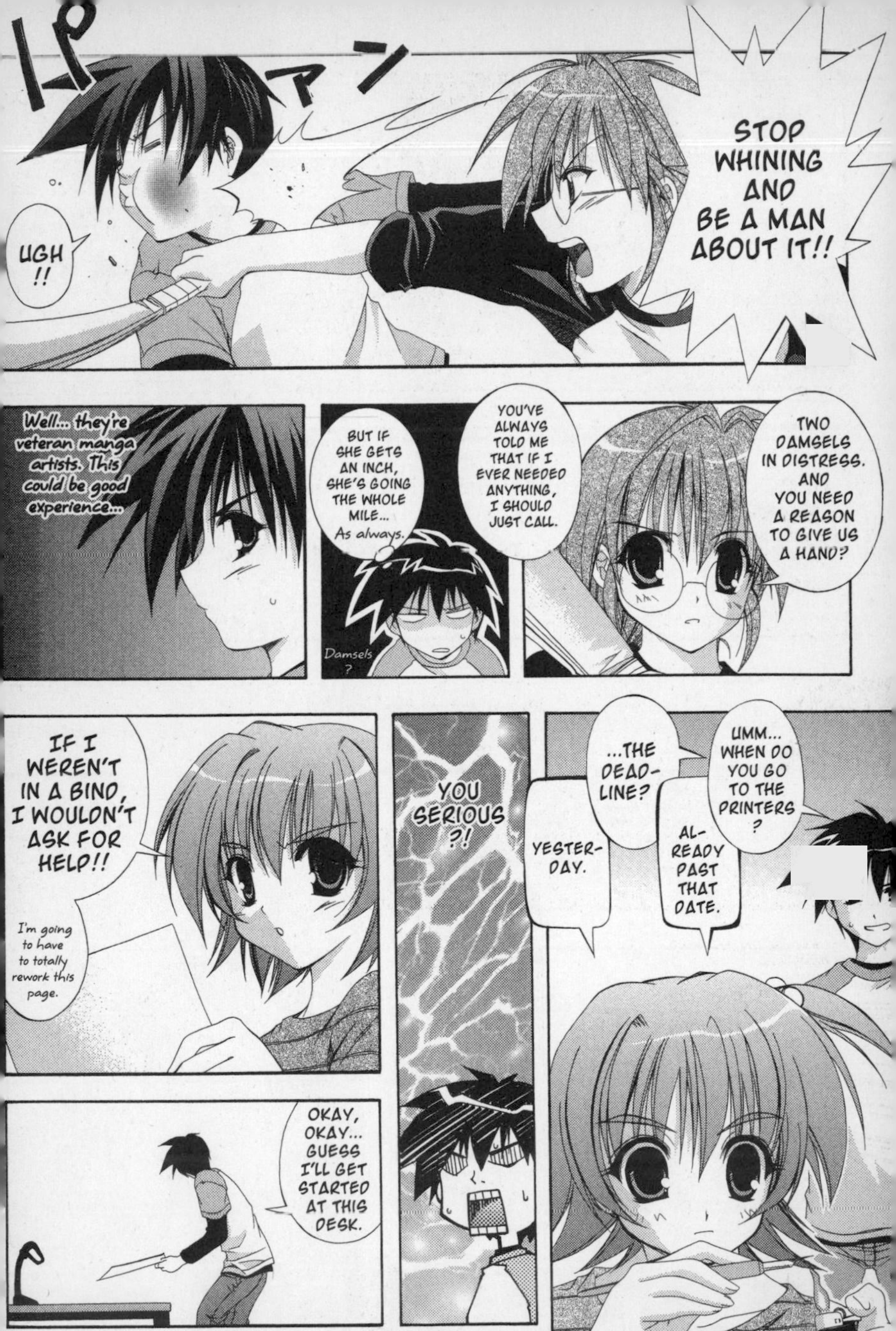
パァン
STOP WHINING AND BE A MAN ABOUT IT!!
UGH!!
TWO DAMSELS IN DISTRESS. AND YOU NEED A REASON TO GIVE US A HAND?
YOU'VE ALWAYS TOLD ME THAT IF I EVER NEEDED ANYTHING, I SHOULD JUST CALL.
BUT IF SHE GETS AN INCH, SHE'S GOING THE WHOLE MILE... As always.
Damsels?
Well... they're veteran manga artists. This could be good experience...
UMM... WHEN DO YOU GO TO THE PRINTERS?
AL-READY PAST THAT DATE.
...THE DEAD-LINE?
YESTER-DAY.
YOU SERIOUS?!
IF I WEREN'T IN A BIND, I WOULDN'T ASK FOR HELP!!
I'm going to have to totally rework this page.
OKAY, OKAY... GUESS I'LL GET STARTED AT THIS DESK.

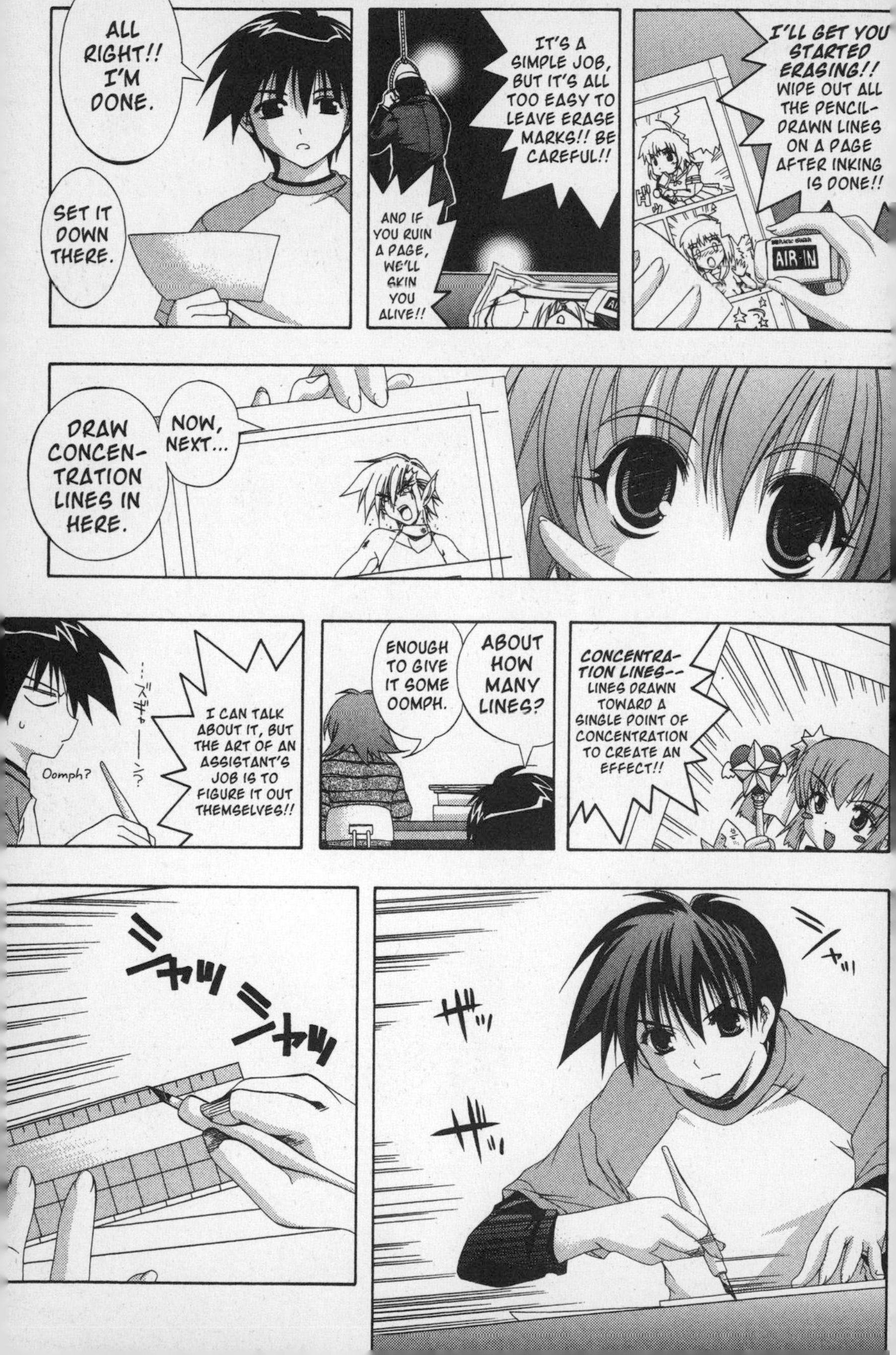
I'LL GET YOU STARTED ERASING!! WIPE OUT ALL THE PENCIL-DRAWN LINES ON A PAGE AFTER INKING IS DONE!!
AIR-IN
IT'S A SIMPLE JOB, BUT IT'S ALL TOO EASY TO LEAVE ERASE MARKS!! BE CAREFUL!!
AND IF YOU RUIN A PAGE, WE'LL SKIN YOU ALIVE!!
ALL RIGHT!! I'M DONE.
SET IT DOWN THERE.
NOW, NEXT...
DRAW CONCENTRATION LINES IN HERE.
CONCENTRATION LINES--LINES DRAWN TOWARD A SINGLE POINT OF CONCENTRATION TO CREATE AN EFFECT!!
ABOUT HOW MANY LINES?
ENOUGH TO GIVE IT SOME OOMPH.
I CAN TALK ABOUT IT, BUT THE ART OF AN ASSISTANT'S JOB IS TO FIGURE IT OUT THEMSELVES!!
Oomph?
シャッ
ザッ
ザッ
シャッ シャッ

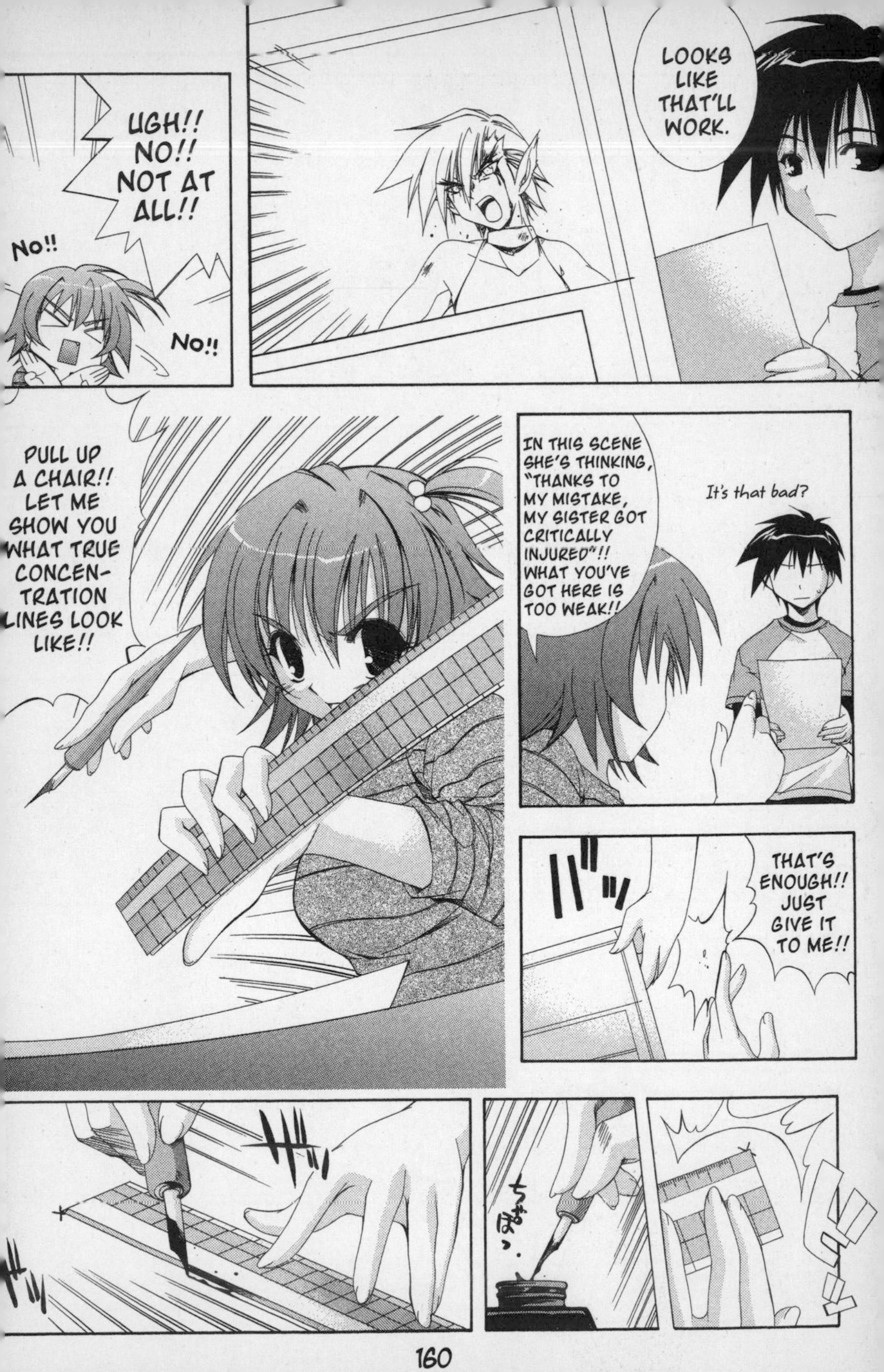
LOOKS LIKE THAT'LL WORK.
UGH!! NO!! NOT AT ALL!!
No!!
No!!
IN THIS SCENE SHE'S THINKING, "THANKS TO MY MISTAKE, MY SISTER GOT CRITICALLY INJURED"!! WHAT YOU'VE GOT HERE IS TOO WEAK!!
It's that bad?
THAT'S ENOUGH!! JUST GIVE IT TO ME!!
PULL UP A CHAIR!! LET ME SHOW YOU WHAT TRUE CONCEN-TRATION LINES LOOK LIKE!!
ちゃぽっ

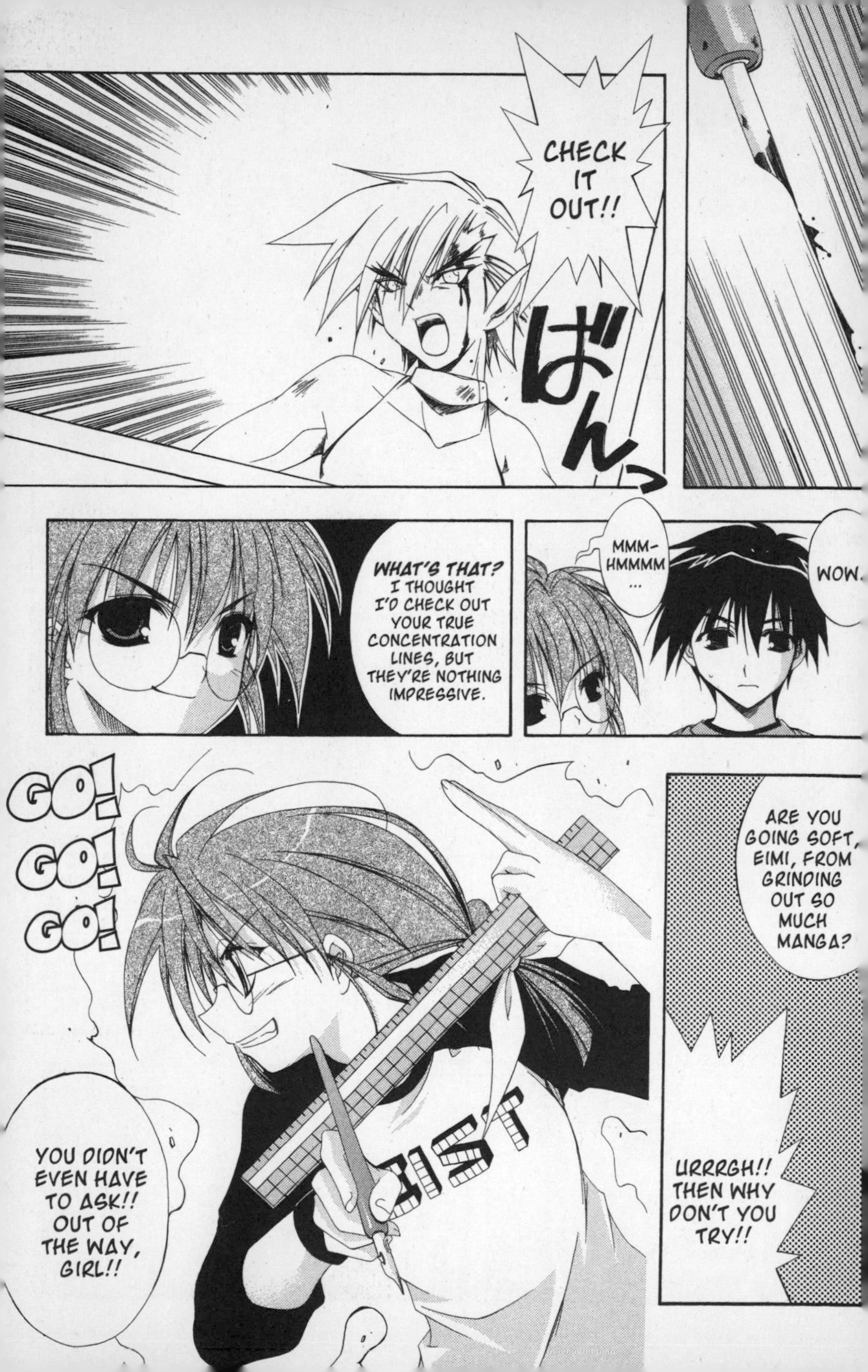
CHECK IT OUT!!
ばんっ
WOW.
MMM-HMMMM ...
WHAT'S THAT? I THOUGHT I'D CHECK OUT YOUR TRUE CONCENTRATION LINES, BUT THEY'RE NOTHING IMPRESSIVE.
ARE YOU GOING SOFT, EIMI, FROM GRINDING OUT SO MUCH MANGA?
URRRGH!! THEN WHY DON'T YOU TRY!!
GO! GO! GO!
YOU DIDN'T EVEN HAVE TO ASK!! OUT OF THE WAY, GIRL!!

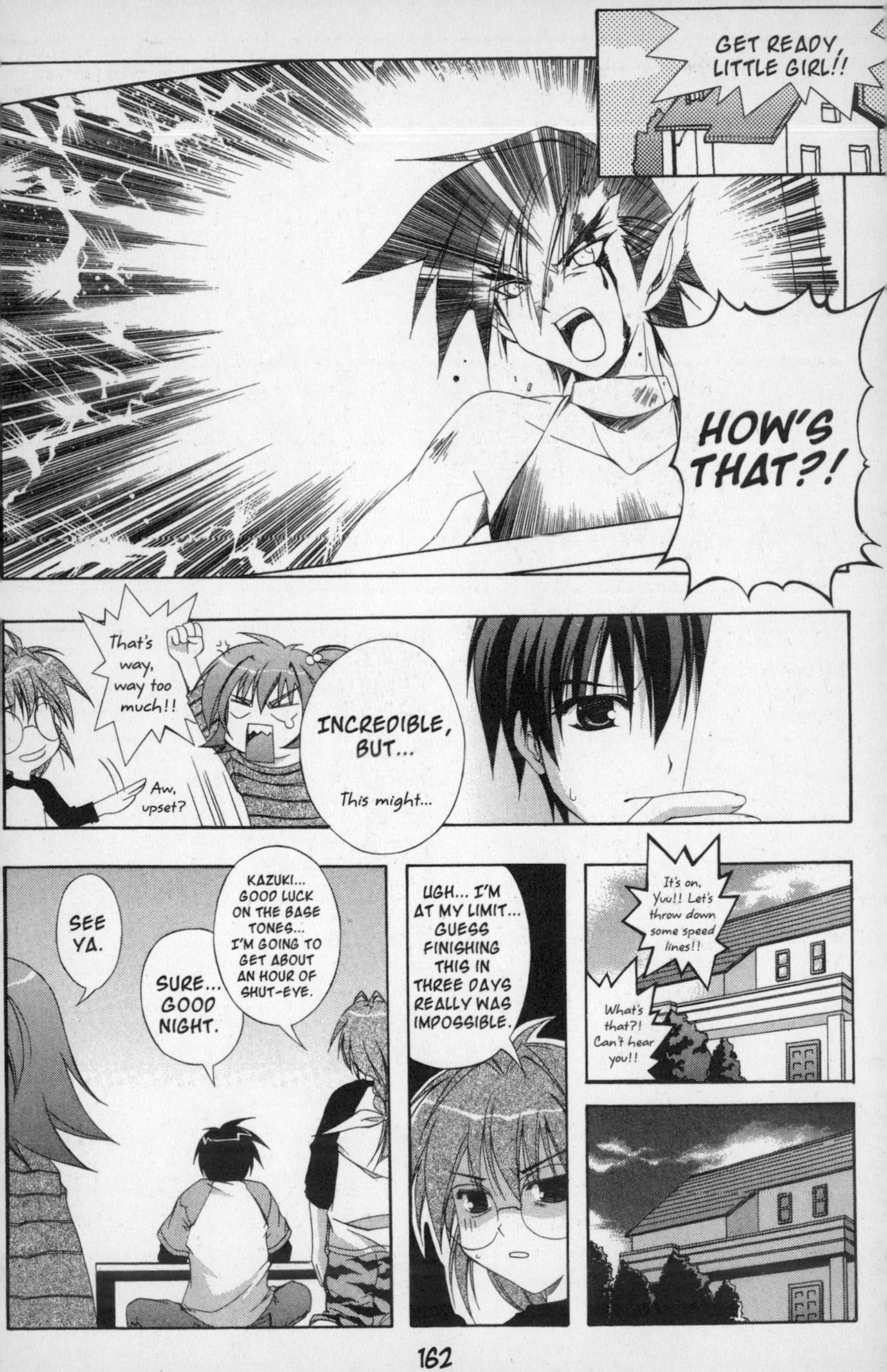
GET READY, LITTLE GIRL!!
HOW'S THAT?!
INCREDIBLE, BUT...
This might...
That's way, way too much!!
Aw, upset?
It's on, Yuu!! Let's throw down some speed lines!!
What's that?! Can't hear you!!
UGH... I'M AT MY LIMIT... GUESS FINISHING THIS IN THREE DAYS REALLY WAS IMPOSSIBLE.
KAZUKI... GOOD LUCK ON THE BASE TONES... I'M GOING TO GET ABOUT AN HOUR OF SHUT-EYE.
SURE... GOOD NIGHT.
SEE YA.

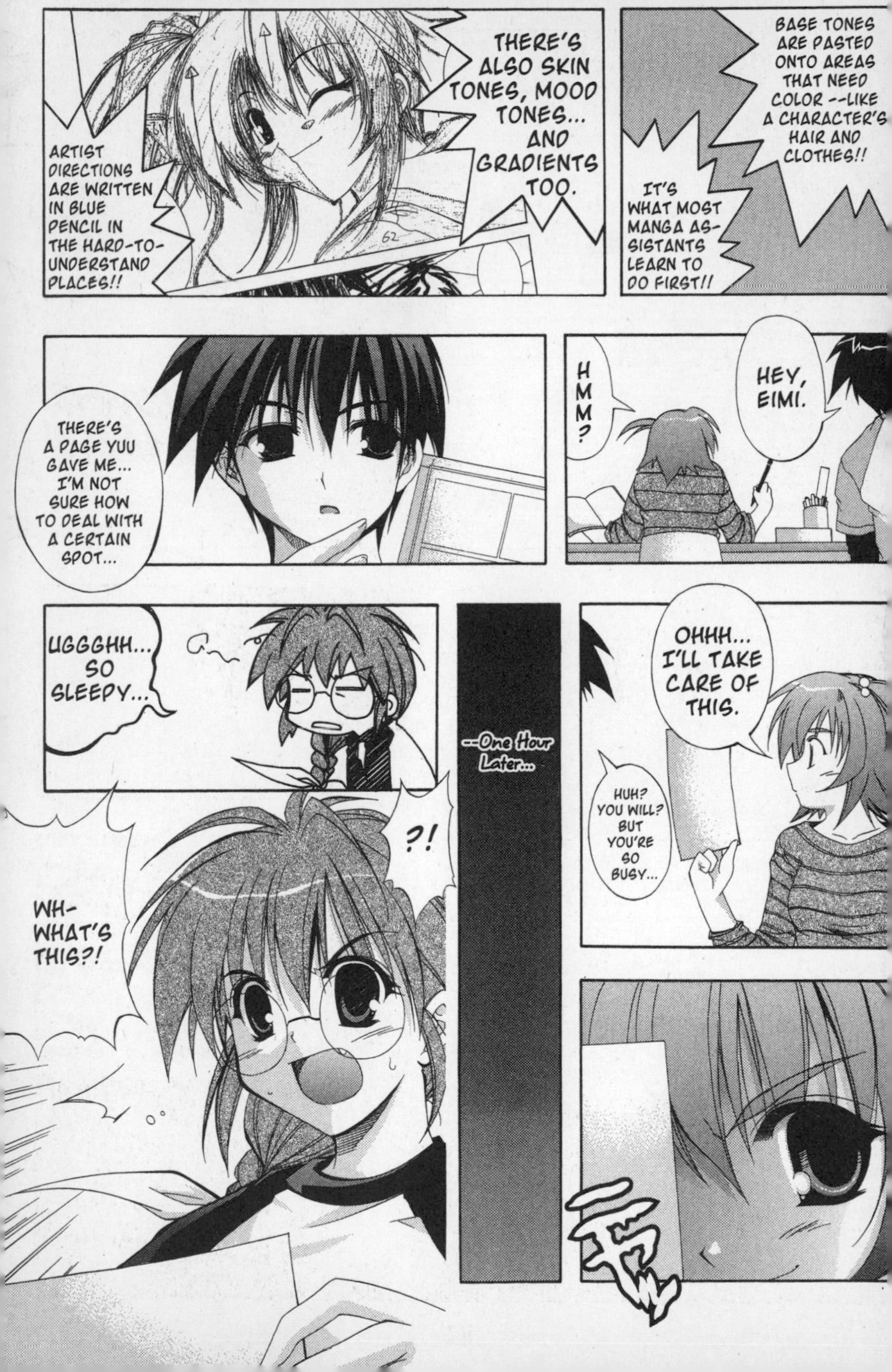
BASE TONES ARE PASTED ONTO AREAS THAT NEED COLOR --LIKE A CHARACTER'S HAIR AND CLOTHES!!
IT'S WHAT MOST MANGA AS-SISTANTS LEARN TO DO FIRST!!
THERE'S ALSO SKIN TONES, MOOD TONES... AND GRADIENTS TOO.
ARTIST DIRECTIONS ARE WRITTEN IN BLUE PENCIL IN THE HARD-TO-UNDERSTAND PLACES!!
HEY, EIMI.
HMM?
THERE'S A PAGE YUU GAVE ME... I'M NOT SURE HOW TO DEAL WITH A CERTAIN SPOT...
OHHH... I'LL TAKE CARE OF THIS.
HUH? YOU WILL? BUT YOU'RE SO BUSY...
--One Hour Later...
UGGGHH... SO SLEEPY...
?!
WH-WHAT'S THIS?!

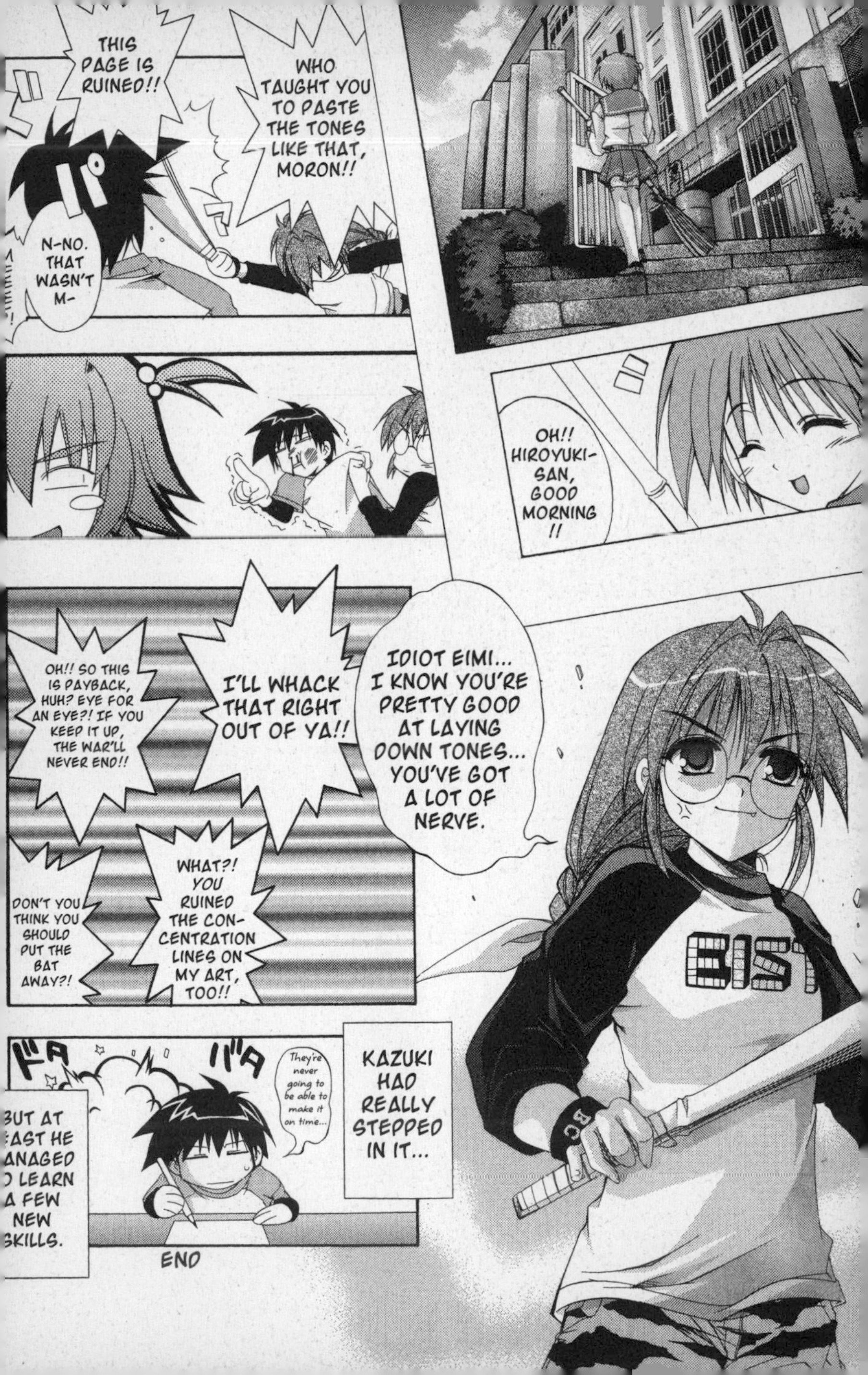
OH!! HIROYUKI-SAN, GOOD MORNING!!
IDIOT EIMI... I KNOW YOU'RE PRETTY GOOD AT LAYING DOWN TONES... YOU'VE GOT A LOT OF NERVE.
BIST
BC
WHO TAUGHT YOU TO PASTE THE TONES LIKE THAT, MORON!!
THIS PAGE IS RUINED!!
N-NO. THAT WASN'T M-
I'LL WHACK THAT RIGHT OUT OF YA!!
OH!! SO THIS IS PAYBACK, HUH? EYE FOR AN EYE?! IF YOU KEEP IT UP, THE WAR'LL NEVER END!!
WHAT?! YOU RUINED THE CONCENTRATION LINES ON MY ART, TOO!!
DON'T YOU THINK YOU SHOULD PUT THE BAT AWAY?!
KAZUKI HAD REALLY STEPPED IN IT...
バA
ドA
They're never going to be able to make it on time...
BUT AT EAST HE ANAGED O LEARN A FEW NEW KILLS.
END

COMIC PARTY

Vol.2

PRESENTED BY
SEKIHIKO INUI
(STUDIO-OZZFEST)

STAFF
SID YATOGAMI
MAKOTO FUGETSU
AHIRUNO MADOKA

EDITOR IN CHIEF
JUN UMEZAWA

EDITOR
NAOKI IIJIMA

DESIGN
MITSUWO SHIIBA
(SHINDOUSYA)

SPECIAL THANKS
AQUAPLUS
MISATO MITSUMI
TATSUKI AMADUYU
TAKESHI NAKAMURA
TSUTOMU WASHIMI
EIJI KAWAKAMI
HIROYUKI SANADURA
TORU ZEKU
RAIYA ARAHABAKI
JUZE
NAGI KAZEKAWA

RYOKUYOUSYA

TOUJI&WHO'S BAD
ALL MY FRIENDS&FAMILY

AND PUNK ROCK MUSIC

THANK YOU FOR READING

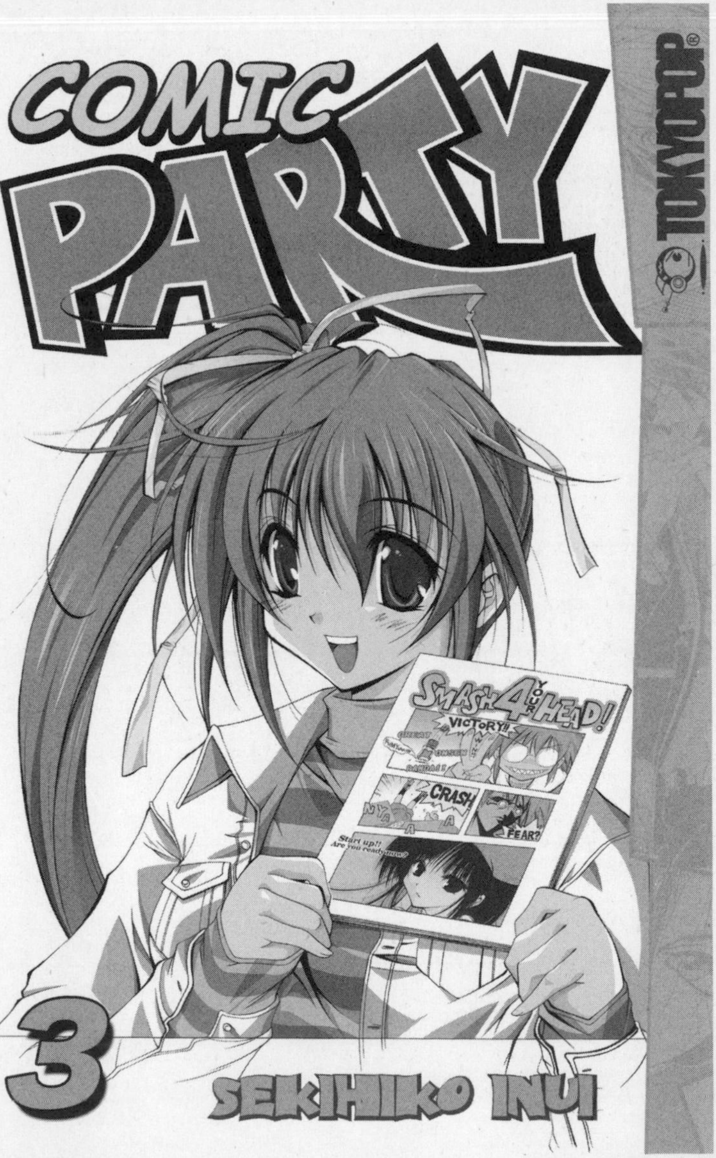
COMIC PARTY
TOKYOPOP
SMASH 4 YOUR HEAD!
VICTORY!!
CRASH
FEAR?
Start up!!
Are you ready now?
3
SEKIHIKO INUI

Preview

IT'S THE COMI RANGERS TO THE RESCUE! WHEN KAZUKI AND COMPANY FIND KINGU JACKY'S BOMB, WILL THEY BE ABLE TO PUT OUT THE COMIC PARTY POOPER? EVEN IF THIS TNT TERRORIST FIZZLES OUT, KAZUKI MUST STILL FIGURE OUT HOW TO MAKE HIS DOUJINSHI LIGHT UP THE BEST-SELLER LISTS BEFORE HE BURNS OUT. MEANWHILE, WILL MIZUKI TURN THE NEXT COMIC PARTY INTO A COSTUME PARTY SUCCESS? STAY TOONED!

ALSO AVAILABLE FROM  TOKYOPOP®

ALSO AVAILABLE FROM  TOKYOPOP®

MANGA

.HACK//LEGEND OF THE TWILIGHT
@LARGE
ABENOBASHI: MAGICAL SHOPPING ARCADE
A.I. LOVE YOU
AI YORI AOSHI
ANGELIC LAYER
ARM OF KANNON
BABY BIRTH
BATTLE ROYALE
BATTLE VIXENS
BRAIN POWERED
BRIGADOON
B'TX
CANDIDATE FOR GODDESS, THE
CARDCAPTOR SAKURA
CARDCAPTOR SAKURA - MASTER OF THE CLOW
CHOBITS
CHRONICLES OF THE CURSED SWORD
CLAMP SCHOOL DETECTIVES
CLOVER
COMIC PARTY
CONFIDENTIAL CONFESSIONS
CORRECTOR YUI
COWBOY BEBOP
COWBOY BEBOP: SHOOTING STAR
CRAZY LOVE STORY
CRESCENT MOON
CROSS
CULDCEPT
CYBORG 009
D•N•ANGEL
DEMON DIARY
DEMON ORORON, THE
DEUS VITAE
DIABOLO
DIGIMON
DIGIMON TAMERS
DIGIMON ZERO TWO
DOLL
DRAGON HUNTER
DRAGON KNIGHTS
DRAGON VOICE
DREAM SAGA
DUKLYON: CLAMP SCHOOL DEFENDERS
EERIE QUEERIE!
ERICA SAKURAZAWA: COLLECTED WORKS
ET CETERA
ETERNITY
EVIL'S RETURN
FAERIES' LANDING
FAKE
FLCL
FLOWER OF THE DEEP SLEEP
FORBIDDEN DANCE
FRUITS BASKET
G GUNDAM

GATEKEEPERS
GETBACKERS
GIRL GOT GAME
GIRLS' EDUCATIONAL CHARTER
GRAVITATION
GTO
GUNDAM BLUE DESTINY
GUNDAM SEED ASTRAY
GUNDAM WING
GUNDAM WING: BATTLEFIELD OF PACIFISTS
GUNDAM WING: ENDLESS WALTZ
GUNDAM WING: THE LAST OUTPOST (G-UNIT)
GUYS' GUIDE TO GIRLS
HANDS OFF!
HAPPY MANIA
HARLEM BEAT
I.N.V.U.
IMMORTAL RAIN
INITIAL D
INSTANT TEEN: JUST ADD NUTS
ISLAND
JING: KING OF BANDITS
JING: KING OF BANDITS - TWILIGHT TALES
JULINE
KARE KANO
KILL ME, KISS ME
KINDAICHI CASE FILES, THE
KING OF HELL
KODOCHA: SANA'S STAGE
LAMENT OF THE LAMB
LEGAL DRUG
LEGEND OF CHUN HYANG, THE
LES BIJOUX
LOVE HINA
LUPIN III
LUPIN III: WORLD'S MOST WANTED
MAGIC KNIGHT RAYEARTH I
MAGIC KNIGHT RAYEARTH II
MAHOROMATIC: AUTOMATIC MAIDEN
MAN OF MANY FACES
MARMALADE BOY
MARS
MARS: HORSE WITH NO NAME
MINK
MIRACLE GIRLS
MIYUKI-CHAN IN WONDERLAND
MODEL
MY LOVE
NECK AND NECK
ONE
ONE I LOVE, THE
PARADISE KISS
PARASYTE
PASSION FRUIT
PEACH GIRL
PEACH GIRL: CHANGE OF HEART
PET SHOP OF HORRORS
PITA-TEN

05.11.04T

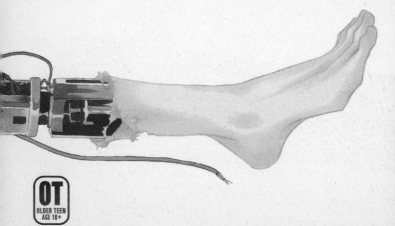

DOLL ™

AVAILABLE IN HARDCOVER AND PAPERBACK EDITIONS

Love,
Compassion,
Circuitry.

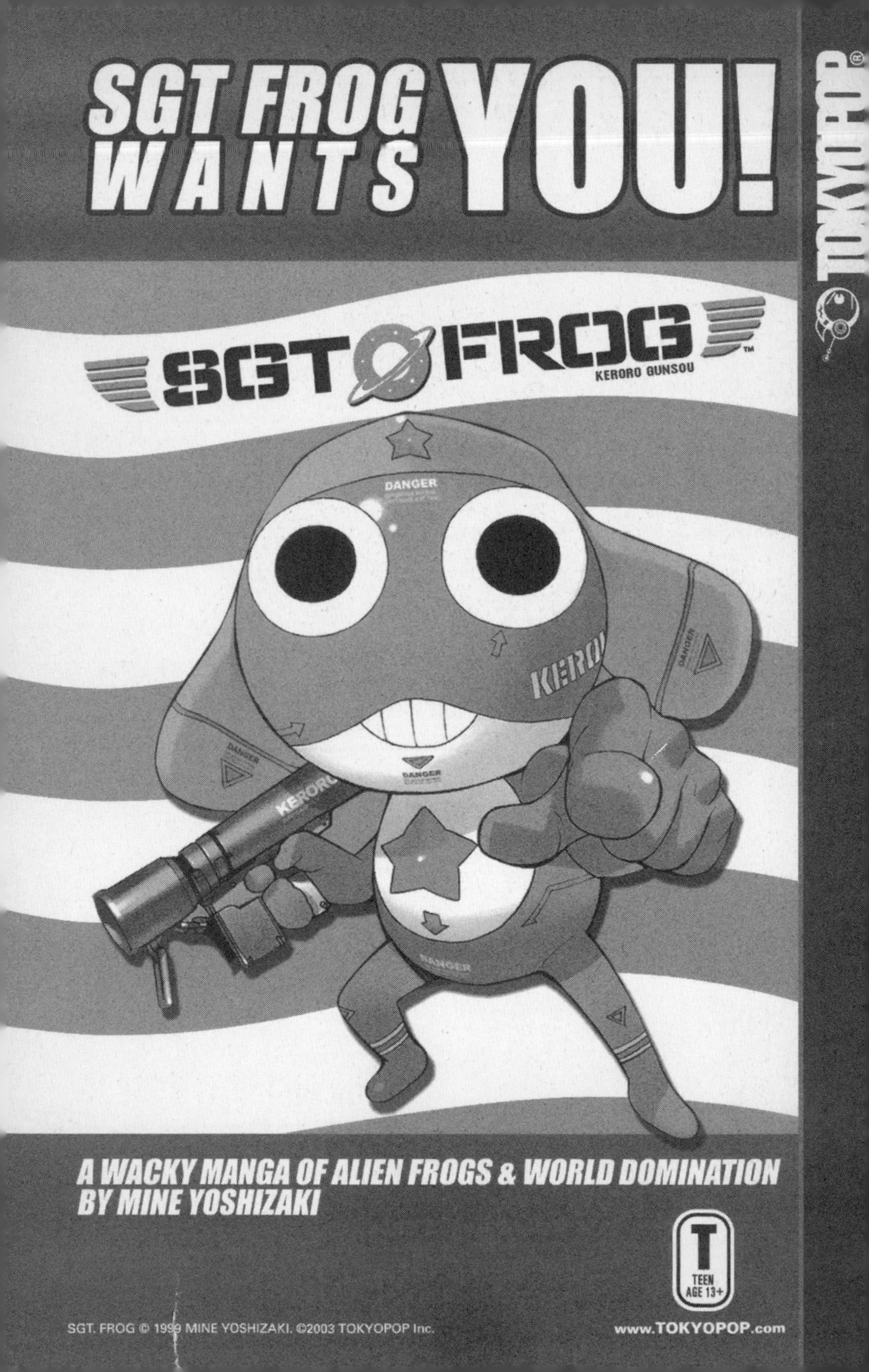
SGT FROG WANTS YOU!
TOKYOPOP®
SGT FROG™
KERORO GUNSOU
DANGER
KERORO
A WACKY MANGA OF ALIEN FROGS & WORLD DOMINATION
BY MINE YOSHIZAKI
T
TEEN AGE 13+
SGT. FROG © 1999 MINE YOSHIZAKI. ©2003 TOKYOPOP Inc.
www.TOKYOPOP.com

PITA-TEN

By Koge-Donbo - Creator of Digicharat

The girl next door is
bringing a touch of heaven
to the neighborhood.

When darkness is in your genes,
only love can steal it away

D·N·ANGEL

STOP!

This is the back of the book.
You wouldn't want to spoil a great ending!

This book is printed "manga-style," in the authentic Japanese right-to-left format. Since none of the artwork has been flipped or altered, readers get to experience the story just as the creator intended. You've been asking for it, so TOKYOPOP® delivered: authentic, hot-off-the-press, and far more fun!

DIRECTIONS

If this is your first time reading manga-style, here's a quick guide to help you understand how it works.

It's easy... just start in the top right panel and follow the numbers. Have fun, and look for more 100% authentic manga from TOKYOPOP®!